Th   P9-CMT-395
A History

Second Edition

Also available from Continuum:

The First Crusade and the Idea of Crusading
Jonathan Riley-Smith

The Crusades
A History

Second Edition

JONATHAN RILEY-SMITH

Yale Nota Bene
YALE UNIVERSITY PRESS
New Haven and London

Second edition published as a Yale Nota Bene book in 2005.
Second edition published in Great Britain in 2005 by Continuum.
First published in the United States in 1987 by Yale University Press.
First published in Great Britain in 1987 by the Athlone Press Limited.

Printed in the United States of America.

Library of Congress Control Number: 2005922281

ISBN 0-300-10128-7 (pbk.)

A catalogue record of this book is available from the British Library.

Ecce quam bonum et quam iucundum
habitare fratres in unum!
(Psalm 132 (133): 1)

Contents

Maps

Drawn by András Bereznay

1. THEATRES OF WAR

BALTIC

NORTH SEA

ATLANTIC OCEAN

POMERANIA

BOHEMIA
MORAVIA
AUSTRIA

Languedoc

Lombardy

BOSNIA

PORTUGAL

ARAGON

CASTILE

PAPAL
STATES
● Rome

K. OF NAPLES

GRANADA

Canary Is.

Algiers

MOROCCO

Tunis

K. OF SICILY

TUNISIA

Malta

MEDITER

Muslim controlled in 1094

Christian controlled in 1094

Pagan in 1094

●●●●●● Maximum advance of Islam during the 1095–1798 period

------- Maximum advance of Christendom during the 1095–1798 period

——— Boundary between Islam and Christendom in 1798

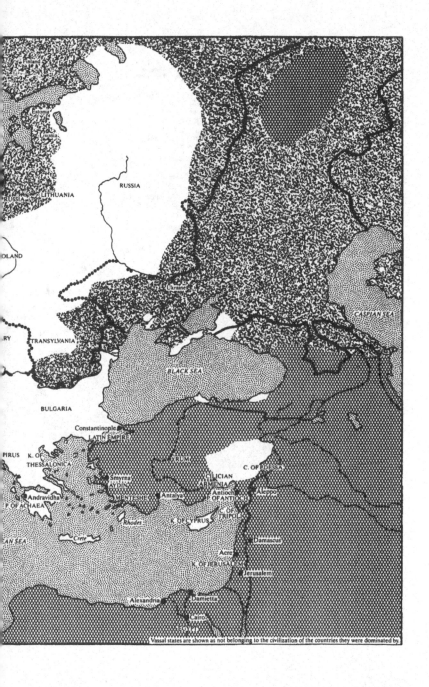

Vassal states are shown as not belonging to the civilization of the countries they were dominated by.

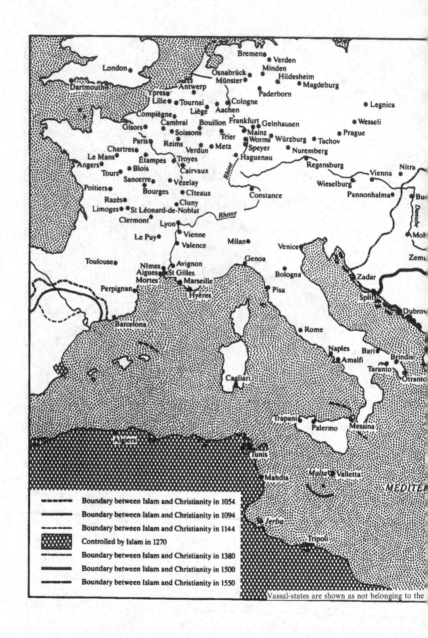

London
Dartmouth

Bremen • Verden
Osnabrück Minden
Münster • Hildesheim
Paderborn   • Magdeburg

Antwerp
Ypres•
Lille • Tournai
Compiègne• Liège Aachen
Gisors• Cambrai Bouillon Frankfurt Gelnhausen
Soissons Mainz
Paris• Reims Trier Worms Würzburg • Tachov
Chartres• Verdun Speyer Nuremberg
Le Mans• Étampes Troyes Haguenau
Angers• • Blois Clairvaux
Tours• Sancerre• • Vézelay
Poitiers• Bourges • Cîteaux
Razès• Cluny
Limoges • St Léonard-de-Noblat
Clermont• Lyon•
Le Puy• • Vienne
Valence

Cologne
• Legnica
• Wesseli
• Prague

Regensburg
Vienna • Nitra
Wieselburg
Pannonhalma• •Bu
Constance
•Moh
Rhone Danube
Milan• •Zemu

Toulouse• Nîmes• • Avignon
Aigues• St Gilles Genoa
Mortes • Marseille Bologna Zadar
Perpignan• Pisa Split
Hyères Dubrov

Barcelona • Rome
Naples Bari
• Amalfi Brindis
Taranto Otranto

Cagliari

Trapani Palermo Messina

Alger Tunis
Mahdia Malta Valletta MEDITE

Jerba
Tripoli

2. EUROPE AND THE NEAR EAST

Timişoara

aradin

Orşova

rade

Niš

Sofia

sovo

zo

Nicopolis

Varna

Nesebŭr

Sozopol

Plovdiv Maritsa

Edirne

Constantinople

Thessaloniki

Gallipoli

Bursa

Lepanto

Alaşehir

Smyrna

Athens

Eskihisar

Ephesus

ha

Üsküdar

Izmit

Nicaea

Dorylaeum

Eskişehir

Amorium

Akşehir

Karaman

Antalya

Alanya

Göksu

Rhodes

Crete

EAN SEA

Azov

Feodosiya

Sudak

Balaklava

BLACK SEA

Trebizond

Niksar

Manzikert

Merzifon

Çankırı

Ankara

Kayseri

Comana

Göksun

Malatya

Maraş

Konya

Ereğli

Adana

Misis

Gaziantep

Edessa

Tarsus

Silifke

Antioch

Aleppo

Cyprus

Nicosia

Damascus

Acre

Jerusalem

Damietta

Alexandria

Cairo

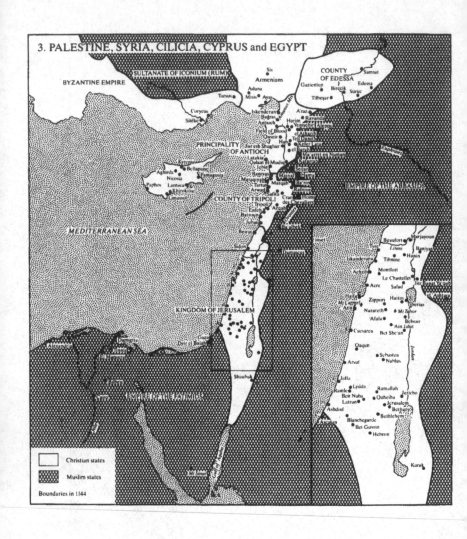

3. PALESTINE, SYRIA, CILICIA, CYPRUS and EGYPT

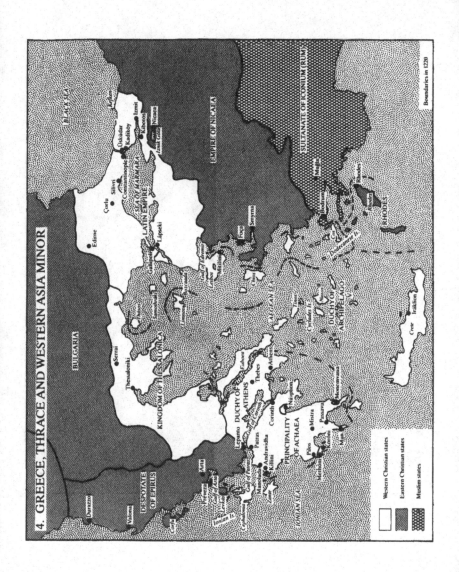

4. GREECE, THRACE AND WESTERN ASIA MINOR

PERSIA

BULGARIA

Edirne

Silivri
Çorlu
Constantinople
Lapseki
LATIN EMPIRE
SEA OF MARMARA

Üsküdar
Kadıköy
İzmit
Nicaea
İznik Gölü

EMPIRE OF NICAEA

Serrai

Thessaloniki

KINGDOM OF THESSALONICA

Gulf of Edremit

Smyrna

SULTANATE OF KONYA (RUM)

DESPOTATE OF EPIRUS

Durazzo

Vlorë

Arta

Lepanto
DUCHY OF
ATHENS
Gulf of Corinth
Patras
Thebes
Euboea
Athens

AEGEAN SEA

Chios

DUCHY OF
ARCHIPELAGO

RHODES

Andravidha
Killíni
Corinth
Nauplia
PRINCIPALITY
OF ACHAEA
Pátras
Mistra
Passava
Methóni
Koróni
Maïna
Monemvasia
Pylos

Cyclades Is.

Crete
Iráklion

IONIAN SEA

Boundaries in 1230

Western Christian states
Eastern Christian states
Muslim states

5. SOUTH-WEST FRANCE AND SPAIN

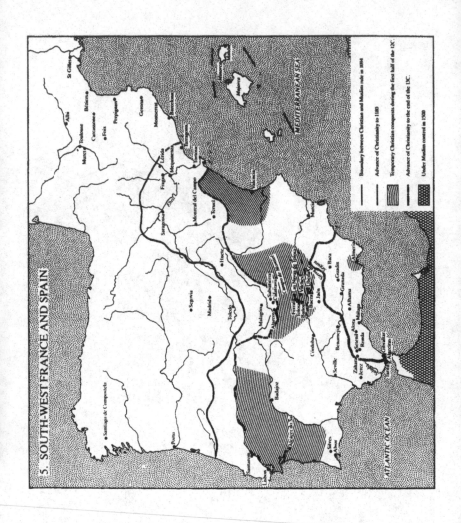

Boundary between Christian and Muslim rule in 1094

Advance of Christianity to 1180

Temporary Christian conquests during the first half of the 13C.

Advance of Christianity to the end of the 13C.

Under Muslim control in 1500

St Gilles
Albi
Toulouse
Béziers
Muret
Carcassonne
Foix
Perpignan
Gerona
Montserrat

Santiago de Compostela

Segovia
Madrid
Toledo

Saragossa
Fraga
Lérida
Monzón
Barbastro
Ebro
Montreal del Campo
Teruel

Huesca

MEDITERRANEAN SEA

Porto

Malagón

Salamanca

Jaén
Baza
Guadix
Granada
Alhama
Málaga

Badajoz

Córdoba

Beaumarchais
Zahara
Jerez
Seville
Setenil
Ronda
Alora
Gibraltar

Lisbon
Silves
Alvor

ATLANTIC OCEAN

6. THE BALTIC REGION

NORWAY

Bergen

SWEDEN

NOVGOROD

Finland

Tallin

Estonia

Novgorod

Lake Peipus

Saaremaa

Livonia

Pskov

PSKOV

BALTIC SEA

Riga

Uxküll

Durbe

TEUTONIC ORDER

Dvina

DENMARK

Memel

Zalew Wislany

Königsberg

Prussia

Lübeck

Rügen

Gdansk

Demmin

Marienburg

Tannenberg

Bremen

Artlenburg

Szczecin

Pomerania

Kulmerland

Thorn

LITHUANIA

Magdeburg

Brandenburg

Elbe

Oder

THE WESTERN EMPIRE

Legnica

Breslau

POLAND

Vistula

Cracow

Pagan in 1095, christianized
gradually to the end of the 14C.

Boundaries in 1390

Milan

Verona

Treviso

LOMBARDY

Mantua

Venice

Piacenza

KINGDOM OF ITALY

Ferrara

Genoa

Bologna

Faenza

Cesena

ROMAGNA

Pisa

Florence

MARCH
OF
ANCONA

TUSCANY

Ancona

DUCHY OF
SPOLETO

ADRIATIC SEA

Viterbo

PATRIMONIUM PETRI

Tagliacozzo

Rome

Ostia

Ferentino

Monte Cassino

Lucera

San Germano

Foggia

Benevento

Bari

Naples

APULIA
(Norman)

Amalfi

Taranto

Brindisi

Otranto

TYRRHENIAN SEA

CALABRIA

Cape Orlando

Bagnara

Palermo

Messina

IONIAN SEA

Trapani

SICILY
(Norman)

7. ITALY

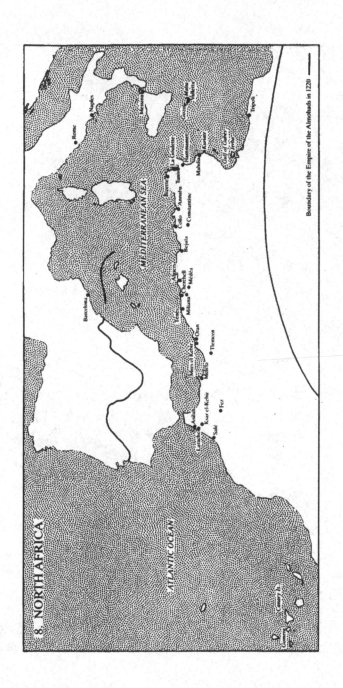

8. NORTH AFRICA

ATLANTIC OCEAN

MEDITERRANEAN SEA

Rome

Naples

Messina

Barcelona

Bougie
Collo
Annaba
Tunis
La Goulette
Constantine
Bejaïa
Mahdia

Algiers
Dellys
Cherchell
Médéa

Tenes
Milan
Oran

Ksar el-Kebir
Melilla
Tlemcen

Arzila
Ksar el-Kebir
Salé
Fez

Larache

Canary Is.
Canary Is.

Tripoli

Gulf of Gabes

Boundary of the Empire of the Almohads in 1220 ——————

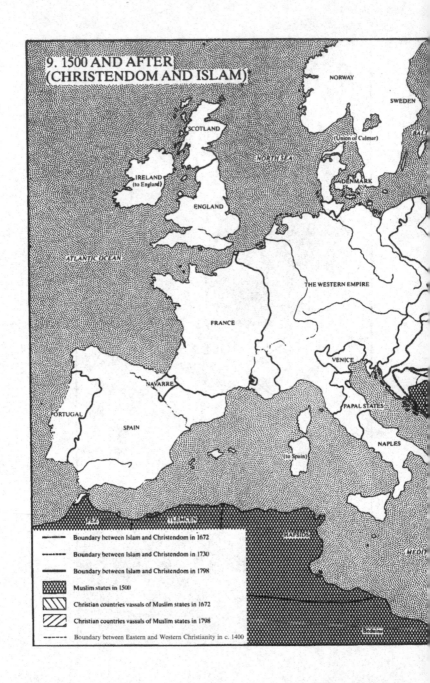

9. 1500 AND AFTER (CHRISTENDOM AND ISLAM)

NORWAY

SWEDEN

SCOTLAND

(Union of Calmar)

NORTH SEA

IRELAND
(to England)

DENMARK

ENGLAND

ATLANTIC OCEAN

THE WESTERN EMPIRE

FRANCE

VENICE

NAVARRE

PAPAL STATES

PORTUGAL

SPAIN

NAPLES

(to Spain)

FEZ

TLEMCEN

HAFSIDS

MEDI

- - - - Boundary between Islam and Christendom in 1672
- - - - Boundary between Islam and Christendom in 1730
———— Boundary between Islam and Christendom in 1798
▨ Muslim states in 1500
▨ Christian countries vassals of Muslim states in 1672
▨ Christian countries vassals of Muslim states in 1798
- - - - - Boundary between Eastern and Western Christianity in c. 1400

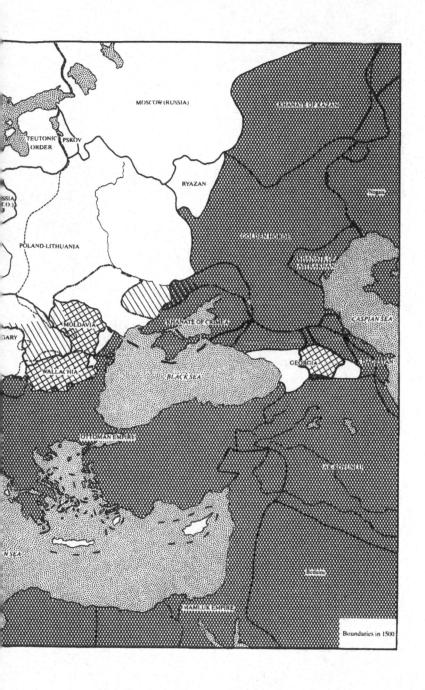

Preface to the Second Edition

The preparation of a second edition of this book has proved to be a much harder task than I anticipated. I knew that an enormous amount of new history had been generated in the last seventeen years, but I had not expected to find so much that needed rewriting. It seems to me that the subject has moved on in a number of ways.

- Controversies which engaged our attention twenty years ago are grinding to a halt. This may be partly because the parties involved are exhausted, but it is also because the priorities of most historians are changing. One of these debates related to definition. Although 'pluralism', one of the approaches which generated so much heat, is now quite influential, is touched on in the Introduction and the Afterword and governed the way this book was written, leading pluralists are much less certain of its general application than they used to be.
- Most historians also seem to have lost interest in the question whether the Latin settlements in the East were colonies or not. This may also be a result of a general disillusionment with Marxism, but it should be added that the conviction that the settlements were examples of early colonialism is still axiomatic in Arab and in some Israeli circles.
- Interest in the motivation of crusaders has grown, as has a conviction that the materialistic explanations for recruitment are no longer sustainable. The penitential nature of crusading is much more clearly understood, because of the evidence provided by sermons, which is increasingly being brought to bear on the subject. Another class of evidence – that provided by liturgical texts – is coming into focus and can be expected to supplement the homiletic material.
- The details of the small crusades to the East, which were fought in the intervals between the large-scale expeditions, are much clearer to us than they used to be. I was tempted to abandon the numbers which have traditionally been given to the great crusades, but in the end decided that this would confuse my readers.
- The history of the western settlements in the East is being transformed by studies of their society and culture. These are leading to a revival of

the nineteenth-century picture of cultural assimilation, although in a modified form. The more one considers the institutions of the kingdom of Jerusalem, the more experimental, even innovatory, some of them appear to be. In this respect there is a need for comparative research, involving Jerusalem alongside similar regions conquered by westerners: Aragon and Sicily spring to mind. In all of these there appears to have been a lively and self-conscious approach to the problems of adapting to the needs of alien subject populations. At the same time the 'constitutional' interpretation of historical developments in the kingdom of Jerusalem, which used to be so influential, is fading away in the face of the detailed studies of the operations of lordships and instruments of government.

- Attention has been drawn to the reappearance of the masses in the revival of peasant armies in the fifteenth and early sixteenth centuries. Along with this there has been an explosion of interest in the history of the military orders. One result is that a much more positive picture of them in the early modern period is coming into focus. Another is that the order-states of Prussia, Rhodes and Malta are beginning to attract a lot of attention.

The extended quotations in the text are extracted from the following works: those on pages xxxiii, 12–15, 79, 112–13, 116, 122, 124–5, 131, 134, 137, 148–9, 163, 170–2, 174, 185–6, 192–3 are taken from L. and J. Riley-Smith, *The Crusades: Idea and Reality, 1095–1274* (1981); that on page 71 is taken from Usamah ibn Munqidh, *An Arab-Syrian Gentleman and Warrior in the Period of the Crusades*, tr. P. K. Hitti (1929); on pages 71–2 from Rabbi Jacob ben R. Nathaniel ha Cohen, 'Account', tr. E. N. Adler, *Jewish Travellers* (1930); on page 184 from P. J. Cole, *The Preaching of the Crusades to the Holy Land, 1095–1270* (1991); on page 277 from Pius II, 'Commentaries', in *Memoirs of a Renaissance Pope*, tr. F. A. Gragg (abridged edn, 1960); on page 302 from E. Siberry, *The New Crusaders: Images of the Crusades in the 19th and Early 20th centuries* (2000); and on page 306 from E. Sivan, 'Modern Arab Historiography of the Crusades', *Asian and African Studies* 8 (1972).

J. S. C. R-S.
July 2004

Preface to the First Edition

Crusades were waged in many theatres of war and it is no coincidence that some of the regions involved have changed hands many times over the centuries. So many places have more than one name. On the assumption that some of my readers may want to visit the more important sites, I have followed *The Times Atlas of the World* (6th comprehensive edition, 1984) for place-names whenever possible, but I have modified its practice for places too well known to readers of English to change (Gdańsk rather than Danzig, but Fez not Fès, and Marienburg rather than Malbork). In every case I have included any alternative name in parentheses after the first mention and also in the index.

The Times Atlas has adopted a system of transliteration which is used widely in Britain and the United States, but it is not one employed by historians and I decided that it would be confusing if I tried to recast Arabic personal names to agree with it. Arabists will not like the way I use one system of transliteration for places and another for persons, but my chief aim has been to make things as easy as I can for the general reader.

Every university historian knows that his greatest debts of gratitude are owed to his undergraduate and post-graduate students. To two of mine, Dr Peter Edbury and Dr Norman Housley, are owed special thanks because they read this book in typescript and saved me from blunders and infelicities. I did not always follow their advice, however, and so take full responsibility for the interpretations and opinions, which are my own. I would also like to thank Janet Daines, who typed the final version.

J. S. C. R-S.

Introduction

In the early thirteenth century the preacher James of Vitry addressed the Knights Templar. His sermon was certainly delivered in the East, probably in Acre, where he was bishop and where the Templars had their headquarters in a massive convent-fortress by the sea. He began by drawing attention to the fact that while the Templars and their fellow Christian soldiers battled on a lesser plane than the first 'soldiers of God', the apostles and martyrs, and the last, those souls who would remain firm during the final trial before Doomsday, they had the important duty of countering a real and present threat to Christians from the devil and his agents: idolators, pagans, heretics and pacifists, the last of whom sought to undermine their role. He justified Christian violence with theological arguments, drawn almost entirely from Gratian's *Decretum*, the standard textbook of canon law. This must have been over the heads of his audience, for most of the Templars were uneducated and would have perceived only dimly, if at all, the intellectual case for force. They must have been relieved when, as was his custom, James told some good stories, including one about a Templar 'in the days when the Templars were poor and most fervently religious' – a typical dig at his listeners – before ending his sermon with an exhortation to eschew their own glory and place their trust only in God.

Reading the sermon now, it does not come across as a great success. There is an artificial break between the scriptural allusions and quotations from the Fathers in the first three-quarters of it and the anecdotes and simple message with which it ends. It manages only to illustrate the deep gulf that has always separated the cerebral abstractions of theologians from the forces that move ordinary men and women. Popes and preachers, who had to present the theology of violence to ordinary Christians in terms they could understand, never succeeded in building satisfactory bridges across the divide. This is one reason why they could never fully control the passions they aroused. But it is important to stress at the start that the crusading movement flourished against a background of ideas on violence which were upheld by most educated men. Without them the Church would never have embarked on the dangerous course of encouraging laymen, let alone religious like the Templars, to resort to arms: it had had enough trouble trying to cope with the anarchic turbulence in contemporary society.

For most of the last two thousand years Christian justifications of war have rested on two premises. The first was that violence – defined crudely as an act of physical force which threatens, deliberately or as a side-effect, homicide or injury to the human body – was not intrinsically evil. It was morally neutral until qualified by the intention of the perpetrator. If his intention was altruistic, like that of a surgeon who, even against the wishes of his patient, amputated a limb – a measure which for most of history endangered the patient's life – then the violence could be regarded as being positively good. The second premise was that Christ's wishes for mankind were associated with a political system or course of political events in this world. For the crusaders his intentions were embodied in a political conception, the Christian Republic, a single, universal, transcendental state ruled by him, whose agents on earth were popes, bishops, emperors and kings. A personal commitment to its defence was believed to be a moral imperative for those qualified to fight. Propagandists gave this theory expression in terms the faithful could understand: within the earthly extension to Christ's universal empire the Holy Land was his royal domain or patrimony; Livonia (approx. Latvia) on the Baltic was the Blessed Virgin Mary's private estate, a kind of queen mother's dower.

God, whether in the person of Father or Son, would approve of acts of force in defence of his wishes, but only if they accorded with criteria which had been developed as early as the fourth century. There should be a right intention on the part of the participants, whose actions should always express love of God and neighbour. There must be a just cause. And there had to be legitimate proclamation by a qualified authority. That authority would usually be a divine minister, such as an emperor, but it was also believed that God could personally authorize violence. He was reported to have done so on many occasions in the Old Testament and on a few in the New Testament, among them Christ's apparent approval of the possession of two swords by the Apostles at the Last Supper (Luke 22: 38), which, when taken together with his indifference to the profession of the centurion (Matthew 8: 5–13; Luke 7: 1–10), suggested that his precepts of mercy and forgiveness had not entirely reversed the physical retribution which was a feature of the old dispensation. Christ was believed to authorize crusades himself – this was one of their characteristic features – and to do so through his chief representative on earth, the pope.

Every crusader took a vow, which he or she was committed to fulfil as a penance; that is an act, often of self-punishment, which constituted an attempt to repay the debt owed to God on account of sin. It was for this reason that each was also granted an indulgence. This privilege, fully developed from c. 1200, and the guarantee of remission of sins which preceded it, distinguished crusading from most other forms of Christian holy war. A crusade was for the crusader as an individual only secondarily about service-in-arms to God or the benefiting of the Church or

Christianity; it was primarily about benefiting himself since he was engaged in an act of self-sanctification. This very radical concept was diluted over time and under the influence of chivalry by the much older ideal of performing service to Christ, but in one form or another penance remained at the heart of crusading throughout its history. According to the thirteenth-century preacher Humbert of Romans service to Christ could only be effective if it was penitential. Because of the penitential nature of crusading and its aboriginal association with pilgrimage to Jerusalem, crusaders always had the status of pilgrims and pilgrimage terminology was often used of them, while some of the privileges they enjoyed, particularly the protection of themselves, their families and properties, were similar to those given to pilgrims.

A crusade was fought against those perceived to be the external or internal foes of Christendom for the recovery of Christian property or in defence of the Church or Christian people. Injuries to Christians and the Church provided crusaders with the opportunity of expressing love for their oppressed or threatened brothers in a just cause, which was always related to that of Christendom as a whole. A crusading army was therefore considered to be international, even when it was actually composed of men from only one region. As far as the popes were concerned, the Muslims in the East and in Spain had occupied Christian territory, including land sanctified and made his very own by the presence of Christ himself, and they had imposed infidel tyranny on the Christians who lived there. The pagans in the Baltic region threatened new Christian settlements. The heretics in Languedoc or Bohemia were rebels against their mother the Church and were denying the responsibility for teaching entrusted to her by Christ, while they and the Church's political opponents in Italy disturbed rightful order. The popes believed that preaching crusades for all these theatres of war was justified, even essential, but not all Christians saw crusading in the same light and while there is general agreement that crusades to the East always had greater prestige and provided the standard against which all others were judged, there has been vigorous debate, which will be referred to below, whether the papal definition of crusading, to which the descriptive term 'pluralist' has been given, reflected general opinion at the time and is useful now. This book is written by a pluralist, but it is anyway the case that so many Catholics took part in crusades within, or on the frontiers of, Europe that the western theatres of war cannot be ignored if one is to give a balanced account of the movement. The popes made judgements on the respective importance of a range of options at a given time. Developments within one theatre could influence events in another and sometimes two theatres would be directly linked, as when Spaniards argued that the best way to reach Jerusalem was to extend the Reconquest into a liberation of North Africa, or when the Teutonic Knights made use of Prussia as a training-ground for Palestine.

Modern pluralism is a model and models invariably break down when the criteria for them are applied too strictly. While it holds good for crusades to the East and the defence of Europe itself against the Turks from the late fourteenth century onwards, some of the campaigns fought during the Reconquest of Spain, the perpetual crusade in Prussia and Livonia and some expeditions on the Finnish-Russian border, the crusades against the Albigensians, Hussites and Mongols, and those against opponents of the papacy and its allies in Italy, it cannot be stretched to encompass many other engagements which have to be considered in this book. The brothers of the military orders were never technically crusaders, since they did not take crusade vows – of their nature temporary commitments – but were professed religious permanently engaged in the defence of Christendom. The secular lords and knights of Latin Palestine and Syria were not crusaders either and the campaigns they fought in defence of their homes and properties were not usually crusades. The leagues formed to combat the Turks from the fourteenth to the late seventeenth centuries were not crusades in the strict sense because, although provided with papal authorization and with participants who had taken vows and were granted indulgences, they were alliances of independent Christian powers, even when support for them was preached outside the borders of the states involved, and they lacked the supranational ethos which was a characteristic of all crusades. But these were all so closely associated with crusading that it would be absurd to treat them separately. It is best, I believe, to consider them all as expressions of a crusading movement which underlay them and only came to an end with the surrender of Malta to Napoleon Bonaparte by the Hospitallers of St John in 1798.

Towards the end of this book I will touch on the challenge pluralism presents to the assumption of two centuries that crusading is defined by its hostility to Islam. Professor Giles Constable has pointed out that pluralism does not 'ask where a crusade was going ... [but] how a crusade was initiated and organized' and another achievement, it seems to me, is the way it has encouraged researchers to look in new directions for different kinds of material. Some of them have been led by it back to Europe, into the minds of preachers and their audiences, to the operation of social networks and the expression of grass-roots ideas, to the strategic and financial discussions in Rome and to the management of the western commanderies, which provided the men and matériel for the fighting convents of the military orders in the East. The work these scholars are doing strikes especially at the foundations of a materialistic interpretation of crusading, because anyone re-examining the reasons for recruitment to such arduous, disorientating, frightening and expensive enterprises is bound to question the validity of a belief in expectations of profit, which anyway rests on very little evidence.

The relevance of ideology – although a very different ideology to our own – is confirmed in the history of the Church's attitude to crusading. From the twelfth century to the seventeenth the consensus among Catholic bishops was that qualified men had a moral obligation to volunteer. This was reinforced by the support of a succession of men and women universally regarded as saints: Bernard of Clairvaux, Thomas Aquinas, Bridget of Sweden, Catherine of Siena, John of Capistrano, even Francis of Assisi. From Urban II in 1095 to Innocent XI in 1684 pope after pope wrote or authorized the despatch of letters, including many general ones, in which the faithful were summoned to crusade, offered spiritual privileges if they responded and threatened with divine judgement if they did not. These letters comprise an impressive, coherent and consistent body of teaching on the theological and ethical value of crusading. The popes also recognized a new type of religious institute in approving of and privileging the military orders, the function of which was justified by St Thomas Aquinas. Two of them, the *Sovereign Military Order of Malta* and the *Teutonic Order*, survive today as Orders of the Church, although both have lost their military functions. The Teutonic Order has a Calvinist version in the *Bailiwick of Utrecht* and the Order of Malta has Anglican and Lutheran/Calvinist versions in the *Most Venerable Order of St John* and the three *Johanniterorden*. At least five general councils legislated for crusades and two of them, the Fourth Lateran Council (1215) and the Second Council of Lyons (1274), published the constitutions *Ad liberandum* and *Pro zelo fidei*, which were among the movement's defining documents. This body of theological and devotional support cannot be ignored or explained away. Some readers were shocked by my use in the first edition of this book of a quotation from a report in the early 1270s by the thirteenth-century preacher Humbert of Romans, who was trying to answer the point that harm was done to Christendom by the deaths on crusade of so many decent men.

> The aim of Christianity is not to fill the earth, but to fill heaven. Why should one worry if the number of Christians is lessened in the world by deaths endured for God? By this kind of death people make their way to heaven who perhaps would never reach it by another road.

But Humbert was stating what nearly all his contemporaries believed. We have to accept that many men and women were prepared to sacrifice wealth, health, life itself, in a cause which they believed to be just, even salvational. Their actions were individual expressions of a piety that may be alien to us but was very real to them.

CHAPTER 1

The Birth of the Crusading Movement: The Preaching of the First Crusade

The casus belli

In the first week of March 1095 Pope Urban II presided over a church council at Piacenza in northern Italy. There was present an embassy sent by the Byzantine emperor Alexius I to ask for help against the Turks, whose advance across Asia Minor had brought them within striking distance of Constantinople (Istanbul). This appeal set off the chain of events that led to the First Crusade.

By the early eighth century the Christians had lost North Africa, Palestine and Syria and most of Spain to the Muslims. The frontier between Christendom and Islam had then stabilized until the Byzantine (or Greek) emperors, ruling from Constantinople what remained of the eastern Roman empire, went onto the offensive in the second half of the tenth century. The comparatively subdued reaction of the Muslims to the First Crusade can be partly explained by the fact that their confidence had already been shaken 130 years before, when the ancient cities of Tarsus and Antioch (Antakya) had been retaken and the Byzantine frontier had advanced into northern Syria. A violent shock had been felt throughout the Islamic world: 600 volunteers had arrived in Mosul from Khorasan, 1,200 miles away, in 963; they were followed three years later by a further 20,000 men. The Christian victories had coincided with internal developments that were to transform the western Islamic scene. The authority of the 'Abbasid caliphs in Baghdad had atrophied and they themselves had fallen under the control of Shi'ite princes, whom the Sunnis regarded as heretics. In 969 Egypt had been occupied almost without opposition by another Shi'ite dynasty, the Fatimids, and a rival caliphate had been established. The Fatimids had struggled to wrest Palestine and Syria from the 'Abbasids, but in the 1060s and 1070s they had to give way to Turks who, taking advantage of seventeen years of internal disorder in Egypt, drove them out of most of their Syrian possessions and left them with only a shaky hold on parts of Palestine. It was these Turks who at the same time revived Muslim fortunes on the Christian frontier.

Far to the east, among the nomadic Turkomans on the borders of the Turkish steppe east of the Aral Sea who had converted to Islam in the tenth century, there had been a large group under a chief called Selchük. Brought into the settled Islamic area as hired warriors, his people were in control of Khorasan by 1037 and their victory at the Battle of Dandanqan in 1040 opened Iran to them. In 1049 the motley following of Tughrul, Selchük's grandson, comprising barely controllable nomadic Turkomans and more regular forces, penetrated Armenia. In 1055 Tughrul entered Baghdad and by 1059 he was master of Iraq as far as the Byzantine and Syrian marches. He established a sultanate which ruled Iran, Iraq and part of Syria in the name of the 'Abbasid caliph. At their conversion to Islam the Selchük Turks had absorbed the aggressive and strict religion of the frontiers and they justified their progress westwards as a campaign against the corruption in Islam which, they believed, had manifested itself in the scandal of the orthodox Sunni caliphate being for over a century under the dominance of Shi'ite princes. Their concern thereafter was to proceed against the heretical caliph in Egypt.

Their early moves against Christian territory were haphazard and spasmodic. From the later 1050s parties of nomads were raiding deep into Byzantine Armenia and by the late 1060s they were to be found in Cilicia and in Anatolia proper. As they moved across the borders they passed beyond the control of Tughrul's nephew and successor Alp Arslan, who was forced to intervene in the region. This in turn provoked a Byzantine military reaction. In 1071 Alp Arslan conducted a campaign which, although it involved capturing several Christian places in order to consolidate his frontier, was concerned primarily with bringing Muslim Aleppo to heel. The city fell to him, but he then heard that the Byzantine emperor Romanus IV Diogenes was preparing an offensive. Rounding on the Greeks, he annihilated them and captured the emperor at the Battle of Manzikert.

Byzantine military power had been in decline. Manzikert opened the empire to the Turkoman nomads, a process hastened by the short-sighted actions of Greek generals competing for the throne, who enrolled Turks in their service and established them in the interior. Asia Minor rapidly passed out of Byzantine control and it was this that lay behind the appeal to the West in 1095.

Pope Urban II

The papacy had for some time been worried about the disintegration of Christendom's eastern frontier. News of Turkish penetration had led Pope Gregory VII in 1074 to propose leading personally a force of as many as 50,000 volunteers to 'liberate' their Christian brothers in the East; he stated that with this army he might even push on to the Holy Sepulchre in Jerusalem. Pope Urban had been in touch with the Byzantine emperor from the beginning of his pontificate, with the aim of improving relations between the Latin and Greek Churches. It is, therefore, highly improbable that his behaviour after the council of Piacenza was a spontaneous response to the appeal just made by the Greeks. It is more likely to have been one that had been long premeditated.

With hindsight one can see how Urban's upbringing and career had prepared him for the step he now took. He had been born c. 1035 into a North French noble family: his father was probably a vassal of the count of Champagne. Educated at the prestigious school attached to the cathedral at Reims, he became canon and archdeacon there, before leaving soon after 1067 to enter the great Burgundian abbey of Cluny, perhaps under the influence of that desire for a stricter religious life which was to lead his teacher St Bruno to found the Carthusians. By 1074 the abilities which had made him archdeacon at a very young age had brought him to the office of grand prior of Cluny, the second-in-command to the abbot. Cluny was at the centre of ecclesiastical affairs and its monks were called upon to serve in Rome under Pope Gregory VII. Urban was appointed to the cardinal-bishopric of Ostia, the senior office in the college of cardinals, succeeding another past grand prior of Cluny. He went to Rome in 1080 and was caught up in the Investiture Contest, particularly during the winter of 1084–5 when he was trying to shore up crumbling support for Gregory in Germany. He was one of three persons nominated by Gregory as his possible successor and after the short pontificate of Victor III he was elected pope on 12 March 1088. His time as canon of Reims and monk and prior at Cluny had brought him into contact with some of the best elements in the reform movement and had exposed him to views associated with Cluny on the functions of secular knights in the service of the Church. His career in Italy and as papal legate in Germany had introduced him to the latest reform ideas and to their application to ecclesiastical politics. But above all by birth he was well qualified to know the minds of the western knights.

After staying in Piacenza for about a month he began a leisurely journey through northern Italy before moving on to France. On 15 August 1095 he was at Le Puy, the bishop of which, Adhémar of Monteil, was to play an important part in the crusade. From there Urban summoned the French bishops to a council to be held at Clermont in the following November. He then travelled south to St Gilles, in the dominions of Raymond of St Gilles, the count of Toulouse and a future leader of the crusade, before travelling up the Rhône valley to Cluny, which he reached on c. 18 October. One of the reasons for his visit to France had been to dedicate the altar of the great new church that had been built at Cluny. He reached Clermont on 15 or 16 November and opened the council on the 18th. On the 27th he proclaimed the crusade to a large but predominantly clerical gathering, after which he journeyed through central, western and southern France, skirting the area directly controlled by the king, whose excommunication for adultery had been confirmed at Clermont. Urban must have preached the crusade a good deal himself and we have references to the sermons he delivered at Limoges at Christmas 1095, at Angers and Le Mans in February 1096 and at Nîmes in July. He also presided over ceremonies at which knights took the cross: possibly at Le Mans, certainly at Tours in March 1096. He recrossed the Alps into Italy in August. By then the crusade was under way. For a man in his sixties his achievement had been astonishing. He had covered about 2,000 miles, entering country towns, the citizens of which had never seen a king or anyone of such international importance in living memory, accompanied by a flock of cardinals, archbishops and bishops, whose riding households must have been immense and whose train must have stretched across miles of countryside. He had timed his arrival to coincide with great patronal feasts: he was at St Gilles for the feast of St Giles, at Le Puy, the greatest Marian shrine of the time, for the feast of the Assumption, at Poitiers for the feast of St Hilary. He had been crowned with his tiara and he had ridden through the streets wearing it. He had dedicated with all the liturgical theatre that could be mustered the cathedrals and monastic basilicas that witnessed to the ambitious building programme embarked on everywhere by French churchmen. He had then preached the cross.

There were many descriptions of the message Urban was trying to get across at Clermont and on his tour of France. Most are not to be trusted because they were written after the crusade had liberated Jerusalem, when no writer was immune from a general euphoria that bathed the immediate past in an artificial glow, but there is enough contemporary material, particularly in his own letters, for us to make out at least the outlines of his appeal. At Clermont and throughout his preaching tour he stressed that he was speaking on God's behalf. He wrote of the crusaders being inspired agents of God who were to be engaged in God's service out of love for him. He told them they were followers of Christ and he may well have referred to them as 'knights of Christ'. The pope was, of course, using the expostulatory language already employed by reformers when they referred to their military supporters, but the crusaders took him literally and became convinced that they were fighting for God.

A war of liberation

Urban called for a war of liberation, to be waged by volunteers who had vowed to fight as an act of penance. This part of his message reflected ideas long held by progressive churchmen. The central power of the state in France had fragmented. Real authority was no longer being exercised by the king, nor by many of the great magnates, but, by a process that is still mysterious but may have had something to do with the fact that by the tenth century a society constructed for war no longer had any function other than to turn its aggression in on itself, many of the provinces had broken into smaller units, based on castles from which castellans and their bodies of knights so terrorized their neighbourhoods that they came to represent the only authorities, violent, arbitrary and demanding, that men knew. This breakdown, even of provincial government, was often accompanied by uncontrollable violence. The Church reacted by taking the lead in a movement for the 'Peace of God', which expressed popular concern in great assemblies of free men, meeting round piles of relics collected from all the local churches and decreeing the immunity of the clergy and the poor from violence and exploitation and banning the use of all force at certain times of the year and on certain days of the week. Attempts were made to force the castellans and knights to accept peace provisions, but they could only be compelled by force and so the peace movement itself engendered military actions against peace-breakers, conducted in the name of churchmen who, if they were bishops and abbots, anyway had their own retinues of knights.

The peace movement had waned in France by the 1090s, but it had spread to Germany which was itself fragmenting. It is indicative of the fear Urban and others felt of the prospect of anarchy at home while the great lords were campaigning in the East that the peace movement was revived in France at the time of the First Crusade. At any rate, out of it had come the conviction that the very aggressiveness that had broken up society could be put to good, God-given purposes if only the laity could be disposed to canalize their energies into the service of the Church. All over Europe churchmen were turning to laymen for military support, while chaplains, concerned to put across the Christian message in terms their employers and their households would understand, drew on the Old Testament stories and Christian hagiography for heroic and martial tales which would appeal to their listeners. Their efforts were rewarded in the sense that, although society in the late eleventh century was still violent, it was less violent than it had been. There was also evidence of growing piety and outward shows of devotion among many armsbearers. If it cannot be said that before 1095 the Church had been outstandingly successful in its appeals for armed assistance, in the response to Urban's call it is as though at last its perception and the laity's aspirations met and the hand it had been holding out to laymen was suddenly grasped. It is surely no coincidence that the pope who engineered this meeting of minds was himself a product of that class the Church had been most concerned to energize.

At the time, churchmen were being driven by a reform movement which had dominated the past fifty years, a half-century that was one of the most extraordinary in Christian history. The reformers wanted to free the Church from corrupt practices, which they imputed above all to an excessive influence of the laity in ecclesiastical affairs. They wanted a purer institution, more akin to the Early Church they perceived in reading the Acts of the Apostles, and since most of them were monks, engaged in a reform of monasticism which pre-dated and ran parallel to the more general reform of the Church, they viewed the Early Church through monkish eyes. It is no exaggeration to say that they wanted to monasticize the Christian world. They dreamed of a clergy, celibate and untainted by worldly values, ministering to lay men and women who as far as they were able lived lives and adopted devotional practices that corresponded to monastic ones. The energy expended on the cause was remarkable. So too were the vigour with which the reformers encouraged the physical transformation of the Church's presence all over Europe through the building of parish churches, each in its way a large conventual chapel for a lay community, and the intelligence that led them to foster scholarship, particularly the study of grammar, history and canon law, to justify their campaign. Most extraordinary of all is the way the papacy was captured by them; it is no coincidence that so many of the popes of this period had been monks themselves. For most of its 2,000-year history the papacy has not been in the forefront of reform. It has supported reformers and it has taken over and controlled reform once it has begun, but only once, in the later eleventh century, can it be said that the popes found themselves in the invigorating but dangerously exposed position of being the leaders of a radical party in the Church.

When Urban called for liberation he was using a concept coloured by its employment in the last half-century by reformers who had an exaggerated notion of liberty, bred in great exempt abbeys like Cluny, communities which had been accustomed to enjoy 'liberties' granted them by the popes, which freed them from the authority of bishops and kings. This pressure for liberation in the West had already led to violence. For over forty years popes had supported the use of force against those who resisted the new ideas, most notably when around 1080 a party of German magnates had dragged Pope Gregory VII into war with their king and emperor-designate Henry IV. The war had spread to Italy. Gregory had been driven from Rome and an anti-pope established there in his place. Urban had begun his pontificate in exile, opposed by powerful forces in Europe. His success in rebuilding support had culminated in his entry into Rome in 1094 and in the council of Piacenza itself, which was attended by a large body of bishops and by a significant number of representatives of lay powers.

Since the summons to liberation in the Latin Church had already led to the use of liberating force, it was only a matter of time before it would be extended to areas in which Christians suffered from far more serious disabilities than any of their western brothers. Urban also used the term 'liberation' of the Norman Count Roger's invasion of Sicily and of the Reconquest of Spain, where the Christians had begun to reoccupy the territories lost to the Muslims in the eighth century: the fall of Toledo to the Christians in 1085 had been a sensation. And it was certain – Gregory VII's proposal of 1074 had shown this – that when reformers, accustomed as monks to constant references to Jerusalem in the psalmody of the divine office, thought of the East their minds turned naturally to the holy city. In this respect the First Crusade hardly required a *casus belli*, since the inner momentum of the reform movement would probably have led to it sooner or later.

In 1095 Urban proclaimed a war with two distinct liberating goals. The first was the freeing of the eastern churches, and especially the church of Jerusalem, from the savagery and tyranny of the Muslims. This was the liberation of people, the baptized members of the Church. Urban apparently painted a lurid picture of life under Muslim rule and exaggerated the threat the Turks now posed to Constantinople – their advance had petered out in 1092 – although it must have seemed real enough to the Greeks. It is clear that he coupled this liberation with that of the whole Church. In this he was like his predecessors, who had always associated the liberation of specific groups of the faithful with the needs and renewal of the Church at large; but there was also another factor which made it impossible for him to treat the crusade in isolation.

The eastern frontier of Christendom was not the only one that had been shaken up in the previous decades. So had the south-western frontier in the Iberian peninsula. After the Umayyad caliphate in Cordoba had collapsed in 1031 Moorish Spain had fragmented into petty kingdoms. As Christian pressure began to grow in the later eleventh century these kinglets sought assistance from Ibn Tashfin, the Almoravid ruler in North Africa. The Almoravids, who had established a powerful kingdom centred on Marrakech, had originated as a militant Sunni movement among the Berber peoples. They were notably zealous, puritanical and intolerant. They crossed over to Spain, took it over and won a victory over the Christians at Sagrajas in 1086, after which carts filled with the heads of Christian dead were trundled round Spain and North Africa to show the faithful that the Christians need not be feared. In response, French contingents, including several future crusaders, marched to a rather inconclusive campaign against them in 1087.

It is not surprising that Urban's eyes should have been also on Spain and since almost the start of his pontificate he had enthusiastically supported – indeed the evidence suggests that he himself had inaugurated – a drive to reoccupy Tarragona, a ghost town in no man's land fifty miles down the Spanish coast from Barcelona. The count of Barcelona, who was being encouraged to take it, made it over to the pope as a 'land of St Peter'. Urban appointed an archbishop, fostered colonization, enjoined the notables of the region to rebuild the town 'in penitence and for the remission of sins', and suggested that those planning to make pilgrimages, even to Jerusalem, should instead work for and make financial contributions to the restoration of Tarragona, which, he assured them, would gain them the same spiritual benefits. Nor is it surprising that when, after he had preached the crusade, he learnt that Catalans were planning to take the cross for Jerusalem, he ordered them to stay at home where, he promised them, they could fulfil their crusade vows, 'because it is no virtue to rescue Christians from Muslims in one place, only to expose them to the tyranny and oppression of the Muslims in another'. Although he was spectacularly unsuccessful, since at least two of the four counts he addressed paid no attention to him, he continued to equate the war in the East with the Reconquest of Spain. Most historians do not interpret Urban's words as signifying the first deviation of crusading to another theatre of war, but at the very least the foundations of the Iberian crusades were laid by the originator of the movement and stemmed from a concern of his to preserve an initiative that pre-dated it.

The other goal of the crusade was the liberation of the Holy Sepulchre in Jerusalem, a specific place and one that appealed to the crusaders far more than the idea of the liberation of their brothers and sisters. It used to be argued that the goal of Jerusalem was secondary, perhaps long term, and that Urban's first concern was to help the Greeks against the Turks, thus improving relations with the patriarchate of Constantinople. There is, however, overwhelming evidence in the descriptions of Urban's tour, the decisions of the council of Clermont and the charters of departing crusaders for Jerusalem being a prime goal from the start. And we now know that in a period when interest in the city – or rather in Christ's empty tomb at its heart – had become obsessive, the Byzantine emperor Alexius had himself been targeting western nobles individually for some years, tempting them with the prospect of its liberation.

A penitential war-pilgrimage

Urban's call on crusaders to engage in arms as a penance had its roots in the Investiture Contest. During it the popes had courageously taken the first steps towards a renunciation of the protection of the western emperors on principle, although this exposed them to the greedy ambitions of local Roman nobles, who had shown in the past that unless checked they were capable of treating their bishopric as a pawn. Faced with conflict within Christendom and fearing the nobility at home the popes had tried to find allies in Italy itself and to build up all over Europe a party of lay supporters. They had also turned to the learned for justification of Christian violence. Particularly important in this respect was what would nowadays be called a think-tank, comprising a brilliant group of men gathered round Countess Mathilda of Tuscany, one of the most committed supporters of radical reform. The Mathildine scholars concentrated on reviving and developing the ideas of St Augustine of Hippo (354–430), the most authoritative theoretician of Christian violence, who in a long career had evolved an intellectually satisfying theory of positive force and a justification for serving God in arms. Anselm of Lucca compiled an anthology of Augustine's statements on the issue. John of Mantua based his argument on the incident in the Garden of Gethsemane when St Peter had been rebuked by Christ for drawing a sword and cutting off the ear of the high priest's servant. John maintained that although as a priest Peter had not been permitted to wield the sword himself, he and his successors the popes had authority over it, since Christ had told him to put it back into its scabbard rather than throw it away. Bonizo of Sutri took up the idea of martyrdom in battle, which had been occasionally expounded by the papacy since the ninth century, when two popes had averred that soldiers who died in the right frame of mind in combat against infidels would gain eternal life. One of them had reinforced this by promising absolution to the dead, a precedent which seems to have persuaded the canonist Ivo of Chartres, writing at the time of the First Crusade, that death in engagements against the enemies of the faith could be rewarded. Meanwhile, the title of martyr had been extended by Pope Leo IX to those who fell simply in defence of justice, when he referred to the 'martyrdom' of those who had fallen in the defeat of his forces by the Normans in the Battle of Civitate in 1053.

Striking as the arguments of the Mathildine scholars were, a crusade was to be much more than the service to God in arms envisaged by them, because it was going to be preached as a penance and this, as the conservative opponent of reform Sigebert of Gembloux pointed out, was a departure from previous Christian teaching on violence. Even into the twelfth century a spectrum of opinions on the question whether fighting could be meritorious, whatever the fate of the fighter, ranged from doubts whether sin could be avoided in any act of war to the conviction that altruistic violence could be virtuous. The idea of penitential warfare was revolutionary, not only because it ended the argument for the time being, but also because it put the act of fighting on the same meritorious plane as prayer, works of mercy and fasting. It used to be thought that the first evidence of it in papal circles was an 'indulgence' granted by Pope Alexander II to Christian soldiers going to besiege the Muslim stronghold of Barbastro in Spain in 1063–4. It has recently been argued, however, that there is no reason to suppose that Alexander's letter was addressed to fighters at all – it was probably written for pilgrims – and it is more likely that Gregory VII was the first to state categorically that taking part in war of a certain kind could be an act of charity to which merit was attached and to assert that such an action could indeed be penitential. This is certainly what Sigebert of Gembloux thought when he wrote that the idea had been Gregory's own.

Gregory had a close spiritual relationship with Mathilda of Tuscany and ideas were being exchanged between his circle and hers. It was in the course of this dialogue that the concept of penitential war appeared, leading one opponent of reform to accuse Gregory of 'inciting to bloodshed ... secular men seeking release from their sins'. Sigebert of

Gembloux wrote that Gregory had first put forward the idea that warfare could be penitential when he 'had ordered ... Mathilda to fight the Emperor Henry for the remission of her sins'. The phrase 'remission of sins', echoing the Nicene Creed's definition of baptism, could hardly have had a more potent sound to it. Gregory's reasoning is revealed in a life of Anselm of Lucca, in which one of Anselm's priests described how he transmitted a blessing from Anselm to Mathilda's army in 1085. 'We were', he wrote, 'to impose on the soldiers the danger of the coming battle for the remission of all their sins'. So Anselm was justifying penitential war with the argument that the act of fighting in a just cause was a penance because it was dangerous.

This created a new category of warfare. For a time crusading was not to be the only manifestation of it, although it was the most important. A Pisan assault on Mahdia in North Africa in 1087 was believed to be conducted 'for the remission of sins' and in the euphoria that followed the liberation of Jerusalem Pope Paschal II appealed to Count Robert of Flanders, who had just got back home, to fight another penitential war against the opponents of reform. In the decade before the First Crusade the idea that one could fight as a penance must have been spreading through the families and networks of papal supporters, and from sympathetic monastic communities into the countryside around. Like so much of the radical thought bubbling up during the Investiture Contest, it would have been hard to defend on theological grounds. It would never have been easy to justify the inflicting of pain and the loss of life, with the consequential distortion of the perpetrator's internal dispositions, as a penance simply because the penitent was exposing himself to danger, however unpleasant the experience might have been for him. It was to be Pope Urban's achievement that he gave the idea a context in which it could be presented more convincingly, because he associated it with the most charismatic of all traditional penances, the pilgrimage to Jerusalem.

Jerusalem

Eighty-six years before, in 1009, the Holy Sepulchre had been vandalized on the orders of the Fatimid caliph Hakim. Christ's cave-tomb had been levelled almost to the ground, so that only the floor and the lower part of its walls survived. When the news of its destruction reached the West a wave of persecution broke on the relatively new Jewish communities in parts of France. Some appear to have been decimated. An outburst of ferocious anti-Judaism, again associated with concern for the Holy Sepulchre, was to feature in the early stages of the First Crusade, but meanwhile the destruction of the Sepulchre and the persecution of Christians in Palestine interrupted a flow of pilgrims to Jerusalem which seems to have been on the way to becoming a flood. The increased traffic had probably reflected anxiety that as the year 1000 approached the Last

Days were near, for it was to be in Jerusalem that the final acts in this dimension – the appearance of Anti-Christ, the return of the Saviour, the earliest splitting of tombs and reassembling of bones and dust in the General Resurrection – would take place. Pilgrims had been visiting Jerusalem for centuries and centres of its cult had already been established in western Europe, but contemporary piety encouraged an almost feverish obsession with the holy places. Enthusiasm was fuelled by the arrival of relics from Jerusalem, which were housed in many churches. There were especially famous collections in the Lateran Palace in Rome and in the abbey of Moissac in Languedoc. In the course of the eleventh century churches were to be dedicated to the Holy Sepulchre or the True Cross, or constructed along the lines of the shrine which housed the Tomb. Some were even donated into the Sepulchre's proprietorship.

This enthusiasm was a by-product of an almost morbid concern with sinfulness. Men and women were acutely conscious that a feature of their society was a predisposition to sin, not only because it was violent and because standards and paths to preferment were conditioned by a martial class, but also because the Church, under the influence of monks and engaged in a programme of evangelizing the secular world, was asking of them impossibly high standards of behaviour. Attendance at Mass and participation in pilgrimages were for most people the natural ways of showing religious feeling and sorrow for sin in a society in which piety tended to express itself publicly. There was a constant traffic between local cult-centres and this was stimulated by, and reinforced, the relations of the laity with their local religious communities, which were often the guardians of shrines and to which they were anyway growing increasingly close. Many pilgrims, however, travelled further afield. What drew them were not only the devotional and penitential aspects of a temporary and often demanding exile on the road, but also the relics held at cult-centres and the miracles performed by the saints they represented, such as Faith at Conques, Benedict at Fleury and Cuthbert at Durham, which ranged from idiosyncratic, sometimes capricious and even vengeful acts of protection to cures. On the other hand, while miracles sometimes occurred at or near the greatest long-distance shrines, Compostela, Rome and Jerusalem, it was not usual to go to Rome or Jerusalem for miraculous assistance but out of devotion and for forgiveness.

Pilgrims to Jerusalem were, broadly speaking, of three types. The first, and perhaps the most numerous, were those performing penances imposed on them by their confessors. By their very nature penances needed no vow. The second, often hard to distinguish from the first because there was a penitential element in their journeys as well, were those engaged in what was called a *peregrinatio religiosa*, an act of devotion undertaken voluntarily and perhaps vowed, but not enjoined by a confessor. The third were those who were going to Jerusalem to live there until they died. The special location of the city in the geography of providence meant that it was a place in which devout Christians wanted to be buried.

After the low point in eleventh-century pilgrimaging which followed Hakim's destruction of the Sepulchre, the stream was bound to swell again, and in the mid-1020s there is evidence for many pilgrims on the move, with enthusiasm reaching fever pitch at times. The year 1033 was considered to be the anniversary of the Resurrection and throughout the 1030s, at a time when the shrines in Jerusalem were being partially restored by the Byzantine emperor, pilgrims from many parts of the West were converging on the city. The next major wave appears to have surged East in the 1050s. Then in 1064 there was a large pilgrimage, recruited in France and Germany and triggered by the conviction that Easter Day 1065 was going to fall on exactly the same date as it had in AD 33. In the 1070s passage across Asia Minor, now being overrun by the Turks, must have become much more difficult, but the traffic does not seem to have lessened. It was certainly on the increase in the 1080s and early 1090s. The departure of the First Crusade in 1096 was, therefore, the last of waves of pilgrims which had regularly surged to the East for seventy years.

It was the goal of Jerusalem, of course, that made the crusade both a war and a pilgrimage. While on the one hand Urban used of it the language of pilgrimage – *iter*, *via*, *labor* – on the other he also employed the military term 'Jerusalem expedition' (*Jherosolimitana expeditio*). For one crusader it was not only 'the Jerusalem pilgrimage', but also 'such a ... great ... expedition of the Christian people contending to go to Jerusalem to fight for God against the pagans and the Muslims'. Two brothers took the cross

> on the one hand for the grace of the pilgrimage and on the other, under the protection of God, to wipe out the defilement of the pagans and the immoderate madness through which innumerable Christians have already been oppressed, made captive and killed with barbaric fury.

Crusaders as penitents

The fact that the First Crusade was also a pilgrimage to Jerusalem reinforced, even perhaps legitimated, the practice of penitential war. The council of Clermont had decreed that whoever joined the army 'for devotion alone, not to gain honour or money ... can substitute this journey for all penance' and Urban himself promised the crusaders that

> if any men among you go there not because they desire earthly profit but only for the salvation of their souls and the liberation of the Church, we, acting as much on our own authority as on that of all the archbishops and bishops in the Gauls, through the mercy of almighty

God and the prayers of the Catholic Church, relieve them of all penance imposed for their sins, of which they have made a genuine and full confession.

Some historians have been worried by apparent contradictions in Urban's declarations. Was he merely dispensing his fighters from the performance of penance imposed in the confessional? Or did the crusaders themselves assume that he had relieved them from the punitive consequences of their past sins in this world or the next? In the context of contemporary penitential theology, however, there can have been no contradiction, because the terms Urban used came to the same thing. His crusade 'indulgence' was not really an indulgence at all. It was an authoritative pastoral statement that the penance the crusaders were taking on themselves was going to be so severe that it would be fully 'satisfactory', in the sense that God would be repaid not only the debt of punishment owed on account of their recent sins, for which penances had not yet been performed, but also any residue of debt left over from earlier penances which had not been satisfactory enough. Urban was not granting a spiritual privilege, which was what the developed indulgence would be in that it presupposed that God would treat a meritorious act as if it was 'satisfactory' even though it was not. He was proclaiming a war in which the fighters would be imposing condign punishment on themselves by their own efforts.

He was, in effect, creating a new type of pilgrimage, like the *peregrinatio religiosa* in that it was volunteered out of devotion, but also like the penitential one in that its performance constituted a formal penance and was set by him in the context of the confessional. The writer of the Monte Cassino Chronicle, probably a curial official who came to know Urban's mind, believed that he had set the crusade in motion to provide a means of satisfying 'the penitence of the princes, ... because they could not do penance at home for their innumerable crimes and as laymen were very embarassed to be seen keeping company without weapons'. The nobles, he continued, 'vowed on the authority and with the advice of Pope Urban to take the road overseas to snatch the Sepulchre of the Lord from the Muslims in penitence and for the remission of their sins'. In other words, the summons to crusade was a pastoral move, giving armsbearers the chance of contributing to their own salvation by undertaking a severe penance which did not entail the abandonment of their profession of arms and the humiliating loss of status involved in pilgrimaging abroad as normal penitents, without weapons, equipment and horses. A commentary on the crusade as something deliberately created so that nobles and knights could function as soldiers, not just for the Church's benefit but also for their own, is to be found in the contemporary historian Guibert of Nogent's famous statement:

God has instituted in our time holy wars, so that the order of knights and the crowd running in their wake ... might find a new way of gaining salvation. And so they are not forced to abandon secular affairs completely by choosing the monastic life or any religious profession, as used to be the custom, but can attain in some measure God's grace while pursuing their own careers, with the liberty and in the dress to which they are accustomed.

There can be no doubt that the crusaders understood that they were performing a penance and that the exercise they were embarking on could contribute to their future salvation. Running through many of their charters is a pessimistic piety, typical of the age, expressing itself in a horror of wickedness and a fear of its consequences. Responding to Urban's emphasis on the need for sorrow for sin, the crusaders openly craved forgiveness. They joined the expedition, as one charter put it, 'in order to obtain the pardon that God can give me for my crimes'. The same sentiments were put more elaborately in another:

Considering how many are my sins and the love, clemency and mercy of Our Lord Jesus Christ, because when he was rich he became poor for our sake, I have determined to repay him in some measure for everything he has given me freely, although I am unworthy. And so I have decided to go to Jerusalem, where God was seen as man and spoke with men and to adore in the place where his feet trod.

On 22 May 1096 Fulk Doon of Châteaurenard in Provence came to the abbey of Lérins, where the abbot handed him the symbols of pilgrimage and 'enjoined the journey to Jerusalem on him as a penance'. While Miles of Bray from Champagne was absent in the East he was reported 'doing penance for his guilt'.

A consequence was that crusading could be considered as a kind of alternative to profession into the religious life. Describing the crusade, contemporaries were to portray the army on the march as a nomadic abbey, its days and nights punctuated by solemn liturgy, its soldiers dedicated to austerity and brotherhood – 'just as in the primitive church, nearly all things were shared in common' – and enduring a religious exile, temporary it is true, which led, as one writer put it, 'not [to] a military but a monkish life as far as frugality was concerned'. In an age in which the monastic life was a measure against which everything tended to be set, it would be tempting to see this monasticization of war in commentaries written after the liberation of Jerusalem as a consequence of a rationalization of the apparently miraculous triumph of the First Crusade, were it not for the fact that at least three men, seriously drawn to religion, changed their minds on hearing about the crusade's preaching and joined the armies to the East as if military service of this kind had already an equivalence to religious profession. So comparisons between monasticism and crusading were being made even before the armies marched.

The crusaders regarded themselves as pilgrims and while on crusade they engaged in characteristic devotional and liturgical exercises. Warrior pilgrims were a novelty, because as penitents pilgrims had always been forbidden to carry arms, but the crusade was anyway a very odd sort of pilgrimage. Urban tried to confine participation to armsbearers. He forbade monks to go:

> We were [he wrote] stimulating the minds of knights to go on this expedition. ... We do not want those who have abandoned the world and have vowed themselves to spiritual warfare either to bear arms or to go on this journey; we go so far as to forbid them to do so.

He wanted to limit the number of priests to as few as was necessary. He stated that the old, the infirm and women were not suitable, although women apparently could accompany their husbands or brothers with permission from church authorities. His statements on the unfit laity could not, however, be prohibitions, merely recommendations. Pilgrimages were devotional exercises for all penitents, whatever their condition – indeed those going to healing shrines were the sick – and it was clearly impossible to limit a pilgrimage to youngish, healthy men, which is one reason why so many of the 'unsuitable' did eventually take part in the crusade.

The introduction of the vow was another very significant innovation. Its exact terms are not known, but it must have involved a promise to pilgrimage to Jerusalem combined with a pledge to liberate it by force. Pilgrims had never been under the general obligation to make vows and one must suppose that most never did. The misconception that the crusader's vow originated in that of the pilgrim probably stems from the fact that in the surviving pontificals and manuals, dating from the third quarter of the twelfth century onwards, actions, which earlier had been separate, had become conflated, so that the cross, the sign of the vow and the symbols of pilgrimage were received at the same time. Reading these led to the belief that the rite for the taking of the cross must have developed out of the ceremony for blessing the insignia of pilgrims, but it can be demonstrated that in the earliest period of crusading there was not one action, but two: the taking of the cross and the granting of the pilgrim's purse and staff, which would follow separately, perhaps some time later.

The introduction of crosses was a stroke of genius. Urban was reported by those who had heard him at Clermont associating the taking and wearing of them in a highly charged way with Christ's precept, 'If any man will come after me, let him deny himself and take up his cross and follow me' (Matthew 16: 24 or Luke 14: 27). The language the pope was reported using suggests that he knew he was doing something new and that he intended the crosses to be distinctive. Crusaders were certainly conspicuous, distinguishable from their contemporaries and perhaps even from other pilgrims, with whom crosses had never been regularly associated before. It is easy to forget how visible the ordinary cloth ones must have been. A mid-twelfth-century sculpture, from the priory of Belval in Lorraine, shows a crusader wearing one made from two-inch strips of cloth on his chest; it looks as though it measured six by six inches. Crusaders were obliged to wear their crosses at all times and were not supposed to take them off until they had fulfilled their vows.

It was important to contemporaries that they should be marked out in this way. Leaders of crusading early armies became convinced that there was a reservoir of additional manpower in the West which could be deployed if only the Church would make laggards, who should have been identifiable, fulfil their vows and attempts were periodically made to establish just how large the force of war-shy was. It was always a lot easier to rail against 'false' crusaders than to make them do what they had promised, but the pressure put on them and the publicity they attracted underlined the seriousness of the commitment they had made.

Urban preached the crusade as a meritorious act of love which laymen were particularly qualified to undertake and he went further in proposing the crusade as a 'way of the cross'. Hitherto that way had been a renunciation of earthly things in a retreat into the cloister, but monastic profession was not a responsible option for many, who knew well that in an insecure environment their families depended on them remaining in the world. Now these laymen were provided with something to do that was almost equivalent to monasticism. The pope had taken a step along the road that would lead the Church to recognize the lay condition as a vocation in itself.

The response

In addition to preaching the crusade personally during his journey through France Urban sent letters or embassies to Flanders, Genoa, Bologna, Pisa and Milan. The crusade was also discussed at councils he held at Bari in October 1098 and Rome in April 1099. At Clermont, and probably at the council of Nîmes in the following summer, he encouraged all the bishops present to preach the cross themselves. Several followed his instructions, among whom the most prominent was Hugh of Die, the archbishop of Lyon and an ardent reformer, but there is evidence that many did not. The council of Clermont had agreed a body of legislation on the crusade, but only one canon – on the remission of sins – survives in the form it was decreed. Very few manuscripts of the council's decisions, which tended to contain only those canons which were of interest to the bishops who had them copied, included it. One which did, a list made for Bishop Lambert of Arras, may not even have reflected Lambert's concern, since he left us his own account of the council, in which no mention is made of the crusade at all; for him the most important result was the pope's confirmation of the standing of his own bishopric. Monks were more enthusiastic and many religious communities were centres of recruitment. There were also free-lancers like Peter the Hermit.

But the news of the pope's appeal seems mostly to have spread by word of mouth – so fast, according to one contemporary, that there was no need of preaching – and it is clear that it was passed within families from member to member. Concentrations of crusaders were to be found in armsbearing families in Limousin, Flanders, Lorraine, Provence, the Ile-de-France, Normandy and Burgundy. Outstanding examples were the comital house of Burgundy and the castellan family of Montlhéry in the Ile-de-France. Of the five sons of Count William Tête-Hardi of Burgundy, three were crusaders and a fourth, as Pope Calixtus II, preached the crusade of 1120. A grandson and granddaughter also took part. Three members of the house of Montlhéry were involved, together with the members of an astonishing array of related families, of which Chaumont-en-Vexin sent four crusaders, St Valéry three, Broyes, Bourcq of Rethel, and Le Puiset two each, and Courtenay and Pont-Echanfray one each. Indeed the two generations of this clan active at the time of the First Crusade produced twenty-three crusaders and settlers, all closely related, of whom six became major figures in the Latin East. We can picture a chain of enthusiasm stretching across northern France.

Elements can be identified which may help to explain why some kin-groups were predisposed to respond strongly to the appeal to crusade. Among them were family traditions of pilgrimage to Jerusalem, attachment to Cluniac monasticism and the reformed papacy, and the veneration of certain saints. Female kindred, moreover, appear to have carried the message to the families into which they married. Of four sisters in the comital house of Burgundy, three were the wives of first crusaders and the fourth was the mother of one. Although there were probably independent traditions in the Le Puiset clan, its matriarch was one of four Montlhéry sisters, all of whom were the wives or mothers of crusaders; so were both her daughters.

The response to the summons to crusade was large enough to cause comment at the time, but just how large is now difficult to judge. Leaving aside the numbers on the third wave of the crusade – the so-called Crusade of 1101 – which were affected by the news of the liberation of Jerusalem, the following can be suggested very tentatively. Around 5,000 knights gathered on the second wave before Nicaea (Iznik) in June 1097.

One should multiply that by a factor of four to include their supporters (grooms, shield bearers and so forth) and add on something for foot soldiers. So c. 25,000 might be a fair estimate of the number of combatants. There were also many poor people with the crusade and with them its size may have reached c. 40,000. Crusaders continued to overtake the army right up to the fall of Jerusalem and beyond, even though the numbers during the siege of Jerusalem had fallen to 15,000. We should add c. 5,000 for late departures. The armies of the first wave were at least as large as those of the second and might have comprised another 40,000 persons. This gives us a total of 85,000, of whom perhaps 7,000 would have been knights. We then have to take into account the substantial number who took the cross but did not leave; perhaps 42,000 or 50 per cent of the number departing would be reasonable. So we end up with an estimate of 127,000 recruits, of whom about 10 per cent would have been knights.

These are guesses, of course, but even much lower estimates produce figures which were very substantial for the time and beg the question why so many responded. The population of Europe, which had been steadily growing, had reached the point at which the systems of inheritance and marriage practices were being put under severe pressure. And by 1096 several years of drought had led to poor harvests in France and shortages, and hence to ergotism, a terrifying condition which could lead to insanity and death and was brought on by eating bread made from rye which had not had ergot removed from it. The age was one of colonization on the frontiers and even in forests and on marginal lands within old Europe and it was natural for a few commentators at the time and for many historians since to assume that the crusade was a colonial venture, that the prospect of new territory for settlement in a land referred to in scripture as 'flowing with milk and honey' and situated in a region of legendary wealth, moved peasants, landless unmarried sons and members of families collectively sharing smaller subdivisions of holdings to opt for a new life. On the other hand, most commentators then and a minority of historians now have maintained that the chief motivation was a genuine idealism.

The poor were very numerous in all the armies of the First Crusade. It is possible that many of them were taking advantage of the chance to seek a new life for themselves, but we know very little about them, let alone their ideas and aspirations. They must have suffered a very high death rate and it is hard to envisage the survivors having the means or energy to return home once the campaign was over. Some remained in northern Syria when the armies marched south. Others must have stayed on in Palestine when the crusaders who could afford it left for home.

The evidence for the armsbearers being knowingly engaged from the first in a colonial venture is weak. Cases can be made for the territorial ambitions of some, including Bohemond of Taranto and Baldwin of

Boulogne, but otherwise there is little to go on. Even the Montlhéry clan, with its remarkable cluster of crusaders, seems to have been drawn to the enterprise primarily by its spiritual benefits. It should be remembered that although the crusade began the process by which western Europeans conquered and settled in many of the coastal territories of the eastern Mediterranean, it is very unlikely that this was planned from the start. The pope and the military leaders assumed that once the armies reached Constantinople they would be elements in a much larger force under the command of the Byzantine emperor, to whose empire Jerusalem had once belonged, and that from then on the campaign would be one which, if successful, would restore Greek rule to the Levant. It was only when the westerners discovered that the emperor was not interested in leading them and was not prepared to send with them anything more than a comparatively small force of Greeks that they made the decision to strike out on their own. This would not have precluded settlement, of course, but the fact is that most of them returned to Europe once the campaign was over.

Another common explanation of motive is that the early crusades were little more than large-scale plundering expeditions, with which western knights were already familiar from their forays into Spain and elsewhere. The bishops at Clermont had certainly been concerned that men might join the crusade 'for money' and there can be no doubt that it attracted violent individuals. There were no means available for screening recruits for suitability, other than the decisions of the magnates on the composition of their households; indeed there could not have been, because, as has already been pointed out, as pilgrimages crusades had to be open to all, even psychopaths. The appetites of the violent may well have been sharpened by disorientation, fear and stress as they sackaged their way to the East. The vicious persecution of Jews in France and Germany, which opened the march of some of the armies, was marked by looting and extortion and the passage of the crusaders through the Balkans was punctuated by outbreaks of pillaging.

On the other hand, the reality was that because the crusaders had no proper system of provisioning foraging was essential for their survival. While in Christian territory they were dependent on hand-outs from local rulers; once in the devastated no man's land that Asia Minor was becoming they were far from any worthwhile rendezvous-point with European shipping until they reached Antioch, and then they were near one which brought them only limited supplies. All the leaders, from great to small, had to live with the fact that their followers expected from them at the very least a subsistence level of provisioning. This alone would have accounted for an obsession with plunder.

A third popular explanation of the attraction of crusading is that rising population was forcing landowning families to take measures to prevent the subdivision of their estates, either through the practice of primo-geniture or through a primitive method of birth-control, according to which only one male in each generation was allowed to marry. The other young men were encouraged to make themselves scarce. Departure on crusade was an appropriate way for a supernumerary to reduce the burdens his family was facing.

An entirely different picture emerges from the documents. Crusaders were not conscripts or vassals performing feudal service. Most of them were volunteers and those who could not attract the support, or were not ensconced in the household, of a rich noble had to finance themselves. Information about the distance to Palestine must have been freely available to them, since many western Europeans had been on pilgrimage and a significant number of knights had served as mercenaries in the Byzantine forces. The distance and consequent expenses may not have deterred the very poor, who expected nothing and could, perhaps, have believed that their situation could only improve, but for knights it was a different matter. They were expected to bring with them the equipment, horses, pack animals and servants required to fulfil their function efficiently. Half a century later a Rhineland knight called upon to serve the western emperor in Italy needed to put by for such a campaign twice his annual income. The factor by which a French knight would have had to multiply his income in budgeting for a campaign in the East can only be guessed at, but a factor of four or five would not be unreasonable. This makes the traditional picture of landless knights departing without a care in the world ridiculous. It is not surprising to find in monastic and cathedral cartularies examples of the steps crusaders and their families took to provide themselves with funds, but land prices were depressed after years of drought. The run of poor harvests was broken by a magnificent one in 1096, after a wet spring that seemed to be a physical expression of God's approval of the enterprise, but this obviously came too late for many of the crusaders, who had already been engaged in selling or pledging their lands, and the seriousness of their situation was compounded by the facts that the disposals were so numerous and the number of individuals or institutions capable of providing ready cash on so large a scale so few that the value of property in France was said to have fallen.

One measure, which seems to have been attractive to the lords and richer knights, was the surrender of disputed claims in return for cash. Renunciations by crusaders of claims and rights unfairly exercised occurred quite commonly – pilgrims did not like to leave behind anyone with a grudge against them – but religious communities could also be persuaded to part with money for them. The benefits to the crusader were multiplied, because he could leave with a clearer conscience as well as with a contribution towards his costs. Some lords had been extremely rough. The co-owners of the castle of Mezenc, in dispute with the monks of

St Chaffre du Monastier but now 'taking the road to Jerusalem to fight the barbarians', had made their point by plundering 'the poor living in our villages, taking everything that belonged to them, to a loaf's crust, as the saying goes'. Churchmen seem to have fastened onto these agreements as good ways of ending what must have been exhausting and stressful contests and the compositions were often expressed in grovelling terms; perhaps these were demanded by the religious in return for their money. The castellan Nivelo of Fréteval allowed the drafter of his charter of renunciation to refer to him, quoting from Pope Gregory I, as being 'raised in a nobility of birth which produces in many people an ignobility of mind', and to his claims as 'the oppressive behaviour resulting from a certain bad custom, handed on to me not by ancient right but from the time of my father, a man of little weight who first harassed the poor with this oppression'.

Property might well also have to be pledged or sold. Some sales were substantial and could include whole lordships. Most pledges appear to have been *vifgages*, agreements according to which the lenders did not receive interest but occupied the properties concerned, enjoying the revenues from them until their loans had been repaid to them. The employment of *vifgages* technically avoided usury and were presumably convenient, but a disadvantage for crusaders and their families was that the lands passed out of their control until the pledges were redeemed. It goes without saying that disposing of property to an ecclesiastical institution would have been a last resort, since it could be lost to the market for ever, but it was often only churches and religious communities which had the funds available, because they were rich or because they could realize cash from the disposal of valuables treasurized in their shrines. Nevertheless, 16 per cent of the surviving pledges and 13 per cent of the sales were agreed not with churchmen but with lay men and women. The percentages may not seem impressive, but it should be remembered that the surviving records are almost entirely ecclesiastical and that it would have been rare for a deal negotiated among the laity to surface in them. They indicate quite a lot of activity in the secular world devoted to raising money for the crusade. A total of 10 per cent of the pledges and 9 per cent of the sales involved the crusaders' close relations and it is notable that some of these were female, including sisters who perhaps could call on their husbands' assets at a time when the male members of the family were short of cash.

The disposal of property was something that involved all the members of a crusader's family, since what was being alienated was patrimony, in which they had an actual or potential interest. They could make difficulties and passionately dispute the arrangements which had been made, but this was unusual. Apparent acts of generosity by relations, particularly maternal uncles, who often had an interest in protecting their sisters' children, as opposed to paternal uncles who were potential competitors, may have been made to prevent the degradation of patrimonies. It is striking that of the surviving agreements with churchmen at least 43 per cent of all disposals for cash were of assets of doubtful value, because possession of them was disputed or questionable, or because they were already pledged. This suggests that many families adopted sensible policies when it came to alienation and in the terms of many documents we may be hearing echoes of conferences of the kindred, summoned to decide whether assets could be saved or, if not, what type of property should be offered for pledge or sale. A record of one such conference surfaces in a Breton document. The crusader Thibald of Ploasme informed his brother William that if he was not helped financially he would have to sell his inheritance. William did not want Thibald's share of the estate to be lost, so he raised money from the monks of St Nicolas d'Angers by selling them part of his share of a mill which was already pledged.

The fact that crusading involved costs rather than gain is confirmed if one looks at the condition of the crusaders when they came home. There is very little evidence for them returning wealthy, which is not surprising, considering the expenses of the return journey from the Levant and the impracticability of carrying riches in kind over long distances; indeed, it was reported that many in the exodus from Palestine in the autumn of 1099 were impoverished by the time they reached northern Syria. Of course, the enhanced standing of many of them on their return could have helped to ease any financial burdens they faced. Amid the dangers and hardships of a crusade close association with a great lord could lead to advancement and in an age when family fortunes could be improved by marriage, ex-crusaders might well have found that they could arrange more advantageous matches for their sons and daughters.

Nevertheless, the disposal of assets to invest in the fairly remote possibility of settlement after a 2,000-mile march to the East or in the hope of improving one's status at home would have been a stupid gamble, especially as the odds could have been lessened simply by waiting until after the agricultural depression had passed and the flood of properties on the market had subsided. It is not surprising that the only strategy for which there is evidence is one in which the kindred cooperated in damage-limitation once a relation had taken the cross. There is no evidence to support the view that crusading relieved families of burdens; on the contrary, the evidence points overwhelmingly to families taking on burdens to help individual members fulfil their vows.

It makes sense, therefore, to suppose that crusaders, and especially their families, were moved by idealism. This was an age of ostentatious and extravagant generosity and monasteries and religious communities benefited greatly from it. If the phenomenal growth of monasticism was due as much, if not more, to those who did not enter the communities but endowed them from outside as to those who did, then the same is true of the crusading movement. Behind many crusaders stood a large body of men and women who were prepared to make substantial sacrifices in agreeing to the disposal of property to help them set out. It is important to bear in mind that the popularity of crusading can be exaggerated. Although it was an activity which appealed to people living in many different parts of western Europe, with a wide range of perceptions, cerebral and emotional, there was always a majority which was not prepared to engage in something so inconvenient, dangerous and expensive. We do not, in other words, have to find explanations for motivation involving all western society. Even among the armsbearers, about whom we have most information, the figure of, say, 12,000 respondents (of whom about half did not actually depart) represents a fraction of the total numbers. In England alone there were c. 5,000 knights and in France and the French-speaking imperial territories at least 50,000. So we are concerned with the reactions not of an entire class but of a fraction of it, defined by its response to the summons of the pope and the support of the kindred.

The 'first Holocaust'

Urban's appeal succeeded because it could be interpreted by lay knights in accordance with their own thinking. This could mean that in their minds it would take on a colouring that churchmen did not like, but which they could do little to control. Western European society consisted of many tight, interlocking circles, made up of families, each of which was bound together by the knowledge that its members were kin and therefore 'friends', obliged to care for each other's interests, and of feudal groupings, of vassals round lords, which made the same demands on their members. Familial and feudal relationships imposed on men the obligation of the blood-feud in which they were bound to draw their swords in the interests of their relatives, lords or fellow vassals. It is significant that the first appeal for crusaders was expressed in intimate, even domestic, terms. Men were called upon to go to the aid of their oppressed 'brothers', the eastern Christians, whom they were obliged to love, and to the aid of their 'father' and 'lord', Jesus Christ, who had been humiliated and disregarded and had lost his 'inheritance' or patrimony. That could be a summons to a vendetta.

> I address fathers and sons and brothers and nephews. If an outsider were to strike any of your kin down would you not avenge your blood-relative? How much more ought you to avenge your God, your father, your brother, whom you see reproached, banished from his estates, crucified; whom you hear calling, desolate and begging for aid.

The idea that the crusade was a form of the vendetta may have contributed to its bloody overture. There were outbreaks of violent anti-Judaism in France shortly after the council of Clermont. These spread to Germany and eastern Europe, where they were associated with the first wave of crusaders leaving for the East. On 3 May 1096 the storm broke over the Jewish community at Speyer, where a South German army had gathered under Emich of Flonheim, the most merciless of the persecutors. Emich proceeded to Worms, where the massacres began on 18 May, and then to Mainz, where he was joined by more Germans and by a large army of French, English, Flemish and Lorrainer crusaders. Between 25 and 29 May the Jewish community at Mainz, one of the largest in Europe, was decimated. Some crusaders then marched north to Cologne, from where the Jews had already been dispersed into neighbouring settlements. For the next month they were hunted out and destroyed. Another band seems to have gone south-west to Trier and Metz, where the massacres continued. It is possible that Peter the Hermit's crusading army forced almost the whole community at Regensburg to undergo baptism. The communities at Wesseli and Prague in Bohemia suffered from the attentions of yet another army, probably that led by a priest called Folkmar.

These pogroms were attributed by some contemporaries to avarice and the crusaders certainly made financial demands of the Jewish communities and despoiled them. But the Hebrew accounts ascribed greed more to some of the local bishops, their officials and townspeople than to the crusaders, who seem to have been more interested in forcing conversions. Everywhere Jews were offered the choice of conversion or death. Synagogues, Torah scrolls and cemeteries were desecrated and the Jews feared that the crusaders intended to wipe their religion out in the districts through which they passed. Two motivations have been suggested. The first was the desire for vengeance. The crusaders seem to have found it impossible to distinguish between Muslims and Jews and if they were being called upon, as they saw it, to avenge the injury to Christ's 'honour' of the loss of his patrimony to the Muslims, why, they asked, should they not also avenge the injury to his person of the Crucifixion – a far deeper disparagement of his 'honour' – particularly in the light of a popular legend circulating at the time in which Christ on the cross had called on the faithful to avenge him? The second was millenarian. Forcing baptism on the Jews may well have reflected the conviction that the Last Days would be ushered in by their conversion. The forcible conversion of non-Christians was prohibited in canon law and the German bishops, with varying degrees of success, tried to stop it. To educated churchmen events from long ago, the Crucifixion in AD 33 and the Muslim occupation of Jerusalem in 638, could not justify retribution. It was a present injury, the fact that the Muslims were still in occupation of the holy city, which justified the crusade, not some woolly concept of past disparagement of honour. But once the crusade had been preached as an expression of love for God and brothers it was impossible for churchmen to control the emotions their appeal had aroused.

Other motives could also have been at work. It is hard to reconcile calls for vengeance with demands for conversion: one is an act of retaliation, the other would have been regarded by the perpetrators as the conferment of a benefit. Focused persecution, moreover, occurred in the preparations for, rather than in the course of, crusades. Emotional anti-Judaism seems to have featured in a European context, but not, or not so much, in a west Asian one, where, at any rate after 1110, there was relative toleration in crusader Palestine. The contradictions may be explained by the fact that holy war always has a tendency to turn inwards. Its participants come to believe that it can never be successful if the society which has bred it is unregenerate and impure. The Christian crusade, like the Islamic *jihad*, led easily to strivings for religious uniformity at home. While the belief that it was part of the divine plan that Jews should survive in a servile condition as providential witnesses made it impossible for church leaders to tolerate the use of force against them, Jews nevertheless constituted an alien group and it is possible that baptism was being forced on them with the aim of creating a uniformly Christian society by eliminating their religion.

CHAPTER 2

The Course of the First Crusade

Three waves of men and women left Europe between 1096 and 1101. In between there was a continuous stream of parties travelling East, so that the forces of the second wave were being overtaken all the time by new recruits and crusaders were still entering Palestine as those who had won Jerusalem were leaving for home. There was, moreover, a counterflow of deserters back along the path and from as early as the winter of 1096 the disillusioned, the sick and the fearful were drifting back to western Europe.

The condition of Islam

Although none of them knew it, the crusaders were marching towards an open door. I have already pointed out that Palestine and Syria had been a theatre in which a resurgent Sunnism, spearheaded by the Selchük Turks who had established a sultanate to rule on behalf of the 'Abbasid caliphate in Baghdad, warred against the Fatimid caliphate in Cairo, which for the last century had been a centre of vigorous proselytizing Shi'ism. The city of Jerusalem had fallen to the Selchüks in 1071, but on 26 August 1098, while the crusade was in northern Syria, it was retaken by the Fatimids. By then the Islamic world had been gravely weakened by a chain of disasters. In 1092 one of the greatest figures in Selchük history, the vizir Nizam al-Mulk, the power behind the sultans for over thirty years, had been murdered. A month later the Selchük sultan Malikshah had died in suspicious circumstances. He was followed to the grave not only by his wife, grandson and other powerful figures, but also by the 'Abbasid caliph al-Muqtadi himself. With this wipe-out the Selchük sultanate disintegrated into principalities in which pretenders and members of the family fought each other for power. Then in 1094 the Fatimid caliph al-Mustansir, who had ruled for fifty-eight years and had fiercely resisted the Selchüks, also died. So did his vizir, Badr al-Jamali.

The first wave

The first wave of crusaders left very early, in fact far too early, in the spring of 1096. The most famous of its leaders, a popular preacher called Peter the Hermit, had begun to recruit for the crusade in central France even before the council of Clermont. This has led a few historians to try to revive the story, believed by one or two of Peter's contemporaries and probably assiduously propagated by himself, that the crusade was his brainchild. He collected a substantial following before moving on to the

Rhineland in April. In advance of him, and probably on his instructions, a large body of foot, led by eight knights under the command of Walter Sansavoir (not 'the Penniless', as is popularly supposed: Sansavoir was the toponym of the lords of Poissy) entered Hungary on 21 May and marched in a fairly orderly fashion to Constantinople. There was a serious outbreak of violence at Belgrade, predictably over foraging, and the absence of more trouble is remarkable considering the fact that Walter's early arrival took the Byzantine authorities by surprise.

At Constantinople Walter was joined by parties of Italian pilgrims and on 1 August by Peter the Hermit, who had left Cologne on 20 April and had had a much more difficult crossing of the Balkans, for which the indiscipline of his followers was largely to blame. His army marched peacefully through Hungary, but at Zemun, the last town in the kingdom, a riot broke out, the citadel was stormed and a large number of Hungarians were killed. The crusaders were naturally anxious to escape retribution by crossing the river Sava into Byzantine territory as soon as possible, and the attempts by a Byzantine force to restrict their movement were resisted. They were in an ugly mood by the time they reached a deserted Belgrade which they probably sacked. Nevertheless the Byzantine governor at Niš, unprepared though he was, tried to be cooperative and allowed them to buy supplies in exchange for the surrender of hostages. As they were leaving, some Germans set fire to mills outside the town and the governor sent troops to attack the rearguard. Many of Peter's followers, ignoring his orders, turned on their attackers and were routed and scattered. The crusaders lost many men and women and all their cash. Luckily, by the time they reached Sofia the Greeks were ready to receive them. They were now kept supplied and on the move and reached Constantinople without further incident.

Walter and Peter were received well by the Byzantine emperor Alexius and were advised to wait until the other bands of crusaders, which were known to be assembling in Europe, arrived. But Peter's impatient followers took to raiding the surrounding countryside and the Greeks decided that the sooner they were moved on the better. On 6 August they were ferried across the Bosporus. They then marched to Kibotos, a suitable assembly-point where they could wait for the rest of the crusade, but differences arose between the Germans and Italians on one side, who elected their own leader, an Italian noble called Rainaldo, and the French on the other. From Kibotos the French raided as far as Turkish Nicaea and Rainaldo's party sought to emulate them. The Germans and Italians broke away and established a base beyond Nicaea, but on 29 September they were surrounded by the Turks and surrendered eight days later. Those who agreed to apostatize were sent to the East, but all who refused were killed. When the news of this disaster reached the main body, Peter the Hermit was away in Constantinople and the French crusaders, ignoring Walter Sansavoir's pleas for caution, advanced into the interior on 21 October. They were ambushed by the Turks and were annihilated.

Walter and Peter at least reached Asia Minor. Three other armies, which marched at about the same time, got no further than Hungary. The force of Saxons and Bohemians under Folkmar was destroyed at Nitra. Another unruly band under a Rhineland priest called Gottschalk was forced to surrender to the Hungarians at Pannonhalma. The large army of Rhineland, Swabian, French, English and Lorrainer crusaders under Emich of Flonheim, which had been persecuting the Jews in the Rhineland, was halted before Wieselburg on the Hungarian frontier where, after taking six weeks to build a bridge over the river in front of the town, its first assault dissolved into panic and flight.

It is wrongly assumed that these forces, 'The People's Crusade', consisted almost entirely of peasants, in contrast to those that left Europe later in 1096. This was certainly an explanation given by contemporaries for their massacres of Jews, their indiscipline in the Balkans and their failure in Asia Minor. But we cannot allow ourselves to be lulled by the comforting belief that these were mere gangs of peasants, prone to riot and unprofessional on the march. Although there may have been more non-combatants than in the later armies, there was a strong knightly element as well. Walter Sansavoir was an experienced knight; so were Peter the Hermit's captains, one of whom, Fulcher of Chartres, was to end his days as a lord in the county of Edessa, the earliest Latin settlement. Emich of Flonheim was an important South German noble. So was Count Hartmann of Dillingen-Kybourg, who joined him at Mainz. They were probably accompanied by at least four other German counts. The army of French, English, Flemish and Lorrainer crusaders, which also met Emich at Mainz, was apparently large and well equipped and was led by an outstanding group of French knights: Clarembald of Vendeuil, Thomas of Marle lord of Coucy, William the Carpenter viscount of Melun, and Drogo of Nesle. They may have made up a French advance-guard, since after the destruction of Emich's forces they joined Hugh of Vermandois, the king of France's brother, and continued their journey to the East with him.

One of the reasons for the catastrophes that befell this first wave of crusaders was that it left Europe before the date set by the pope, which was 15 August 1096. Leaving while western Europe was still in the grip of near famine conditions, before the marvellous harvest of that summer, the crusaders were short of food from the start. In the Balkans they had to pillage when the markets were not available to them. Even with access to markets they were anxious about supplies and over and over again it was disputes about provisions that led to disorder. The Byzantine government, moreover, was unprepared. It had not set up the organization to guide the crusaders; nor did it have the supplies to give them. And the failure of the armies of Folkmar, Gottschalk and especially Emich of Flonheim to get through at all meant that Peter the Hermit and Walter Sansavoir did not have adequate forces in Asia Minor.

The second wave: the march to Constantinople

The second wave of crusaders began to leave western Europe in the middle of August, on or after the date fixed by the pope. At this stage they travelled in separate corps, each mustered from a region and many under the leadership of great magnates. Hugh of Vermandois left France in the middle of August and travelled by way of Rome to Bari, from where he set sail for Durazzo (Durrës). But a storm scattered his fleet and Hugh, who was forced to land some way from Durazzo, was briefly detained before being escorted to Constantinople. At about the same time Godfrey of Bouillon, the duke of Lower Lorraine, left with his brother Baldwin of Boulogne and a party of Lorrainer nobles. Godfrey is the most famous of the first crusaders, but the one we can understand the least. He had been born c. 1060, the second son of Count Eustace II of Boulogne and Ida of Lorraine. His elder brother, Eustace III, who crusaded at the same time, had inherited Boulogne and the family's great estates in England a little after 1070. Six years later Godfrey's maternal uncle left him the duchy of Lower Lorraine, the marquisate of Antwerp, the county of Verdun and the territories of Bouillon and Stenay. But King Henry IV of Germany postponed confirmation of the grant of Lower Lorraine and Godfrey only acquired the duchy in 1087, while he had to fight what amounted to a ten-year war against his aunt, the formidable Mathilda of Tuscany, who had no intention of renouncing her claims to her husband's lands, and the bishop of Verdun and the count of Namur, who backed her, before he was firmly in control of his other properties. Until he took the cross he had not shown any marked piety and it is clear from the terms of the pledge agreements he drew up that in 1096 he had no definite intention of settling in the East. In ecclesiastical politics, moreover, he had been firmly on the side of the German king and against the reforming papacy. His maternal grandfather and uncle had been imperialists, and those who had stood in the way of his inheritance, Mathilda of Tuscany and the bishop of Verdun, were partisans of Pope Gregory VII. He himself had fought for Henry IV and had probably taken part in the seizure of Rome from Gregory in 1084.

The personality of Godfrey's younger brother Baldwin is clearer to us. Born between 1061 and 1070, he had been destined for the Church and had been presented with prebends at Reims, Cambrai and Liège. But in the new climate of reformist opinion such pluralism was intolerable and it may be that he was forced to surrender some of his benefices. At any rate he had left the Church by 1086, too late to enjoy a share in the family inheritance which had already been divided between his brothers. This helps to explain the animosity Baldwin was to show later to reformers and reform ideas. He was poor and his need for money may have led to his marriage in c. 1090 to Godehilde of Tosny, the child of a powerful Anglo-Norman family, who was to die during the crusade. He was an intelligent, calculating and ruthless man. He was not pleasant, but his strength of personality and quickness of mind were to be of great value to the crusaders and the early settlers in the East.

Passing through southern Germany, the brothers and their following reached the Hungarian border in September. Here they delayed to get clearance from the king, who had already smashed three crusading armies. Baldwin was persuaded to be a hostage for the crusaders' behaviour and Godfrey issued strict instructions against plundering. Late in November he reached Byzantine territory. Hearing a rumour that Hugh of Vermandois was being held prisoner by the emperor, he allowed his followers to pillage the region around Silivri until he was assured that Hugh was free. He reached Constantinople on 23 December and camped outside the city near the head of the Golden Horn.

Bohemond of Taranto crossed the Adriatic with a small force of South Italian Normans a fortnight after Hugh of Vermandois. About forty years old, he was the eldest son of Robert Guiscard, the duke of Apulia, and had played a leading part in his father's invasion of Byzantine Albania in 1081. Robert had left him his conquests on the eastern shore of the Adriatic, which the Normans were already losing, and in consequence Bohemond had found himself effectively disinherited, since his younger brother Roger had been left Apulia. Although in the late 1080s he had carved out for himself a large lordship in southern Italy, there can be no doubt that he wanted a principality, possibly to be won at the expense of the Greeks who had retaken the lands he should have been enjoying in Albania. One hostile contemporary believed that this was the sole reason for him taking the cross. According to an admirer he was 'always seeking the impossible'. The Greeks, who believed that he had also inherited from his father designs on the Byzantine empire itself, recognized that he was very able; in fact he was to prove himself to be one of the finest generals the crusading movement produced. He was also intelligent and pious, and he was perhaps the only leader who really understood the motives of the reforming papacy. Byzantine officials were prepared for his arrival, but the local inhabitants, who had after all experienced a Norman invasion quite recently, refused to sell him provisions. So his followers had to forage until they were assured of supplies by the Byzantine government once they had passed Thessaloniki. They also destroyed a small town which they thought was occupied by heretics and had a brush with imperial troops who tried to hurry them along. Bohemond had to spend time and energy trying to restrain his followers from looting even in Thrace and when he went on ahead to

Constantinople, which he reached on 10 April 1097, his nephew Tancred, who was to prove himself to be one of the ablest of the early rulers of the settlements in the East, allowed the Normans to forage in the countryside not far from the Byzantine capital.

Bohemond was closely followed by the count of Toulouse, Raymond of St Gilles, who was now in his mid-fifties and was by the standards of the time an elderly man. He had spent thirty years patiently reassembling his ancestral lands, which had been scattered into other hands, and was now master of thirteen counties in southern France. He belonged to an extraordinarily complicated kinship-group, resulting from the marriages of his mother, Almodis of La Marche, who was wedded in turn to Hugh V of Lusignan, Pons of Toulouse and Raymond Berengar I of Barcelona. She bore Hugh of Lusignan two sons, of whom Hugh VI was the elder, Pons of Toulouse a daughter and three sons, of whom Raymond of St Gilles was the second, and Raymond Berengar of Barcelona two sons. She did not lose touch with the children of her previous marriages: in 1066-7 she travelled to Toulouse to be present at the wedding of her daughter. A century later she had a reputation for having been a bolter, but in fact it may have been that her husbands found it hard to cope with her personality, which appears to have been overbearing. She was excommunicated by Pope Victor II for encouraging Raymond Berengar to challenge his grandmother's possession of his county and she was eventually murdered by one of her stepsons. But a feature of her offspring from three husbands was how many of them were committed supporters both of papal reform and of the crusade. Hugh VI of Lusignan and Raymond of St Gilles were *fideles beati Petri*, recognized supporters of the papacy, and Hugh, Raymond and probably their half-brother Berengar Raymond II of Barcelona took the cross for the crusade, as did the husbands of their nieces Philippa of Toulouse and Ermessens of Melgueil.

Raymond was also connected by marriage to the Spanish royal houses and it is possible, though not certain, that he had fought in the Spanish Reconquest. Although it is by no means clear that he really understood what the cause of church reform entailed, Pope Urban regarded him as an ally and had picked him to be the leader of the crusade before it was proclaimed at Clermont. The pope visited St Gilles before the council and may have discussed the expedition with Raymond there since, in what must have been a pre-arranged *coup de théâtre*, the day after Urban's sermon the count's ambassadors arrived at Clermont to commit their master to the enterprise. There were rumours that Raymond had vowed never to return home. Whether they were true or not this elderly man had made the decision to desert the lands he had taken so long to consolidate, leaving his eldest son in charge of them, and to go with his wife on a hazardous journey to the East. He had prepared for this more efficiently than any of the other leaders and his followers fared better in the ordeals ahead than did the other crusaders, but he seems to have been chronically ill, which is not surprising when one considers his age. He shared leadership of perhaps the largest force with Bishop Adhémar of Le Puy, who had vigorously upheld the cause of reform in southern France from the 1080s, had been appointed papal legate on the crusade by Urban, and was to dominate the councils of the leaders until his early death. Raymond and Adhémar marched through northern Italy, round the end of the Adriatic and through Dalmatia, where the locals were hostile. Escorted by imperial troops, who were prepared to treat roughly any who diverged from the route, they reached Thessaloniki at the beginning of April. Raymond himself arrived in Constantinople on the 21st, but before his troops joined him six days later they were severely bruised in a clash with their Greek escorts, who were doubtless trying to prevent them from foraging.

Duke Robert of Normandy, Count Robert of Flanders and Count Stephen of Blois left France in the autumn of 1096. They journeyed by way of Rome and Monte Cassino to Bari. Robert of Flanders crossed the Adriatic almost at once and reached Constantinople at about the same time as Bohemond. Robert of Normandy and Stephen of Blois wintered in southern Italy and joined the others in Constantinople on c. 14 May after a markedly peaceful passage through the empire. The reason for this seems to have been that the Byzantine government, realizing that the heavy-handed way its troops had shepherded the earlier contingents had been counter-productive, had got its act together.

The second wave: Constantinople to Antioch

The crusaders' experiences at Constantinople affected the rest of the campaign. No one was certain what part would be played by the Greeks, but it seems that most of the leaders were expecting their full participation and even that the emperor Alexius would himself take overall command. In the spring of 1097 Alexius discussed with Godfrey of Bouillon, Robert of Flanders, Bohemond and perhaps also Hugh of Vermandois the possibility of taking the cross himself and assuming leadership of the expedition. This may simply have been politic on his part; certainly when Raymond of St Gilles arrived and made the emperor's captaincy a precondition of his acknowledgement of his subordination to him, Alexius excused himself on the grounds that his presence was needed in Constantinople. Although there was cooperation between Greeks and Latins during the siege of Nicaea and then a Greek presence as far as Antioch – which was more than token and was welcome because the Byzantine government's representative, a Hellenized Turk and experienced military commander called Tatikios, provided guides – there remained, after Tatikios's withdrawal in February 1098, only a few Greek officers and clergy, while, in the crusade's wake, an imperial army concentrated on re-establishing Byzantine control over the coast of Asia Minor as far as Antalya. By June 1098 Alexius himself had moved with an army of Greeks and lately arrived crusaders only as far as Akşehir, under half-way from Constantinople to Antioch. Erroneous reports of the situation in Antioch and rumours of the mustering of a large Turkish army in Anatolia led him to withdraw even from there, abandoning the crusade to its fate. By the summer of 1098 Greek participation had shown itself to be half-hearted at best.

As far as Alexius himself was concerned, another issue was paramount. Help of a very different sort to that he had envisaged had arrived and the crusaders had already caused him major problems as they had advanced through the Balkans and approached Constantinople. He was thoroughly suspicious of them, particularly of Bohemond of Taranto, and he must have felt that he had to find some means of controlling them. He may have worked out a method of doing so in the late autumn of 1096 when Hugh of Vermandois was his prisoner-cum-guest. His tactics were to try to isolate the leaders in order to deal with each of them separately – his daughter Anna in her encomium of him wrote that he feared for an attack on Constantinople if they mustered together – and to demand two oaths, in return for which he presented them with large sums of money, gifts not as lavish as they might seem, since he obliged them to pay for the goods they had to buy in his markets. They were, of course, desperate for supplies and therefore at a disadvantage, which was compounded by the fact that the only real alternative to a refusal of the emperor's demands was to return home.

The first of the oaths was a promise to hand back to the empire all the lands they liberated which had once belonged to it. This provided Alexius with legitimate grounds for claiming sovereignty over the territories likely to be won, since it is clear that the crusaders had no intention of trying to conquer land that had not once been Christian. The second was an oath of homage and fealty, similar to the contracts entered into by *vassalli non casati* in the West, which were not accompanied by the reciprocal grant of a fief. It gave Alexius a measure, admittedly limited, of control. The leaders' reactions to the demands for these oaths were not consistent. Hugh of Vermandois (as far as we know), Robert of Normandy, Robert of Flanders and Stephen of Blois raised little objection. Godfrey of Bouillon and Raymond of St Gilles made difficulties, and although Bohemond of Taranto did not, his second-in-command Tancred did, perhaps revealing Bohemond's real attitude. It has been suggested that it was no coincidence that the objectors were the men who eventually settled in the East and that the divisions among the leaders that surfaced in Constantinople continued for the rest of the crusade, but it was not at all clear at this stage who would settle in the Levant and it is more reasonable to look at the leaders' predicaments in turn.

Hugh of Vermandois was a near prisoner when the oath was demanded of him. He was also virtually alone. As for Godfrey, it has already been pointed out that he had set out in 1096 with every intention of returning to Europe, at least if the East was to offer him nothing better. It is, therefore, unlikely that the oaths were unattractive because they might limit his freedom of action in the future. He was obviously distrustful, concerned that Hugh of Vermandois's agreement had been extorted from him, and unwilling to take any step before consulting the other leaders whose arrival was expected. Alexius put pressure on him by cutting off his supplies. Godfrey responded to this threat to his force's existence by authorizing his brother Baldwin to raid the suburbs of Constantinople. Supplies were restored and there followed three months of relative peace until Alexius, hearing of the approach of more crusading armies, cut off supplies once more. Again the crusaders' response was to use force, the only weapon at their disposal. This culminated in an attack on the city on Maundy Thursday, which was beaten off by the Greeks. Godfrey must have realized that force would not get provisions restored and so, in a desperate situation, he and his leading followers took the oaths and his troops were immediately transported out of the way, across the Bosporus.

By the time Bohemond of Taranto arrived, therefore, Alexius had successfully wrung oaths from Hugh of Vermandois and Godfrey of Bouillon. So Bohemond was in no position to refuse outright, although Tancred managed to slip through Constantinople without submitting. Bohemond was not well off and his force was a small one. If the report that he requested the office of Grand Domestic – commander-in-chief of the Byzantine army – is true, it was quite a sensible move on his part, because he could then have ensured adequate Greek military support for the crusade.

Since Raymond of St Gilles may have made a vow never to return to his native land he may have hoped for an eastern principality, but it was the performance of homage and the oath of fealty rather than the promise to return territory to the empire that raised difficulties for him. He appears to have believed that the making of homage conflicted with his crusade vow to serve God, and in spite of the efforts and irritation of the other crusade leaders he would not change his mind. He compromised by taking a more limited oath to respect and maintain the emperor's life and honour, for which there were parallels in the region of France from which he came. We know nothing of Robert of Flanders's reaction, but by the time Robert of Normandy and Stephen of Blois arrived the precedents had been set and, whether they liked them or not, there was little option but to follow them. The various parties were shipped separately across the Bosporus from April 1097 onwards and in early June they assembled in one army before Nicaea, the first important city in Asia Minor which was in Turkish hands.

The events in Constantinople had left the crusade leaders frustrated and disillusioned. After long marches they had arrived short of supplies and unsure of the future role of the Greeks. They found the emperor reluctant to take on the burden of leadership, apparently only interested in the recovery of imperial territories – which, to be fair, was what he had wanted in the first place – and prepared to use every measure at his disposal, from the distribution of largesse to the denial of supplies, to force each prince in turn to take the oaths before his confrères arrived. Although Alexius gave them generous gifts of cash, these only provided the means to buy provisions in his own markets. No wonder that from this time onwards most of the crusaders distrusted and disliked the imperial government.

Although its inhabitants were still mostly Christian, Nicaea was the chief residence of the Selchük sultan of Rum, Kilij Arslan, the most powerful Turkish prince in Anatolia. The capture of the city was essential before the crusade could advance down the old military road to the East. It had been well fortified by the Greeks and was held by a strong Turkish garrison. But Kilij Arslan himself was away with the bulk of his forces, disputing Malatya with his chief rival, an emir called Danishmend, and was out of touch. By the time the first of his troops had been rushed back the city was invested and the main body of his army failed to break through the cordon on 21 May, although it inflicted heavy losses on the crusaders. Kilij Arslan withdrew, leaving the city and his wife, family and much of his treasury to their fate, but it was not until Greek ships had been launched on Iznik Gölü (Lake Ascanius), on the shore of which it stood, that Nicaea was entirely isolated. The garrison opened negotiations with the Byzantines and on 19 June, the day appointed for a general assault, the crusaders saw imperial banners flying over the town. Alexius had avoided any embarrassment by having Nicaea surrender directly to himself, but he took the opportunity to demand and receive oaths from those leaders, including Tancred, who had not yet made them.

The crusaders must already have made the very courageous decision to break into Asia on their own, without proper support or any prospect of provisioning until they reached Syria. Between 26 and 28 June they set out across Asia Minor, marching in two divisions. The first, under Bohemond's command, consisted of the Normans from Italy and France together with the followers of Robert of Flanders and Stephen of Blois, and the Greeks. The second, under the command of Raymond of St Gilles, was made up of the southern French and the Lorrainers and the force of Hugh of Vermandois. These became separated and lost contact, for reasons which were unclear even then, since they were still being debated in Syria a decade later. Close to Dorylaeum at dawn on 1 July Kilij Arslan's soldiers, supplemented by troops provided by other Turkish princes, who had surrounded Bohemond's corps during the night, launched an attack, forcing the Christian knights back onto the mass of armed and unarmed pilgrims with them. This confused crush of men, although unable to strike at the enemy, could defend itself quite effectively and the battle remained deadlocked for two or three hours until the second corps, hurrying up in separate columns, each of which was answering Bohemond's call for help as best it could, surprised and routed the Turks.

The crusaders rested for two days. They then resumed their advance by way of Akşehir and Konya through a country already laid waste in the aftermath of the Turkish invasions and further devastated by a scorched-earth policy adopted by their enemies. On a march of 105 days (including 15 rest days) they averaged just over 8 miles a day, which was good going, considering the number of non-combatants they had with them. At Ereğli on c. 10 September they put an army blocking their way to flight. Tancred and Baldwin of Boulogne now broke away to raid Cilicia, taking advantage of the existence in that region of a string of petty Armenian principalities, established precariously out of the chaos of the last few decades. The crusaders did not cooperate with one another, but their quarrelsome progress was welcomed by the Armenian population which had recently settled in the area and they took Tarsus, Adana, Misis and Iskenderun before rejoining the main army. Baldwin left again almost at once with a small force and with an Armenian adviser who had attached himself to him, to follow the seam of Armenian principalities eastwards. He took two fortresses, Ravanda and Tilbeşar, with the assistance of local Armenians and was then invited by Toros, the prince of Edessa (Urfa), whose position was newly established and very insecure, to become his adopted son and partner. On 6 February 1098 he reached Edessa, but a month later the Armenians in the city rioted, perhaps with his connivance. On 9 March Toros was killed by the mob while trying to escape and on the following day Baldwin took over the government entirely. He had established the first Latin settlement in the East, comprising Edessa, the fortresses of Ravanda and Tilbeşar and, within a few months, Birecik, Sürüc and Samsat.

The region was prosperous and from the autumn of 1098 money and horses poured out of it to the crusaders in Antioch. Godfrey of Bouillon himself was given the castle and estates of Tilbeşar and his comparative wealth was very apparent in the later stages of the crusade. By means of it he was able to augment his following, significantly at the expense of Raymond of St Gilles, and this may have contributed to his election as ruler of Jerusalem. We shall see that Baldwin at Edessa was able in another way to contribute to the crusade's salvation at a vital moment, but, given the bitterness later felt by the Greeks at the refusal of the crusaders to abide by their oaths and restore Antioch to the empire, it is of interest to note that although Tarsus, Adana, Misis, Iskenderun,

Ravanda, Tilbeşar and Edessa had all been Byzantine, no move was made to restore them to Greek rule or even to recognize Greek suzerainty. The Greeks were far away, of course. Their only detachment was still marching with the main crusading army, which was why a western knight was appointed to hold Comana 'in fealty to God and the Holy Sepulchre and the princes [of the crusade] and the [Byzantine] emperor' when it was reached. The apparent refusal of Tancred and Baldwin even to consider the issue of Byzantine sovereignty was a pointer to the future.

The leaders of the main force, meanwhile, must have been advised that passage through the Cilician Gates in the Taurus mountains and particularly through the Syrian Gates, the Belen pass which cuts the Amanus range north of Antioch, was hardly possible if these were adequately defended. They decided to add about 175 miles to their journey by swinging north to Kayseri and then south-east by way of Comana and Göksun to Maraş (Kahramanmaraş), by-passing the main bulk of the Amanus. This brought them onto the open plain north of Antioch, which they reached on 21 October. They were in a moderately good state as far as provisions went, and a Genoese fleet, which in a remarkable example of forward planning had left Europe on 15 July and docked at Mağaracik (Suwaidiyah; Port St Simeon), the port of Antioch, on 17 November, brought more supplies. But already, during the march across the wastelands of Asia Minor, horses and beasts of burden had been dying like flies in the summer heat. This was disastrous, particularly to the knights who needed chargers to fulfil their functions and maintain their status and pack animals to carry their baggage. By the time the crusaders reached Antioch there were not more than 1,000 horses left – so already four out of every five knights were horseless – and by the following summer the numbers had shrunk to between 100 and 200. Most knights, among them powerful men at home, were now fighting on foot or riding donkeys and mules; even Godfrey of Bouillon and Robert of Flanders had to beg for horses before the Battle of Antioch in June 1098. Moreover, the loss of pack animals meant that the knights had to carry their own heavy sacks of arms and armour and this had led to embarrassing scenes of panic as they struggled up steep paths during the crossing of the Anti-Taurus mountains.

The second wave: the siege of Antioch and its aftermath

An army of possibly 30,000 men and women now found itself engaged in a siege that was to last until 3 June 1098. Situated between Mount Silpius and the river Orontes, with its citadel on the mountain-top 1,000 feet above it, Antioch could never be completely surrounded. During the siege the crusaders built camps and forts across the river and before the northern and southern gates, but these must usually have been lightly garrisoned, because most of the force was occupied with hunting for rations. Having marched into Asia without any proper system of provisioning – indeed it would have been impossible to devise one – the crusaders had to rely on foraging and it is not surprising that within a short time the countryside around the city was stripped bare. They were obliged to search further and further afield, travelling in foraging parties fifty miles and establishing foraging centres at great distances from Antioch: northwards towards Cilicia, north-eastwards towards Edessa, to the east to Yenişehir and Harim, to the south to the Ruj and Latakia. The abiding impression one has of the siege is not one of warfare but of a constant search for food. Predictably, there was famine and death from starvation, illness and disease. Other crusaders besides Raymond of St Gilles seem to have been chronically sick. There was also impoverishment and even lords of some standing in the West found themselves compelled to enter service with the greater princes. Providing for circles of followers, which were never constant but enlarged and contracted as sources of food became available or scarce, imposed great pressures on the princes. Already by January 1098 Bohemond was threatening to leave the siege because he did not have the resources for it. By the following summer both Godfrey of Bouillon and Robert of Flanders were temporarily in penury. In these stressful circumstances it is not surprising that there were manifestations of homesickness and fear, leading to panic and desertion.

The siege of Antioch lasted for seven and a half months, through a winter during which the crusaders suffered dreadfully. Late in December 1097 and early in February 1098 Muslim forces of relief, the second of which launched an attack in conjunction with a sortie from the garrison, were beaten off, but a third, and very large, army, including detachments from Iraq and Iran, left Mosul under the command of its governor Kerbogha in May. It spent three fruitless weeks trying to reduce Edessa – the other example of the importance to the crusade's survival of Baldwin's initiative – and, collecting additional troops from Aleppo on the way, arrived in the vicinity of Antioch on 5 June. By that time the crusaders' situation had been transformed. Bohemond, whose ambition to possess Antioch himself was already apparent, had entered into negotiations with one of the garrison captains, probably a renegade Armenian, who had agreed to deliver the city to him. He persuaded all his colleagues, except Raymond of St Gilles, to promise him the city if his troops were the first to enter it and if the emperor never came to claim it in person. He then revealed the conspiracy and received their support. Before sunset on 2 June the crusaders engaged in an elaborate diversionary manoeuvre before returning to their positions after dark. Just before dawn on the 3rd sixty knights from Bohemond's force swarmed over the walls under the traitor's command, a section of the fortifications half-way up the slopes of Mount Silpius around a tower called the Two Sisters. They then dashed down the hill to open the Gate of St George and their confrères poured into the city, which was in their hands by evening, although the citadel still held out. The governor, who had fled, fell from his horse and was beheaded by some Armenian peasants.

The crusaders were now in occupation of a city that had suffered a long siege and they were almost immediately besieged themselves, as Kerbogha's army came up and camped across the river. Kerbogha was in touch with the citadel, from which an assault was launched on 9 June. A crusader sortie failed on the 10th and that night the Christians' morale sank to its lowest. There were so many desertions or attempted desertions that the leaders, fearing a mass break-out, were forced to seal the gates. Those who fled joined Stephen of Blois, who had only recently been elected commander-in-chief but had retired to Iskenderun just before Antioch fell, probably because of ill-health. He was now panicked into flight. Reaching the imperial headquarters at Akşehir, he and his companions persuaded Alexius of the hopelessness of the crusade's situation, whereupon the emperor, anyway fearing a Turkish counter-attack in Anatolia, led his army northwards again, back to the safety of Constantinople.

Within Antioch, however, morale had begun to rise. Two visionaries had approached the leaders. One of them had seen Christ on the night of 10 June and had received the assurance from him that the crusaders would prevail, provided they repented of their sins. The other reported a series of visits from St Andrew, who had shown him the hiding-place of the Holy Lance, the tip of the spear with which Christ's side had been pierced during the Crucifixion. This relic was 'discovered' on 14 June at the bottom of a trench dug in the floor of the newly reconsecrated cathedral and, in spite of the fact that many of the leaders, including the papal legate, were sceptical, the ordinary crusaders were elated. It was decided to resolve the crisis in which they found themselves by seeking battle. One last embassy was sent to Kerbogha to seek terms and on 28 June the crusaders sortied out of the city under Bohemond's command. They were marshalled in four divisions, each made up of two squadrons of horse and foot: given the few horses left, the number of mounted knights must have been very small. Each division engaged in turn in a complicated manoeuvre, switching from column to line, so that in the end three of them were advancing side by side, with the infantry in front masking the few mounted knights, and with their flanks covered, on the right by the river Orontes and on the left by high ground. The fourth division, under Bohemond himself, marched in reserve. The crusaders attacked in echelon, presumably at walking pace, and the Muslims fled, whereupon the citadel surrendered to Bohemond. This extraordinary victory has never been explained, although it may be that Kerbogha, who should never have allowed the whole Christian army to emerge from a single gate across a bridge before engaging it, could not prevent his forces being sucked piecemeal into the mêlée. The crusaders rationalized it by ascribing it to the appearance of a heavenly army of angels, saints and the ghosts of their own dead, which intervened on their side.

It was, in fact, the turning-point of the crusade, but that cannot have been apparent at the time. The princes sensibly decided to wait until 1 November, when the summer heat would be over, before continuing their march, but an epidemic, probably of typhoid, broke out, claiming the life of Adhémar of Le Puy and scattering the other leaders to their foraging centres. When they returned in September there were signs of division over two issues and in November these surfaced.

The first was the possession of Antioch, which Bohemond claimed for himself. Raymond of St Gilles, who still held some parts of the city, including the governor's palace and a fortified bridge over the Orontes leading to the road to the port, spoke up for the oaths sworn to the Byzantine emperor. He may have wanted Antioch for himself and envisaged that the only way of achieving this was by an imperial grant, but no one could deny that oaths had been sworn and homage had been paid to the emperor. Before the city fell it had been agreed that it would be surrendered to him if he came in person to claim it and after the Battle of Antioch a high-powered embassy, led by Hugh of Vermandois and Baldwin of Mons, was sent to invite him to present himself and take the leadership of the crusade. His reply did not reach the crusaders until the following April. He promised to join them in June and asked them to delay their advance until his arrival. He demanded the return of Antioch and his ambassadors complained bitterly about Bohemond's usurpation of the city in breach of his oath. In the meantime Bohemond's supporters argued that the Byzantine emperor was indifferent, even hostile, to the crusaders and had failed as the leaders' feudal lord, which he was; that the oath to him had been extorted from them by force; that the departure of Tatikios and the withdrawal of Alexius and his army from Akşehir when the crusade was most in need had shown that the Greeks had not kept their side of the bargain; and that Alexius's failure to reply so far to the embassy of July 1098 revealed the military unpreparedness of the empire.

Of course this was special pleading, but the crusaders had been let down by the Greeks and their need was pressing. They were conscious of, even obsessed by, the large number of men whom they believed had taken the cross but had never left Europe. The existence of this reserve of manpower was often in their thoughts and the bishops with the crusade excommunicated those who had not fulfilled their vows and expressed the hope that their colleagues in the West would do the same. At the same time some new recruits were coming out to join the army. Most of these were travelling overland and the crusaders expected that many others would follow the same route, as indeed they were to do in the crusade of 1101. Antioch, dominating the passes from Asia Minor into Syria and holding the northern coastal road open against the Muslim powers in Syria and Iraq, had to be held by someone reliable. Alexius had not proved himself to be that; on the contrary he appeared to the crusaders to have cynically manipulated them to serve his own ends. It is important to remember that although Bohemond stayed behind in Antioch and did not fulfil his own vow at the Holy Sepulchre until five months after its liberation he was not at all blamed in the West for what he had done; in fact his visit to France in 1106 was a triumph.

The second issue was the date at which the march to Jerusalem should be renewed. As a step in this direction the ordinary crusaders forced the princes to agree to the investment of the town of Ma'arret en Nu'man, sixty miles south of Antioch. This fell on 11–12 December 1098, but the princes still could not bring themselves to make a firm decision and a conference in the Ruj early in January 1099 came to nothing.

One of the chief reasons for this paralysis of will was the fact that the crusade had no proper leadership. On four separate occasions attempts were made to provide the army with a commander-in-chief. Alexius turned down the proposal in the spring of 1097. It was put to him again by the embassy that left Antioch in July 1098. In the spring of 1098 Stephen of Blois was elected over-all commander, but he deserted soon afterwards. In January 1099 Raymond of St Gilles, under pressure from his followers to continue the journey, offered to take the other leaders into his service for large sums of money, but most of them refused to serve him. The fact was that not one of the princes was strong enough to dominate the others. It is generally supposed that these men led 'armies', but that is far from the truth. Each was accompanied by a household, including relatives and dependants, and each came to provide for a wider body of men as the shortages began to bite; but the bulk of effective soldiery, the petty lords, many of them commanding their own little forces, and the knights, were independent and their allegiances constantly shifted as circumstances changed and the ability of the princes to reward them and their little entourages came and went. The crusade was characterized by a kaleidoscopic shifting of allegiances as minor figures moved from one contingent to another. No leader's following was coherent or permanent enough to provide him with a platform from which he could dominate the rest. A result was that the crusade was run by committees and assemblies. Each prince took counsel with his leading followers and there were general assemblies of the whole army, but most important of all was a council of the princes. This was quite effective while Adhémar of Le Puy was alive, for he had the personality and authority to dominate it. His death on 1 August 1098 removed the only objective and authoritative leader and the committees became deadlocked.

The paralysis was reflected in the breakdown of discipline. Lawlessness bore particularly hard on the poor, who suffered in the anarchy and feared starvation if the crusade remained becalmed much longer. In the middle of November 1098, with the princes dithering, they became fiercely critical and threatened to elect their own commander. They forced Raymond of St Gilles and Robert of Flanders to lead them to Ma'arret and when on c. 5 January Raymond of St Gilles's followers heard that the conference in the Ruj was going badly they pulled down Ma'arret's walls, depriving him of his base. Raymond had no option but to recommence the march to Jerusalem on the 13th. The ordinary crusaders still in Antioch also began to raise their voices and Godfrey of Bouillon, Robert of Flanders and Bohemond had to bow to public pressure. They convened a general assembly on 2 February which decided on a muster at Latakia on 1 March as a prelude to an advance from there.

The second wave: the liberation of Jerusalem

Syria was in as disorganized and unready a state to meet the crusade as Asia Minor had been and the crusaders faced very little opposition to their advance. The Turkish rulers of Aleppo and Damascus were at odds with one another. The Arab dynasties in control of Seijar (Shaizar) and Tripoli were even more hostile to the Turks than to the Christians. The Egyptians, who had only just regained control of Jerusalem, reacted to the developing threat by resorting to diplomacy. Early in 1098 an Egyptian embassy spent several weeks in the Christian camp at Antioch, before returning to Cairo with Christian envoys, who were then detained in Egypt for a year. These men were only released in the spring of 1099, when they accompanied another Egyptian mission to the crusade, which by this time was besieging 'Arqah, fifteen miles from Tripoli. Raymond of St Gilles had marched there by way of Kafartab, where he met Robert of Normandy and Tancred, and Rafniye. Before the end of March he was joined by the other crusade leaders, except Bohemond who remained behind to guard Antioch. The investment of 'Arqah did not go well and the crusaders were demoralized by the failure and by the death of Peter Bartholomew, the visionary to whom had been revealed the whereabouts of the Holy Lance. His visions had become so eccentric that he had antagonized a large section of the army and he had volunteered to undergo an ordeal by fire, which he did not survive. The crucial factor, however, which led the crusaders to raise the siege of 'Arqah appears to have been a breakdown in the negotiations with the Egyptians. Realizing that should they delay their advance on Jerusalem they would have to face another, and very formidable, army of relief once they were besieging it and knowing that this was the harvest season, which would provide them with the wherewithall they needed, they took the road south again on 13 May.

Up to this point – and two years had elapsed since the siege of Nicaea – they had moved quite slowly. They had been concerned to cover their rear by reducing some of the major fortresses which could have barred their communications back through Antioch and Asia Minor to Constanti-nople. Now all caution was abandoned and in another reckless decision they decided simply to by-pass the great strongholds in front of them and make a dash for Jerusalem. Their progress changed from a crawl to a gallop. They crossed the Dog river north of Beirut six days after leaving 'Arqah and marched rapidly south by way of Tyre, turning inland north of Jaffa and reaching Ramle on 3 June. They arrived before Jerusalem on the 7th. On the previous day Bethlehem had fallen to Tancred, who had deserted Raymond of St Gilles, whom he had agreed to serve, and had transferred his allegiance and that of the South Italian Norman contingent to Godfrey of Bouillon.

Jerusalem was, like Antioch, far too large to be surrounded, but whereas Antioch had been besieged for seven and a half months and then occupied only through treachery, Jerusalem was taken by assault after five weeks. The crusaders at first concentrated most of their strength against the western wall, but then divided their forces between the western section of the northern wall, where Robert of Normandy, Robert of Flanders, Godfrey of Bouillon and Tancred took up positions, and Mount Zion to the south, where Raymond of St Gilles, bitterly at odds with Godfrey over the desertion of Tancred and probably of others in his following, took his post. For a time the siege went badly, in spite of the arrival of Genoese and English ships at Jaffa and an expedition to the north into Samaria, which provided wood and other materials for the construction of two siege-towers, a battering-ram and some catapults. Meanwhile news arrived of the march of the Egyptian relief force that everyone, not least the garrison of Jerusalem, had been expecting. On 8 July, following the instructions transmitted by a visionary, a great penitential procession of crusaders wound its way from holy place to holy place outside the city walls and gathered to hear sermons on the Mount of Olives. The 14th was spent filling in the ditch to the south and by evening Raymond of St Gilles's tower was closing on the wall, but on the 15th Godfrey of Bouillon's men, who had switched their point of attack eastwards to level ground slightly to the east of the present-day Herod's Gate, succeeded in bridging the gap between their tower and the wall. Two knights from Tournai were the first across, followed by the Lorrainers. The trickle became a torrent as crusaders poured over the wall and through a breach already made by the ram, some making for the Temple area and some beyond, down to the south-west corner where the Muslims defending against Raymond of St Gilles were forced to withdraw. Jerusalem, which was not well populated but had become a place of refuge for the inhabitants of the countryside around, was given over to sack. Although the only contemporary Muslim evidence suggests that the number of deaths may not have been as high as has been supposed, the eyewitness Christian writers wallowed in their descriptions of a massacre.

On 22 July Godfrey of Bouillon was elected ruler of the new settlement. His first task was to organize its defence against the Egyptian counter-invasion. He had some difficulty in persuading the other crusade leaders to commit themselves and their forces entirely, but by the evening of 11 August the whole Christian army was at Ashdod, where the herds the Egyptians had brought to feed their troops were captured. At dawn the following morning the Christians surprised the Egyptian host, still encamped just north of Ascalon (Ashqelon), and a charge by the European knights, who seem by now to have been able to replace their horses, routed the enemy.

The achievement of the second wave

To western European armsbearers of the central middle ages the second wave of the First Crusade was the single most important event of the recent past. Celebrated in a cycle of epic poems, illustrated in frescos, tapestries and carved tympana, it quickly became legend and those who had taken part were celebrated as heroes. The exploits of Hugh of Chaumont-sur-Loire, lord of Amboise, were remembered by his descendants decades later. The family of Arnold II of Ardres, which was correctly maintaining a century later that he been there, explained the absence of his name from the lists of knights recorded in the epic *La Chanson d'Antioche* by asserting that he had refused to bribe the author to include it. In many ways the course of military actions on the crusade does have a heroic quality about it. The campaign was marked by great sieges: Nicaea, Antioch, Ma'arret en Nu'man, 'Arqah, Jerusalem; and before Jerusalem every advanced technique of warfare and every form of siege-engine available at the time were deployed to ensure a speedy end to the investment. Battles were won on the march at Dorylaeum and Eregli. Even more impressive were the defeats of armies of relief – one at Nicaea, three at Antioch, one after Jerusalem had fallen – because it was generally held that the most dangerous situation in which any force could find itself was when it was attacked from the rear while laying siege to a city. All this was achieved by an army that had lacked provisions and had constantly to forage, had lost its horses and had to fight for much of the time on foot, had no firm leadership, had sometimes disintegrated into anarchy and had to endure heavy losses. The most recent estimate of mortalities concludes that just under 40 per cent of the armsbearers died. The fatalities among the poor must have been much higher.

The third wave

After this triumph most of the crusaders decided to return home. From the winter of 1099–1100 they began to reappear in Europe, bringing with them not riches but relics, which they gave to local churches, and the palms which they had collected as evidence that they had fulfilled their vows. But already in the spring of 1099, even before they had reached Jerusalem, Pope Urban had commissioned the archbishop of Milan to renew crusade preaching in Lombardy. There was a fervent response and as the news of the liberation, which Urban, who died on 29 July 1099, never heard, swept the West new armies were raised. Urban's successor, Pope Paschal II, threatened, as Urban had done, to excommunicate those who had not yet fulfilled their vows and this was taken up by the bishops. Paschal also threatened to excommunicate deserters. Hugh of Vermandois and Stephen of Blois were among the individuals in this humiliating condition who now decided to retrace their steps to the East. Of course those who had fled from the crusade had brought dishonour not only on themselves but also on their kindred. Miles of Bray and his son Guy Trousseau deserted in 1098. It cannot have been coincidence that when Miles went again with the 1101 expedition he was accompanied by the other senior member of the family, his brother Guy of Rochefort.

Many men and women in France, Italy and Germany who had not taken the cross before now flocked to the banners. Papal legates were sent to France. They held a council at Valence in September 1100, went on to Limoges, where Duke William IX of Aquitaine and many of his vassals took the cross, and from there moved to Poitiers where, at a council assembled on 18 November, the fifth anniversary of the opening of the council of Clermont, they preached the crusade.

The armies of the third wave were probably as large as those which had left in 1096. The ecclesiastical contingent under the chief papal legate, Hugh of Die, archbishop of Lyon, was stronger. The lay princes were of equal or greater rank than their predecessors: William of Aquitaine, Stephen of Blois and Hugh of Vermandois, William of Nevers, Odo of Burgundy, Stephen of Burgundy and Welf of Bavaria. Under the surface glitter of light-hearted knight-errantry that may be a reflection of William of Aquitaine's ebullient personality, there are indications of a serious religious purpose and of attempts to learn from the mistakes of their predecessors. The very wealth, carried in cash and jewelry, that gave these crusaders such a bad name for luxury was one of them.

The first to depart were the Lombards, who left Milan on 13 September 1100. Their wintering in Bulgaria and encampment outside Constantinople for two months in the spring of 1101 were marked by disorder, as they waited for other crusaders from Germany and France. Alexius, as before, tried to force them to cross the Bosporus by refusing them licences to buy supplies. As their predecessors had done, they reacted violently and launched an attack on his palace of Blachernae, but this so embarrassed their leaders that they agreed to be ferried across to Asia. At Izmit (Nicomedia) they were joined by the first and smaller of the German armies, by men from Burgundy and northern France under Stephen of Blois, and by Raymond of St Gilles, who had reached Constantinople in the summer of 1100 with his household and had reluctantly allowed himself to be attached to them as an adviser. He was not very successful. Against his advice and that of the Greeks and Stephen of Blois, the new crusaders decided not to wait for the rest of their confrères but to march for Niksar, where Bohemond, who had been captured in the previous summer by the Danishmend Turks of eastern Anatolia, was incarcerated. It is even possible that, fired by wild talk in Europe as news of the successes had come in, the Lombards, who alone among the new crusaders had been inspired to further conquest rather than to lend aid to the Holy Land, were planning to enter Iraq from the north and lay siege to Baghdad itself. In June they marched from Izmit to Ankara and then north-east to Çankiri (Gangra) before swinging east again. In the early part of August, somewhere near Merzifon, they were met by an army raised by a coalition of the Turkish princes, who had at last buried their differences. There followed several days of fighting before the crusaders panicked and fled.

An army under William of Nevers reached Constantinople in June 1101 and, overtaking the force of William of Aquitaine which was already there, crossed the Bosporus and on the 24th set off to catch up with the Lombards. At Ankara it gave up the chase and turned south towards Konya, which it reached in the middle of August, after a three-day running battle. William failed to take the town and moved on to Ereğli, which was deserted, its wells blocked. After several thirsty days the crusaders were routed. Meanwhile the third army, under William of Aquitaine, which had left France in the middle of March and had joined the Bavarians under Welf before marching in an unruly fashion through the Balkans, had reached Constantinople at the beginning of June. It remained near the city for five weeks, purchasing supplies and taking advice from the Greeks, although a number of Germans wisely chose to go directly to Palestine by sea. In the middle of July William and Welf set off eastwards, along the route followed by the second wave of crusaders, but the way had been devastated by the Turks and by the constant passage of crusaders. In spite of careful planning they soon ran out of food. Near Ereğli their army was ambushed and annihilated.

William of Aquitaine and Welf of Bavaria escaped, as had William of Nevers, Stephen of Burgundy, Stephen of Blois and Raymond of St Gilles from the earlier disasters. Hugh of Vermandois died of his wounds at Tarsus. Some of the survivors joined Raymond of St Gilles in Syria and took the town of Tartus, which was to be his base for the creation of another settlement. Then most gathered in Jerusalem where they fulfilled their vows. Some, delayed from departure by adverse winds, joined the settlers' forces to meet another Egyptian invasion. Unlucky to the last, they were heavily defeated on 17 May 1102 and poor Stephen of Blois was killed.

Developments in the idea of crusading

The course of events from 1097 to 1099 established that a crusade was a pilgrimage on which knights could fulfil their normal function as warriors. With its elaborate liturgies, penitential processions and fasts – it is remarkable that fasting was imposed upon the starving soldiers before every important engagement – the crusade struck articulate contemporaries, who were mostly monks, as having the features of a quasi-monastery on the move. Laymen had made vows, temporary it is true but with similarities to monastic profession, while the exigencies of the campaign had imposed poverty on them and ought also to have imposed celibacy. Like monks they were 'exiles' from the normal world. They had taken up their crosses to follow Christ and had abandoned wives, children and lands for the love of God, putting their bodies at risk out of love for their brothers. Like monks they engaged in regular communal devotions and just as monks made an 'interior' journey to Jerusalem, they made a corporeal one. Since an aim of the reform movement had been to monasticize the whole Church, it seemed that here at last the laity was falling into line. There was, in fact, an extraordinarily rapid transfer to crusading of phrases and images traditionally associated with monasticism: the knighthood of Christ, the way of the cross, the way to a heavenly Jerusalem, spiritual warfare. The monastic interpretation of crusading was not going to last, but it provided the Church with a starting-point in its approach to the questions this revolutionary new form of warfare inevitably raised.

One of the problems highlighted by the crusade was that of control. Parish priests had been given the job of regulating recruitment – no one was to take the cross without going to his parish priest for advice – but the parochial system was not yet adequate to cope with mass recruitment. Bishops were supposed to enforce the fulfilment of vows if need be, although it is impossible to decide whether those who carried out their vows on the third wave did so because of threats of excommunication or because they were inspired or shamed by the news of the liberation of Jerusalem. The papal legates and clergy on the crusade should have exercised some control, but the clergy were mostly of poor quality and as the house-priests of magnates they were not the men to challenge or discipline their employers. Churchmen failed to prevent the massacres of Jews in the spring and summer of 1096 or the establishment of a secular state in Palestine in 1099. One can discern among the laity, moreover, a certain independence of attitude. It is clear that it was the seizure of a relic, the Holy Sepulchre, which attracted them, rather than any expression of fraternal love for fellow Christians in the East, and the pope could not convince them that those who had expired before their vows had been fulfilled would enjoy the remission of sins. Quite a large number of individuals seem to have taken the cross in 1100 because close relatives had died on the second wave before reaching Jerusalem. The faithful continued to be anxious about this as late as the middle of the thirteenth century, when Thomas Aquinas tried to answer to their concerns.

The traumatic experiences of the crusaders on the second wave were crucial to the development of the belief that their enterprise really was divine. The conviction that everything they did was subject to the benevolent, if stern, control of God seems to have grown among them once Asia Minor had been crossed. It was reinforced by the discovery of relics, the veneration of sites familiar to every Christian mind and by fortuitous disturbances in the night skies – auroras, comets, shooting-stars – most of which were preludes to an intense period of solar activity, 'the medieval maximum', which began around 1120. The crusaders were not fools. They knew how much at a disadvantage they had been and yet they had still won through. There could be no satisfactory explanation of this other than that they had experienced God's interventionary might. It is not surprising that it was with the crossing of Asia Minor that the visionaries in the army began to see apparitions – Christ himself, angels, saints and the ghosts of their own dead – and that their dead began to be treated as martyrs. The failures of the third wave in 1101 actually reinforced this impression, for they suggested that the opposition crushed in 1097–9 had been more powerful than it was. The disasters that overtook William of Aquitaine and his confrères could be attributed to their own luxury, pride and sinfulness and therefore to the judgement of God.

The idea of the crusade as a divinely inspired and directed war comes across vividly in the letters and eyewitness accounts of the crusaders, but it was crude and occasionally untheological. It was taken up by a second generation of commentators, particularly three French Benedictines, Robert the Monk, Guibert of Nogent and Baldric of Bourgueil. Writing ten years later, these men placed the crusade in the context of providential history. To Robert it was the clearest sign of divine intervention in this dimension after the Creation and the Redemption of mankind on the Cross. To Guibert the crusaders outclassed the Israelites of the Old Testament. The Benedictine commentators also put all the elements firmly into a theological context, relating martyrdom, for example, to Christian love. In their writings the idea of the crusade as a war for Christ, which had been elaborated maladroitly by the crusaders themselves, was given proper theological expression.

And yet there was much that was still amorphous and unformed. Crusading took a long time, almost a century, to reach maturity, and many questions had still to be answered. What distinguished a crusade from any holy war, or armed pilgrimage for that matter? Under what circumstances and in what theatres of war could crusades be fought?

Could they be proclaimed only by popes? What powers of control over crusaders did the Church have? How did the assurance of the remission of sins actually work and to whom did it apply? How were crusades, which were very expensive, to be financed? The twelfth century was to be taken up with providing answers to these questions.

CHAPTER 3

The Holy Places and the Patriarchates of Jerusalem and Antioch

The founding of the settlements

Early in the twelfth century four West European settlements were coming into existence in Syria and Palestine. Their future was still uncertain. The rulers' protocols were imprecise. There is no good evidence that the title of advocate of the Holy Sepulchre, supposedly assumed by Godfrey of Bouillon, was ever adopted by him; he appears to have called himself 'prince' or 'duke'. His successor, Baldwin I, who sometimes called himself 'king of the Latin people of Jerusalem', was once entitled, with wild hyperbole, 'king of Babylon and Asia'. The future counts of Tripoli called themselves 'commanders of the Christian army in Asia'.

The first settlement to be established was, as we have seen, the county of Edessa, which straddled the Euphrates, stretching from the fortresses of Gaziantep and Ravanda in the west to an indeterminate frontier in the east. Edessa was 160 miles north-east of Antioch and 45 miles east of the Euphrates, a Latin salient in an area that had for centuries been borderland between Muslims and Greeks. The countryside was fertile, but it was very exposed and the European settlement was sparse and confined to isolated fortresses. The population was mostly Christian, Jacobite and Armenian, and the counts, who were comparatively rich, tended to get on quite well with their subjects.

Between Edessa and the sea lay the principality of Antioch. Its control over Cilicia was spasmodic, but it came to hold the Syrian coastline as far south as Baniyas. It extended inland to Maraş and 'Azaz in the north-east and, with its frontier skirting Aleppo which always remained in Muslim hands, to el Atharib and Ma'arret en Nu'man in the south-east. The bulk of this territory had been gained against the interests as much of the Greeks as the Muslims. During the crusade the southern ports of Latakia and Baniyas were handed over to Byzantine officials by Robert of Normandy and Raymond of St Gilles. In 1099 and 1100 the emperor Alexius, smarting under Bohemond's refusal to recognize his claims to Antioch, reoccupied Cilicia by force and also took Maraş, but the Greek occupation did not last. In August 1099 Bohemond laid siege to Latakia, assisted by a Pisan fleet, which had brought with it the new papal legate, Archbishop Daimbert of Pisa, had raided Greek islands on its way to the East and had fought an engagement with a Byzantine fleet sent to intercept it. The Pisans helped to blockade Latakia and Byzantine occupation was only preserved for the time being through the intervention of Raymond of St Gilles, Robert of Normandy and Robert of Flanders, who arrived there on their way back from Jerusalem. Within a few months Bohemond had been taken prisoner by Danishmend, but after a dangerous interregnum of seven months his nephew Tancred assumed the regency and at once embarked on a policy of expansion, recovering Cilicia and re-investing Latakia, which fell to him in 1103 after a long siege.

The climax in the early conflicts with the Greeks came in 1108. Bohemond had been released by the Muslims in 1103, but he had to deal with renewed Byzantine invasions that autumn and in the summer of 1104, when the Greeks reoccupied Tarsus, Adana, Misis and Latakia. At the same time the Muslims were advancing from the east. Bohemond travelled to Europe where, as we shall see, he himself organized a new crusade openly aimed against the Byzantine Greeks. In October 1107 his crusaders invaded the empire, but after a year of near inactivity he was compelled to surrender and agree to the Treaty of Devol, in which he recognized that he held Antioch, the territories of which were defined, as the emperor's vassal.

Long before then, any advance to the south had been blocked by the activities of Raymond of St Gilles, who was in the course of founding the county of Tripoli. Ever since he had first entered the region Raymond had probably been looking for territory. Foiled at Antioch and again at Jerusalem, it is possible that he had tried to establish a principality in southern Palestine around Ascalon or Arsuf. On his way south in 1102, with the remnants of the third wave of crusaders, he had laid siege to Tartus. In doing so he was, strictly speaking, in breach of an oath he had been forced to make to Tancred, who had briefly imprisoned him after the disasters in Asia Minor and had made him promise not to take any territory between Antioch and Acre ('Akko); he doubtless considered this oath to be invalid since it had been made under pressure. Tartus soon fell and, although moves against Husn el Akrad (later to be known as Crac des Chevaliers) and Homs failed, Raymond, who considered himself to be still on crusade, set up a siege-camp on high ground about three miles inland from the important port of Tripoli, which he gradually enlarged into the castle of Montpèlerin. Tripoli was not to fall until 1109, long after his death, but in 1104 he collaborated with the Genoese in taking Jubail, which was to the south of it.

This brings us to the kingdom of Jerusalem. The election of Godfrey of Bouillon on 22 July 1099 to the rulership is a shadowy affair. The formal decision seems to have been made by the leaders of the crusade after a debate in the presence of the whole army, but informal approaches had been made beforehand to Robert of Normandy, Raymond of St Gilles and Godfrey of Bouillon. Of these Robert may well have been the favourite. Our knowledge of his situation is sketchy, because no one in his following wrote an account of the crusade, but it is surely indicative that the first two Catholic bishops appointed in Palestine, whose roles were to be crucial in military as well as in ecclesiastical terms, were his chaplains. Before the crusade had even reached Jerusalem Robert of Rouen was consecrated bishop of Lydda (Lod) and given control of the strategically important crossroads of Ramle; and Arnulf of Chocques, the duke's chancellor, was chosen to be patriarch of Jerusalem. It was reported later that Robert of Normandy turned down the offer of Jerusalem through 'fear of the work involved', thereby staining 'his nobility with an indelible blot' and incurring divine punishment. Raymond of St Gilles also refused the offer, but this must have been intended by him to have been merely a matter of form. He was certainly not pleased when Godfrey of Bouillon accepted it and he was only persuaded with difficulty to hand over the Tower of David, the citadel of Jerusalem, to the Catholic bishop of el Barah, one of his own followers, who surrendered it immediately. Raymond was old and chronically unwell, whereas Godfrey was now comparatively rich, thanks to the efforts of his brother Baldwin.

When most of the crusaders left Palestine in August 1099 Godfrey was in control of Jerusalem and a belt of land stretching through Ramle to Jaffa on the coast. By the following year three other regions seem to have been entrusted to leading figures who had remained in the East with him. Galdemar Carpenel, a rich nobleman from near Lyon, who had decided to dedicate the rest of his life to the defence of Jerusalem, held the south-eastern frontier, including the towns of Hebron and Jericho. North of Jerusalem the territory round Nablus may have been given to Garnier, count of Grez in Brabant, who was related to Godfrey by birth and probably also by marriage and was a prominent member of his entourage. Further north still Tancred held Bet She'an and Tiberias; the latter had been occupied by Godfrey probably early in September 1099 and was granted to Tancred first as a castellany and then as a fief. That was the limit of Godfrey's conquests when he died on 18 July 1100, although he had forced the ports of Ascalon, Arsuf, Caesarea and Acre to become tributaries and was planning a campaign against Haifa and Acre in concert with a Venetian fleet that had just arrived.

His brother Baldwin and Bohemond were the two obvious candidates for the succession. Both had played important and positive parts in the crusade and had already consolidated their hold over substantial territories. Of the other possible competitors Raymond of St Gilles was away in Constantinople and Godfrey's elder brother Eustace had returned to Europe. Within the little settlement there was a division of opinion. Tancred naturally supported his uncle Bohemond. So did Daimbert of Pisa, the new patriarch of Jerusalem. There can be little doubt that from the point of view of church reformers, of whom Daimbert was one, Bohemond was preferable to a representative of a family which had provided partisans of the imperial cause in the Investiture Contest and, as events were to show, was unenthusiastic about reform. On the other side were the members of Godfrey's household who held positions of trust in Palestine. Appeals were sent to both candidates by their adherents and the Lorrainers took the precaution of seizing control of Jerusalem in Daimbert's absence, for the patriarch and Tancred were with the army besieging Haifa, which fell to the Christians on c. 20 August. Daimbert's message to Bohemond was intercepted by members of Raymond of St Gilles's household, who were still at Latakia, and Bohemond was anyway withdrawn from the scene in August when he fell into the hands of the Turks. It was Baldwin himself who saved the principality of Antioch by coming swiftly to its aid and reinforcing the Armenian garrison of Malatya, which blocked any Danishmendid advance. Before starting his journey south on 2 October he arranged for his cousin Baldwin of Bourcq to be invested with the county of Edessa. He entered Jerusalem on 9 November, assumed the title of king on the 13th and was crowned in the Church of the Nativity in Bethlehem on Christmas Day.

The embellishment of the holy places

The First Crusade had been fought to recover Jerusalem and its shrines. It had originally been assumed that they would be restored to the Byzantine Greeks. The first western settlers, few and isolated, were unprepared for the task that faced them, although they knew well that the *raison d'être* of their settlement was the maintenance and protection of the holy places. They found them deserted. The only shrine-churches in Jerusalem and its neighbourhood which seem to have been staffed by Greek priests were the Holy Sepulchre compound, the Church of the Nativity at Bethlehem, the Church of the Ascension on the Mount of Olives, and the monastery of the Cross and possibly St John's at 'Ain Karim. In addition, there was already a Catholic Benedictine community of Italian Cassinese monks in the abbey of St Mary of the Latins just to the south of the Holy Sepulchre. Godfrey of Bouillon installed twenty secular canons at the Holy Sepulchre, colleges of secular canons of unknown size at the Temple (the Dome of the Rock) and Mount Zion – these, together with the community on the Mount of Olives, were later converted into houses of Augustinian canons regular – and Benedictine monks at St Mary of the Valley of Jehoshaphat, the chief Marian shrine. The installation of canons at the Holy Sepulchre, the Temple and Mount Zion must have made it easier to make use of the clerics of all kinds who had arrived with the crusade, and some of the monks of St Mary of the Latins, with its small daughters of St Mary Major and St John, could have been transferred to the Valley of Jehoshaphat to provide the nucleus of a new community: by 1103 they, together with canons from the Holy Sepulchre, were already establishing new houses at Montpèlerin, outside Tripoli. Even so, the new rulers and senior churchmen must have found it hard to provide the manpower they needed.

It is not surprising to find that of the 89 known first crusaders who settled permanently in the East, 21 were churchmen. Of the ten bishops who had left for the East, however, only one stayed in Palestine and he withdrew from active life, living there for ten years as a hermit. Most of the rest of the clergy were not of high quality, as we have seen. Their low standard is illustrated by two of the most important early appointments. Arnulf of Chocques, the first Latin patriarch of Jerusalem, was quite a well-known scholar who had been tutor to Robert of Normandy's sister, Cecilia of England. Robert had already promised him the first vacant bishopric in Normandy. He was an admired preacher, but he was also reputed to be a womanizer and he was very quickly supplanted as patriarch by Archbishop Daimbert of Pisa. The first abbot of St Mary of the Valley of Jehoshaphat, a man called Baldwin who had been an abbot in Europe and had been Godfrey of Bouillon's chaplain, was a scandalous figure. He had branded a cross on his forehead, had pretended that he had been marked by an angel and had financed his crusade out of oblations made to it by the faithful. It must have been clear to everyone but themselves that these early clerical settlers badly needed supplementing.

Of the settlers in and around Jerusalem who can be identified before 1131, over 51 per cent were churchmen. It is clear from their toponyms – Barcelona, Barres, Beauvais, Bridiers, Brittany, Bure, Chartres, Chocques, Gascony, Le Mans, Messines, Picquigny, Prévenchières, Rouen, St Omer – that many of them had come directly from France. Some senior churchmen were sent by the papacy. Daimbert of Pisa has already been mentioned. Archbishop Gibelin of Arles, who arrived as legate in 1108, also became patriarch of Jerusalem. Others may well have been summoned to Palestine by the leaders of the settlement themselves. Gilduin of Le Puiset, a cousin of King Baldwin II, who had been a monk of Cluny and prior of the Cluniac house of Lurcy-le-Bourg before travelling east at a time of crisis in 1120 to become abbot of St Mary of the Valley of Jehoshaphat, had probably been invited by the king. Stephen of Chartres, abbot of St Jean-en-Vallée at Chartres and another cousin of Baldwin, came on pilgrimage in 1128 and was immediately elevated to the patriarchate.

A prime objective was to encase the great shrines in proper buildings. A feature of Jerusalem was the careful location of events recorded in Scripture. They included the Crucifixion on Calvary and the Resurrection in the Holy Sepulchre, the Last Supper in a room which also doubled as the place where the Holy Spirit had descended on the Apostles at Pentecost, Christ's conversation with the doctors and anger at the money-changers in the Temple, his Agony in a Garden near the site of his arrest at Gethsemane, the Blessed Virgin Mary's Assumption from a tomb in the valley of Jehoshaphat – another resurrection shrine and the house of her parents, SS Joachim and Anne, near the sheep pool where Christ had cured the paralytic. Many of the sites had been located long before, but some were pure invention – the Hospitallers of St John came to identify their headquarters with a hospice supposedly founded by the Maccabees, ruled by Zachary, the father of St John the Baptist, and frequented by Christ – but localization was essential, because only at an identifiable spot, radiating with power and focused on by the saints, would the pilgrims' prayers be truly efficacious.

When the crusaders arrived most of the holy places were in a sorry state. Some were in ruins and others needed reconstructing, or at least restoring. The building programme seems to have begun relatively slowly, but it reached a crescendo in the 1140s under the patronage of Queen Melisende. The planners did not express publicly what they intended to do – at any rate no description of their intentions survives – but it is fairly clear that their programme was governed first by their own respect for the sanctity of the shrines now in their care and secondly by the requirements of pilgrims, whose own devotion enhanced that sanctity. More pilgrims than ever were now coming to Jerusalem. They wanted to venerate the relics of Christ and others at identifiable locations, the assurance that their own prayers would be supplemented by those of the religious resident at the site concerned and a sympathetic environment which would assist their devotions. This did not necessarily mean that the atmosphere should be reverentially quiet. The twelfth century was an intensely theatrical age, in which every technique was used to heighten public emotion, through dramatic display in liturgy, ritual and situation. A shrine-church, reached at the end of a long and wearisome journey, was rather like stage-set on which the holiness of the events or people it commemorated could be theatrically reproduced, generating public displays of fervour.

In Jerusalem liturgical drama was to be experienced almost every day, as, for example, in the Vespers processions in the Church of the Holy Sepulchre every Saturday from Easter to Advent. The most theatrical of the pilgrim dramas in that church took place each year with the miracle of the Holy Fire, the auto-lighting of one of the seven lamps in the Aedicule, a small free-standing chapel enclosing the Tomb, which stood under a rotunda built in the eleventh century. The miracle occurred on Holy Saturday, during the Liturgy of the Sacred Fire which throughout the rest of Christendom depends on the striking of a flint. This, a wonder to Muslims as well as to Christians for centuries, was preceded on Good Friday by the extinguishing of the lamps in the Aedicule, which was locked and would not be opened again until the miracle had taken place, although it had little windows through which the flickering light of one of the wicks could be seen once it had been kindled. The liturgy would begin in a crowded church at nine o'clock in the morning. Although the timing of the arrival of the fire could be erratic, and it was even known to flare up at one of the other holy places in the city such as the Temple or the Church of St John, it usually came to the Sepulchre in the afternoon. At about three o'clock, after the appointed readings, sung alternately in Greek and Latin, and their associated psalms and prayers, a Greek cantor standing in one part of the rotunda would start to chant the triple appeal *Kyrie eleison* with its response, which heralded the fire's appearance. At the same time the patriarch would approach the Aedicule, carrying a candle and preceded by the relic of the True Cross. Once the miracle had taken place he would enter and light his candle from the lamp, before passing the light on to the candles of all those present and then processing with it across Jerusalem to the Temple.

There was already a tradition in the West of reproducing the Holy Sepulchre in stone as a backdrop to liturgical representations of Christ's entry into Jerusalem on Palm Sunday and his Passion, Death and Resurrection in the Easter Triduum. The reality aimed for in these western examples was not, of course, that of the scene in first-century Jerusalem, but of the structure now enclosing its physical remains. The intention of men and women in the central middle ages was representation, not imitation. Their reality was more like that to be found in icons, the purpose of which was to provide gateways to the unchanging truth that lay beyond them. The new rulers in Jerusalem never had the intention, therefore, of reproducing accurately in tableau form the physical actuality of the scenes the locations represented. They wanted to give an impression of them if possible and to enhance reality through the use of other elements. In some places their aims had already been adequately met and the buildings were anyway so familiar that drastic alterations would have been counter-productive. They converted the Dome of the Rock into a church, but left it and the Church of the Nativity at Bethlehem more or less untouched in architectural terms, although they decorated the interiors, introducing at Bethlehem what has been described as one of the most extensive and complex programmes of mosaic, fresco and sculpture decoration in the Mediterranean world.

Christ's Tomb, or what remained of it, had been detached in the fourth century by the emperor Constantine's engineers from the rest of the quarry wall out of which it had been hollowed and had been encased in the Aedicule. The twelfth-century Aedicule was to all intents and purposes the one constructed by the Greeks in the 1030s after the cave-tomb had been destroyed by Hakim. The Greeks had recreated the cave artificially and the Aedicule remained a tomb-like chamber, decorated, of course, in a suitably sumptious manner, with a throughway in an eastern compartment, so that pilgrims could enter by one door and leave by another. All the settlers did was to embellish this little building with mosaics, cover it with silver and add a cupola; it was, after all, only about sixty years old when they arrived.

They adopted the same approach with respect to the Calvary Chapel, on top of the rock column to which the hill of Golgotha had been reduced by Constantine's engineers. The actual site, the summit of Calvary, was, like the rock of the Tomb, visible, but was encased in marble. Unlike the Aedicule, there had never been, for obvious reasons, any attempt to recreate the actuality of the top of a mound of living rock, open to the sky in the middle or at the edge of a disused quarry. Within the chapel all was gloom, exaggerated for pilgrims who entered directly from the sunlit outdoors, with a dim view above and around of mosaic glittering in the candle light. All attention could be focused on the rock summit enclosed by an altar with one element of actuality – the hole into which the cross had been inserted – visible and touchable.

When they felt it to be necessary, however, the Latins did engage in major building works and these often demonstrate how their minds worked. The site of the Cenacle on Mount Zion, the 'Upper Room' in which the Last Supper and the Descent of the Holy Spirit at Pentecost were supposed to have taken place, had been identified for centuries. The scriptural narratives made clear that it was part of a two-storied building, but the Church of the Dormition to which it was attached was in ruins in 1099. So here the Latins had to reconstruct. Little remains of their church except the Cenacle itself, which turns out to be a late twelfth-century Gothic gallery chapel. Contemporaries would have been disappointed with the first-century reality of a small, dim, rather low-grade chamber and the room had probably been redesigned by the Latins at least twice before taking its final shape. The four ribbed vaults, carried on slim columns, obviously represented what contemporaries thought a room suitable for the Last Supper should look like: one of the pilgrims, commenting on the size of an earlier version, pointed out that it was large enough for Christ and the Apostles to dine in. Its success can be measured by the way its form was echoed in the refectories of Augustinian canons in the West.

A concern of the builders was to ensure that a continuous stream of prayer heavenwards reinforced the pilgrims' petitions. The common Christian practice of placing a high altar or choir over a crypt in which lay the body of a saint or over a particularly holy place was often to be found in Palestine, as at St Anne's in Jerusalem, where a slightly irregular Romanesque church was built so that its sanctuary was directly over the crypt in which the Blessed Virgin Mary was believed to have been born. An ambitious example of the practice was to be found at Bethany, just outside the city, which was believed to be the site of several Gospel stories. It was the place from which Christ had begun his triumphal entry into Jerusalem on Palm Sunday and the village of the sisters Martha and Mary (identified with Mary Magdalene). Here had stood the house of Simon the Leper, where Mary had anointed Christ with oil. It was also the village where Christ had raised Lazarus, the sisters' brother, from the dead. It was integrated into the Jerusalem liturgical round, for on Palm Sunday and also on other days in the year there were processions to and from the city. There was already a sixth-century church, which was thought to stand over the house of Simon the Leper. To the west of it and across a yard was the cave-tomb believed to be that of Lazarus. In 1138 this site passed to the Benedictine nunnery of St Lazarus of Bethany, newly founded by Queen Melisende as a fitting community to be ruled by her sister Yveta as abbess. The nuns fronted the cave-tomb with a large barrel-vaulted room, but on the rock level above they built a three-aisled basilica. Its east end had three apses supported on three barrel vaults, the central one being the entrance to Lazarus's tomb. The abbey church was destroyed by Saladin in 1187 and hardly any decorative details survive, but it is surely significant that the nuns' choir was situated immediately above the cave-tomb, so that their intercessions could draw on and reinforce the sanctity of the place.

Most important of all, of course, was the Church of the Holy Sepulchre, which was dedicated, if not yet entirely completed, on 15 July 1149, the fiftieth anniversary of the liberation of Jerusalem. When the crusaders took the city there had not been one church but a compound containing several separate shrines around an open courtyard, including the Tomb, Calvary nearby, and, somewhat apart, the ruins of Constantine's basilica, built over the spot where his mother had reputedly discovered the wood of the True Cross in 320. The settlers' building programme, in which masons, sculptors, mosaicists and painters from Europe and Asia were engaged, was strikingly original. A pilgrim would have been familiar with the details of a narrative in which Christ was led outside the city walls to Golgotha or Calvary, which some believed had also been the site of the burial of Adam, the first man, many centuries before. Christ was confined in a spot nearby while his cross was erected. He was then crucified. Once he was dead, his body was hurriedly anointed with spices and was laid in an unused cave-tomb nearby. The Sepulchre overlooked a garden in which, after discovering the empty tomb on Easter morning, Mary Magdalene had asked a man, whom she thought was a gardener but was in fact the risen Christ, where the body had been taken. Nearly three centuries later, the emperor Constantine's mother had discovered the actual cross used at the crucifixion buried in a pit not far away.

The Latins decided to roof over the courtyard. The locations of Christ's death and resurrection were henceforward to be physically related to one another for the first time under a single roof in one enormous, sumptuously decorated building, which would have the familiar elements of a great European road-church, including an ambulatory, but would also contain a number of additional and associated holy sites. Each of these – the Chapel of Adam, the Chapel of St Helena and the Grotto of the Cross, Christ's Prison and the Place of Anointing – would have been the centre of a major cult in the West. The work had to be achieved in an urban setting and on a built-up site, cluttered with previous Constantinian and Byzantine structures. The holy places within were at fixed points, since they had been firmly identified, and so could not be moved to more convenient locations.

The decisions on what to preserve or demolish and what the ground plan would be seem to have been made at the start. The Byzantine rotunda around the tomb was kept, although its eastern apse was dismantled, so that it could be linked to a new transitional Gothic church to the east. The Aedicule and the Calvary Chapel were preserved but embellished, as we have seen. The Byzantine Prison of Christ was kept and this led, perhaps for aesthetic reasons, to the retention of a Byzantine arcade and a Constantinian wall. On the other hand it was decided to destroy three small shrines on the east side of the old courtyard and replace them with three radiating chapels off the ambulatory.

The Holy Sepulchre church is, in fact, the best illustration of the settlers' devotional policies. The decision to roof over the courtyard and construct one building unifying all the disparate elements described in the Gospels meant that an enclosed stage-set had been created in which visitors could wander at will. The advantages were obvious. The pilgrims would no longer be distracted by having to cross an open court outside when going from one shrine to another. In an enclosed space, recollection (that focusing of the mind) could be more easily maintained, while everything that would contribute to a favourable ambience – the smell of incense, the sound of bells and chant – could be controlled. It is indicative that the Latins placed the choir, from which rose the solemn intercessions of the office, right in the centre of the church: east of the Sepulchre, north of Calvary, south of the Prison and west of the Grotto of the Cross.

On arrival, pilgrims would be confronted with the double doorway. They would not usually enter the church by that way, but would climb an external staircase up to the Calvary Chapel. After venerating the site of the Crucifixion there, they would descend into the body of the church, past the Chapel of Adam and a crack in the living rock, which was said to have split open at the moment of Christ's death and was considered to be still spattered with the dried remnants of his blood. They could then cross directly to the Aedicule of the Tomb itself, about eighty-five feet away, walking under a dome which complemented the Byzantine one over the rotunda and was placed over the spot where Christ's corpse was supposed to have been anointed before burial. They could then explore the church, which was believed to stand on the site of the garden (possibly hinted at by the foliage capitals of the tree-like columns), visiting Christ's Prison and passing along an ambulatory out of which opened chapels, two of which contained reliquaries of the True Cross. They would go down a flight of steps that led to the site of the original discovery of the Cross or climb up to the galleries linking the new church and the rotunda.

Wherever they went inscriptions, sculptures, mosaics and frescos would remind them of the event that had taken place at the particular spot they were venerating. For most pilgrims the representations in mosaic and paint would have meant more than the inscriptions, and the scenes depicted seem to have been quite straightforward and easy to understand. Nearly all of them have been destroyed and we are so reliant on fragmentary references to them that we can only identify a few. Again, the Latins do not seem to have done away with those already in place which they admired or found helpful; they even transferred a great Byzantine Anastasis from the rotunda to the new eastern apse over the high altar. They liked to supplement rather than replace. Over one of the two doors at the entrance to the church was a mosaic tympanum representing the Risen Christ appearing to Mary Magdalene in the garden near his tomb. The significance of the fact that the first witness to the Resurrection had been a converted sinner would not have been lost on those on penitential pilgrimage. Under it a sculpted frieze on one lintel illustrated scenes from the raising of Lazarus to the Last Supper. It may have been intended to continue the frieze over the other door, completing the series with scenes of the Passion, but if so the work was never finished and a vine-scroll entwined with humans and birds was put in its place. Over the entry to the Sepulchre itself were mosaics showing Christ in his tomb, the Blessed Virgin Mary, and The Three Maries with their phials of ointment at the empty Sepulchre confronted by the angel who had just rolled back the stone from its entrance. The Latins did not disturb a traditional scheme of images in the Calvary Chapel, including a Byzantine crucifixion over the altar, but they increased the number of figures of Old Testament prophets and kings and added the magnificent surviving mosaic of the Ascension. At the spot where the True Cross was supposedly found by St Helena, they painted a fresco depicting the Crucifixion. It has been written that 'one must imagine the church of the Holy Sepulchre glowing with all the subdued richness with which we are familiar in St Mark's at Venice'.

Although Greek and indigenous craftsmen were employed, the design of the churches and monastic quarters throughout the settlements was recognizably western. First-rate sculptors were recruited in Europe to work on particular commissions, such as the capitals and doorway of the cathedral at Nazareth, or to create semi-permanent workshops in the East in which their artistry inter-reacted with that of other western immigrants, as in the 'Temple workshop' in Jerusalem, active from c. 1170 to 1187 and assembled round a core of Provençal craftsmen. And the splendour of the churches was reflected in their furnishings. A magnificent series of liturgical books survives, one a superb product for Queen Melisende herself, others witnessing to the presence of skilful masters in the scriptorium of the Holy Sepulchre.

The cost of restoring the holy places must have been stupendous, at a time when building projects were in train throughout the settlements. Money of this sort could never have been raised within the kingdom of Jerusalem itself, the existence of which was always under military threat, or from taxes or levies on the pilgrim traffic or from the oblations of pilgrims. Enormous subsidies must have come from overseas, although no records of their despatch or arrival have survived. But the result was surely worth all the expense. The impression one has of Catholic Jerusalem in the twelfth century is of a cult-centre which was being intelligently managed. Shrines already well known to western pilgrims were not disturbed, but were further beautified. Some of the most prestigious were related to one another and others nearby in a great church which combined all the best features of a major shrine, including the assurance of regular intercessory prayer. The Cenacle and Bethany were cleverly developed. The building programme in Jerusalem demonstrates how sensitive the settlers were to the needs and predispositions of the pilgrims, whose arrival twice a year provided the city with its *raison d'être*.

The establishment of the Latin Church

The Latin Church in Palestine and Syria was formed in the two decades after the conquest and retained until the end of the thirteenth century features it had by then developed. The crusaders had entered a region in which many creeds somehow managed to co-exist. In the north the majority of the indigenous population may well have been Christian, mostly Monophysite Armenians and Jacobites, although there were also strong Orthodox communities, particularly around Antioch. In the south, leaving aside an unknown number of converts to Catholicism – including from the 1180s onwards whole Uniate communities, the Maronite and a section of the Armenian – the indigenous peoples consisted of various Christian groups – Orthodox Greeks who were generally Arabic-speaking, Monophysites of different kinds, particularly Jacobites, Armenians and Copts, and Nestorians – but there were more Muslims – Sunni and Shi'a of various types, including Druses – than in the north, although it has been suggested that they were still not yet a majority. There were also Jews of several schools and Samaritans, and a few Zoroastrians.

In time the settlers had to get on with all the religious groups who were now subject to them, but at first they were determined to expel all infidels, whether Muslims or Jews, from centres of religious or military significance. The policy can already be seen in operation in the winter of 1097–8. At Tilbeşar, Ravanda and Artah the Muslims were slaughtered or driven out, but the indigenous Christians were allowed to remain. The crusaders adopted the same approach in the following June when they took Antioch, although it was said that in the darkness before dawn they found it hard to distinguish between the Christian and Muslim inhabitants of the city, and again in July 1099 when they took Jerusalem. The Muslims and Jews who had survived were expelled and were not permitted to live in Jerusalem thenceforward, although they could visit it as pilgrims; in fact a few were in residence later in the twelfth century. The indigenous Christians of Jerusalem were allowed to stay, but the relatively small number of inhabitants led later to extraordinary measures to increase the size of the population, including the relocation of Christian villagers from Transjordan. Where elsewhere there was an indigenous Christian population, of whatever denomination, that could remain; where there was not there was to be settlement by western Europeans.

In many of the earliest examples – el Barah in Syria, taken by Raymond of St Gilles in the autumn of 1098; Ramle in Palestine, reached by the crusade in June 1099; and Caesarea, which fell to the settlers in May 1101 – settlement was accompanied by the foundation of a Catholic bishopric, the incumbent of which was also expected to exercise military command along the lines of some frontier sees in western Europe. At the same time the crusaders were careful not to displace the existing Orthodox bishops, whose legitimacy and authority they recognized. The Orthodox patriarch of Antioch, John IV, who had been inside the city and had suffered during the siege, was restored to his cathedral, once it had been reconsecrated, and was accorded the full honours of the patriarchate. But a ruling at the council of Clermont, made with reference to Spain, stating that liberated churches would 'belong' to the principalities of the princes who conquered them, was used to justify the appointment of Catholic bishops where no Orthodox see existed or where there were vacancies. The Catholic patriarch of Jerusalem, who was elected a fortnight after the city's liberation, was appointed in the knowledge that there was a vacancy, for the Orthodox patriarch Symeon, who had accompanied the crusade for part of its journey, had just died in Cyprus.

Ethnic cleansing, born of desperation and isolation, could not be maintained indefinitely once it became clear that western immigration was not to be on a large enough scale to create a state solely for Christians. The taking of Sidon (Saïda) in 1110 marked a change of policy and the acceptance of the residence of non-Christians in the larger cities. On the other hand, the toleration of existing Orthodox bishops was already breaking down. At Christmas 1099 Daimbert, now patriarch of Jerusalem, consecrated Catholic archbishops of Tarsus, Misis and Edessa and a Catholic bishop of Artah. These towns had substantial native Christian populations and it is hard to believe that in all of them the

Orthodox bishoprics were vacant. All, moreover, were in the patriarchate of Antioch and it may be that the Orthodox patriarch John had refused to consecrate them, which is why Daimbert did so by virtue of his legation from the pope. The new bishops had accompanied their temporal masters, Bohemond of Antioch and Baldwin of Edessa, and also Daimbert himself, south to Jerusalem; their consecration was obviously an act of full deliberation. It was followed six months later by the forcing of the Orthodox patriarch out of Antioch and his replacement by a Catholic. John's position became, or was made, intolerable and he retired to the monastery of Oxeia. This was treated by the Latins as abdication. The change in policy towards resident Orthodox bishops has been put down to Daimbert's supposed Hellenophobia, but the background to it was the Byzantine invasions of Cilicia and the empire's manifest desire to gain control of Antioch. Tarsus and Misis commanded the roads in and out of Cilicia. Artah watched the road east of Antioch. Edessa had already proved its strategic worth in the summer of 1098. Back in Normandy it was said that the settlers feared that Patriarch John would betray Antioch to the Byzantine emperor after Bohemond had fallen into the hands of the Turks. The setting up of lines of Catholic bishops in place of existing Orthodox ones was, therefore, a response to military and political pressure from the Byzantine government and it is surely no coincidence that in the early twelfth century Catholic dioceses were established much more rapidly in Syria than in Palestine, where as late as 1120 there were only four Catholic bishops besides the patriarch.

Most of the early appointments were of poor quality, as we have seen. Standards in the settler church were not helped by the political consequences of the conquest. The crusade had been preached by a reforming papacy, but the pope's chief representative, Adhémar of Le Puy, had died in 1098 and the first rulers of Jerusalem had in the past supported the imperialists in the Investiture Contest. That would not necessarily have precluded sympathy for reform ideas, for many of the imperialists were themselves reformers, differing from the papalists only on the means by which reform should be achieved. But neither Godfrey of Bouillon nor Baldwin I showed any sympathy for reform ideas; indeed Baldwin, who had been trained for the priesthood and so must have been conscious of some of the issues, was clearly antipathetic.

It is against this background that Baldwin's conflict with Daimbert of Pisa should be viewed. Pope Urban had appointed Daimbert as his chief legate to replace Adhémar of Le Puy and it was in this capacity that on his arrival in Jerusalem before Christmas 1099 Daimbert chaired a council which refused to confirm the election to the patriarchate of Arnulf of Chocques. Daimbert was then elected patriarch himself and presided at a ceremony at which he invested Godfrey and Bohemond with their principalities. It is possible that in their minds and his was the idea either of vassal-states of the papacy, of which Daimbert was still the legate, or of vassal-states of the Holy Sepulchre, along the lines of the lands of St Peter in Europe, or merely the confirmation of the princes' rule by a representative of the papacy, a power qualified to grant this recognition. We cannot now tell what was the intention of those present, although the future rulers of Jerusalem and Antioch were never to be regarded as vassals of the popes or the patriarchs.

Daimbert seems to have decided on a radical solution to the problem of the endowment of his church. He wanted to create a patriarchal patrimony, centred on Jerusalem, not unlike the papal patrimony in Italy. To provide for the twenty Catholic canons, who had already been installed in the Holy Sepulchre, the Orthodox clergy there were deprived of their benefices; but Godfrey, who was very short of cash, was probably reluctant to give way to demands to restore to the church of Jerusalem all the properties and rights it claimed to have enjoyed in the past. He was persuaded by Daimbert to confirm it in its ancient possessions at the same time as the new patriarch was consecrated – although his inventory may have been less extensive than Daimbert's – and six weeks later he granted it a fourth part of Jaffa. In ecclesiastical circles in Jerusalem there was a tradition that at Easter 1100 Daimbert had forced Godfrey to cede to him the whole of the city of Jerusalem, including its citadel, and the remaining three-quarters of Jaffa, although Godfrey's need for resources was recognized to the extent that he was allowed to retain usufruct until the settlement was enlarged. Godfrey was also believed to have promised that should he die without an heir Jerusalem and Jaffa would pass immediately to the patriarch and to have confirmed this on his deathbed; it was said that only the quick action of his household frustrated Daimbert and assured their possession by Baldwin. The church of Jerusalem briefly revived its claims to Jerusalem and Jaffa thirty years later. Irrespective of the accuracy of the tradition, it is clear that Daimbert was ambitious, even if the only consequence seems to have been the development of a patriarchal lordship around the Church of the Holy Sepulchre in the north-western part of the city of Jerusalem.

Godfrey's death and the failure to ensure the succession of Bohemond greatly weakened Daimbert's position. Pope Paschal, moreover, had now appointed a new legate, Maurice of Porto, who arrived at Latakia in September 1100 and met Baldwin on the latter's journey south to claim the kingdom. Baldwin was crowned king by Daimbert himself on Christmas Day 1100 and he clearly had no intention of surrendering what he regarded as his rights. When the new legate arrived in Palestine in the following spring he went onto the offensive. He accused Daimbert of various crimes, including plotting his assassination after Godfrey's death, and he engineered his suspension from the patriarchal office. Then, after allowing Daimbert to buy himself back into his grace, Baldwin demanded money to pay the stipends of knights; at this time the settlement was very precarious and a large Egyptian army was mustering on the southern frontier. Daimbert made a contribution which was considered to be too small. When the king made an angry scene and demanded more, he retorted by raising the issue of the Church's liberty, asking Baldwin whether he dared make her a tribute payer and bondswoman when Christ had freed her and threatening the king with excommunication by the pope. But Baldwin insisted. A compromise worked out by Maurice of Porto failed because Daimbert only half-heartedly fulfilled his side of the bargain.

Baldwin then struck ruthlessly, accusing Daimbert of embezzling money sent to the East by Roger of Sicily and forcing him into exile in Antioch. Although in 1102 Daimbert was briefly restored to power, in fulfilment of a condition Tancred had made in return for military aid from Antioch, he was almost immediately tried again by a council presided over by another papal legate, Robert of Paris, and deposed. He appealed to the pope and accompanied Bohemond to the West in 1104. His successor in the patriarchate, Evremar, was summoned to the papal curia to defend his election, but neither he nor Baldwin sent representatives to Rome and the case went by default to Daimbert, who died at Messina on his way back to the East. Evremar now travelled to Italy to plead his case, but he was followed by Arnulf of Chocques, bringing letters from those very people who had written the references with which Evremar had been armed, calling for his deposition. The pope was scandalized and chose a new legate, Gibelin of Arles, to decide the matter. In 1108 Gibelin declared Evremar's election to have been invalid because Daimbert had been deposed under royal pressure. Gibelin in his turn was elected patriarch.

Daimbert, who had had a distinguished career as a reforming politician in Italy, met his match in Baldwin. He has had a bad press from historians, who have relied on sources hostile to him, but on his arrival in the East he must have been horrified to find a newly established church that was inadequately endowed and staffed by clergy of poor quality, with some dioceses doubling as military frontier-posts, reminiscent of the bad old days in western Europe. He must have been struck by the fact that power in Jerusalem was held not by a supporter of the reforming popes, like Bohemond, but by a man who had been closer to their arch-enemy, Henry IV of Germany. His remedies had been nullified by Baldwin and although Pope Paschal's decision was in his favour the two papal legates sent to the East had not given him wholehearted support. The problem was, of course, that neither they nor the pope could afford to assent to anything that might damage the settlement, the situation of which was perilous enough.

Paschal took the step of confirming Baldwin's assumption of the crown and he later went further. The archbishopric of Tyre with its suffragan sees, including Acre, Sidon and Beirut, was part of the patriarchate of Antioch. Baldwin was naturally anxious that the church in the northern part of his kingdom should not be subject to a patriarch outside his control and he and Patriarch Gibelin appealed to Rome. In 1111 Paschal ruled that the boundary between the patriarchates should be the political frontier between Jerusalem and the northern settlements, thus detaching a large part of the southernmost province of one ancient patriarchate and incorporating it into another. In the process Tyre lost its three northern sees, Tripoli, Jubail and Tartus, which became directly subject to Antioch. The patriarch of Antioch protested and Paschal gave signs of changing his mind, but the rights of Jerusalem were confirmed by Pope Honorius II in 1128. This messy decision, which was always unsatisfactory and remained controversial until at least the middle of the century, shows how far Paschal was prepared to go to meet the king's desires. It is not the only example in his pontificate of compliance with the wishes of secular rulers, but it also demonstrates how the need for strong government in the new settlements tended to take precedence over other considerations.

Relations with the indigenous after 1110

A feature of the Latin Church in Palestine and Syria was that it was relatively small in numbers. In the aftermath of the First Crusade there cannot have been more than between 2,000 and 4,000 western Europeans in the whole of the Near East and although the numbers increased substantially, so that there may have been eventually more than 150,000 in Palestine, the settlement was always small. There were some converts to Catholicism, perhaps a significant number, from among the indigenous peoples – the mere fact of native names appearing in the witness lists to charters testifies to this, since in law only the testimony of Catholics carried full weight in court – but it is impossible to estimate the size of the convert community because there was a natural tendency for convert families to adopt the names of Latin saints and so merge into the crowd. For instance, the Arrabi family first made its appearance in 1122, when Muisse Arrabi was a knight of Jaffa. Muisse had a son called George, whose four children were named Henry, Peter, John and Maria: had they not chosen to use their distinctive cognomen their origins would have been lost to us. A burgess of Acre called Saliba made a will in 1264 which reveals him to have been a Catholic, or perhaps a Maronite, since he made endowments to several Latin churches. His sister was called Nayme. His brother Stephen, who was no longer living, had been married to a woman called Settedar. He had two daughters, Katherine and Haternie (Hodierna), four nieces, Vista, Caolfe, Bonaventura and Isabellona, and six nephews, Leonard, Thomasinus, George, Dominic, Nicholas and Leonardinus.

The legal inferiority of non-Catholics, about which more below, obviously encouraged conversions and in the thirteenth century there was active proselytizing, and diplomatic pressure, from missionaries and legations from the West. The Franciscans and Dominicans were active in the Holy Land and the Dominican *studium* in Acre was a school for missionaries. Much the most important submission was that of the Maronite Church, a Monothelete community under its own patriarch and bishops which held the allegiance of most indigenous Christians in the county of Tripoli. In c. 1181 it entered into full religious union with Rome and thirty years later its status was regularized. It became the first Uniate Church with its own rites, canon law and hierarchy, being directly subject to the popes without the intermediation of the local Catholic bishops. In spite of a party within the community hostile to union, the Maronites remained sentimentally attached to the Holy See even after the Latins had been driven from Lebanon. The other cases, however, were less impressive. In 1198 an important segment of the Armenian Church, that in Cilicia, formally entered into union with Rome. This was engineered by the ruler who was being made a king by representatives of the western emperor, but the agreement had been reached without the consent of the majority of the Armenian bishops, who resided outside Cilicia, was misunderstood by most of the Armenian people, caused anxiety to those who did understand it and had few results, as the reforms requested by the papacy were never implemented. The Armenians remained in a state of semi-independence. Professions of Catholic faith made to the Dominicans in 1237 by the Jacobite patriarch and archbishop of Jerusalem and by a Nestorian archbishop were of even less consequence, being personal. In fact the work of the Dominican and Franciscan missionaries brought to light the fact that the Jacobite and Nestorian communities, although technically heretical, consisted of ill-educated, devout people who had very little understanding of, or concern about, the theological disputes which had led to separation. But this discovery of the realities of the situation came too late for anything to be done about it.

Even allowing for convert or Uniate families we are still left with very few Catholics, a fact that is confirmed by the small number of Latin parish churches – usually one to each settlement – and by the practice of making the cathedral double as the sole parish church in the larger towns: even in Jerusalem the only Latin church with the *jus parochiale* was the Holy Sepulchre. Jaffa had two parishes after 1168 and Acre and Antioch had multiple parishes in the thirteenth century, but these were very much exceptions. A full Catholic hierarchy was eventually established, but it stood on a very small base and its responsibilities were further reduced by the system of exemptions, which freed the greater monasteries and religious orders and in the thirteenth century some of the churches in the Italian merchant quarters from episcopal jurisdiction.

It is true, of course, that the Catholic bishops retained formal authority over members of other Christian denominations, although there was a distinction made between the Orthodox, who were regarded as relatively sound at least until late in the twelfth century, and the others, who were technically heretical. The Orthodox had their own churches and monastic communities. There is no good evidence that they were ever expelled from the greatest cult-centres, although their priests there were deprived of their benefices and presumably had to subsist on offerings from the faithful. They were actually present in the Church of the Holy Sepulchre and witnessed the failure in 1101 of the auto-lighting of the Easter fire in the Aedicule, which has wrongly been attributed to their absence. Throughout the period of Catholic occupation the Orthodox liturgy seems to have been celebrated daily before the Sepulchre at a large altar in a prominent place in the church and at an altar in the church of Our Lady of the Valley of Jehoshaphat. It is noteworthy that when the Church of the Nativity at Bethlehem was redecorated by Greek mosaicists at the expense of the Byzantine emperor Manuel, the *filioque* clause, a contentious issue between Orthodox and Catholics, was omitted according to Orthodox practice from the formula of the Procession of the Holy Spirit inscribed on the walls. Titular Orthodox patriarchs of Antioch and Jerusalem lived in exile – although for a brief period, from 1165 to 1170, the Orthodox patriarch Athanasius was restored to Antioch – but many Orthodox bishops remained in residence and some sees must have had new appointments after hundreds of years of vacancy. In the patriarchate of Antioch it seems that their presence was not recognized and the Catholic bishops, who regarded themselves as in every sense the legitimate successors to the apostolic lines, appointed vicars to watch over their Orthodox flocks. In the patriarchate of Jerusalem Orthodox prelates seem to have been treated by the Catholics as coadjutors: we know of individual bishops at Gaza and probably also at Sidon and Lydda. The only Orthodox prelate recognized by the Latins as a full diocesan bishop, however, was the archbishop of Sinai, far to the south and outside their direct control.

Of the other Christians the most numerous were the Jacobites and the Armenians. In practice they were left alone. In the north, where most of them lived and where the Jacobite patriarch and the Armenian catholicos resided, they were not interfered with by most of the Catholic bishops, although the vicar appointed to supervise the Orthodox in at least one diocese also oversaw them. In the south they were regarded as being under the authority of the Catholic patriarch and their archbishops of Jerusalem were treated as his suffragans, although this seems to have been no more than a legal technicality. Both communities had cathedrals in Jerusalem. The Jacobites were not admitted to the Holy Sepulchre but were allowed to have a chapel at the entrance, with a separate door in the outer wall, while the Armenians had a chapel in the Parvis, the open space to the south of the church.

Like the army of a banana republic the Latin Church had far too many generals for the troops available. It was markedly monastic as a result of the granting of the custody of so many of the holy places to religious communities and this, combined with the fact the laity were not very numerous, meant that the Catholics directly subject to the bishops were so few that the bishops themselves had very little to do. In the winter of 1216–17 James of Vitry, who as bishop of Acre was responsible for the largest Catholic community in the East, described his daily round: Mass first thing in the morning; then the hearing of confessions until mid-day; then, after a meal – he claimed to have lost his appetite since he had come to Palestine – visiting the sick until the hours of None or Vespers; then a sitting of his court, which took up much of the rest of the day. He wrote that he had no time for reading other than from the lectionaries at Mass or Matins and that he had to reserve the night-time for prayer and meditation, but his responsibilities in a city crowded with ecclesiastical refugees from the interior, with all the disputes over rights that followed, were exceptional.

By the time he was writing the situation had become absurd. As the Christians began to lose territory to the Muslims, exiled bishops and their chapters crowded into the cities on the coast, particularly Acre, and there most of them remained, either because their sees, like those of Hebron and Sebastea, were not recovered, or because, like those of Nazareth, Lydda, Tiberias and Jerusalem itself, they were too exposed to be safely reoccupied. Some lines of bishops lapsed, two were joined to other dioceses, but several continued, largely because their churches had been endowed with properties along the coast and in western Europe. The cathedral churches of the Holy Sepulchre, Sebastea, Nazareth and Bethlehem, along with the abbeys of St Mary of the Latins and St Mary of the Valley of Jehoshaphat, the priory of Mount Zion and the military orders, had been endowed with estates throughout Christendom, from which revenues continued to flow in. Their administration provided a living for some of the canons and religious. In new statutes drawn up in 1251 for the chapter of Nazareth it was laid down that if the archbishop's own lordship in Galilee did not provide a living for him and prebends for the chapter

> only the prior should remain living with the archbishop in Syria. The other canons shall be provided for as is honestly seen to be expedient or they will be sent overseas to govern the priories and churches belonging to the cathedral of Nazareth.

Even without cathedral churches and pastoral duties these chapters were independently endowed, like modern Oxford and Cambridge colleges, and would have remained in existence for that reason alone. A curious result was that the walls of thirteenth-century Acre contained, besides its own clergy and the brothers of the military orders and the friars, the Augustinian chapter of the Holy Sepulchre, religious communities like Mount Zion and St Mary of the Valley of Jehoshaphat exiled from Jerusalem and titular bishops *in partibus infidelium* with their chapters.

The plethora of idle bishops was only one of several odd features of the Church. Representing a minority in a potentially hostile population it was forced, after the brutal depopulations of the first decade, to express toleration, not only with respect to other Christians but also with respect to those of other faiths, which continued to be openly practised. Mosques at Tyre were mentioned by the traveller Ibn Jubayr. Hanbali Muslim peasants had gathered for Friday prayers with the *khutba*, invoking the name of the 'Abbasid caliph, in the village of Jamma'il near Nablus, before some of them migrated in 1156. They left because of extortionate taxation and because their Friday prayers were under threat: their Latin lord was apparently telling them they should be working. This was, it is true, a case of discrimination, but it stemmed from the behaviour of one landlord – and incidentally the drawing power of a Muslim teacher who was attracting many people in the district – and it demonstrated that up to that time religious practice had been undisturbed. Muslim visitors were struck by the way local shrines continued to flourish. Writing about the Nablus region 'Imad ad-Din commented that the Franks 'changed not a single law or cult practice of the [Muslim inhabitants]', a phrase echoed by the geographer Yaqut, who wrote with reference to a mosque in Bethlehem that 'the Franks changed nothing when they took the country', and by the traveller Ibn Jubayr when describing a shrine at 'Ain el Baqar (the Ox spring) in Acre: 'in the hands of the Christians its venerable nature is maintained and God has preserved it as a place of prayer for the Muslims'. A new synagogue was constructed by the Samaritan Jews at Nablus in the 1130s and the magnificence of the synagogues at Meiron near Safad (Zefat) was commented on by a Jewish traveller c. 1240. The Western Wall of the Temple and the tombs of the kings on Mount Zion were visited by Jews, although the latter had been sealed, and local shrines venerated by both Muslims and Jews included the tombs of Jonah at Kar Kannah and of Hanona b. Horkenos in Safad. Non-Christians, who were technically forbidden to live in the city of Jerusalem, certainly visited it as pilgrims. In the Temple compound Muslims went to the Dome of the Rock, now an Augustinian church, and the el Aqsa mosque, now the headquarters of the Templars. The news of the discovery at Hebron in 1119 by the recently established Augustinian canons of what were supposed to be the tombs of the patriarchs Abraham, Isaac and Jacob was a sensation and Jews and Muslims could gain entry to them after the Christian pilgrims had left on payment of a *douceur* to the custodian. The same sort of arrangement was to be found at Sebastea, where the clergy benefited from gifts made by Muslims wanting to pray in the crypt of St John the Baptist there.

Shared holy places were not unusual in the Near East. In the kingdom of Jerusalem the evidence for some assimilation and even syncretism includes a church shared with Syrian Christians near Tiberias. In Acre the cathedral of the Holy Cross, which was built on the site of a mosque, had inside it an area set aside for Muslim prayer and just within the walls of the city at 'Ain el Baqar there was a mosque-church with a Frankish eastern apse, incorporating the *mashhad* (oratory) of 'Ali (the prophet's son-in-law), used by Muslims – presumably Shi'ites – Jews and Christians, who believed that this was the spot where God had created cattle for Adam's use: 'Muslim and infidel assemble there, the one turning to his place of worship, the other to his'. The traveller 'Ali al-Harawi put the popularity of this site down to a ghostly appearance by 'Ali, who had terrified the Franks. In Jerusalem the Templars allowed Muslims to pray in one of their churches close to the el Aqsa mosque. The account by Usamah ibn Munqidh of his experience there is very well known.

> Whenever I visited Jerusalem I always entered the Aqsa mosque, beside which stood a small mosque which the Franks had converted into a church. ... The Templars, who were my friends, would evacuate the little adjoining mosque so that I might pray in it. One day I entered this mosque ... and stood up in the act of praying, upon which one of the Franks rushed on me, got hold of me and turned my face eastward saying, 'This is the way thou shouldst pray'. A group of Templars hastened to him, seized him and repelled him from me. I resumed my prayer [whereupon the Frank rushed in at him again]. ... The Templars ... expelled him. They apologized to me, saying, 'This is a stranger who has only recently arrived from the land of the Franks and he has never before seen anyone praying except eastward'.

Less well known is a similar incident, described by the Jewish traveller Jacob ben Nathaniel, at Rav Kahana's tomb near Tiberias, a healing shrine which attracted Christian as well as Jewish pilgrims.

> When a knight from Provence came and saw that the uncircumcised [the Christians] lit many lights upon the grave he asked 'Who is this one?' and they answered, 'It is a righteous Jew, who heals the sick and helps the barren'. He said to them, 'Why do you thus in honour of a Jew?' and took a stone and threw it on the ground and raised his hand to throw another stone. He was on horseback but fell and died. Immediately the captains and monks [acc. to another trans: the clergy

and bishops] gathered and said that he [the Provençal knight] was not punished because of the Jew, but because he wounded the honour of the teacher of Jesus, and Jesus was wrath with him and killed him; and they said all this before the country folk.

This is a typical *miraculum*, of course, but the report of the anxiety of the clergy to head off trouble by giving a Christian twist to the death of the apoplectic knight confirms that this shrine was the centre of a syncretic cult. So shared places of worship were features of popular religion in Palestine and Syria and were tolerated by the Latin clergy. Some were deep in the countryside, but others were in, or were close to, the towns.

Toleration must have been partly a response to this popular syncretism, but of course there were limits to it. Only Catholics had full rights in law, because only their witness was fully valid in court and the weight given to the testimony of the members of other communities was graded according to their creeds. While all Christians originally had the intrinsic right to freedom, non-Christians did not. This so hindered conversions, because lords, even when they were churchmen, were reluctant to allow their slaves to be baptized and therefore freed, that Pope Gregory IX ruled that baptism would not affect their servile status, a measure also applied in Spain and along the Baltic shores. Non-Christians suffered further disabilities which seem to have stemmed from a modification of the Muslim *dhimmi* laws, which the crusaders had found on their arrival. Strictly speaking, the status of a *dhimmi* was in Muslim law open only to an individual who could be classed among the 'people of scripture': Jews, Christians and Sabaeans (interpreted to cover Zoroastrians). Each adult, male, free, sane *dhimmi* had to pay a poll-tax, the *jiziya*. His real estate could, but did not necessarily, pass to the whole community of Islam, but he could have the use of it and anyway he had to pay on it and its crops a land tax (*kharaj*), while he was liable for other levies for the maintenance of the Muslim armies. He had to distinguish himself from believers in dress. He was not permitted to ride a horse or carry weapons. He suffered legal disabilities with respect to testimony in the law courts, protection under criminal law and marriage. He and his family were not citizens of the Muslim state, but members of a quasi-self-governing community, under its own responsible head, such as a rabbi or bishop, although all serious cases, and those involving the members of different faiths, had to be dealt with by the Muslim courts. On the other hand, *dhimmis* were guaranteed security and protection in the exercise of their religion, although they should not cause public offence by it. They might repair and even rebuild existing places of worship, but could not erect new ones.

In the kingdom of Jerusalem we find that *kharaj* was levied on lands, although given its ubiquity in Islam and the fact that the Latins maintained their predecessors' system of revenue-collection this may not mean much;

that Jews and Muslims, but not Christians, paid a poll-tax; that they were supposed to be differentiated in dress and could not witness in cases involving Latins, except to prove a Latin's age or descent, or to provide evidence on estate boundaries. On the other hand they could practise their own religion. Rabbinical tribunals and Jewish academies flourished in Acre and Tyre, and although no record survives of a *qadi* (a Muslim judge) in post in the kingdom, there was one at Jeble in the principality of Antioch in the 1180s. Professor Kedar has pointed out that the absence of any reference to *qadis* in Palestine should not surprise us, since we would have known nothing about the rabbinical tribunals had they not been so prestigious that their *responsa* were circulated and preserved.

The settlers innovated in two ways. The first of their modifications concerned non-Latin Christians, from whom the restraints of *dhimma* seem to have been only partially lifted. There is no evidence that any Christian had to pay the capitation tax. Nor, indeed, were they subject to tithes, which were levied only on Catholics; in practice this meant that only the lord's share of a village crop was tithed. But the testimony of non-Catholic Christians as witnesses was graded and was never treated as being as authentic as that of the Latins. They also seem to have had some community status with their own bishops continuing to act as their leaders. On his arrival in Acre in 1216 James of Vitry wrote that he had been able to address the Greeks and Jacobites because their bishops were in residence. The Greeks gathered to hear him 'at the orders of their bishop', but 'I have not yet been able to assemble the Nestorians, Georgians and Armenians, because they have no bishop or other head [in the city]'.

In their treatment of the Orthodox Arabic-speaking *Suriani*, who seem to have been the most numerous of the indigenous Christians in the kingdom of Jerusalem, the settlers went further. Special courts, called *Cours des Syriens*, were established for them throughout the kingdom. It was believed in the thirteenth century that during the early decades of the settlement these had been instituted at the request of the *Suriani* to judge according to their customs. Like any *dhimma* courts they had no rights of high justice or of jurisdiction over the properties of freemen. In thirteenth-century Acre and in some other towns the *Cour de la Fonde*, a market court, had absorbed the local *Cour des Syriens*, but there is evidence for the court surviving in Jerusalem, Nablus, Tyre and Bethlehem, all of which, except possibly Nablus, had substantial Orthodox populations. Whether or not the *Suriani* had really asked for these minor courts, it is noteworthy that they must have dealt with those 'secular' cases which under Muslim rule would have been heard by their bishops. It may be that western reform ideas on the separation of temporal powers from the spiritual were being imposed by the Catholics on an indigenous Christian community.

The establishment in many places of the *Cours de la Fonde* was the second innovation. The settlers seem to have taken the existing offices responsible for collecting market taxes, and to have added to their functions the judgment of minor commercial cases involving the members of different indigenous communities. In Acre the bailli, two Latin and four indigenous jurors of the *Cour de la Fonde* heard cases concerning debt, pledge or leases, or

> anything else a Syrian or Jew or Muslim or Samaritan or Nestorian or Greek or Jacobite or Armenian has done. Know well that right judges and commands us to judge that none of the aforesaid peoples ought to plead in any court concerning any [small] claim they make among themselves save in the *Cour de la Fonde*.

Jewish claimants could take oaths on the Torah, Samaritans on 'the five books of Moses', Muslims on the Quran, Jacobites and Greeks on an image of the cross and Gospel books written in their own script. Cases 'of blood', including murder, treason and theft, had to be heard in a higher Latin court.

The creation of special small-claims courts, existing alongside the higher courts of the kingdom, the rabbinical and episcopal tribunals and the courts of the *qadis*, was a departure from *dhimma* legislation, because in a Muslim state all inter-communal cases, and not only the major ones, had to go before a government judge. It has been argued with respect to the Jews that so reluctant would they have been to allow hearings outside their own community that resort to the governmental courts would have occurred only when adherents of different religions were involved, but it has also been demonstrated that although in Egypt Christian and Jewish community leaders profoundly disapproved of cases passing outside their own arbitration, individuals who thought they might gain did appeal to Muslim courts. There is anyway evidence for commercial partnerships in the Latin East involving men of different communities and a prime reason for the establishment of the *Cours de la Fonde* must have been to resolve inter-communal disputes.

An experimental approach to the management of non-Latins, whether Christian or not, and a studied toleration were not particularly exceptional in the twelfth century, but it is significant that they were maintained in the thirteenth, in spite of a drive for Christian uniformity on papal terms, which began during the pontificate of Pope Innocent III, first in southern Italy and then in Greece. Pressure for change was resisted by the Catholic hierarchies in Palestine and Syria – although not in Cyprus – probably because the bishops did not want to antagonize the indigenous population. So although conversions were made and Uniate churches formed, the picture of the Church on the Levantine mainland is one of an extraordinarily passive body. A result was a generally quiescent, because relatively well treated, subject population.

The contribution of the Latin Church

In the twelfth century the Latin patriarchate of Jerusalem was also one of the most unreformed in Latin Christendom. No doubt this was due to the poor quality of the first generation of churchmen and to the fact that the early secular rulers were unsympathetic to reform. The picture we have, above all from the pioneering work of Professor Mayer, is not unlike that which confronts us in the more backward parts of Europe. In Palestine there were proprietary churches in the hands of laymen as late as the middle of the twelfth century. It was not until the council of Nablus in 1120 that the king and lords could be induced to give up their control of tithes. Until the end of the twelfth century the kings kept a tight control of episcopal elections through the enjoyment, like their European counterparts, of honorary canonries which gave them a share in elections, through influence and by means of the disreputable practice of dual postulation by which an electoral body secretly submitted two names to the king, although on the surface there followed a free canonical election. Dual postulation was gradually driven out after it had drawn from the papacy a condemnatory decretal in the 1190s, while the translations of bishops from Europe to eastern sees – something only the pope could do – reduced state interference in the thirteenth century, when anyway there was an absentee and often powerless monarchy. But one is left with the paradox of an old-fashioned, unreformed Church created by one of the greatest initiatives of the reformed papacy.

It remained low in quality and provincial, in spite of occupying magnificent buildings and being so well endowed with lands thousands of miles away. It is true that by 1103 the Church of the Holy Sepulchre had established a master of schools and that there was another in Antioch by the late twelfth century. Theology was taught in Acre by 1218 and canon and probably civil law in Tripoli in the middle of the thirteenth century. By the 1120s Nazareth was a cultural centre of some importance, referred to as a 'famous religious community' in a papal document of 1145 and providing livings to two figures of minor literary significance, Rorgo Fretellus and Gerard of Nazareth; its library, the catalogue of which survives, bears comparison with those of western schools. But bright young men like William of Tyre, who spent nearly twenty years studying at the best schools and under the best masters in France and Italy, had to go to Europe for their education; and this was still the case in the thirteenth century. Although their society is now considered to have provided a better channel for the transmission of Arabic learning than used to be thought, the settlers looked to Europe for their scholarship and culture, and to judge from the literature that attracted them the interests of the lay nobility were practically indistinguishable from those of their contemporaries in the West. The *Chanson des Chetifs*, commissioned by Prince Raymond of Antioch and composed by a priest who was rewarded with a canonry there, belongs in its legendary story of crusaders captured by the Muslims to a western genre.

It would be wrong, however, to deny this small, isolated and backward institution, in the pockets of the twelfth-century kings, any contribution to the Church at large. Apart from the confraternal orders of the Holy Sepulchre and Bethlehem, the Latin kingdom also provided Christendom with the Carmelites and with two important new forms of the religious life, the hospitaller and the military, which then fused.

From the First Crusade onwards Palestine naturally attracted large numbers of fervent westerners, who wished to live out their days as hermits in caves near Jerusalem, or in Galilee, or on the Amanus mountain chain north of Antioch, where some of them formed themselves into particularly strict communities, or on Mount Carmel, a tongue of hillside extending to the sea-shore by Haifa, where they settled in imitation of the prophet Elijah. Early in the thirteenth century Patriarch Albert of Jerusalem drew up a rule for a group of Carmelite hermits, which was later confirmed by Pope Honorius III and became the primitive Rule of the Carmelite Order. This was soon to transform itself into a brotherhood of mendicants and in future centuries was to produce some of the greatest saints in Christian history.

The hospitaller way of life is particularly associated with the Order of the Hospital of St John of Jerusalem. This body came into existence soon after the First Crusade, when the administrators of a pilgrim-hospice in Jerusalem, run by the abbey of St Mary of the Latins, broke away from their parent and, benefiting from the general enthusiasm for pilgrimages to the Holy Land, were endowed with property in the East and in western Europe and in 1113 were recognized by the papacy as belonging to an independent institute. The ethos of the early Hospitallers stemmed directly from the concerns of the eleventh-century reformers, who had encouraged foundations committed to charitable and pastoral work. The Hospitallers venerated the 'holy poor', whom they regarded as their 'lords'. They thought of themselves as the 'serfs of the poor of Christ'. Their Rule laid down that their clothing had to be humble 'because our lords the poor, whose serfs we acknowledge ourselves to be, go about naked and meanly dressed. And it would be wrong and improper for the serf to be proud and his lord humble'. Their master was, and still is, known as 'the guardian of the poor'. In their abject humility and loving respect for the poor they foreshadowed the Franciscans. They made their ideal a reality by ministering to the poor when they were sick and by burying them when they died. The uninterrupted history of hospitals as we know them in western Europe only began in the eleventh century and the greatest of the early ones was that managed in Jerusalem, together with a large orphanage, by the brothers (and sisters) of St John. It was run on a staggering scale, with almost unimaginable luxury for the time. We know a lot about it, partly because it is referred to in the order's statutes, but also because of a treatise on Christian love composed in the 1180s by a man who had lived there for a while.

A feature of Hospitaller nursing was this: because every poor man and woman *was* Christ, he or she should not just have good treatment, but the best and most luxurious treatment possible. This was, of course, a religious imperative, but it was also the application of the basic nursing principle that patients get better if they are well fed, comfortable and contented. The hospital in Jerusalem took in the poor, whatever their illness (except leprosy), nationality or sex.

> This holy house [of the Hospital], knowing that the Lord, who calls all to salvation, does not want anyone to perish, mercifully admits men of the Pagan faith [that is Muslims] and Jews ... because the Lord prayed for those afflicting him, saying: 'Father, forgive them for they know not what they do'. In this blessed house is powerfully fulfilled the heavenly doctrine: 'Love your enemies and do good to those who hate you'; and elsewhere: 'Friends should be loved in God and enemies on account of God'.

The admission of Muslim and Jewish pilgrims may help to explain why the sick were to be given chicken if they could not stomach pork and why there are references to a second kitchen, a *coquina privata*, in which the chicken was cooked. It may be that the Hospitallers were respecting the dietary laws of their non-Christian patients.

If the poor fell ill in the streets of the city and had not the strength to admit themselves the Hospital's servants would search them out and bring them in. On reception each patient made confession and received communion; thereafter he or she seems to have been encouraged to receive the Sacrament every Sunday. Every day the wards were inspected and blessed with holy water, brought to them in procession. There were eleven of them, but the hospital could be enlarged to take 2,000 patients, twice the number normally allowed for. The treatise-writer reported that it had happened many times that, when the hospital was overflowing, the brothers' dormitory was occupied by the sick and the brethren had to sleep on the floor. Sick women had their own wards, where they were looked after by female servants. One was devoted to obstetrics. Newly born babies were bathed as soon as they were born and wet nurses were provided for those whose mothers could not feed them through poverty or illness. There were separate beds for the sick at a time when only the grandest lords had their own and in the obstetrical ward there were little cots so that the babies should not be disturbed by their mothers. The beds had feather mattresses and coverlets, which were changed every fortnight, and the patients were provided with cloaks and sandals, so as to protect them when they went to the latrines.

Each ward was overseen by a brother, assisted by twelve servants, whose duties included making the beds, looking after the patients, giving them wine, hot and cold water, towels, and feeding them. Their diet was lavish. At a time when very few people ever had white bread or a meat diet, white loaves were issued to them and meat was served on three days a week. The range of food available is astonishing. Besides pork, mutton and chicken, the brothers served doves, partridges, lambs, eggs, fish, pomegranates, corn cakes, chick-peas, pears, plums, chestnuts, almonds, grapes, dried figs, dried lettuce, chickory, radishes, purslain, rock-parsley, parsley, cucumbers, lemons, gourds and melons. Following medical doctrine, however, certain foods were never on the menu, such as beans, lentils, shrimps, moray eels and the meat of breeding sows.

Four physicians and four surgeons were employed, together with a number of bloodletters. The wards were distributed among the physicians so that each had sole charge of the patients in his care. He was obliged to visit them each morning and evening to inspect their urine and take their pulses. The surgeons had responsibilities not only in Jerusalem, but also when a Christian army campaigned against the Muslims. They staffed a mobile tented hospital. If the wounded could not be treated properly there, they would be sent on beasts of burden to the hospital in Jerusalem or to the hospital nearest to the battlefield. If there were not enough animals available to move them, 'the wounded mount the horses of the brothers [-at-arms] themselves, and the brothers, even the noble ones, return on foot', thus openly demonstrating that all they had belonged to the sick.

One has only to imagine the logistics involved in an institution where the standards of nursing care must have been highly labour intensive and which catered for far more patients than any modern hospital would consider admitting. These patients would probably have been sleeping in separate beds for the first time in their lives and would certainly never have eaten such good food so regularly or have had such close spiritual supervision. It has often been suggested that the influences on the hospital were eclectic; that its organization into wards reflected Byzantine traditions and that the medicine practised in it was Arabic. But its physicians seem to have been Latin Christians and there is no evidence that its standards and practices were anything but western. The nursing regime seems to have been based on the doctrines taught at Salerno, the greatest of the western medical schools.

The expenses must have been enormous and it is all the more remarkable that within decades of their foundation the Hospitallers had taken on another function as well and were on the way to transforming their institute into a military order. In this they were following a path already taken by the Knights Templar. These had their origins in 1119–20, when a knight from Champagne called Hugh of Payns formed eight companions into a regular community of lay brothers, committed to defend the pilgrim roads through Palestine to Jerusalem, which were still very insecure. The Templars gained the support of the king, Baldwin II, who gave them part of the royal palace in the Temple enclosure, and of St Bernard, the influential Cistercian abbot of Clairvaux, who persuaded a papal legate, two archbishops and ten bishops attending the council of Troyes in 1129 to recognize them and draw up a rule for them.

With the Templars warfare as a temporary act of devotion became warfare as a devotional way of life. Whereas crusaders were laymen directing their everyday skills for a time into a holy cause, Templars were religious as permanently at war as those in other religious institutes were at prayer. They were members, they and their apologists admitted, of a new kind of Order of the Church, although they insisted that its foundation was foreshadowed, and therefore justified, in scripture. Wearing the cross, they appropriated for themselves the monastic, and then crusading, title of 'knights of Christ'. St Bernard took up the theme already present in the First Crusade of the comparison of the new knight, saving his soul in a worthy cause, with the old violent reprobate.

> Oh, this is a truly holy and secure knighthood and it is certainly free from that double peril which often and habitually endangers one sort of man, in so far as he fights for some other cause than Christ. For how often do you who fight the knighthood of the world come to grips with a most dread situation, in which either you may kill the enemy in body while in fact killing your own soul, or by chance you may be killed by him and die in body and soul simultaneously.

Motivated by love, the Templars died, he believed, as martyrs.

> How glorious are the victors who return from battle! How blessed are the martyrs who die in battle! Rejoice, courageous athlete, if you live and conquer in the Lord, but exult and glory the more if you die and are joined to the Lord. Life indeed is fruitful and victory glorious, but according to holy law death is better than either of these things. For if those are *blessed who die in the Lord*, how much more blessed are those who die for the Lord?

Nevertheless, the early apologies and *Omne datum optimum*, Pope Innocent II's charter for them (now redated to 1138), cannot hide the fact that what the Templars were doing was considered abhorrent in some circles. The founding of a religious order, the professed members of which took familiar vows, said the office and then rode out to kill their enemies was just as unprecedented as penitential war had been forty years before. The proposition that fighting was a charitable activity for religious on an equivalent level to the care of the sick was revolutionary. It is astonishing that the section of clerical opinion which disapproved was not larger, particularly as the foundation of the Templars could be said to have undermined the argument that crusading was something particularly suitable for laymen to undertake, to which the conservatives must have been coming to terms. In fact, so small, or so discreet, was the opposition to the Templars that we do not even have the names of any critics; we know only of their existence from the apologists' reactions to their views.

A reason for this may be that the Templars quickly gained powerful supporters, not only in the eastern settlements but also in the West. It was this popularity and the endowments it generated that enabled them to take on major responsibilities in the East from very early on. They were granted their first important frontier march, in the Amanus mountains north of Antioch, as early as the 1130s. The scale of the benefactions to them throughout Christendom probably exceeded those to the Hospitallers in the twelfth century. It is, therefore, not surprising that the Hospitallers themselves began to adopt the features of a military order from the 1120s onwards. In 1136 King Fulk of Jerusalem, who was trying to confine Ascalon, the last Muslim stronghold on the Palestinian coast, with a ring of fortresses, gave them one of these castles at Bet Guvrin (Beit Jibrin; Bethgibelin). Recent archaeology has revealed how large this castle was. I used to believe that the order garrisoned it with mercenaries, but I am now convinced that it was far too important a commitment to have been left unsupervised. It was followed by others, especially Crac des Chevaliers (1144), Belvoir (1168) and Marqab (1186). Between 1163 and 1170 there was a rapid expansion of military activities, an expansion which was temporarily halted with the order in debt and its master suffering from a nervous breakdown. But the military wing then resumed its growth, in spite of worries expressed by Pope Alexander III, and the statutes issued by a chapter-general which probably met in 1206 show that by that time the Hospital of St John was a fully-fledged military order. The association by these brothers of hospitaller and military functions was imitated by the Teutonic Knights, who came into existence in 1198 and will be described in a later chapter, and by the 1230s by another hospitaller body, the Order of St Lazarus, which had originated in a leper hospital outside the St Lazarus postern gate in the walls of Jerusalem. The house seems to have been a large one – it will be remembered that the only sick the hospital of St John did not admit were lepers – and became a normal house of refuge for leprous knights. This may be the reason why in the thirteenth century, now based like the other orders in Acre, it assumed a military role, with both healthy and leprous knights serving in its force, which must have been quite small. By then the brothers followed the Augustinian Rule and had been endowed with lands and leper hospitals in the West. They were privileged by the papacy, although an attempt in the 1260s to put all the leper houses in the West under their protection was never implemented and with the collapse of the Latin settlement in Palestine they ceased to have much to do with crusading. Other military orders came to be founded, especially in Spain and Germany, as we shall see. There was also an English order: that of St Thomas of Acre.

The Hospitallers and Templars were members of great international institutions, the first truly centralized Orders of the Church. They were freed from the authority of diocesan bishops by papal privilege, becoming answerable only to Rome. In the East they increasingly took on their shoulders an important share of the burden of defence. They have been described as over-powerful 'states within a state', contributing to that fragmentation of authority which in the end so weakened the kingdom of Jerusalem; but this picture of them is a caricature. Constitutionally their position was no different from that of other great ecclesiastical institutions in Latin Christendom, most of which held property under terms that exempted them from feudal services and the jurisdiction of secular courts. The difference, of course, was that they were relatively stronger. They were competitive, sometimes selfish, occasionally quarrelsome. Their leaders, while often good administrators, were not usually subtle or reflective men. They appreciated, however, that the survival of the Christian settlement was the reason for their existence. Even at the height of their power in the thirteenth century there were in the Levant never more than c. 300 brothers of the Hospital and rather more brothers of the Temple, but their commitment involved them in great expenses. They operated as the commanders of mercenary troops who made up the bulk of their garrisons and field regiments and had to be paid for, while the maintenance of their fortifications was very costly. Safad, one of the largest Templar castles in Palestine, was rebuilt in the 1240s. An estimate made within the order put the bill, over and above the income from the villages nearby, at 1,100,000 Saracen besants. Thereafter the annual cost of maintaining the castle ran to 40,000 Saracen besants. Since mercenary knights were serving in Acre a few years later for 120 besants a year, the expenses of raising this large and quite complicated structure was the equivalent of paying a year's wages to over 9,000 knights and thereafter bearing a permanent establishment of 333 knights. At the time the Templars had another six castles of roughly the same size; the Hospitallers had three. The costs these generated were crippling. In spite of their great estates in the West and the elaborate machinery evolved for exploiting them, the military orders were often over-burdened by their commitments and in financial difficulties.

CHAPTER 4

Settlement, Government and Defence of the Latin East, 1097–1187

Countryside and town

The region settled by the crusaders, nearly 600 miles from north to south, has a geographical unity. Mountains, in some places two parallel mountain ranges, bounded or broken by a depression carrying the watercourses of the Orontes, Litani and Jordan, run parallel to and at some distance from the coast, towards which, every now and then, rocky fingers of hillside extend. Since the wind is a prevailing westerly, winter rainwater is deposited on the high ground which retains it (better then than now because there were greater numbers of trees) and gradually releases it back to the coast throughout the dry season. The plains between the mountains and the coast are, therefore, relatively fertile and were well populated. Some areas beyond the mountains, the land east of the Sea of Galilee for instance, are quite fertile too, before they merge into the desert which borders the region to the east and south.

The native villagers were technically serfs, being tied to the land, unable in ordinary circumstances to leave or alienate their shares in the arable fields. Each village seems to have been run by a council of elders presided over by a headman whom the Europeans called a *ra'is*, a common Arabic title for one who had authority over a community and acted as intermediary between government and governed. His office carried with it more land and a larger house than the other villagers had and he presided over the agricultural decisions made by the community as a whole, levied the returns owed to the lord and was almost certainly the community judge.

A village of this type consisted generally of an inhabited nucleus, a knot of houses huddled together, with a cistern, perhaps a mill, an oven and threshing-floors, around which were vineyards, gardens and olive-groves held in personal possession by the villagers. Beyond were arable lands, which were communally farmed and often stretched so far that abandoned settlements some distance away were occupied for a few weeks each year to work the fields around them. In certain districts, at least, a two-year crop rotation was practised, the fields being divided into those sown in mid-November with wheat or barley and those which were partly left fallow, until sown in the following spring with a summer crop like sesame, and partly given over to vegetable cultivation. The harvest was threshed on the village threshing-floors before it was divided into piles of grain, of which each family had a share, expressed in terms of a fraction of the village lands. Before the division took place the lord's share was subtracted, to be subdivided if the village had several lords. This was the ancient tax of *kharaj*, which usually amounted to one-third or one-quarter of the arable crop and one-half or one-quarter of the produce of vineyards, olive-groves and orchards. To it was added a poll-tax on Muslims and Jews, a 'personal gift', again very ancient, called *mu'na*, a charge on those who owned goats, sheep and bees, and various minor impositions. It was quite common for these dues to be combined and commuted for a cash payment, but it was also usual for them to be paid in kind, which is why one can still occasionally see in the countryside the ruins of great barns in which the returns from several villages could be stored.

There were also settlements of European peasants, which were strikingly different in appearance and were very similar to western 'newtowns (*villeneuves*)'. Instead of a formless huddle of houses one would come across a planned development along a street, with a tower, courthouse and Latin church. At Qubeiba there are still the foundations of very superior stone houses of two storeys, each with an elaborate cistern. Our understanding of the scale of this European colonization has recently been transformed. Whereas we used to think of about twenty examples of colonial settlements, Dr Ellenblum has identified 200, ranging from villages to independent farmsteads, surrounded by extensive irrigation systems and other signs of advanced landscape management. Most of these were to be found in districts where there was an indigenous Christian majority, suggesting that the settlers felt safer living where their co-religionists were predominant.

They came from all over Europe. At Bet Guvrin in the mid-twelfth century, for instance, one can identify among them men from France, the western empire, Italy and Catalonia, attracted by generous terms. Each colonist received a reasonably large parcel of land to cultivate, which he was free to alienate if he wished. The returns he paid were not burdensome – 10 per cent together with certain other dues at one settlement – and were treated as rent. His community had its own system of justice. As in the West, it was presided over by an official called a *dispensator* or *locator*, who combined the responsibilities of president of the court and agent of the lord in the advertising and disposal of shares in the settlement. All the newtowns which have been identified were established in the twelfth century and the movement must have run out of steam in the thirteenth, as the territories under Christian control diminished. But a *dispensator* was still active around 1200 and some of the old communities survived for much of the thirteenth century.

Whether indigenous or immigrant, one feature of the village economy was significantly different from that in western Europe. There was very little demesne land, the home farm which in the West involved a lord in the agriculture of his village and on which the peasants performed labour services for him. In the East demesne land was generally only to be found in the gardens and sugar-cane plantations that lined the coast; and very few villages were coastal. The villagers owed little in the way of labour services – usually not more than one day a week – and in many districts these seem to have consisted of transporting the lord's share of the harvest to collection centres, together with some work on roads and aqueducts. A consequence was that there was very little reason for a lord to involve himself directly in the agriculture of his villages since his chief concern would be to get his due share of the crop. Although a few buildings have been identified as 'manor houses', landlords did not generally live in the countryside, but tended to congregate in the towns, where so many of them anyway had money fiefs.

The region, in fact, was one in which there was still a flourishing urban life. Its hinterland contained great cities, Damascus and Aleppo, for which the coastal ports in Christian hands were necessary outlets. Its own products, especially sugar, were in demand throughout the Mediterranean region and beyond. It straddled a major trade route to the Far East. Spectacular excavations have revealed how sophisticated was the town-planning in Acre, the greatest of the city-ports, where fine buildings and elaborate sewage and water systems have been uncovered. It was to towns like this that most of the Europeans came: of c. 150,000 Latins resident in Palestine, c. 120,000 lived in the towns, the majority being burgess freemen. These burgesses, members of a class which included the Europeans in the colonial villages as well as those in the towns, paid rent rather than servile dues for their properties, called *borgesies*, which they had the right to buy and sell, and cases concerning them were subject to their own courts, the *Cours des Bourgeois*. They were not vassals and were therefore not tied by feudal obligations. They were subject to public law, the *Assises des Bourgeois*, which varied a good deal from place to place, because each settlement had its own. Only two collections of these laws have survived, one from Antioch, which is incomplete, and one from Acre, where there was the largest burgess community. The latter, strongly influenced by a Provençal treatise on Roman law which had a wide diffusion in Europe, has been dated to the early 1240s.

In spite of the early attempts to drive Muslims and Jews away there were also substantial indigenous communities in many towns, not only of proletariat but also of shopkeepers, merchants and artisans. In the twelfth century, the dyeworks at six towns were in Jewish hands, although the most famous, those at Tyre, were owned by Syrians, the *Suriani* referred to in the previous chapter. Jews played a part in the great glass industry at Tyre and engaged in trade as money-lenders and ship-masters. There were also Muslim sea-captains and a safe-conduct from a king of Jerusalem for one trading between Egypt and Tyre has survived. In the thirteenth century there was an important Syrian trading community in Tyre. The most impressive evidence for indigenous participation in trade concerns a company which successfully appealed to Genoa in 1268 for compensation for a ship taken by the commune's fleet off the Cilician coast five years earlier. The city government of Genoa agreed to pay damages of 14,900 Genoese pounds. Partners in the enterprise, which seems to have been organized from Mosul, deep in Islamic territory, were twenty-three men, all indigenous, of which six resided in Ayas (Yumurtalik) in Cilician Armenia, five in Antioch, two in Tyre and six in Acre. One of them was the burgess convert or Maronite Saliba referred to in the last chapter. He was obviously prosperous: his will revealed that he had 1,275 Saracen besants invested in property and 1,156 Saracen besants and 10 royal pounds of Acre in cash; but he must have had more since he left the residue of his estate, for obvious reasons not itemized, to the Hospitallers, and one of his daughters, to whom he had left nothing, sued them for it.

Administration

Throughout history conquerors have adapted rather than destroyed the institutions in the territories they have conquered. The crusaders took over a region accustomed to fairly advanced government. Since most of the native population stayed on to live under their rule it is not surprising that some of the outlines of the previous administration remained in place, if occasionally altered to suit the westerners' preconceptions and requirements. Syria and Palestine had been Roman and Byzantine before falling to the Muslims. Much of northern Syria had, in fact, been Byzantine until recently and the survival of the imperial system there is evidenced by the appearance under the Latins of dukes, praetors and judges, the administrators of the late eleventh-century themes or provinces, although the role of the dukes in Antioch was very similar to that of the viscounts in Jerusalem, who presided over burgess justice. Elsewhere, the changes over the centuries had been less drastic than one might suppose. The basic Roman unit of administration had been the *civitas* – a city with the territory run from it – and several *civitates* combined to form the Roman province, of which there had been seven in the region. Roman provinces had become, with some changes, Muslim *junds* and as late as 985 some of the outlines of the old Roman provincial system could still be discerned. The stability of administrative boundaries can be illustrated with examples from Latin Palestine. The lordship of Caesarea exactly corresponded to the *civitas* of Caesarea on the eve of the Muslim invasions and must have survived as an entity. The same is probably true of the lordships of Ascalon and Arsuf, while the Palestinian boundaries of the principality of Galilee ran more or less along the line of the borders of the Roman province of Palaestina Secunda.

Mediating between the new Latin lords and the villagers were two officials whose offices, in one case certainly, in the other probably, predated the conquest and suggest that organs of Muslim local government had survived. One of these officials was called a scribe (*scriba*), an accurate translation of the Arabic *katib*, the officer in Muslim treasury departments. He was responsible for the collection of revenues, which were mostly traditional ones, and the overseeing of property boundaries. A high proportion of those whose names are known to us – 14, perhaps 16, out of 25 – were indigenous, but among them were men called *scribani* who appear to have held their offices in fief; perhaps here too there are parallels with the Muslim *daman* or tax-farm. The second official was called a *dragoman*, or *interpres*, which confirms that his name was a corruption of the Arabic *tarjuman* (interpreter). He may have been descended from the Muslim *mutarjim*, an assistant of the judge in his dealings with the many peoples under Muslim rule, and it looks as though his responsibilities were judicial. In lay fiefs the dragomanate was usually held, like the scribanage, in fief as a sergeantry.

In the towns too the old taxes and returns continued to be levied, including a tax in Tyre paid by pork butchers, which must have been a survival of a Muslim tax on the purveyors of unclean meat. Again, it is not surprising to find scribes very much in evidence, operating particularly at the points of entry or departure – the gates, and the harbour in the case of a port – and the markets, where goods were registered for taxation or taxation was levied. Goods being exported were charged an exit tax. Imported goods seem to have been initially registered for taxation, since the entry tax was combined with the sales tax and levied later in the markets. The harbour office, known in Acre as the *Chaine*, from the chain that could be raised to close the harbour entrance, also ran the port and imposed an anchorage tax and a capitation levy on the crew and passengers in a ship, which in a pilgrim port must have been profitable. Some markets, such as those in which products like meat, fish and leather were sold for domestic use, were independently run, but in large towns the chief markets involved in international trade were administered collectively by an office called the *Fonde*. In them the goods were weighed by official measurers and the duties were taken after sale in one of two ways: either, when man-to-man bargains were being struck by the merchants, charges were levied on the goods' official value after consulting price lists which were regularly brought up to date; or there were public auctions conducted by official auctioneers, after which the duty was taken before the proceeds were divided among the vendors. Most of these taxes were *ad valorem* – only wine, oil and grain seem to have been taxed according to quantity – and in Acre the percentages varied from just over 4 per cent to 25 per cent.

These procedures were typical of Byzantine and Muslim practice and underline the continuity between the old and new systems. The offices responsible had sophisticated accounting methods. They not only collected the taxes but also paid out annual sums in money fiefs and rents to those individuals granted them by the king or lords. It was even possible for a man who held a money fief to create rear-fiefs or make alms grants out of his income, which were paid on his behalf by the office involved. The offices made returns to central and local treasuries, known as *Secretes*, of which the most important was the *Grant Secrete* of the kingdom, an office of record, registration and revenue supervision and collection, which was so like the Muslim central treasury, the *bait* or *diwan al-mal*, that it was given this name by Muslim contemporaries.

The old Islamic system was not left unaltered, however. The westerners found it hard to come to terms with the fact that in Byzantium and Islam justice and finance were separately administered. In the West these were usually conjoined and it is not surprising to find the European settlers giving at least two of the revenue offices, the *Chaine* and the *Fonde*, additional judicial functions. The *Chaine* in Acre was from at least the mid-twelfth century also a maritime court, concerning itself with the law of the seas and mercantile cases, although all major matters – those involving claims of more than one silver mark – went to the *Cour des Bourgeois*. The *Fonde* also dealt with minor cases of commerce and debt, but we have already seen that in Acre the four native and two Latin jurors, under the presidency of a *bailli*, also functioned as a court for the indigenous.

Cours des Bourgeois bound the non-feudal judicial system together in the same way as the *Secretes* bound the financial. All major cases concerning men and women who were not vassals went to them, and the minor courts, the *Chaine*, the *Fonde* and the *Cour des Syriens*, may have held preliminary hearings on these before they were transferred. A *Cour des Bourgeois* was established in every place where there was a European population of a reasonable size. It was a public court with full rights of jurisdiction, including high justice, the ability to impose the death penalty, over all the non-feudal population and in all issues concerning property held by burgess tenure. It judged according to its own local law. It was presided over by an official, commonly called a viscount, appointed by the king, or a lord in his lordship, who also had police duties, and its decisions were made by burgess jurors. In Acre there were twelve of these, all men of some standing in the town.

So far we have considered the adaptation of an ancient and fairly sophisticated system to cope with an influx of free European settlers. But just as important were the effects of the superimposition of feudalism. This process began during Godfrey of Bouillon's one-year reign. It has been suggested that the conquest was a free-for-all and that the existence of allods, freehold properties, in Latin Palestine is evidence for this; but there is no evidence for allods at all and although there was certainly some uncontrolled land-grabbing as the crusaders marched on Jerusalem in June 1099 it ended once Godfrey had been elected ruler. His own resources were not large enough for him to carry alone the burden of defending what had been taken. We have already seen that Ramle, the key point on the road from the sea to Jerusalem, was held by a bishop. Godfrey granted out two districts, Hebron/Jericho and Galilee, in fief and he may have created a third fief around Nablus. He had promised to make a fourth at Haifa before he died. He also began the practice of granting money fiefs.

Although the existence of feudal institutions as early as 1100 has recently been challenged by Professor Reynolds on the grounds that contemporary terminology was not as precise as it was later to become, her arguments have not in my opinion been convincing enough to counteract the evidence for something similar to a feudal system being imposed on Palestine at least embryonically from the start. The reasons for it are obvious. Few crusaders had stayed on in the East: by the summer of 1100 it was reported that in the area under Godfrey's immediate control there were no more than 300 knights and the same number of foot. Godfrey's household was fully stretched administering Jerusalem and the tongue of land extending from it to the coast. He needed the support of individuals who had men at their disposal or were rich enough to recruit them. Tancred, who was put in charge of Galilee, and Galdemar Carpenel, who was given the stretch of south-eastern frontier from Hebron to Jericho, were collaborators with Godfrey in the defence of the settlement, but they naturally needed freedom to reward their own men and provide themselves with secure bases. Only the granting of the territories to them in fief would give them this freedom. The sequence of events is clear in the case of Galilee. Tancred seems originally to have been given the castellany – that is to say an office, not a lordship – of Tiberias, the chief town in the region, but he ran into difficulties trying to extend Christian control east of the Sea of Galilee. A few months later Tiberias (in other words Galilee) was reconstituted as a fief. It is clear that these great fief-holders were permitted considerable latitude in the decisions they made with regard to conflict with their Muslim neighbours and in the disposal of properties within their territories. This was to be expected since there were few initiatives Godfrey could have taken outside his own domain, where his hands were full. There already existed in western Europe precedents for this in the marches in Germany, Spain and Britain, the lords of which always had a more privileged position than the magnates in more peaceful regions.

A consequence of this process was that while under the settlers the instruments of government survived, the state was fragmented. This was less apparent in Antioch, where some sort of provincial system seems to have been imposed, partly because the demesne of the prince was relatively large and comprised all the greater towns. But in the kingdom of Jerusalem the great lordships became palatinates, free of royal control in day-to-day affairs, in which the lords could administer full justice in their seigneurial and public courts with hardly any reservation of cases to the crown. The kings were powerless to intervene as long as feudal services were not threatened. The lords could also conduct their own foreign policy, making peace or war with their Muslim neighbours without reference to the central government. These privileges were in evidence by the late twelfth century. It has been argued that they were gradually accumulated as the nobility stabilized and gained in power from c. 1130 onwards, but there is some slight evidence – references to the title *princeps*, the existence of *Cours des Bourgeois* in their hands, their free-ranging activities with regard to neighbouring Muslims – to suggest that they were enjoyed from the first. It has also been supposed that the settlers, coming on the whole from a decentralized region like France, simply brought with them their understanding of a natural order of things, but contemporaries clearly understood the advantages of centralized government, as the aspirations of the Normans in England and Sicily show. It is much more likely that in a frontier region the only system that was thought to be workable was that of marcher lordships and that this was established at the start, when the rulers would anyway have been hard-pressed to find any other solution to their problems.

The workings of feudal law reinforce the image of a frontier society. Among the services required from fief-holders was, of course, military service. In Europe it became common for this to be commuted for money payments, known in England as scutage. Only one example of scutage survives – it is from the county of Tripoli – and there is no evidence that the kings of Jerusalem ever allowed it, in a region, significantly, where the commutation of village-returns for money was common. It is clear that military service was a precious commodity and its performance could not be done away with. The kings also had the right to demand of female fief-holders aged between twelve and sixty the 'service' of marriage, so that suitable men could perform knight's service for their fiefs. On the other hand, feudal incidents, which assumed such importance in the West, were rarely to be found in the East. There is no evidence for payments of relief, the sums of money rendered to the lord on entry into a feudal inheritance. The lords, including the king, appear to have had no control over inheritance, although the customs concerning it were extremely complex and were treated in the finest detail in the lawbooks written in thirteenth-century Palestine. Nor did they, in the kingdom of Jerusalem, have the right to wardship of minors. Nothing was to be allowed to discourage potential fief-holders from taking over their tenancies and the obligations that went with them. When considered alongside early legislation to ensure that fiefs were occupied and not held *in absentia* by heirs living in the West, we can perceive an isolated society, worried about the numbers of well-to-do settlers and concerned to see that fiefs were occupied and military services performed in all circumstances.

The crown and the lords

The kings of Jerusalem presided over a confederation of lordships, in which the ties binding lords to them were not uniform. In the far north, Antioch was legally independent, being a vassal-state not of Jerusalem but of Constantinople. That is not to say that the kings were powerless there. Baldwin I established himself as the arbiter of the affairs of all the Latin East by his intervention in a succession dispute which followed the death of Raymond of St Gilles on 28 February 1105. Raymond's successor in the new county of Tripoli was his cousin William Jordan, count of Cerdagne, but at the beginning of March 1109 Raymond's son, Bertrand of St Gilles, arrived from France with a large army to claim his father's estate. William Jordan called for the support of Tancred, who was now prince of Antioch. In his turn Bertrand appealed to Baldwin, who summoned Tancred in the name of the church of Jerusalem to treat with him not only on the future of Tripoli, but also on complaints made by the count of Edessa, against whom Tancred had already been involved in armed conflict. Tancred agreed to recognize the integrity of the county of Edessa in return for the grant of an enormous fief in the kingdom of Jerusalem, comprising all of Galilee, which he had once held, and Haifa, together with proprietary rights over the Temple in Jerusalem. As far as Raymond of St Gilles's territories were concerned, William Jordan was to keep the northern part, consisting of 'Arqah and Tartus, and was to become Tancred's vassal, while Bertrand was to hold Tripoli itself and the region around and was to become Baldwin's vassal. William Jordan died soon afterwards and Bertrand extended his rule over the territory ceded to his cousin. This dispute and its resolution highlighted problems that were always to dog the settlements, since the needs of adequate government and defence were so acute that the claims of the 'heir apparent', an individual present in person and ready to take over at once, weighed heavily and often in derogation of the legitimate rights of a nearer heir who happened to be in Europe. But it also demonstrated the prestige of the crown of Jerusalem, which even the ruler of Antioch, who was not a vassal, could not ignore.

In fact, as long as the princes of Antioch were in conflict with their legitimate overlords, the Byzantine emperors, they would be forced to treat Jerusalem's claims to paramountcy seriously. Baldwin I was prepared to commit the military resources of the south to the defence of the north in 1110, 1111 and 1115, while the rulers of Antioch and Tripoli in their turn joined him in the defence of Palestine in 1113. No sooner had Baldwin II come to the throne than he had to hurry north to take the regency of Antioch in the name of Bohemond II, the infant son of Bohemond of Taranto, after the disaster that overtook the forces of the principality at the Battle of the Field of Blood in June 1119. Baldwin's regency lasted for seven years and every year from 1120 to 1123, when he was taken prisoner by Belek of Aleppo, and again in 1124–5 after his release from gaol, and in 1126, he had to campaign in the north, although his withdrawal of armies from Palestine was not popular with his vassals in Jerusalem. He had to intervene in Antioch again in 1130 after Bohemond II's death, and his successor Fulk did so in 1131–2 and 1133. In 1149 Baldwin III had to rush to the north to save the principality and what by then was left of the county of Edessa after another military disaster. He went again in 1150, 1152, 1157 and 1158. These visits were, of course, those of a paramount chief, the head of a confederation, not those of a suzerain.

On the other hand, Edessa and Tripoli were vassal-states, although both had been founded independently of the crown of Jerusalem. In the case of Edessa, the first two counts became kings and ensured the homage of their successors. In the case of Tripoli, homage was given in consequence of Baldwin I's arbitration in the succession dispute of 1109, although Count Pons (1112–37) made determined efforts to break free. Lordship gave the kings rights and obligations in both counties – for instance King Amalric was regent of Tripoli for ten years while the count was a prisoner of the Muslims – but the way these settlements had been established allowed them a large measure of independence. They were not generally regarded as constituent parts of the kingdom, at least in the twelfth century, and it seems that in them the king of Jerusalem was treated as the personal overlord of the counts rather than as king.

The kingdom of Jerusalem proper began at the Nahr el Mu'almetein, just north of Beirut. South of that the lordships were palatinates. If, as seems very likely, the kingdom was fragmented from the start into independent principalities, the lords of which were royal vassals but otherwise exercised full authority in their lordships as marcher barons, the notion of a pushing, constitutionally strong monarchy in the first two-thirds of the twelfth century cannot be upheld. Detailed studies of the lordships have demonstrated that that constitutional model, proposed by Professor Prawer, breaks down at grass-roots level. And a law, probably dating from the reign of Baldwin II (1118–31), which was supposed to have given the king the power to disinherit vassals without formal trial in a wide range of cases, was actually, it is now suggested, merely establishing fixed penalties for felonies which would have been subject to trial in the ordinary way. Far from freeing the king from the burdensome need to hear a case formally in his feudal court, it actually presupposed that even open treason would be subject to the ordinary processes of law, which in a case involving the king as lord and his vassal meant the decision of his other vassals advising him in his High Court.

It was also the case that the king was extraordinarily dependent on his greater vassals. Since he had no public courts and therefore no apparatus of public justice outside the royal domain, he could only reach the bulk of his subjects through their mediation. On the other hand, he had legal obligations towards them in consequence of the feudal contracts between him and them. In particular he had the duty to maintain them in their fiefs unless it could be proved in his court that they had failed in their duties to him. This court, the High Court, combined the functions of a court for the whole kingdom – although on occasions of national importance it was the nucleus of a much larger gathering, a *parlement* attended by the representatives of other interests in the kingdom – and a seigneurial court of the royal domain. The feudal obligations of the crown meant that power legitimately rested with this body and a result was that constitutional development was stifled. Although general taxes were levied by *parlements* in 1166 and 1183, there never developed, as there did in the West, a regular system of national taxation by consent and therefore no Third Estate. The king's central government, superimposed over the Arab bureaucracy, remained primitive, consisting of great officers with traditional titles – seneschal, constable, marshal, butler, chamberlain and chancellor – although in the case of the seneschal, who controlled the *Grant Secrete*, the department concerned was anything but conventional in western terms.

The power of the lords was reinforced by the nature of the feudal system and by developments in feudal society in the twelfth century. In a community in which money fiefs were prevalent, because of the availability of cash-revenues and commutations, it was common for fiefs to be composite rather than uniform in make-up. For instance, only one of the twenty-seven fiefs listed in the lordship of Arsuf in 1261 was held entirely in land and only one other was a pure money fief; the rest were made up of various combinations of money, produce, rations, land and the profits of offices. Similarly, in 1243 a fief-holder near Tyre had three villages and one-third of the revenues of another, two gardens and some land near the city and in Tyre itself a house, an oven and a rent of 60 besants a year. The great fiefs were also composite. Arsuf, which was one of the smaller of them, extended over the coastal plain of southern Palestine from the el 'Auja' river in the south to the Wadi Faliq in the north and reached inland to the foothills of Samaria, but outside it the lord also had lands in the royal domain near Nablus and a house and probably money fiefs in Acre. A large fief built up for the king's uncle in the early 1180s – the only lordship for which we have many of the foundation charters – was a collection of lands and castles in northern

Galilee and rents in Acre and Tyre. This diversification of assets gave the magnates some financial stability and helped them to survive the territorial losses of the late 1180s.

Some of the laws should have worked very much in their favour. One forbade the tenant of a fief owing the service of several knights to subinfeudate a larger proportion of it than he retained himself. The thirteenth-century jurists could not agree whether the value of all rear-fiefs combined should amount to less than half the total value of the fief or whether a lord had simply to hold in his own hands more than the greatest of his vassals. This law, which was supplemented by the custom of allowing what was called *service de compaignons*, according to which a fief-holder raised a troop of mercenaries in place of rear-vassals, ought to have meant that seigneurial domains could not be dissipated by alienation. For much of the history of the kingdom it did so, but by the thirteenth century the lords' territorial holdings were gravely reduced as they granted lands to the military orders and religious communities in exchange for badly needed cash. Their expenses must have become back-breaking, since most of the castles with their attendant expenses were in their hands.

After an early period marked by instability and waves of immigrants, in which fiefs rapidly changed hands, the greater lordships settled into the possession of families which held them for several generations. After c. 1130 succession became regular, genealogies became continuous and clear and there began a process of consolidation through marriage and inheritance into the hands of a few families. By the third quarter of the twelfth century no more than ten families held the twenty-four most important lordships. Stability manifested itself in a consciousness of class and in the gradual whittling away of the prerogatives the kings had enjoyed in the early decades. They alone could mint coins, levy shipwreck and exploit international trading ports and the roads from them into the interior. They perhaps had control of the highways. Already by the time of Baldwin II, however, only the rights of minting and the control of ports and their communications were mentioned as royal prerogatives and within a few decades even these were challenged. The lords of Haifa and Caesarea were developing their ports and it is possible that before 1187 the lords of Transjordan and Sidon had begun to mint their own coins. Shipwreck was formally surrendered by King Amalric in the 1160s and by the thirteenth century the magnates seem to have usurped whatever rights the kings had had over their highways.

It would be wrong to think of the twelfth-century kings as powerless. They *were* kings, first of all, and kingship implied more than feudal overlordship. Whatever the realities it suggested a ministry for God, symbolically conveyed through the use of vestments and regalia, a public authority relating to all subjects, whether vassals or not. Kings could legislate. Their court had reserved for itself the right to judge minors who were accused of theft and rear-vassals who were accused of stealing from another lord. They could summon a *levée en masse* of all subjects in a moment of crisis. They had a large say in the appointment of bishops. They were, moreover, the possessors of the holiest city in Christendom, even if it had nothing in economic and little in strategic terms to commend it, and they sat on the throne of David. This gave them immense prestige. And they were autonomous. Papal approval was sought and given for Baldwin I's assumption of the crown in 1100, but in no sense was Jerusalem a vassal-state of the papacy; and although it is almost certain that in 1171, during a crisis that followed the collapse of his ambitious plans to conquer Egypt, Amalric acknowledged the overlordship of the Byzantine emperor, this meant nothing in practice. The kings were also richer than their vassals. The royal domain was vast in comparison to the fiefs. It consisted of Jerusalem, Acre and Tyre, with the lands around them, and at times it also encompassed Ascalon and Jaffa, Samaria, Beirut, Hebron and Blanchegarde (Tel es Safi), although these were sometimes apanages, sometimes independent fiefs, and Deir el Balah (Darum). The cities of Acre and Tyre gave them wealth through the taxes that could be levied on trade. Being richer than their vassals, the kings could always buy mercenaries to supplement their armies and this gave them a certain independence of their subjects, since they were not completely reliant on their services, however important these might be. They could also make great use of money fiefs and could therefore have a large number of direct vassals. This gave them patronage and political power. During the succession crisis of 1186, one claimant, who had possession of most of the royal domain and the support of some important magnates, had at her disposal nearly half the feudal knights in the kingdom. And, as we shall see, the kings were less affected by the disasters of the late 1180s than their vassals, because the rising prosperity of the ports of Acre and Tyre led to growing profits that could offset the territorial losses.

Baldwin I to Baldwin V

Looking at the Latin East at this time one clearly discerns a type of society, rapidly disappearing in the West, which depended crucially on a king's personal vigour and military skill. In this exposed frontier region his power as an individual to change events was great and his political position still rested on old-fashioned virtues like military leadership. Baldwin I was a tough personality, a conqueror whose attitude to the granting of fiefs and to the Church was dominated by self-interest. He had ruthlessly exploited the county of Edessa for his own ends and for those of the First Crusade. He greatly extended the area left him by Godfrey of Bouillon and his prestige was such that he was recognized throughout the

Latin East as paramount ruler. But he was probably homosexual and in spite of three marriages, one bigamous and all apparently entered into for material gain, he had no children. His death on 2 April 1118 threw the kingdom into a second succession crisis, which provided the Montlhéry family – that kindred which had produced so many of the early crusaders and settlers – with the opportunity to stage a *coup d'état*. On Palm Sunday (7 April), the day the king's body was brought into Jerusalem to be buried, Baldwin of Bourcq, a member of the Montlhéry clan but also a relative of the king, who had given him the county of Edessa, arrived suddenly and unannounced. He had come down on pilgrimage to celebrate Easter and had heard of the king's death on the way. The vassals and leading churchmen of the kingdom met at once, presumably in what was later to be called a *parlement*, to discuss to whom the succession should be offered. A party headed by Joscelin of Courtenay, Baldwin of Bourcq's first cousin, and the patriarch, Arnulf of Chocques, proposed that the throne should be offered to Baldwin who, Joscelin argued, was present in the East, was related to the previous king and had shown himself to be the kind of person who would make a good ruler. Most of those taking part in the assembly, however, were in favour of the late king's eldest brother, Count Eustace of Boulogne, who had returned home after the First Crusade, and an embassy was immediately despatched to western Europe. After it had left, a second meeting of the *parlement* was demanded by Joscelin. In the absence of at least some of Eustace's partisans this reversed its earlier decision and Baldwin was anointed king on Easter Day, although he was not crowned for another twenty-one months. Eustace and the mission from Jerusalem had reached Apulia when they heard the news. The envoys were indignant, but Eustace, who had not been enthusiastic, turned back to avoid scandal.

There can be no doubt that Joscelin of Courtenay, who as lord of Galilee was the greatest magnate in the kingdom, had manipulated a *parlement* to get his first cousin the throne. He and the rest of the kin were rewarded, as they had to be, given the importance to a new king whose legitimacy was questionable of having his 'natural friends' in positions of trust. Joscelin was granted the county of Edessa in the late summer of 1119 and another cousin, William of Bures-sur-Yvette, was made lord of Galilee in his place. Two other members of the family soon arrived in the East, no doubt hurriedly sent to bolster the king's position. The Cluniac prior Gilduin of Le Puiset was at once made abbot of St Mary of the Valley of Jehoshaphat and Hugh of Le Puiset, who had spent his childhood in Apulia, had taken possession of Jaffa by January 1120, when he witnessed the king's grant to his uncle Abbot Gilduin, although he was 'not yet a knight'. The recognition of the lordship of a boy, who cannot have been more than thirteen years old, over one of the most strategically important frontiers of the kingdom is an indication of Baldwin's reliance on his relatives. Later in his reign he strengthened his position further by marrying one daughter to the new prince of Antioch and probably betrothing another to the son of the count of Tripoli.

The way a *coup d'état* in Palestine had evoked an immediate response in support from the kindred in Europe demonstrates the strength of the ties which bound the settlers to their families 2,000 miles away, although the western kinsmen must also have been expecting patronage. The new king was a nicer man than his predecessor. He was genuinely pious and he was happily married. He was an active and responsible leader of men. But he was exceptionally miserly and he does not seem to have been very popular. His reign was never a secure one and it was haunted by the problem of succession because he sired only daughters. The nobles of Jerusalem showed discontent at his intervention in Antioch after the catastrophe of the Field of Blood. The council of Nablus marked a surrender by him to the Church. In 1122 he had to use force to make Count Pons of Tripoli recognize his overlordship. While he was held prisoner by the Muslims a party in the kingdom may even have offered the crown to Count Charles of Flanders. He probably had to face a revolt from the lord of Transjordan and towards the end of his reign he was in conflict with the patriarch of Jerusalem, who made vast claims on the basis of the promises to Daimbert supposedly made by Godfrey of Bouillon, demanding the town of Jaffa for the patriarchate immediately and the city of Jerusalem itself once Ascalon was conquered.

It was perhaps to deflect criticism that Baldwin adopted a highly aggressive policy towards his Muslim neighbours. In the seven years from 1124 the great port of Tyre was occupied; the two chief enemies, Cairo and Damascus, were taken on at the same time, with major attacks on Damascus or its territory being launched in 1126 and 1129; and two raids into the countryside around Egyptian Ascalon were accompanied by the granting of Ascalon itself to Hugh of Jaffa, the closest Christian marcher lord. It must be indicative that no record has survived of any action, or threat of action, by the usually aggressive Muslim raiders from Ascalon between 1126 and 1132. It may also be that now an Egyptian government sued for peace. The Fatimid caliph al-Amir was assassinated in 1130. His son, only a few months old, was proclaimed his heir, but was soon murdered and his cousin and future successor, the regent al-Hafiz, was imprisoned by the new vizir, Abu Ali Ahmad ibn al-Afdal, known as Kutaifat. Since the direct line of the Fatimid dynasty had been extinguished and there was no caliph, the Egyptian empire was placed under the sovereignty of the Hidden Imam, but the Imam regarded by Kutaifat as being in hiding until he would reappear on the Last Days was the Twelfth, the mahdi of the Imamis, and it has been pointed out that this effectively abolished Egypt's state religion, since the Fatimids claimed descent from Isma'il, the seventh Imam. Kutaifat was murdered by guards loyal to the Fatimids in December 1131, but three months before his death he sent an embassy to Jerusalem, although any offers it made were refused by Fulk of Anjou, who by this time had succeeded to the throne.

Baldwin had done what he could to assure a peaceful succession. Count Fulk V of Anjou's acceptance of the hand of his eldest daughter Melisende had followed long negotiations, the matters at issue being the legitimacy of Baldwin's position and Melisende's status as an heiress to the throne. This would have been on everyone's mind because of the parallel case of Mathilda of England, another woman whose succession was raising doubts. Mathilda had been betrothed to Fulk's son Geoffrey in the summer of 1127 and she had married him in June 1128, shortly after Fulk had taken the cross for a new crusade. It has been suggested that an English precedent, in which King Henry I declared Mathilda to be his heir on 1 January 1127, was echoed in Palestine in the recognition of Melisende as *heres regni*, an act which overcame any doubts that Fulk might have had about his future.

Fulk was a relatively powerful nobleman, who was free to marry since his first wife had died. He had already shown himself to be an enthusiastic supporter of the Latin settlements during and after his first crusade in 1120. But there was probably more in his favour than that. Eustace of Boulogne, the 'rightful heir' displaced by Baldwin in 1118, had died in 1125, but in that year his daughter and heiress, another Mathilda, had married Stephen of Blois, who took the title of count of Boulogne and was to underline the Boulogne inheritance by naming his first son Eustace. Stephen, who was a younger son of the first crusader Stephen of Blois and had been brought up and favoured by his uncle Henry of England, was also a claimant for the English throne and in the end resolved to compete for that, but the mere fact of Mathilda of Boulogne's marriage must have caused anxiety in Palestine and Stephen would inevitably have been seen as a threat to Melisende's future succession. This may have persuaded Baldwin and his advisers to make their proposal to Fulk, a man who, they must have known, had already taken on and defeated Stephen on the borders of Normandy in one of the petty wars which plagued French political life.

Here again the Montlhérys were deeply involved. The offer of Melisende's hand was carried to France by the Montlhéry William of Bures-sur-Yvette and the crusade of 1129 which followed was encompassed, like the *coup d'état* in 1118, by Montlhéry activity. In 1127 Guy I of Dampierre-sur-l'Aube, whose mother was a Montlhéry, appeared in the East, together with another cousin, Guy of Le Puiset. In 1128 Stephen of Chartres, the abbot of St Jean-en-Vallée of Chartres who was Baldwin's blood relative, came to Palestine on pilgrimage. He was waiting for a ship home when the patriarch of Jerusalem died. He was promptly elevated to the patriarchate, although this move was not a success, because his desire to reclaim what he believed to have been the rights of his church led to a bitter quarrel with the king. By March 1129 Guitier of Rethel, the son of Baldwin's sister Mathilda, had arrived; he witnessed a charter of his uncle's, together with his cousins Melisende of Jerusalem, Gilduin of Le Puiset and Hugh of Jaffa, in the presence of his cousin the patriarch. Then Viscount Hugh III of Chartres crusaded. If he travelled with Count Fulk and the Angevins, which is likely, Fulk arrived in Palestine flanked by two Montlhérys, because William of Bures-sur-Yvette also returned with him. It looks as though the choice of Fulk was a Montlhéry device to shore up the government established in 1118.

The crusade of 1129, which accompanied Fulk to Palestine, was, moreover, a Montlhéry creation. William of Tyre, who wrote several decades later but was chancellor of the kingdom of Jerusalem and had access to governmental records, looked on the departure on a preaching tour of the West by the master of the Templars, Hugh of Payns (who owed so much to Baldwin's favour that he could be regarded as the king's creature), as a consequence solely of a decision made by Baldwin and his advisers. The role of Pope Honorius II, who certainly knew of the crusade since in one of his letters he referred to recruitment in Anjou, seems to have been passive and there is no evidence of papal initiative or of papal legates at work.

Fulk faithfully served Baldwin until the latter's death on 21 April 1131. By that time a son had been born of the marriage and Professor Mayer has suggested that, no doubt to ensure his inheritance, almost the king's last act was to alter the conditions of future government slightly by conferring royal power jointly on the three persons involved, Fulk, Melisende and her baby son, another Baldwin. It is clear, however, that from the start of his reign Fulk was determined to change the direction in which the kingdom had been moving and to reverse the policies of the 1120s. He signalled this by choosing to be crowned not in Bethlehem, as his two predecessors had been, but in Jerusalem, under the Sepulchre rotunda. This may have been because the date chosen for his coronation was 14 September, the feast of the Exaltation of the Holy Cross, commemorating the discovery of the True Cross; but whatever it meant, his coronation marked a clean break with his predecessors. He brought in new men of his own and the change can be particularly clearly traced in his chancery. This upset the Montlhérys and must have contributed to a revolt early in the reign, involving Hugh of Jaffa, whom Fulk had accused of treason. William of Tyre was later to suggest that it was the rumour that Hugh was having an affair with Melisende – William knew, of course, that they were both Montlhérys – that led to bad blood between him and the king. It may be, however, that the '*familiaria colloquia*' which Hugh and Melisende were suspected of having were family discussions about how to retrieve a situation that was getting out of hand. At any rate,

Hugh rebelled with the support of a dispossessed lord of Transjordan, although the sentence he incurred of exile for three years was an extraordinarily light one. It is possible that his rebellion was caused not only by the king's determination to bring in new men of his own to replace the old household officials, but also by Fulk's refusal to consider whatever the Egyptian embassy had proposed. If Kutaifat had been feeling so isolated that he had been prepared to surrender the beachhead at Ascalon and the offer had been turned down, Hugh, who had already been granted rights over it, would have felt aggrieved.

Fulk died in 1143, but Queen Melisende remained dominant even after her son Baldwin III came of age in 1145. A great patron of the arts, as we have seen, she was also a true Montlhéry and she governed with the assistance of another cousin, Manasses of Hierges. The young king was pushed more and more to the periphery until he asserted himself in the spring of 1152. He demanded that the kingdom be formally divided with his mother, who in 1150 may even have prevented her own vassals obeying his summons to service in northern Syria, and he then questioned the way the division had been made. He moved swiftly to occupy his mother's territories and by the late spring he was in control. Melisende was confined to dower land round Nablus. The dominance of the Montlhérys, a family of middle-ranking French nobles who had taken over the Latin East and had been responsible for initiating one, and perhaps two, crusades, came to an end.

Once in charge Baldwin answered an appeal from the north, where the Muslims had taken Tartus. The town was liberated and an assembly of nobles from the kingdom, the county of Tripoli and the principality of Antioch met in Tripoli. This did not accomplish its chief purpose – to persuade Constance, the heiress of Antioch, to marry – but it attested to the young king's strength, not least because he had been able to summon his vassals to a general assembly outside the borders of the kingdom. He proved himself to be another clever and vigorous king, under whom the final coastal conquest, of Ascalon, was made, but he died young, on 10 February 1163, before he had time to complete ambitious plans which included perhaps an alliance of all the Christian powers in the eastern Mediterranean region to conquer Egypt.

He was succeeded by his brother Amalric, who was as able and certainly as energetic. The most striking feature of Amalric's reign, the attempt to take Egypt, will be considered below. But the king also tried to find a solution to the main legal impediment to royal control, the impenetrable thickets of privilege which surrounded the great fiefs and shielded them from intervention. His most important legal act, the issuing of a law entitled the *assise sur la ligece*, was a response to a crisis in his predecessor's reign. Gerard, lord of Sidon, had dispossessed one of his vassals without a judgment in his seigneurial court. King Baldwin had taken steps to redress the vassal's grievance, and Gerard had been forced to submit, return the fief and compensate his vassal for the damage done. Now, at a solemn meeting of the High Court, Amalric decreed that in future all rear-vassals were to make liege homage to the king, in addition to the simple homage they made to their own lords, and that the king had the right to demand oaths of fealty from freemen in any fief held in-chief from him. It is true that in the long run this *assise* encouraged solidarity among the feudatories, since those who had made liege homage to the king, great lords and rear-vassals alike, were peers of one another, bound to each other by the common oaths they had taken, and that this solidarity found expression in the use of the *assise* against the crown itself in ways that Amalric could never have envisaged. But when it was issued the *assise* was an expression of royal strength. In theory the king could now call on the support of rear-vassals if their lord was in conflict with him: after forty days they were bound to come over to his side if their lord was in revolt or was plotting against him or had refused to stand trial in the High Court, on condition that their fiefs be restored to them within another forty days. More important than this, a formal channel of communication to the ruler was opened, since a rear-vassal was now a member of the High Court itself and could raise an issue of injustice in a lordship directly with the king. Everywhere in Christendom royal jurisdiction tended to operate at the initiative of plaintiffs and it followed that kings could only realize their potential when they ruled a state in which ordinary men and women could easily take their cases to royal judges through an apparatus of provincial courts. In Jerusalem this was impossible, for the great fiefs were jurisdictionally autonomous and there were no royal courts outside the royal domain. So Amalric took the only action open to him: he made it possible for cases to be brought out of fiefs by plaintiffs and presented to him. Presumably through the oaths of fealty he envisaged similar channels of communication for non-feudal freemen.

Like many strong kings Amalric left his successor a bitter legacy. He had been married to Agnes of Courtenay, the daughter of the last count of Edessa, and by her he had had two children, Sibylla and Baldwin. On his accession he was persuaded to have this marriage annulled on the grounds of consanguinity and he later married Maria Comnena, the great-niece of the Byzantine emperor. By her he had another daughter, Isabella. There is some evidence that in his reign opinions among the nobility and at court began to polarize between those who sympathized with Agnes and those who supported the king or were building careers under him and his Greek wife, among whom must be included the great historian William, archbishop of Tyre. On Amalric's death on 11 July 1174 the two sides began to stake out their positions. The new king, Baldwin IV, was a minor. Of the two men entrusted by Amalric with the regency for, and custody of, his son, one was assassinated, the other put aside, and Count

Raymond III of Tripoli, Baldwin's nearest adult relative of the royal line, assumed the regency until the king came of age in 1177. Baldwin naturally favoured his mother's adherents and in fact created a great fief for his uncle, Joscelin III of Courtenay, in northern Galilee. Those close to Maria Comnena and many of those associated with the last years of Amalric's rule found themselves deprived of power and influence. But the new king himself was already known to have contracted leprosy. He was assured only of a short life, punctuated by periods of prostrating illness, during which lieutenants would have to be found to rule for him. He was certain to have no children.

In 1176 his sister Sibylla married William of Montferrat in what was the best match yet made by a member of the royal house, because William was related to the western emperors and the French kings. He died in the following year, leaving Sibylla with a son, the future Baldwin V. This child was himself sickly and the parties which had already come into existence gathered behind the two heiresses to the throne, Agnes of Courtenay's daughter Sibylla and Maria Comnena's daughter Isabella. The king tended to favour Sibylla and her second husband, Guy of Lusignan, until 1183 when, deeply hurt by Guy's grudging attitude to his desire for adequate revenues while Guy held the lieutenancy on his behalf, and encouraged by Guy's political opponents who were determined to destroy him, he removed Guy from the lieutenancy. He then crowned Baldwin V as his co-ruler, passing over Sibylla's rights, gave Raymond of Tripoli the lieutenancy with the expectation of the regency after his own death and sent an extraordinary embassy to the West under the patriarch of Jerusalem, which went so far as to offer the overlordship of the kingdom to the kings of France and England. Baldwin even agreed to a proposal that in the event of his nephew Baldwin V's early demise the pope, the western emperor and the kings of France and England should decide which of his two sisters was to have the throne; he seems to have had such a hatred of Guy of Lusignan that he allowed his sister's, and therefore his own, legitimacy to be questioned.

Baldwin IV died in March 1185 and Baldwin V in August 1186. The kingdom, which had always badly needed the rule of a strong personality, had been subjected to twelve years of ineffective government. It was now split over the claims of the two half-sisters, each with her own party of supporters, at a time when the Muslims were stronger and more united than they had ever been.

The defence of the settlements

In frontier societies of this kind life was bound to be dominated by military necessity. The Latin occupation of the region does not seem to have been governed by high strategic principles, other than the absolute need to hold the coastline. Occupation proceeded piecemeal as the opportunity arose for land or control of a trade route from which tolls could be collected. Effective authority over a district depended on the possession of castles or walled towns from which it could be administered and defended. This factor, and a chronic shortage of manpower, which demanded fortifications so strong that they could be garrisoned with comparatively small bodies of men, led to remarkable programmes of castle-building. The countryside was dotted with stone castles of every size, from fortified halls and simple towers, often surrounded by single outer walls, and ridge-top fortresses with large walled enclosures attached to them in which the local inhabitants and their livestock could take refuge, to town citadels and advanced concentric castles, the evolution of which, Dr Ellenblum has recently suggested, was in response to the Muslims' adoption of stone-throwing artillery as an instrument of attack rather than defence. If faced by counter-invasion, the first objective of which would be to invest and take these strong points, it was important to have an army in the field which could threaten the invader. On the other hand, a long-term aim could be gradually realized by hemming in the approaches to some important goal, such as Aleppo or Ascalon, with forts that kept up pressure on its defenders.

The Latin occupation and the Muslim counter-attack were characterized, therefore, by the occupation of strong points and the building or improvement of fortifications. The haphazard nature of this process can be illustrated by reference to any atlas. Edessa was taken early on, which accounts for the eastern salient to the north of the settlements. By 1153 the whole coast as far south as Deir el Balah had been occupied, but inland the rift valley marked by the rivers Orontes, Litani and Jordan had only been crossed in certain places, particularly the approaches to Aleppo in the north and the great fief of Transjordan in the south, which reached down to the Gulf of 'Aqaba. Elsewhere the settlement was confined to the land along the coast and the absence of any strategic thinking is shown by the fact that all attempts to prove that the settlers had a coherent system of frontier defence have failed. Some important passes through the mountain chain to the coastal plain, such as in the neighbourhood of Jisr esh Shughur and around Crac des Chevaliers, contained an unusually large number of castles, but others, like the main routes from Damascus to Tyre and Acre, were for most of the time lightly defended.

The western settlers were dependent on resources which were never adequate. An incomplete list of knights' services to the kings of Jerusalem of c. 1180 produces 675 knights; we would probably not be far wrong if we assessed the total at c. 700. In its early years the principality of Antioch seems to have been able to raise about the same number, although this must have been reduced by the losses of territory in the middle of the twelfth century. The number of knights in Edessa was possibly 500. Tripoli could certainly raise 100. The total knights' service provided by the feudal system in the whole of Latin Palestine and Syria at its greatest extent was probably no more than 2,000. This is a very inadequate figure for such exposed settlements and there can have been few occasions when even a substantial proportion of it could have been mustered. From a comparatively early date the vassals of Jerusalem showed a marked aversion to service 'abroad', in which they included Antioch. Summons to service of this kind had to be preceded by negotiations and it was established that they could not be constrained to serve by unsubstantiated statements of military necessity. Even for service within the kingdom, which theoretically could be demanded for up to a year, no king could ignore the desires or financial capacities of his vassals, while at any given time a number of fiefs would be in the possession of minors or old men who had passed the age of service or heiresses who were not yet married or vassals who were sick. It would be very surprising if Jerusalem could count on putting more than perhaps 500 fief knights into the field.

In addition the kings of Jerusalem could call on the service of sergeants from churches, monasteries and towns. The sum of such service c. 1180 was 5,025 men, but the fact that they served in contingents mustered only in an emergency suggests that they were not highly trained. A *levée en masse* of the population could also be summoned in a crisis, but little is known about the quality of the force that resulted or the use to which it was put. Far more important, as the twelfth century wore on, was the contribution made by the military orders, but we have already seen that the brother knights and sergeants were never very numerous, that they acted more as the commanders of bodies of mercenary troops and that their military obligations often overstretched them.

It is clear that the war-resources of the settlers were thin. They were supplemented in five ways. First, increasingly heavy use was made of mercenaries, among whom there was an important group who fought with Muslim equipment and were called turcopoles. The Latin East was a prime source of employment for them, but it was naturally dependent on the cash that could be raised to pay them, which was never enough. This is the reason why large sums of money were periodically sent from Europe – for instance Henry II of England's monetary expiation for the murder of Thomas Becket – and why there was a national tax in Jerusalem in 1183. Secondly, there were *milites ad terminum*, para-crusaders, who are to be found from the earliest settlement onwards. These came out to serve for a time as an act of devotion. They were establishing a tradition which lasted as long as crusading did and their heirs were the men who were to travel to fight in support of the Teutonic Knights and the Hospitallers in Prussia, Rhodes and Malta in the fourteenth, fifteenth and sixteenth centuries. Thirdly, the pilgrims who arrived from Europe each year were often called upon to help out in an emergency, but we will see that a condition of their pilgrimage seems to have been that they should take up arms only after they had visited the holy places. Fourthly, the Italian merchant communities, especially those of Genoa, Venice and Pisa, would sometimes respond to an appeal, particularly if it involved the reduction of a coastal city. Fifthly, there were the crusaders who will be considered in the next chapter. What is relevant here is that the settlers regularly appealed to Europe for help and very irregularly received it, in spite of the increasingly innovative ways they underlined their appeals from the 1160s onwards.

They were, of course, isolated, for they had alienated the Byzantine empire, the only strong Christian power nearby. They were also unable to influence the course of political events in the Muslim world, on which their existence depended. In the early twelfth century Near Eastern Islam was still fragmented and in turmoil. Antioch and Edessa faced Aleppo and Mosul and, after 1133, a small but fiercely independent enclave established by the Assassins, members of an Isma'ili Shi'ite sect which used murder to further its ends. On the borders of Tripoli were a group of lesser cities and principalities, Seijar, Hama and Homs. Jerusalem faced Damascus to the east and Egypt to the south. After the initial shock of the First Crusade the reaction of most of the petty Muslim states had been to reach a *modus vivendi* with the settlers, although not a peaceful one, since the Christians had forced themselves upon an already kaleidoscopic and violent system of local politics and were themselves on the offensive. There were counter-invasions from Egypt immediately and from the Selchükid sultanate in Iraq from 1110 onwards, and there soon began to develop on the Muslim side the idea of *jihad*, or holy war, which was at first confined to a few religious leaders in Damascus and Aleppo, but came to the surface in the army that faced the Latins at the Field of Blood in 1119. It surfaced again in Aleppo in 1124, at a time when the city was besieged by the Christians. Aleppo was relieved by Aksungur al-Bursuki, the governor of Mosul, and incorporated into a personal state he was creating for himself before he was murdered by the Assassins in November 1126. On the sudden death of his son Ma'sud in May 1127 the coalition he had created might have broken up had not 'Imad ad-Din Zengi been appointed governor of Mosul. Zengi entered Aleppo in June 1128 and then embarked on a series of conquests which were not confined to Christian territory – he was far more occupied in Iraq than in Syria – but in 1135 he cleared the western and south-western approaches to Aleppo of Christian forces by taking el Atharib, Zerdan and Ma'arret. In 1137 he took Ba'rin on the frontier of the county of Tripoli. In 1144, when the count of Edessa became involved in a defensive alliance against him with a Muslim neighbour, he occupied the eastern fortresses of the county and, taking advantage of Count Joscelin II's absence and the temporary weakness of the garrison, came before Edessa itself on 24 November. He broke into the city on Christmas Eve and sacked it. The citadel fell two days later.

The loss of the capital of the first Latin state in the East made a great impression in the West as we shall see, but there was widespread and spontaneous reaction on the Muslim side as well. In the tumult of praise and propaganda, the concept of the *jihad*, voiced only intermittently in Zengi's camp before, became prominent. Showered with honours by the caliph, Zengi pressed home his advantage, taking Sürüc and laying siege to Birecik, but he was assassinated by one of his slaves on the night of 14 September 1146 and his territories were divided between two of his sons. The younger of them, Nur ad-Din, received Aleppo. Since he had not succeeded to Mosul, he was not distracted, as his father had been, by the politics of the eastern Fertile Crescent, but on the other hand his resources were fewer. In spite of his inexperience, he showed his mettle at once by rushing to the aid of the garrison at Edessa, which was threatened by Christians hoping to gain some advantage from his father's death. He then entered into an offensive alliance against Antioch with the Selchükid sultan of Rum and took Hab and Kefer Lata, which guarded the passage from the Aleppan plain. He renewed hostilities after the failure of the Second Crusade. His army, reinforced by troops from Damascus, utterly defeated a force from Antioch which was inferior in numbers on 29 June 1149. This was a turning-point for him. In his own eyes and in the opinion of his contemporaries he became a champion of the faith. The propaganda of the *jihad* was exploited by him in every possible way, through poetry, letters, treatises, sermons and inscriptions, and in it two themes stand out: the obligation to reconquer the coastlands, and especially Jerusalem, from the Christians; and the conviction that this could only be achieved through Muslim religious and political unity. As the leader of a resurgent moral rearmament, Nur ad-Din took measures against the Shi'ites and others whom he regarded as deviants and he positively encouraged the founding of schools, mosques and Sufi convents.

Unur, the ruler of Damascus, died in the early autumn of 1149; so did Nur ad-Din's brother, the ruler of Mosul. Nur ad-Din was thwarted at Mosul, where another brother was set up as governor – he did not gain the city until 1170 – but he forced Damascus to recognize his suzerainty and, in alliance with the sultan of Rum, he occupied all the remaining territory of the county of Edessa, the surviving fortress of which, Tilbeşar, surrendered on 12 July 1151. In April 1154 he was at last able to take direct control of Damascus and with the fall of Ba'albek in June 1155 the unification of Muslim Syria was complete. The next few years were spent consolidating his empire, although he also took advantage of Jerusalem's preoccupation with Egypt to raid the northern settlements, laying siege to Harim and in August 1164 inflicting a major defeat on the Christians at Artah, in which Bohemond III of Antioch, Raymond III of Tripoli, the Byzantine *dux* Coloman and the western visitor Hugh VIII of Lusignan were taken prisoner. Harim surrendered a few days later. Nur ad-Din, however, was also very concerned by King Amalric's invasions of Egypt and in the end he was much more successful there than in the kingdom of Jerusalem. In 1164, 1167 and 1168 his general Shirkuh intervened in Egypt, becoming its vizir in 1169. Egypt now recognized Nur ad-Din's suzerainty.

He died on 15 May 1174. Under him the Muslim political scene had been transformed. In place of a confused jumble of petty states there was now a powerful and united Syria, with Egypt under its shadow. The Christians had always dreaded the unification of the Muslim Near East, but Nur ad-Din's death led, as might be expected, to a struggle for power among his officers, nominally over the guardianship of his young son. One of these officers was Saladin, who had succeeded his uncle Shirkuh as vizir of Egypt and had, in obedience to Nur ad-Din's orders, abolished Shi'ite Fatimid rule and proclaimed the orthodox Sunni 'Abbasid caliphate there in September 1171. In the name of the unity of Islam Saladin occupied Damascus in October 1174 and then marched on Aleppo by way of Homs and Hama. Resisted at Homs and gaining control of Hama only with difficulty, he failed in his first attempt to take Aleppo, but in April 1175 he routed his Muslim opponents at the Battle of the Horns of Hama. Formally invested by the caliph with the government of Egypt and those parts of Syria he now held, he took up the themes of Nur ad-Din's propaganda, the *jihad* against the Christian settlements and religious and political unity.

Saladin was a practical and down-to-earth man and his chief aim, the reunification of Nur ad-Din's territories, took a long time to achieve. By the time Aleppo fell to him in June 1183 some of Mosul's dependencies were also in his hands. Mosul itself recognized his suzerainty in February 1186. His campaigns against the Christians in these years were frequent, but they do not seem to have engaged his energy and resources to the same extent. In 1177 he planned a large-scale raid on Ascalon and Gaza, which was surprised at Mont Gisard on 25 November and thrown back. In the spring and summer of 1179 his forces gained notable victories at Tell el Hara and Marjayoun after which a half-completed Christian fortress at Jisr Banat Ya'qub was taken and destroyed. But in 1182 he made an unsuccessful raid on Beirut and in 1183 he failed to bring the kingdom's forces to battle during a razzia into Galilee. Karak in Transjordan held out against him in November of that year and again in August and September of 1184, even though he brought with him on the latter occasion the most powerful army he had yet assembled. For invasions of the Latin settlements in 1170, 1171, 1173, 1177, 1179, 1180, 1182, 1183 and 1184 all Saladin had to show was the occupation of 'Aqaba on the Red Sea in 1170 and the destruction of the castle at Jisr Banat Ya'qub in 1179.

His ambitions, however, had set him on an endless road, since the warfare to which he was committed could only be financed out of further conquest. It has been said that he 'used the wealth of Egypt for the conquest of Syria, that of Syria for the conquest of Jazira and that of the Jazira for the conquest of the coast', the 'coast' being, of course, the Latin settlements. He was always in financial difficulties and it goes without saying that his 'empire' was very precariously constructed, resting on the force of his personality and on uncertain relations with the 'Abbasid caliphate; but it was his good fortune that at the moment his career reached its climax the Christians were exceptionally weak and divided.

The political background to the warfare in the region can, therefore, be summarized as follows. Until 1128 Antioch, Edessa and to a lesser extent Tripoli faced the Byzantine empire, which was never fully reconciled to the Latin occupation of Antioch and parts of Cilicia and entered the region in force in 1099, 1100, 1104, 1137, 1138, 1142 and 1158-9. It also faced a number of Muslim statelets from out of which emerged the coalition of Mosul and Aleppo, the sultanate of Rum in Asia Minor and the small, independent and idiosyncratic principality of the Assassins. Until 1169, on the other hand, Jerusalem confronted two major powers, Damascus and Egypt. With Nur ad-Din's addition of Egypt to an empire that already included Damascus the Latin settlements faced on their eastern and southern borders a unified coalition which, however precariously bound together, presented them with a real threat.

Their own military activities fall into four phases. The first lasted until c. 1130, ending with the deaths of the two leaders who were survivors of the first generation of settlers, Baldwin II of Jerusalem and Joscelin I of Edessa, and the coming to power of Zengi. It was characterized by Latin advance. At first, of course, the rulers of Jerusalem had to beat off determined attempts by the Egyptians to recover the territory they had lost. The Christians met invasions from Egypt, which often made use of Ascalon as a forward base, in 1101, 1102, 1103, 1105, 1106, 1107, 1110, 1113, 1115, 1118 and 1123. After 1107 most of these irruptions were razzias conducted by Ascalon's garrison, which constituted so real a threat that in the 1130s the patriarch and citizens of Jerusalem built a castle, Chastel Hernaut, in the foothills of the Judaean hills to protect the road to their city from Egyptian raiders and King Fulk constructed a ring of fortresses to contain its garrison; they included the one he granted to the Hospitallers.

The Christians also tried to reduce the coastal ports, which were progressively taken in a strategy which dominated the next twenty-five years. The coast of the principality of Antioch and much of its hinterland were occupied as far south as Baniyas. Meanwhile the gap from Baniyas to Beirut was bridged by the establishment of the county of Tripoli. In the south Haifa fell after Godfrey of Bouillon's death. Arsuf and Caesarea were taken in 1101, Acre in 1104, Beirut and Sidon in 1110, Tyre in 1124, and finally Ascalon in 1153. The Christians now held the whole of the Levantine coast from Iskenderun to Gaza. This assured a land-line back to Antioch and from there into Asia Minor, but far more important in the long run was the effect on maritime traffic.

The geography of the eastern Mediterranean is conditioned by a prevailing west to north-west wind; by currents, set up by water flowing through the Dardanelles and the Straits of Gibraltar and running down the Greek coast and rather treacherously along the North African one; and by the contrasting southern and northern shore-lines. The African shores are dangerous, with shoals at some distance from the land and without the easily recognizable physical features that made the rocky northern coast of the Mediterranean so attractive to navigators. It was customary, therefore, for ships from the West to sail in the northern part of the sea for as long as possible before directing their course for the Levant. A potent weapon in the hands of the Muslims was the Egyptian galley fleet in the Nile Delta, which could be used to intercept western shipping and cut what increasingly became the main line of communication between the settlers and the West. To be effective the fleet needed, of course, regular watering, and the occupation of the coast so deprived it of water that it no longer had the range to operate effectively against the northern Mediterranean shipping lanes and especially at their point of convergence, the seas around Cyprus.

In the north, the settlements at Antioch and Edessa expanded and met, but some regions closer to the coast were reduced slowly. The pilgrim roads to Jerusalem were still insecure in 1118 and the hinterlands of Sidon and Beirut were only gradually mastered in the late 1120s. Meanwhile the settlers were driving into the interior. Tancred was already pushing to the east of the Sea of Galilee as early as the autumn of 1099 and the eastern bank of the Wadi Araba as far as the Red Sea was garrisoned from 1115 to 1116. Latin expansion east of the sea of Galilee aroused the anxieties of Damascus. There was endemic petty warfare on the eastern frontier until 1115 and hostilities were resumed in 1119. Baldwin I sustained a major defeat at es Sinnabra in 1113 and in that year, 1121 and 1124 there were Muslim raids into Galilee.

The Latin settlers in the north had to face counter-invasions, organized on behalf of the Selchükid sultanate in Iraq, for five successive years from 1110. In every year, except 1112 and 1114 when the incursions were minor, the Christian rulers combined their forces and held them back to threaten rather than engage the enemy, although in 1115 Roger of Salerno, the regent of Antioch, was able to surprise the Muslims and gain a victory over them near Tell Danith. This ended the invasions for the time being, but Roger's disastrous exposure of his army without its allies to the Muslims in the Battle of the Field of Blood in 1119 was followed by the loss of the Christian strongholds which threatened Aleppo, although some of them were later recovered. Pressure was maintained on the two chief prizes still to be won in the interior, Aleppo, which was threatened in

1100 and besieged in 1125, and Damascus, which was attacked in 1126 and 1129. It says much for the confidence of the Christians in this period that Baldwin I died in 1118 while invading Egypt and that Baldwin II took war to the Muslims on two fronts, as we have seen.

The second phase lasted from c. 1130 to 1153. It was one in which the Christians were on the defensive, although they were still capable of sporadic, opportunist attacks. A feature of this period, it has been pointed out, was their inability to recover what they now lost, in marked contrast to the first phase. Edessa, Ba'rin and Qalaat el Mudiq (Afamiyah) were lost for good; Harim and Baniyas were reoccupied only for a short time. There were, moreover, only two major offensives, both made possible by foreign aid: against Seijar in collaboration with the Greeks in 1137 and against Damascus, undertaken with the Second Crusade in 1148.

The third phase, from 1153 to 1169, opened with the occupation of Ascalon by Baldwin III and was characterized by the invasions of Egypt by Amalric in alliance with the Greeks. These naturally involved the Christians in sieges: of Bilbeis in 1163, 1164 and 1168, Alexandria in 1167, Cairo in 1168 and Damietta (Dumyat) in 1169. They strained the kingdom's resources and led to serious divisions of opinion among the Christians. From 1164 onwards every invasion was opposed by an army sent to Egypt's aid from Syria and the Christians' failure left the country to Nur ad-Din.

The fourth phase, from 1169 to 1187, was one in which the settlers were back on the defensive. Saladin regularly, if rather half-heartedly, invaded the kingdom and the only major offensive undertaken by the Christians was an assault on Hama and Harim in 1177, taking advantage of the presence of Count Philip of Flanders and the arrival of a Byzantine fleet. The hero of these years was the young leper king, Baldwin IV, who even in illness ensured that every attack was met by a Christian army, the duty of which was not to seek battle but to challenge any attempt by the enemy to take castles or towns.

The Battle of Hattin and the loss of Jerusalem

Then came Saladin's invasion of 1187. Just before it occurred, the political crisis in Jerusalem had come to a head. After Baldwin V's death in August 1186 Raymond of Tripoli, the regent-elect, lord of Galilee through marriage and leader of the claimant Isabella's partisans, was persuaded to go to Tiberias while the little king's body was sent to Jerusalem in the care of the Templars. Acre and Beirut were seized in Sibylla's name, while she and her knights hurried to Jerusalem, where they were joined by Reynald of Châtillon, the lord of Transjordan. Sibylla, who also had the support of the master of the Templars and the patriarch, was crowned in the Church of the Holy Sepulchre and she herself then crowned her husband, Guy of Lusignan.

Isabella's adherents had been outwitted and as they gathered defiantly at Nablus, planning to go as far as crowning Isabella and her husband Humphrey of Toron (Tibnine), Humphrey destroyed their position by taking flight and submitting to Guy and Sibylla in Jerusalem. This ended the rebellion, which was over by October. Most of the feudatories made their peace, although Raymond of Tripoli retired in fury to Tiberias, holding out until the following summer, when a disaster for which he was held responsible made his position untenable. He had, as was his right as lord, made an independent treaty with Saladin and in late April 1187, in accordance with this, he allowed a Muslim reconnaissance force to enter Galilee. At precisely this time a mission sent by Guy, led by Balian of Ibelin, who was Maria Comnena's second husband and lord of Nablus, the archbishop of Tyre and the masters of the Temple and the Hospital, was approaching. Ignoring Raymond's warning to stay behind the walls of the castle of 'Afula until the Muslim troops had left the area, the Templars and Hospitallers rashly attacked them and were cut to pieces. The master of the Hospital and the marshal of the Temple were killed.

In the meantime Saladin had been looking for a reason to put aside a truce he had made with the Christians in 1185. This was provided by Reynald of Transjordan, who had pursued an extraordinarily adventurous and aggressive policy of his own against the Muslims for some years, launching attacks across Sinai and into northern Arabia as far as Tayma', and even sending a naval squadron into the Red Sea to pillage merchant shipping and to land an invasion force at Rabigh in the Hijaz; it was apparently stopped only a day's march from Mecca. Reynald had now attacked a caravan travelling from Cairo to Damascus and had refused to return the spoil. In late May 1187 Saladin reviewed his troops at el 'Ashtara in the Hauran. It was the largest army he had ever commanded, probably c. 30,000 men, of whom 12,000 were regular cavalry. On 30 June he crossed the Jordan just south of the Sea of Galilee. The Christians made what had become a conventional counter-move, assembling their army at Zippori. This was smaller than Saladin's, but it was much larger than usual. They had stretched the resources of the kingdom to put c. 20,000 men into the field, of whom 1,200 were knights, drawn from Jerusalem and Tripoli and the military orders, together with 50 from Antioch. As was customary in times of crisis they had brought with them the kingdom's holiest relic, the fragment of the True Cross discovered in Jerusalem by Arnulf of Chocques in 1099.

Saladin now divided his forces. On 2 July he attacked Tiberias. A tower on the walls was quickly mined and the town was seized, although the garrison, with Raymond of Tripoli's wife Eschiva, withdrew to the citadel. The bulk of Saladin's army was held back from Tiberias at Kafr Sabt, some six miles away. In the Latin camp an anguished debate began. Raymond of Tripoli, by now thoroughly discredited, advised King Guy not to move and even to allow Tiberias to fall. Quite apart from his obligations as a feudal overlord to a vassal in peril, Guy's experiences four years before may have led him to reject this apparently sensible and disinterested advice. He had been severely blamed, when he was Baldwin IV's lieutenant, for not engaging Saladin in battle when the latter had invaded Galilee in September 1183 and this criticism had marked the start of an unscrupulous campaign which had contributed to his fall from favour, his wife's exclusion from the inheritance of the kingdom and the appointment of Raymond of Tripoli as lieutenant in his place and as regent for Baldwin V. At any rate, Guy made the decision to move and the Christian army marched on 3 July, by way of the spring of Tur'an, about nine miles from Tiberias. It found itself having to fight a two-day battle on the march. As it continued its advance it was engaged by the wings of the Muslim army, which cut off its retreat and a chance of returning to the water at Tur'an, while Saladin held the high ground between it and the steep drop from the escarpment down to Tiberias. By evening the Christians had been forced to halt at a spot far from their goal and without water. When, hot and thirsty, they tried to resume their march on the following morning, they were gradually forced off the road onto the rough ground to the north. Raymond of Tripoli and a small party that included the lords of Sidon and Nablus managed to break through the Muslim lines and escape, but most of the Christians gathered round Guy in a hopeless stand on a hill crowned with two peaks, known as the Horns of Hattin. The demoralized survivors were taken prisoner. The relic of the True Cross was seized and was paraded through Damascus fixed upside down on a lance.

The results of this disaster were catastrophic. Fortresses and cities had been deprived of their garrisons to swell the Christian army and Saladin could storm through Palestine and Syria with impunity. By September all the important ports south of Tripoli, except Tyre, had fallen to him. Inland from the Palestinian coast only the castle of Beaufort (Qalaat esh Shaqif) remained in Christian hands by January 1189, and it was lost in 1190. In the county of Tripoli, only the city, the town of Tartus, two Templar castles and the Hospitaller castle of Crac des Chevaliers were still Christian; in the principality of Antioch, only the city itself and the castles of Quseir and Marqab. The city of Jerusalem fell on 2 October 1187 after a fortnight's siege, during which Balian of Nablus, who had taken charge of its defence, resorted to the knighting of all noble boys over sixteen years of age and thirty burgesses. Saladin allowed the population, swollen by refugees from the surrounding countryside, to ransom themselves on quite generous terms, so that at least a proportion was freed, although many of these people faced further hardship as they tried to find shelter in the few towns still under Christian control. The Temple area was restored to Islam. The Hospital of St John became a Shafi'ite college. Jerusalem had been lost after an occupation of just over eighty-eight years.

CHAPTER 5

Crusading in Adolescence, 1102–1187

Crusaders or pilgrims

In the responses of western Europeans to the news of the disasters in Palestine in 1187 crusading came of age. That was ninety years after the First Crusade and for most of the twelfth century the movement had been inchoate. I have already described how around 1107 three intelligent French monks, Robert the Monk, Guibert of Nogent and Baldric of Bourgueil, had reforged the crude ideas of the earliest crusaders into a theologically acceptable interpretation of their triumph, in which the events were shown to be evidence of God's miraculous interventionary power and the crusaders were portrayed as laymen who had temporarily taken a kind of monastic habit, leaving the world for a time to enter a nomadic religious community, the members of which had adopted voluntary exile in a war for the love of God and their neighbours, were united in brotherhood and followed a way of the cross that could lead to martyrdom. This presentation was to be useful to the Church – the histories of Robert and Baldric were widely read – but it could not be a lasting solution to the theological issue of the role of laymen, which required the greater understanding of their particular 'vocation' that developed in the course of the twelfth century. It was no real answer to treat them as if they were not laymen at all.

This theorizing was anyway on a high plane and when we look at the crusading movement in practice we find such confusion that it has been possible for one historian to question whether it existed at all. It may have been possible for individuals to take the cross at any time, without the precondition of papal proclamation. In the wake of the liberation of Jerusalem there was a tendency to transfer the ideas and extravagant language of crusading to any conflict about which the promoters or the participants felt strongly. Count Helias of Maine, who was devout and had taken the cross, refused to join the First Crusade because King William II of England was threatening his county and he was said to have defended it wearing the cross, as though engaged in a personal crusade. A remarkable piece of propaganda, composed in Magdeburg in 1108, tried to present the German war against the pagan Wends across the Elbe in crusading terms:

Follow the good example of the inhabitants of Gaul and emulate them in this also. ... May he who with the strength of his arm led the men of

Gaul on their march from the far West in triumph against his enemies in the farthest East give you the will and power to conquer these most inhuman gentiles [the Wends] who are near by.

Penitential warfare had evolved out of the Investiture Contest, as we have seen, and advocates of church reform were not slow to reapply the idea, now reinforced by the crusade's success, to the older struggle against simoniacs.

On the other hand, crusaders were readily identifiable and the sight of those who 'had taken the cross', the act which signified the making of the vow, would have led everyone to know that an expedition was being planned or was in train. Our problem is that we often do not have the visual information available to men and women at the time and are reliant on written evidence, which is so oblique that it is sometimes hard for us to distinguish crusades from pilgrimages. During the First Crusade the rules relating to penance and the carrying of weapons had been modified. Before it pilgrims to Jerusalem had been supposed to travel weaponless and this feature of penances was so deeply embedded in contemporary thinking that once Jerusalem had been secured in the Battle of Ascalon the ordinary rules of penitential pilgrimage again prevailed. Casting their weapons away, many, if not all, the crusaders started for home carrying nothing but their palm fronds, which were evidence that they had completed their pilgrimage, notwithstanding the fact that the return journey, at least in its initial stages, must have been as dangerous as the crusade itself had been, if not more so now that Islam had been aroused. A graphic description of its perils was provided by a Norman crusader, who was one of more than 1,400 passengers crammed into a large ship at Jaffa. Cruising north it ran into a storm and was wrecked off Tartus, which was in ruins and empty. The travellers ransacked the town, but, worried that they might be attacked by the Muslims, nearly 100 of them boarded an Armenian boat bound for Cyprus.

The reversion to the traditional rules for penitents is illustrated by a famous letter written in 1102 by Bishop Ivo of Chartres to Pope Paschal II. Raimbold Croton, a hero of the crusade, had had a monk in charge of a nearby abbey estate seized and castrated for permitting, or probably ordering, the abbey servants to mow hay from a field which Raimbold claimed was his own. Ivo described his decision and its consequences.

We took away Raimbold's weapons and imposed a fourteen-year penance on him, in such a way that he should abstain from the more luxurious foods during the prescribed period. ... He accepted this obediently, but afterwards, having sent for many and great men to intercede for him, he exhausted us with much earnest pleading that he be allowed the use of arms on account of the way his enemies disturbed him.

Since Raimbold had lost a hand in the assault on Jerusalem it is highly unlikely that he could have used a sword effectively. The point was that his status would have been affected if for fourteen years he had to go about unarmed. Ivo, pestered beyond endurance, sent Raimbold on pilgrimage to Rome with this letter; he wrote that the penance of the pilgrimage might induce the pope to be merciful. A later case was the pilgrimage of Henry the Lion in 1172. Henry was perhaps accompanied by as many as 1,500 persons, who, finding their way barred by a Serbian force in Bulgaria, resorted to arms, but only reluctantly and somewhat inconclusively, since the Serbs soon fled. The German pilgrims felt they had to justify their action in the light of the threat they faced.

It is true that after 1100 men described as pilgrims were quite often engaged militarily in Palestine. Some of them turn out to have been crusaders; these included Bertrand, the son of Raymond of St Gilles, who was finishing off the reduction of the Lebanese coast in 1108 and had vowed to serve 'God and the Holy Sepulchre'. There were also men who were not crusaders, but were obviously pilgrims prepared to fight. Fulcher of Chartres, who was in Palestine at the time, stated that in 1105 the Egyptians were planning an invasion 'because we were so few and were without the help of the usual pilgrims' and he wrote with respect to the year 1113 that 'it is usual in these overseas parts for our army to grow daily at this time, because the pilgrims have arrived'.

Pilgrims, therefore, had access to weapons, but their military service can be shown to have conformed to a particular pattern. They do not seem to have volunteered for action until after they had fulfilled their religious obligations. A party of English, Flemings and Danes, which arrived and after visiting the holy places helped prepare an attack on Sidon, was probably made up of pilgrims, as were the Norwegians who left Bergen in 1107 in a large fleet under the command of Sigurd, who shared the throne with his two brothers. After a leisurely journey by way of England, France, Spain and Sicily they reached Acre in the summer of 1110. Sigurd was persuaded to help King Baldwin take the city of Sidon, but the Norwegians agreed to assist the kingdom only after they had been to Jerusalem, because Christ had ordered 'his faithful followers first to seek the kingdom of God and afterwards to find all the beneficial things they sought'. In 1153, when the kingdom's army was laying siege to Ascalon, pilgrims were forbidden to return to the West before they had supplemented the besieging force and in October 1183, when the departure of the homeward passage was near, others, who must have already been to Jerusalem, were called upon to serve as foot soldiers in an army facing Saladin in the valley of Jezreel. So twelfth-century pilgrims behaved in precisely the opposite way to so many of the first crusaders, who had self-consciously reverted to an unarmed state once they had liberated the Holy Sepulchre.

While Jerusalem was in Christian hands there appear to have been, broadly speaking, two patterns of behaviour. Those on crusade, such as the soldiers in 1101 and 1147–8, fought on the march to the East and again, if need be, once they had visited the holy places. Those who came as pilgrims pure and simple only felt free to take up arms after they had achieved their goal by venerating the Holy Sepulchre. The distinction is important, because it seems that for half a century after the First Crusade pilgrimaging was far more appealing to European armsbearers than crusading, which attracted only sporadic interest. Although there were some centres of continuing zeal, such as one which has been located among leading castellan families in the district immediately to the north of Angers, elsewhere the establishment of traditions had to wait until later. The Bernards of Bré in the Limousin, who sent three men in 1096 and four on the Second Crusade in 1147, provided no recruits in the interim and the descendants of Count William Tête-Hardi of Burgundy, who were very active at the time of the First Crusade and were to contribute no less than ten crusaders to the Second, seem to have provided only one between 1102 and 1146, although it was William's son, Pope Calixtus II, who proclaimed the crusade of 1120. Although most crusaders did not feel the urge to crusade again, a number of them returned to Jerusalem as pilgrims. Their enthusiasm for Jerusalem as a cult-centre had not dimmed and the fact that the old eleventh-century tradition of pilgrimages there had reasserted itself is confirmed by an examination of regional activity. The Limousin, where there had been great enthusiasm for the First Crusade, provides us with the name of only one crusader for the period from 1102 to 1131, and he is doubtful, but it generated many pilgrims and an intense emotional attachment to Jerusalem was still in evidence. No crusader has been identified in the period between 1103 and 1147 from Provence, where there had again been an enthusiastic response in 1096, but there were many pilgrims to Jerusalem, especially from the nobles in the district of Marseille. Much the same picture is to be found in Champagne, which had sent many men to the East between 1096 and 1102. Few crusaders can be found in the region between 1102 and 1147, but there was enthusiasm for pilgrimages to Jerusalem, the lead being taken by Count Hugh I of Champagne.

One is left with the impression that in much of western Europe crusading became dormant after all the efforts associated with the First Crusade. To many armsbearers that expedition must have seemed a unique chance to engage in a particularly appropriate meritorious activity. Now they turned back to their traditional devotions, to be recalled only in 1146, when Bernard of Clairvaux preached the new crusade as another once-and-for-all opportunity of self-help on one's passage to heaven:

[God] puts himself into a position of necessity, or pretends to be in one, while all the time he wants to help you in your need. He wants to be thought of as the debtor, so that he can award to those fighting for him wages: the remission of their sins and everlasting glory. It is because of this that I have called you a blessed generation, you who have been caught up in a time so rich in remission and are found living in this year so pleasing to the Lord, truly a year of jubilee.

The early crusades of the twelfth century

Nevertheless, the years between the First and Second Crusades were not without incident. They witnessed the definitive extension of crusading to Spain, although one of the most important campaigns there may not have been a crusade at all. In 1118 Pope Gelasius II formally legitimized a war, to be led by King Alfonso I of Aragon, against Saragossa (Zaragoza). The city, the most important prize to be seized since Toledo, fell on 19 December to a large army which included in its ranks the first crusaders Gaston of Béarn and Centulle of Bigorre, and also Alfonso Jordan, the count of Toulouse, who had been born in Syria, and the viscounts of Carcassonne, Gabarret and Lavedan. It is noteworthy that this campaign, organized and led by a king who could put the resources of his state at its disposal, was successful not at the expense of some debilitated petty kingdom, but against the Almoravids, who now controlled most of Moorish Spain and were routed in battle on 8 December. No statement from Pope Gelasius that the assault on Saragossa was a crusade survives, although a precedent had been created by Paschal II, when he granted the use of crosses and remission of sins for the participants in a war launched in 1114 against the Muslims in the Balearic Islands, waged by Catalans and Pisans under Count Raymond Berengar of Barcelona, which was then switched in 1116 to a campaign down the mainland coast.

We are on much firmer ground with the crusade preached by Pope Calixtus II. This was to be fought concurrently in the East as well as in the Iberian peninsula and on 2 April 1123 Calixtus issued a letter calling on crusaders in Spain to fulfil their vows, granting them the same remission as that conceded to crusaders to the East and appointing Oleguer, archbishop of Tarragona, as papal legate. This letter was issued at the time the First Lateran Council was in session and the council's decree on the crusade referred to both Jerusalem and Spain. The crusade was also discussed at a council at Santiago de Compostela, presided over by Archbishop Diego Gelmírez, who may have been appointed legate alongside Oleguer. Diego issued a stirring summons, the first expression of a justification for Spanish crusading which was to be resorted to over and over again through the centuries.

Just as the knights of Christ and the faithful sons of Holy Church opened the way to Jerusalem with much labour and spilling of blood, so we should become knights of Christ and, after defeating his wicked enemies the Muslims, open the way to the same Sepulchre of the Lord through Spain, which is shorter and much less laborious.

The crusaders were granted remission of sins 'through the merits of SS Peter, Paul and James'. In the end it was Alfonso I of Aragon, from another part of the peninsula, who in a feat of arms much admired at the time led a major raid into southern Spain in the winter of 1125–6, marching by way of Teruel, Valencia, Murcia, Gaudix, Granada and Malaga, where he embarked on a boat to demonstrate that he had crossed the peninsula. He returned to Saragossa bringing with him 10,000 Andalusian Christians and their families, who had decided to emigrate and whom he settled in the Ebro valley.

Within a decade another field for crusading was at least the subject of discussion. From the late 1120s the papacy was engaged in a struggle against the South Italian Normans, which was accentuated by Roger of Sicily's support for the anti-pope Anacletus, and papal propagandists were resorting to language reminiscent of the reformers half a century before. In May 1135 Pope Innocent II presided over a council at Pisa which decreed that those who fought against the pope's enemies 'for the liberation of the Church on land or sea' should enjoy the same remission of sins as that granted to the first crusaders by Urban II at the council of Clermont. There is no evidence that these fighters had to make crusade vows, but this isolated grant of a crusade privilege to those who fought against the political opponents of the papacy links the struggles of the reformers of the eleventh century to the 'political crusades' of the thirteenth. It led to controversy in the years that followed, with on the one hand a body of highly critical opinion and on the other an avant-garde, a representative of which was Peter the Venerable, the great abbot of Cluny, prepared to argue that violence against fellow Christians could be even more justifiable than the use of force against infidels.

Meanwhile a new crusade to the East was diverted off course, foreshadowing the events of 1202–4. Bohemond of Taranto and Antioch, who had been held prisoner by the Danishmend Turks from the summer of 1100 to the spring of 1103, arrived in France early in 1106. After a melodramatic visit to the shrine of St Leonard, the patron saint of captives, at St Léonard-de-Noblat, to fulfil a vow he had made in captivity, he embarked on a triumphant tour of France, lecturing to large audiences. His progress was marked by gifts of relics and silks to churches; he had stripped the treasury of Antioch on his departure. Many French nobles wanted him to be godfather to their children and it was said that Henry I of England discouraged him from visiting his kingdom because he was worried that he might tempt away his best knights. In April or May 1106 he married Constance, the daughter of King Philip of France, a match that demonstrated the reputation he now had. He despatched agents to regions he could not visit himself, even to England. He may also have made use of the written word. A version of the anonymous account of the First Crusade, the *Gesta Francorum*, which had been written by someone in his contingent, may have been circulating France and it is possible that a forged letter purporting to be from the emperor Alexius to Count Robert I of Flanders, which suggested that the Greeks had become so desperate in the 1090s that they had been prepared to envisage Latin rule in Constantinople, was being publicized at the same time. A legendary account of Bohemond's experiences as a prisoner of the Muslims was soon incorporated into the *miracula* of the shrine of St Leonard.

At a council held at Poitiers Bohemond and the papal legate, Bruno of Segni, formally proclaimed a new crusade, with the support of Pope Paschal whom Bohemond had met on his journey. They described it in First-Crusade terms as a journey to the Holy Sepulchre with the aims of helping the Christians in the East and forcing the Muslims to disgorge their Christian prisoners, but Bohemond's intentions were already greater. He had travelled to the West to seek aid for his principality of Antioch, which was threatened by the Greeks as well as by the Muslims. We have seen that soon after his release from prison he had had to face Byzantine invasions of Cilicia and Syria. In June 1104 much of his eastern frontier had fallen to Ridvan of Aleppo. He had held a council in Antioch at which it was decided that the only course open to him was an appeal to the West. The Greeks certainly loomed as large in his thoughts as did the Muslims and he was accompanied on his tour through France by a pretender to the Byzantine imperial throne with his Greek entourage. There is an account of Bohemond speaking on a dais before the Lady Altar in the cathedral of Chartres on the day of his marriage. He began by telling the story of his adventures and in calling for a crusade to Jerusalem he also proposed an invasion of the Byzantine empire, promising rich pickings to those who would go with him. Over the next few months he developed his case and when on the eve of his departure he wrote to the pope, he referred to the usurpation of the Byzantine throne by Alexius and justified an attack on the Greeks as vengeance for their treatment of the crusaders and as a means of ending schism between the Catholic and Orthodox Churches.

By October 1107 his army, which contained several of his companions from the First Crusade, was mustered in Apulia. It was large enough for the monastic historian Orderic Vitalis to write of it as the 'third expedition ... to Jerusalem'; Orderic must have considered the forces of 1096 and 1100–1 to have comprised the first and second. On the 9th it landed on the

Albanian coast at Valona (Vlorië) and then marched for Durazzo, which the Italian Normans had held for a short time twenty-five years earlier. Bohemond laid siege to Durazzo, but the Greeks cut off his communications across the Adriatic and in the spring of 1108 the Byzantine forces closed around him. As the summer wore on his army became prone to disease. In September he surrendered and was forced to sign the Treaty of Devol, to which reference has already been made. Some of his fellow crusaders travelled on to the East. Most, without the means to continue, returned to western Europe. Broken by his defeat, Bohemond did not go back to Syria but retired to his estates in southern Italy, where he died in 1111.

News of a disaster for the Christians in northern Syria eight years later, the Battle of the Field of Blood in which the prince of Antioch was killed, reached the West in the autumn of 1119. Pope Calixtus II, who heard of the disaster while travelling through France, immediately proclaimed a new crusade. The speed of his reaction is not surprising considering that he was not only from the family of the counts of Burgundy, which had shown itself to be strongly predisposed to crusading, but was also the cousin of Baldwin II of Jerusalem and was therefore related to the Montlhéry clan. At this crucial moment the Montlhérys had a natural ally on the papal throne, who responded to the threat to Latin rule in the East, and therefore to the family, by preaching the first crusade to be formally proclaimed since that of 1107. It must be significant that this crusade never seems to have been intended to engage itself in Syria, where the westerners had been defeated, but was to travel instead to the Holy Land, 400 miles to the south, where Baldwin's seat of government was.

Calixtus planned the new crusade on a large scale. He wrote to Venice and probably also to Germany and France, which suggests that a general letter was composed to summon the faithful to take the cross. He also decided to promote a crusade in Spain at the same time, as we have seen, and the decree of the First Lateran Council, which granted the remission of sins and the Church's protection to crusaders, imposed sanctions on those who would not have left for Jerusalem or Spain by Easter 1124. In Venice, to which Baldwin had also directly appealed, there was an enthusiastic response. The doge and the leading citizens took the cross and were granted a banner of St Peter by the pope. On 8 August 1122 a large fleet left for the East. The Venetians paused to attack Byzantine Corfu in retaliation for an attempt by the emperor John Comnenus to reduce their privileges in the empire, but they left hurriedly on hearing that Baldwin had fallen into the hands of the Muslims. They reached the coast of Palestine in May 1123, destroyed an Egyptian fleet off Ascalon, spent Christmas in Jerusalem and Bethlehem and helped besiege Tyre, which fell on 7 July 1124. They were rewarded with a third of Tyre and its territory and with important commercial privileges which must have been already promised them by Baldwin as inducements to crusade. The Venetians returned home by way of the Aegean, sacking Greek islands and territory as they went. Their pillaging brought the Byzantine government to heel and in August 1126 John Comnenus confirmed and extended their privileges. They were, however, not the only crusaders in the East at the time. They carried others in their ships and there is evidence for men from Bohemia, Germany and France taking the cross. It is also possible that a Genoese squadron took part.

A few years later more crusaders were sought by the settlers in the Levant, when the embassy was sent from Jerusalem to offer the hand of Baldwin's daughter Melisende to Fulk of Anjou. The Templar master Hugh of Payns toured the West recruiting crusaders and a substantial number of them accompanied Fulk to Palestine in 1129 and joined an army of settlers in an unsuccessful assault upon Damascus. The initiative for the new expedition seems to have been Baldwin's own. The crusade was launched without any authorization by Pope Honorius II, who remained a bystander, as we have seen. This underlines the difference between the unregulated early expeditions and their thirteenth-century successors, over which the authority of the popes had been firmly established. Already in 1103 the western emperor Henry IV had committed himself to a penitential war in the East without reference to the papacy and had authorized the preaching of it by the bishop of Würzburg. Henry must have been trying to reassert his traditional authority as defender of Christendom, an authority which had been usurped by Pope Urban when he had summoned Christians to fight to recover Jerusalem. He was not successful, but the Church, which had invented crusading, had not yet established control over it, partly because preaching, recruitment and oversight demanded unprecedented responsibilities of the clergy, who were often at sea when trying to cope with the unfamiliar issues they had to face.

In the long run the publication, probably around the year 1140, of Gratian's *Decretum* was highly significant in this respect. It was to become the standard compilation of church law and was to lend weight to the establishment of the Church's right to direct the movement. A long section, Causa XXIII, was devoted to violence. Although on the surface Gratian did not deal with crusading – the Causa's process of argument started with the issue of the suppression of heresy by force – consciousness of it lay behind an armoury of justifications for the Church's authorization of violence provided to its readers, who were led inexorably through a panoply of authorities to the conclusions that war need not be sinful, could be just, and could be authorized by God and, on God's behalf, by the pope. Gratian provided a source-book for all future crusade propagandists.

The Second Crusade

The capture of Edessa by Zengi on Christmas Eve 1144 has already been described. An embassy from the Latin East, led by Bishop Hugh of Jeble, reached the papal court at Viterbo shortly after the election of Pope Eugenius III in November 1145, to be followed by a delegation of Armenian bishops. On 1 December the new pope issued a general letter, *Quantum praedecessores*, in which, after touching on the success of the First Crusade and the grave situation now confronting the East, he called for crusaders, granting them a remission of sins which was more advanced than that issued by Urban II. He also decreed the protection of crusaders' property, declared a moratorium on the payment of interest on their debts and eased the way, as Urban had done, for the raising of money from the disposal of land to cover their expenses.

Although it can no longer be maintained with certainty that *Quantum praedecessores* was the first general crusade letter, because there may have been a precedent issued by Calixtus II, its careful delineation of privileges for crusaders set the tone for all later letters of this sort. It was addressed to France, but there is no evidence that it had arrived there when the next event occurred. The news of the disaster had reached France independently in embassies from Antioch and Jerusalem. King Louis VII was one of the most attractive of the medieval French monarchs. Tender-hearted and courteous, pious and serious, he was a loyal son of the Church, but he was not weak, particularly where royal rights were concerned: in many ways he displayed the combination of rectitude and strength which was so marked in his great-grandson, Louis IX. It is probable that he was already considering making a pilgrimage to Jerusalem. He may also have feared that if he did not act the Montlhéry clan would, since the counts of Edessa were their kin. At his Christmas court at Bourges he presented the bishops and magnates, whom he had invited in larger numbers than was usual, with a plan to go to the aid of the Christians in the East and the bishop of Langres preached a sermon, calling on all to assist the king in the enterprise. The response of the court was not enthusiastic and it was agreed that the issue should be discussed again the following Easter after Abbot Bernard of Clairvaux had been consulted.

It was Bernard who transformed the situation. By this time he was the leading figure in the western Church. He had been primarily responsible for the growth of the Cistercian type of reformed Benedictinism, the most fashionable monasticism of the age. He had engineered the victory of Pope Innocent II over his rival Anacletus and the new pope Eugenius had been one of his monks and his pupil. He was the greatest preacher of his day. Fearless and a brilliant speaker and writer, he was at the height of his reputation. No wonder he was consulted by Louis 'as though he were a divine oracle'. He was likely to be sympathetic – he had, after all, already brought his considerable influence to bear in support of the Templars –

but he characteristically replied that a matter of this importance should be referred to the pope, thereby ensuring that papal initiative was preserved. Eugenius's response was to reissue *Quantum praedecessores* on 1 March 1146, with a few minor changes, and to authorize Bernard to preach the crusade north of the Alps. At Vézelay on 31 March, in a dramatic scene played, as at Clermont, in a field outside the town, Bernard read the general letter to the crowd and delivered the first of his crusade sermons with Louis at his side, wearing a cross sent to him by the pope. The audience became so enthusiastic that Bernard ran out of cloth for crosses and in a probably deliberate piece of theatre had to tear pieces from his own habit to make them. After Vézelay he energetically promoted the crusade in letters and sermons. The letters that have survived are among the most powerful crusade propaganda of all time, in which a highly developed concept of the remission of sins was combined with a marvellously appealing description of the crusade as an opportunity presented by God to sinful and violent men of redeeming themselves.

> This age is like no other that has gone before; a new abundance of divine mercy comes down from heaven; blessed are those who are alive in this year pleasing to the Lord, this year of remission, this year of veritable jubilee. I tell you, the Lord has not done this for any other generation before, nor has he lavished on our fathers a gift of grace so copious. Look at the skill he is using to save you. Consider the depth of his love and be astonished, sinners. He creates a need – he either creates it or pretends to have it – while he desires to help you in your necessity. This is a plan not made by man, but coming from heaven and proceeding from the heart of divine love.

Here is Bernard playing on the image of the Holy Land as Christ's own.

> The earth has been shaken and has trembled, because the Lord has caused his land to lose territory. His land, I repeat, where he was seen and in which he lived among men for more than thirty years. His land, which he honoured by his birth, embellished by his miracles, consecrated with his blood and enriched by his burial. His land, in which the voice of the turtle-dove was heard when the Son of the Virgin praised the life of chastity. His land, where the first flowers of his resurrection appeared.

At first sight this passage looks fairly conventional, but what is striking about it is the constant repetition of the words 'His land (*Terram suam*)', which open each sentence like drum beats. Bernard must have wanted to remind his listeners of the importance to them of their own freehold properties and therefore of the need to protect Christ's patrimony.

Bernard was drawn into northern France and Germany to curb the passions aroused by the unauthorized activities of another Cistercian monk called Radulf, whose preaching bred the same violence against Jews as that which had marred the First Crusade. In November he reached Frankfurt, where King Conrad III of Germany was holding his court. Conrad was another admirable ruler – shrewd, sincere, intelligent, pious, courageous and hard-working – and he had already shown interest in crusading, for he had taken the cross in 1124, but Germany was torn by internal feuding, and powerful interests, which he was never able to overcome, had been opposed to his accession. It used to be thought that he initially refused to join the crusade and to take the leadership of the Germans who were now being recruited in large numbers, but historians are now not so sure. What is certain is that enthusiasm, which had spread to Italy and England, now had a momentum of its own and that after a dramatic sermon, preached by Bernard during Mass at the Christmas court at Speyer, in which he directed a personal and highly charged appeal to the German king, drawing attention to his prospects on the Day of Judgement should he fail to answer Christ's summons, Conrad took the cross.

The two most powerful rulers in western Europe were now committed to the crusade, which was looking as though it would be a really major expedition. It also began to assume the features of Calixtus II's ambitious enterprise of a quarter of a century before, although this time on an even larger scale. Eugenius responded favourably to a request from King Alfonso VII of Castile for an extension of the crusade to Spain and he allowed the Genoese and the citizens of the ports of southern France to join that campaign. Then, at an assembly at Frankfurt on 13 March 1147, some German crusaders, mostly Saxons giving expression to ideas current in Saxony since the early years of the century, petitioned to be allowed to crusade against the pagan Wends east of the Elbe rather than against the Muslims. Bernard agreed to their proposal and persuaded Eugenius, whom he met on 6 April at Clairvaux, to authorize it formally. He justified crusading in the new theatre in a startling way, forbidding the fighters to make any truce with the Wends 'until such time as, with God's help, either their religion or nation shall be wiped out'. This extraordinary statement, which was echoed, somewhat more ambiguously, in Eugenius's formal authorization of the Wendish Crusade, looks like the proclamation of a missionary war, corresponding well with what had for long been a feature of the German drive to the east. It has never been satisfactorily explained, especially since Bernard expressed opposition to forcible conversion on another occasion. One of the problems we have to face with crusade propaganda is the underlying contradiction between the desire for conversion, or perhaps the conviction that the success of a crusade would establish political conditions favourable to it, and the Christian tradition that infidels should not be forced, but only persuaded, to abjure their errors. Faced with the need to arouse an audience which did not appreciate subtlety, Bernard and Eugenius were not the only propagandists of German crusades who found themselves drawn into making statements of doubtful theology.

Eugenius's letter, *Divina dispensatione*, issued at Troyes on 13 April 1147, revealed the strategy that was developing, for in it the pope referred to the eastern and Iberian expeditions at the same time as he authorized the German campaign against the Wends. The crusade was now being planned on a gigantic scale. Eventually five armies converged on the East: those of Louis of France, Conrad of Germany, Amadeus of Savoy, Alfonso Jordan of Toulouse and an Anglo-Flemish force that helped the king of Portugal to take Lisbon on the way. Four more armies took the field in north-eastern Europe: a Danish army which joined one under Henry the Lion of Saxony and the archbishop of Bremen, and forces led by Albert the Bear of Brandenburg and a brother of the duke of Poland. In the Iberian peninsula four campaigns were conducted: by the Genoese against Minorca, by Alfonso VII of Castile against Almeria, by the count of Barcelona against Tortosa and by Alfonso Henriques of Portugal against Santarem and Lisbon. Contemporaries saw all these expeditions as parts of a single enterprise: 'To its initiators it seemed that one part of the army should be sent to the eastern regions, another to Spain and a third against the Slavs who live next to us.' At the same time, although not technically part of the crusade, a powerful Sicilian Norman fleet extended Roger of Sicily's rule over the North African coast from Tripoli to Tunis. Nothing like this had been seen since the fall of the Roman empire; nor was it often to be seen again.

In many respects great care was taken in its preparation. The pope joined Bernard in preaching and recruitment and, although they may have differed slightly in their theologies of penance, the two men proposed a very advanced type of remission of sins. We have seen that Urban II's remission had been simply a guarantee that the labour of crusading was so unpleasant that it would constitute an entirely satisfactory penance. With Eugenius and Bernard the emphasis shifted from the penitent's self-imposed punishment to God's merciful kindness, confirmed by the Power of the Keys, by means of which the pope could assure sinners of the remission of punishment as a reward for the action undertaken.

> If you are a prudent merchant, if you are a man fond of acquiring this world's goods, I am showing you certain great markets; make sure not to let the chance pass you by. Take the sign of the cross and you will obtain in equal measure remission of all the sins which you have confessed with a contrite heart. If the cloth itself is sold it does not fetch much; if it is worn on a faithful shoulder it is certain to be worth the kingdom of God.

They exploited pride in the past crusading experiences of previous generations, which had been locked into the collective memory of some cousinhoods.

It will be seen as a great token of nobility and uprightness if those things acquired by the efforts of your fathers are vigorously defended by you, their good sons. But if, God forbid, it comes to pass differently, then the bravery of the fathers will have proved to be diminished in the sons.

The success of their propaganda can be measured not only by the response to it – the so-called Second Crusade was much the largest since the First – but also by the number of those taking the cross who came from families which had provided recruits to earlier expeditions. This suggests that by the middle of the twelfth century there was a pool of potential crusaders, drawn especially from those committed kindred-groups in which recruitment had been concentrated at the time of the First Crusade, even if it had been dormant since. At this stage the movement was developing as much below the surface in the collective consciousness of certain noble and knightly families as in action and in the thinking of the theoreticians.

Eugenius appointed Cardinals Theodwin of Porto and Guido of San Chrysogono as legates in the French army, to be assisted by Bishops Arnulf of Lisieux, Godfrey of Langres and Alvis of Arras. Bishop Anselm of Havelberg was made chief legate for the Wendish Crusade, to be assisted by Bishop Henry of Olmütz, who had originally been appointed legate for Conrad of Germany's army, and Wibald of Stavelot, the abbot of Corvey. Eugenius and Louis wrote to the kings of Hungary and Sicily and the Byzantine emperor Manuel Comnenus, informing them of their plans and asking for provisions and passage. Manuel replied cautiously, suggesting in one letter to the pope that the crusaders take the same oaths of homage to him as their predecessors had made to Alexius and asking in another for guarantees from the French that they would not harm the empire and would return to it cities which had once been under its control. Louis adopted a practical measure to cope with the problem of expenses by raising a levy, perhaps the imposition of feudal aids, which was the first example of the subsidies and taxes that were to transform crusading in the thirteenth century. Conrad saw to it that roads through Germany were improved and bridges were repaired. There were splendid and solemn assemblies in France and Germany at which plans were discussed. But from all this planning there was a glaring omission: there was no consultation with the Latin rulers in the East. Twelve years later Pope Adrian IV was to remind Louis forcefully of this, pointing out the harm that resulted. The only possible explanation is that, although of course they planned to end their crusade with a pilgrimage to Jerusalem, Louis and Conrad were intending to march directly across Anatolia to Edessa, by-passing even the principality of Antioch.

This must have been in the minds of those who took part in the French assembly at Étampes on 16 February 1147, which had to make the final choice of a route to the East. It had before it two options: to follow the overland road by way of the Balkans, Constantinople and Asia Minor, or to travel by sea from Sicily. Conrad of Germany, who was on very bad terms with Roger of Sicily, had apparently only considered the overland journey, which made sense if the prime target was Edessa. At Étampes there were divisions of opinion and a heated debate – it seems that one party, with the support of an embassy from Roger, warned the king of France against putting himself at the mercy of the Greeks by going to Constantinople – but the overland route was decided upon and departure was set for 15 June. The German assembly at Frankfurt on 13 March was informed of the French decision, announced an itinerary through Hungary and set the middle of May as the date for departure, so as to march a few weeks ahead of the French. The two armies which, like those of the First Crusade, contained many unarmed pilgrims as well as crusaders, were to join forces at Constantinople.

The Germans left on the appointed date and passed through Regensburg and Vienna into Hungary, the king of which had been persuaded that their passage would be more peaceful if he paid Conrad a large sum, levied from his church, with which to buy provisions. This measure, which must have been insisted on by crusaders who knew of the experiences of their predecessors, ensured that there was no trouble. The Germans then came to the frontiers of the Byzantine empire. Manuel was on good terms with Conrad, with whom he was bound by an alliance against the South Italian Normans; he had, moreover, recently married Bertha of Sulzbach, Conrad's relative and, it seems, his adopted daughter. He does not appear to have feared and distrusted the Germans as he did the French and his emissaries merely demanded an oath from them that they would not harm his interests in any way. When they had given this assurance the Germans were promised provisions and they marched by way of Niš, Sofia, Plovdiv and Edirne to Constantinople, which they reached after a journey free from major incident, although there were some instances of plundering and a few brushes with the imperial forces.

On good terms with Conrad Manuel might be, but he was not careless. Like his grandfather Alexius he was determined to deal with the crusade leaders separately by shipping them and their armies across to Asia as soon as possible after their arrival. He had even wanted Conrad to by-pass Constantinople and to cross the Dardanelles at Sestus. Conrad had demurred when this was first put to him, probably because he did not want to miss his rendezvous with Louis, but at the end of September, after about three weeks at Constantinople, he agreed to be transported across the Bosporus, perhaps because the Byzantines had asked him to help them against Roger of Sicily, who had now invaded Greece, and the request put him in an embarrassing position. At any rate his army, supplemented by a force from Lorraine which had now arrived, crossed the straits and pressed on into Asia Minor. At Nicaea it gathered provisions for an advance on Konya. But it was so large – Conrad's followers had rejected his sensible suggestion that the non-combatants should be sent separately to Jerusalem – and its advance was so slow that its supplies were soon exhausted. Somewhere near the site of the victory at Dorylaeum in 1097 it was ambushed and defeated. The German retreat became a rout, with the Turks harrying the columns at will, and the shattered army reached the relative safety of Nicaea at the beginning of November. Most of the crusaders now tried to return home, leaving Conrad and a much reduced force to send messengers begging Louis of France for aid.

Louis had taken splendid leave on 11 June when, at the abbey church of St Denis and in the presence of the pope, he had venerated the relic of St Denis, under whose patronage he was to believe himself to be throughout the crusade, had received the oriflamme, the sacred war-banner of his kingdom, and had been presented with his pilgrim's purse by Eugenius himself. From Metz, which had been chosen as the French mustering-point, his army marched by way of Worms to Regensburg, where it found boats ready to carry the baggage down the Danube as far as Bulgaria and where it began to follow the road already taken by the Germans. It was amply supplied by the Hungarians, with whose king Louis was on good terms, and, greatly to his personal cost, Louis was able to keep his army provisioned in Byzantine territory until it reached Constantinople on 4 October; like Conrad he refused to by-pass the city. Throughout the march he was forced to conduct negotiations with Manuel, whose ambassadors had met him at Regensburg. Manuel feared and distrusted the French. He knew there had been dealings with Roger of Sicily – in fact a party of French crusaders did travel to Constantinople by way of southern Italy – and he must have been conscious of the ties of sentiment and nationality that bound the French and the settlers in the Latin East. The latter included the prince of Antioch, who was the queen of France's uncle. Manuel's representatives may well have informed him of the statements made by members of a party within the crusade headed by Bishop Godfrey of Langres, which was bitterly hostile to the Greeks. So it is not surprising that he made more stringent demands of the French than of the Germans. Louis's advisers were prepared to agree not to seize any town or castle in Byzantine territory, but they were not ready to promise to return any place which had once belonged to Byzantium, which is understandable given that their intention was to recover Edessa, which in the distant past had been within the empire. The crusaders were bewildered by the news, which reached them when they were a day's march from Constantinople, that Manuel had made a treaty with the Turkish sultan at Konya, through whose territory they would have to pass. In their camp before Constantinople, the fortifications of which Manuel had strengthened, the bishop of Langres's party even proposed launching an attack upon the Byzantine capital.

The French waited for a fortnight for other armies they knew were coming from the West. Rumours of German successes ahead of them, which turned out to be false, made them restive and Louis had to agree to a crossing of the Bosporus. Further negotiations with the Greeks then held him up on the Asiatic side until the reinforcements arrived. In the end his agreement with Manuel did not specify the return of all past imperial territory. The crusaders made homage and promised not to take any place under imperial jurisdiction; in return they were promised guides and supplies and the Greeks recognized that they would have to plunder where provisions were not made available. At Nicaea the crusaders heard of the rout of the Germans and they were joined by Conrad and the remnants of his army. At Esseron they turned for the sea, hoping for an easier and better-supplied passage if they marched through Byzantine lands along the coast, although this meant the abandonment of the aim of recovering Edessa. At Ephesus Conrad, who was ill, left for Constantinople, but the French pressed on, ignoring a warning that the Turks were gathering to oppose them. By the time they reached Eskihisar on 3 or 4 January 1148 they were desperately short of provisions and the march to Antalya, which they reached on 20 January, was a terrible one. They suffered severely from Turkish harassing attacks which the Greek inhabitants and garrisons were unwilling to hinder, until the Templars who were with them were put in charge of order on the march. At Antalya, on the edge of Byzantine territory, the French found little in the way of supplies, particularly for their horses which were now being decimated by starvation. A fleet promised by the Greeks to transport them all to Antioch proved to be so small that it could only take a fraction of them.

In the end Louis embarked for Antioch having tried, as far as he could, to ensure that the bulk of his force was fitted out for the overland journey; in fact, only a small number managed to get through. It must be stressed that although for most of his march Louis had been leading his army through a region supposedly under Byzantine control, it had received little support from the population, the government or its officers, and the survivors can only have remembered the frustration and broken promises. A recent historical judgement is that Manuel's fear of the French was so great that he connived at their destruction. The French had been distrustful of the Byzantines before they had left France. Their experiences in the Balkans and Asia Minor had borne out the complaints of their predecessors and left them with an abiding bitterness.

Louis reached Antioch on 19 March. Refusing to take part in any campaign in Syria he wished only to press on to Jerusalem to fulfil his vow. Conrad and other German crusaders were already there, together with new arrivals from the West, and a council of war, held in Acre on 24 June and attended by a galaxy of Christian rulers and nobles from the Levant and Europe, decided to try to take Damascus. The proposal, which was only one of several discussed, was not as foolhardy as it is often supposed to have been. The destruction of the crusading armies in Asia Minor had put an end to any hope of retaking Edessa. Damascus had already been attacked by the settlers in 1126 and 1129, on the latter occasion with the aid of crusaders. There were strong religious and strategic reasons for occupying the chief city in Syria and there were sound political arguments as well. Zengi's career had shown how dangerous a united Muslim Syria could be and it could only be a matter of time before his son, Nur ad-Din, who had just married the governor of Damascus's daughter, took the city over unless he was forestalled.

In the middle of July the largest army yet put into the field by the Latins assembled at Tiberias under the command of Louis, Conrad and Baldwin III of Jerusalem. The leaders decided to attack Damascus, which had sent appeals for help to Nur ad-Din and his brother. The Christians approached the city from the west, where the suburban orchards would provide them with supplies of timber, food and water. Driving the Muslims back from the banks of the Barada river on 24 July, they occupied a good position from which to launch an assault, but they now made a bad decision. Knowing that the eastern wall was less well fortified and conscious that the impending arrival of Muslim armies of relief made a rapid capture imperative, they shifted their camp on 27 July to an exposed site with no water and little food. They were trapped as a result. The eastern walls may not have been recently improved but they were strong enough to hold besiegers up. The crusaders could not return to the western side, which was quickly reoccupied by the Muslims. They had placed themselves in a position from which they could only withdraw, which is what they did.

This ended the crusade and there were bitter recriminations and accusations of treachery, especially against individuals and institutions in the Latin East. The Greeks, of course, were roundly condemned for their treatment of the crusaders in Asia Minor and hostility towards them was fanned when a Sicilian squadron, in which the French king and his entourage were returning home, was attacked by a Byzantine fleet, which was still at war with Roger of Sicily. Louis narrowly escaped capture. His wife Eleanor of Aquitaine, whose behaviour at Antioch during the crusade had been atrocious enough to start the train of events which would lead to the annulment of the marriage a few years later, was in another ship and was detained by the Greeks for a time. On his arrival in

Italy Louis began to plan a new crusade with Roger of Sicily and Pope Eugenius, which, like Bohemond of Taranto's, would wreak vengeance on the Greeks on its way to the East.

Meanwhile in north-eastern Germany a large army under Henry the Lion set out from Artlenburg in the middle of July 1147 and laid siege to the Wendish stronghold of Dobin, before which it was joined by the Danes. The siege, marked by a Wendish sortie that routed the Danes, ended inconclusively with a peace treaty according to which the Wends renounced idolatry and the Wendish prince Niklot became an ally and tributary of Count Adolf of Holstein, with whom he had had good relations before the crusade had disrupted them. Early in August the main force under Albert the Bear, which was certainly massive, left Magdeburg and, crossing the Elbe, raided enemy country before dividing, with one part laying siege unsuccessfully to Demmin and the other marching on Szczecin (Stettin), which was in fact already Christian.

More was achieved in Spain. The first party of crusaders to leave home, men from the Low Countries, the Rhineland, northern France and Britain, set sail from Dartmouth and arrived at Porto (Oporto) in Portugal in June 1147. The Portuguese, who had taken Santarem from the Moors three months before, persuaded them to take part in the siege of Lisbon, which fell to them on 24 October. In the east of the peninsula, Almeria, the chief Andalusian port for trade with Africa and the Near East, fell to a combined Castilian, Aragonese, south French, Genoese and Pisan force on 17 October. At the end of 1148 the Aragonese, south French and Genoese went on to take Tortosa and in the autumn of 1149 they occupied Lérida, Fraga and Mequinenza, the last Muslim outposts in Catalonia.

But the Spanish crusade was the only success, as contemporaries, particularly English ones who were proud of their compatriots, were quick to point out. Elsewhere this huge burst of activity had had nugatory results and the crusading movement plumbed depths of despair to which it did not return until the fifteenth century. A strategy on this scale was never to be attempted again. Two German commentators even took the view that the whole enterprise had been accursed. To a Würzburg annalist it had been the work of the devil, a revolt against God's righteous punishment, inspired by 'pseudo-prophets, sons of Belial and witnesses of Anti-Christ, who by stupid words misled the Christians and by empty preaching induced all sorts of men to go'. To Gerhoh of Reichersberg there was link between the disasters and the presence in this world of Anti-Christ. The Latin settlers had displayed avarice and the crusaders, who had deviated from rectitude, had been allowed by God to be deceived by preachers and false miracles to perish in the East. Other commentators, echoing the interpretations of the disasters of 1101, also explained the failures in the East as a punishment meted out on the crusaders themselves, whose wicked behaviour had led God to withdraw his favour, and they tended to attribute the successes in Spain to the humility of the crusaders there. In this storm of protest and obloquy the dignity and forbearance of two leading Cistercian participants stand out. Bishop Otto of Freising, Conrad's half-brother and the leader of one of the German armies in Asia Minor, attributed failure to the mysterious but always benevolent ways of God: 'Although our expedition was not good for the extension of boundaries or for the comfort of our bodies, it was good for the salvation of many souls.' So did Bernard of Clairvaux, the 'pseudo-prophet' on whom, most woundingly but expectedly, the opprobrium fell. Bernard was inspired to write one of the finest expositions of resignation to the will of God in Christian literature.

How can human beings be so rash as to dare to pass judgement on something that they are not in the least able to understand? It might perhaps be a comfort for us to bear in mind the heavenly judgements that were made of old. ... For ... it is true that the hearts of mortal men are made in this way: we forget when we need it what we know when we do not need it. ... The promises of God never prejudice the justice of God.

Low morale

The failure of the Second Crusade ushered in a period in which for nearly forty years Christian demoralization was reflected in a low level of crusading. Papal authority over the movement may have been established by Bernard and Eugenius, but its benefits must have seemed doubtful even to the popes. The planning of a new crusade after Louis of France's return to the West came to nothing. Crises in the East continued to occur and they were invariably followed by embassies to the West begging for help. Most of the appeals were directed to Louis VII of France, because of his known piety and commitment, and Dr Phillips has demonstrated how under King Amalric particularly interesting experiments in public relations were made, including the despatch to Louis of the keys of the city of Jerusalem, recalling an offer made by the patriarch to Charlemagne three and a half centuries before. In response, as in 1120 and 1145, the popes issued general letters, formally summoning the faithful to crusade in the East, in 1157, 1165, 1166, 1169, probably in 1173, in 1181 and 1184. It would be wrong to say that these had no effect. In 1166 Henry of England and Louis of France planned the levying of an income and capital tax, similar to the Saladin Tithe of 1188; some money was eventually sent to Jerusalem. And several small expeditions, like that of Philip of Flanders in 1177, did reach the East. But on the whole the papal appeals fell on deaf ears and with good reason. While Jerusalem and most of the territory conquered in the first half of the century was still in

Christian hands, crusades, that is to say large armies of temporary soldiers who would return home once their vows had been fulfilled, were not the answer to the settlers' predicament, because they required not the conquest of new land, but an increase in the forces permanently garrisoning the territory already held. This is why there was so much emphasis in these years on measures to increase the standing defence, for example Henry of England's promise in 1172 to maintain 200 knights in Jerusalem for a year as part of his penance for the murder of Thomas Becket. Furthermore, until 1170 the kingdom of Jerusalem must have appeared quite strong to the European public, since it had been prepared to embark on its own campaigns of territorial aggrandizement.

The popes who tried vainly to rouse Christians to service in the East made few efforts to intervene in other theatres, where warfare continued spasmodically, whether dignified with the title of crusade or not, and historians are faced with great problems when they try to distinguish crusades from other engagements in this chronic violence. Remissions of sin, for example, were still occasionally granted without formal papal authorization. Papal legates in Spain, and even Spanish bishops, issued them on their own initiative and in 1166 the council of Segovia was prepared to offer the same remission as that granted to pilgrims to Jerusalem to those who would defend Castile against, apparently, Christian invaders. The participants in a high point in the Moorish wars in these years, the defence of Huete in 1172, were granted remission of sins, but no letter of authorization was apparently written. Almoravid power collapsed and gave way to representatives of another North African religious movement, the Almohads, who seized Morocco in 1145, crossed into Europe and occupied Cordoba, Jaén, Malaga and Granada. They retook Almeria in 1157, together with Ubeda and Baeza. During fifty-five years of bitter warfare, from 1157 to 1212, the Christians were forced onto the defensive. In the north the Danes under King Valdemar I, often in alliance with Henry the Lion of Saxony, were particularly active, stung by raids on their coastline by Wendish slave-traders. Their efforts culminated in the capture of Rügen in 1168. They then began to attack the peoples living at the mouth of the Oder and the conquest of Pomerania was accompanied by the foundation of monasteries as centres of active missionary work.

Against this background, the scarcity of papal crusade letters issued for theatres other than the East is striking and is perhaps another sign of demoralization. With respect to Spain there were only three papal crusade authorizations, written in 1153, 1157–8 and 1175, and there was only one authorizing crusading in northern Europe. Issued by Pope Alexander III, probably in 1171, it offered only a limited remission and its wording suggests that the pope thought the conflict with the Slavs was over and that the next enemies to be dealt with were the Finns and Estonians further east, although it was not until 1184 that the Danes began to think seriously of carrying war to the eastern Baltic and even then their plans did not materialize.

The most significant development in the Iberian peninsula in this period was the establishment of national military orders, drawing their inspiration partly from the Hospitallers and Templars, partly from short-lived societies founded by Alfonso I of Aragon to defend Saragossa in 1122 and Monreal del Campo c. 1128. The first Spanish military order came into existence when in 1157 the Templars returned the exposed frontier castle of Calatrava to King Sancho III of Castile. At the king's court in Toledo was Raimundo, abbot of the Cistercian abbey of Fitero. One of his monks, Diego Velázquez, who had been a knight, persuaded him to ask for the castle and volunteers were summoned to defend it. Many of these men were formed into a confraternity and in 1164 they were admitted into the Cistercian Order and were given a modified Cistercian rule. The foundation of the Order of Calatrava was followed by those of Evora, later known as Avis and affiliated to Calatrava soon after 1166; Santiago in 1170; Montegaudio, which was absorbed by Calatrava c. 1221, c. 1173; and San Julian del Pereiro, which was also affiliated to Calatrava and in the thirteenth century took the name of Alcántara, shortly before 1176. These orders flourished in Castile, León and Portugal, but not in Aragon, where the Templars, who after much soul-searching decided to fight in Spain in 1143, and the Hospitallers were predominant. They were used to defend the invasion routes leading from Almohad territory, but they also undertook military campaigns, ransomed prisoners and actively settled the frontier regions under their control with Christian peasants. Their emergence signalled a developing feature of the crusading movement in Spain, its national character. Half a century before, the Spaniards had been joined by many volunteers from across the Pyrenees, but now these came less, partly because the Spaniards themselves resented them. In February 1159 Adrian IV had to discourage Louis of France and Henry of England from campaigning in the peninsula unless they had the permission of the kings there and he made it clear that they would not be welcome without prior negotiations. The Spanish Reconquest was becoming a war of national liberation and the Spanish crusades were with a few exceptions to be nationalistic and under the control of the local rulers.

In papal pronouncements on the remission of sins, whether for crusades to the East or elsewhere, there was a drawing in of horns, which may be further evidence of a lack of morale. Two approaches to penance were now competing with one another. The first, the old view, was that if a penance was severe enough – a six-month fast on bread and water, for example, or a pilgrimage on foot to Rome – it could be 'satisfactory', by which was meant that it could make adequate satisfaction to God for sin.

The second was that it was doubtful whether any penance could ever be satisfactory. The sinner, therefore, had to rely on God's mercy to make good any deficiency and a free and generous remission of all punishment, detached, in a sense, from the nature of the penance performed, could be granted by the pope on God's behalf. It was the old view that had been expressed in the earliest 'indulgences', among them Urban II's grant of full remission of sins to the first crusaders in 1095. The second, and increasingly popular, opinion was already implicit in the writings of Bernard of Clairvaux at the time of the Second Crusade and was also to be found in Eugenius III's *Quantum praedecessores*, perhaps written under Bernard's influence. In 1157, 1165 and 1166 Adrian IV and Alexander III resorted to variations of the very advanced formulation to be found in *Quantum praedecessores*. This must have worried the papal curia, because by 1169 the decision was made to return to the old-fashioned concept that the crusade was simply a satisfactory penance. In Alexander's appeal of that year this was stressed by referring explicitly to 'that remission of penance imposed by the priestly ministry which Urban and Eugenius are known to have established'. For the next thirty years the papacy was to stick to this conservative formulation in spite of the vast strides being made in penitential theology. As late as 1187 and the great letter *Audita tremendi* which launched the Third Crusade it was still being firmly expressed:

> To those who with contrite hearts and humbled spirits undertake the labour of this journey and die in penitence for their sins and with right faith we promise full indulgence of their faults and eternal life; whether surviving or dying they shall know that through the mercy of God and the authority of the apostles Peter and Paul, and our authority, they will have relaxation of the satisfaction imposed for all their sins of which they have made proper confession.

A contemporary propagandist, Peter of Blois, explained that this was a declaration of the worth of the exercise as a satisfactory penance:

> By the privilege of the apostle Peter and the general authority of the Church the Lord had intended in this sign [of the cross] a means of reconciliation; so that the assumption of the commitment to journey to Jerusalem should be the highest form of penance and sufficient satisfaction for sins committed.

The development of traditions

The years from 1102 to 1187, therefore, witnessed some decades of confusion, an extraordinarily ambitious fiasco and then a period in which the movement was at a low ebb in spite of activity in all the theatres of war. Crusading still lacked maturity, but it was developing all the time. It had diversified to include wars against Muslims in the Iberian peninsula and pagans beyond the north-eastern frontier of Christendom. It had threatened papal enemies in the interior of Europe. In Spain it had begun to develop individual features. European rulers were beginning to take part and there had been the first steps in organizing financing. The popes had established their right to authorize these wars and they had got into the habit of issuing general crusade letters in which the remission of sins had been formulated and reformulated. However unsuccessful many of these letters had been in recruiting crusaders, they had given the draftsmen at the curia practice in drawing up the privileges of protection, legal immunity and spiritual benefits which came to be so precisely expressed in the thirteenth century. And a stream of pilgrims, unarmed and armed, and of little parties of crusaders had flowed out to Palestine, demonstrating that although Christians had been demoralized by the failure of the Second Crusade and were not inspired to mount a major expedition, their faith and commitment to the Holy Land had not been shaken.

It was during the twelfth century, moreover, that European noble and knightly families built up traditions of crusading which were to benefit the movement in the thirteenth. Countless examples are to be found. For instance, Count Thierry of Flanders, a nephew of the Count Robert who had played a distinguished role in the First Crusade, took part in the Second Crusade and also visited the East in 1139, 1157 and 1164. His wife, Sibylla of Anjou, King Fulk of Jerusalem's daughter by his first marriage, ended her days as a nun at Bethany. His son Philip led an armed company to the East in 1177 and died during the Third Crusade. His grandson Baldwin was a leader of the Fourth Crusade and became the first Latin emperor of Constantinople. The careers of the ancestors of John of Joinville, who accompanied Louis IX of France to the East in 1248, demonstrate how an example set before 1187 bore fruit in commitment later, although it should be noted that the family provided seneschals to the counts of Champagne, a line of men obsessed with crusading. Geoffrey III of Joinville took part in the Second Crusade. Geoffrey IV died on the Third Crusade. Geoffrey V, who had accompanied his father on the Third Crusade, took the cross again for the Fourth and died on it. Simon, John's father, took the cross for the Albigensian Crusade and again for the Fifth. In the development of these traditions European laymen were appropriating crusading for themselves at a time when churchmen were expressing a growing respect for the idea of a lay vocation. We have seen that theologians working just after the liberation of Jerusalem in 1099 had been concerned to monasticize the movement and to treat crusaders as temporary quasi-monks. Echoes of this attitude can still be found at the time of the Second Crusade, which is not surprising in view of the influence on it of the Cistercians Eugenius and Bernard, but by the Third Crusade the movement's character was much more clearly that of a lay devotion. The element of religious profession had anyway been channelled into the ethos of the military orders, while the idea and practice of chivalry were beginning to dilute the notion of the crusade as a penitential exercise. The family traditions built up before 1187 meant that crusading was now part of the secular concerns of lineage, reputation and domestic custom. In this, as in other respects, western Europe had been unconsciously preparing itself for its response to the loss of Jerusalem to Saladin.

CHAPTER 6

Crusading comes of Age, 1187–1229

The Third Crusade

The news of the catastrophe at Hattin and the fall of Jerusalem reached the West in the early autumn of 1187. The old pope, Urban III, died, it was said of grief, on 20 October. Within ten days his successor, Gregory VIII, was sending out an appeal for a new crusade. This general letter, *Audita tremendi*, is one of the most moving documents of crusading history. It must have been drafted by Urban before his death, since the eight days that elapsed between Gregory's election on 21 October and the date of the earliest surviving versions of it is too short a time for such an important document to have been composed, approved, corrected and copied. It opened with a lament over recent events in Palestine and then in a profoundly theological passage attributed the disasters to punishment for the sins not only of the Latin settlers but also of all Christians, whom it summoned to acts of penance:

> Faced by such great distress concerning that land, moreover, we ought to consider not only the sins of its inhabitants but also our own and those of the whole Christian people. ... It is, therefore, incumbent upon all of us to consider and to choose to amend our sins by voluntary chastisement and to turn to the Lord our God with penance and works of piety; and we should first amend in ourselves what we have done wrong and then turn our attention to the treachery and malice of the enemy.

It went on to remind Christians of the transitory nature of this world and appealed to them to 'accept with an act of thanksgiving the opportunity for repentance and doing good', by going to the aid of the Latin East 'according to the will of God who taught by his own action that one ought to lay down one's life for one's brothers'. It ended with a conventional list of privileges for crusaders, including an old-fashioned remission of sins, and a sumptuary clause. It was echoed in the preaching of the crusade, which was everywhere characterized by calls to repentance. This marked an important stage in the development of crusading thought, for the papacy was now associating success in war directly with the spiritual health of all Christianity, a train of thought which manifested itself until the sixteenth century in the way general councils, summoned to reform Christendom, were often associated with the need to assure crusading success.

The news had been brought to Rome by Genoese merchants. Hard on their heels came Joscius, the archbishop of Tyre, the only city on the Palestinian coast still in Christian hands. Tyre was being energetically defended under the leadership of Conrad of Montferrat, the younger brother of Sibylla of Jerusalem's first husband, who had arrived in Palestine in the wake of the disaster and himself showered the West with appeals for aid. Archbishop Joscius sailed in the late summer to Sicily, where King William II responded by immediately despatching a fleet. In the spring and summer of 1188 this saved Tripoli and provisioned Antioch and Tyre, making an important contribution to the survival of the settlements. Joscius must have reached Rome in the middle of October. He then travelled in winter-time to France and on 22 January 1188 met Henry II of England and Philip II of France at Gisors, on the frontier between the duchy of Normandy and the royal domain, where the kings were meeting to discuss the drafting of a truce between them. Presented with his appeal, the kings and Philip of Flanders and the other magnates who were with them took the cross and began to make plans. Following a practice begun on the Second Crusade, when the Wendish campaigners had worn distinctive crosses, it was decided that the crusaders of each nation would wear crosses of different colours: the French red, the English white and the Flemish green. Henry and Philip agreed to levy a general tax for the crusade, the second, in fact, of the decade and known as the Saladin Tithe.

The vicious politics of western Europe then intervened. War broke out between Henry's eldest surviving son, Count Richard of Poitou, and the count of Toulouse. The kings of England and France became embroiled and relations between them reached a low point when Richard switched support to the king of France and by the summer of 1189 was in open revolt. Henry died on 6 July, shortly after reaching a settlement on the crusade with Philip, and Richard was crowned king of England on 3 September. A storm of protest had blown up at the delays and the reasons for them. Richard had taken the cross earlier than had his father and the force of public opinion was such that he could no longer put off the expedition, even had he wanted to. In November he agreed to join forces with Philip at Vézelay on 1 April 1190. The date of mustering was later put back to 1 July, but the English and French crusades were at last in train.

The vacillation of the English and French kings looked very bad when compared to the response in Germany. The emperor Frederick I was now nearly seventy and had governed Germany for thirty-six years. He was a vigorous old man, with tremendous physical stamina, and he was intelligent and adaptable, with a strong personality and a penchant for flamboyance that had sometimes led him into scrapes. He had been on the Second Crusade forty years before and his mind had occasionally turned to crusading in the interim. How far his commitment to the movement was conventional piety, or speculative and associated with conceptions of the duty of emperors to defend Christendom, or even eschatological and influenced by the idea of the last Christian emperor who would rule Jerusalem before the advent of Anti-Christ, is now hard to tell. But he was in the mood to respond to Henry of Marcy (Cardinal Henry of Albano), himself a distinguished crusade theoretician, who was sent by Pope Gregory to preach the cross in Germany. Frederick was deeply moved by a crusade sermon preached by Bishop Henry of Strasbourg in December 1187 although, being the man he was, he took a few months to make up his mind that Germany could survive his absence. In a typically theatrical gesture he then summoned a special court, a *curia Jesu Christi*, to be presided over not by himself but by Christ, and on *Laetare* Sunday (27 March 1188), when the introit of the Mass begins 'Rejoice Jerusalem and come together all you that love her. Rejoice with joy you who have been in sorrow!', he and many German nobles took the cross in Henry of Marcy's presence; this was predictably the signal for an anti-Jewish riot. Their date of departure was set for the feast of St George, 23 April 1189, and the land route was again chosen. The Hungarians, Serbians, Greeks and even the Turks of Konya were told of their plans. The Greeks received the assurance that there would be a peaceful passage through their empire and they in turn promised to provide guides and supplies. Final arrangements were made at Regensburg, where the crusaders gathered on the appointed date, and on 11 May 1189 the army began its march.

It contained many leading figures in the German Church and nobility and it must have been one of the largest crusading armies ever to take the field. It was very well organized and discipline was strictly enforced, but it began to be harassed by brigands as it passed through regions of the Balkans under Byzantine control. The markets which had been promised were not opened and there was no evidence of preparations for the Germans' arrival. In fact the Byzantine emperor Isaac Angelus had made a pact with Saladin in which he had agreed to delay and destroy them, and obstacles were deliberately, though not very effectively, put in their path. Isaac foolishly tried to bring pressure to bear by arresting Frederick's ambassadors and holding them as hostages, while his officers' vain attempt to use regular troops to block the advance was brushed aside. By the time the Germans occupied Plovdiv on 26 August they were in no mood to be thwarted, and Isaac's refusal of passage across the Dardanelles until Frederick sent him more hostages and promised to surrender half his future conquests was ignored. The Germans resorted to plundering and Frederick, who was negotiating with Serbian and Vlacho-Bulgarian rebels against Byzantium, also began to think seriously of attacking Constantinople itself. On 16 November he wrote to his eldest son Henry, asking him to persuade the Italian maritime cities to raise a fleet to join him before Constantinople in the following March to lay siege to the city.

Isaac had been forced to return the German ambassadors at the end of October, but the next few exchanges were soured by his refusal to address Frederick by his proper title, another issue on which he had to climb down. Frederick moved his winter quarters to Edirne and now held a large area of Thrace, while negotiations with an increasingly panic-stricken Byzantine government continued. On 14 February 1190 Isaac at last agreed to furnish ships for transport across the Dardanelles from Gallipoli (Gelibolu) – at least, unlike his predecessors, he had persuaded the Germans to by-pass Constantinople – to provide markets, supplies and hostages, to release the western prisoners he held and to pay reparations, and he accepted that the Germans would expect to forage in those regions where provisions were not supplied.

The Germans left Edirne on 1 March and crossed the Dardanelles between the 22nd and the 28th. In Byzantine Asia Minor, however, they met with the same harassment and non-cooperation they had experienced in Europe. Leaving Alaşehir on 22 April, they entered Muslim territory and made straight for Konya. On the march they suffered as their predecessors had done – their horses and pack animals died and they ran out of food – but Konya fell to them on 18 May. Refreshed by the stores they found there and promised adequate supplies by the Turks, who were now anxious to let them through in peace, they reached Karaman, on the borders of Cilicia, on the 30th. Here they were again in Christian territory and they were greeted with friendliness by the Armenians, but on 10 June Frederick, who had proved that it was still possible to march an army through Asia Minor and was exuberant and hot, succumbed to the temptation of one last *coup de théâtre*, this time fatal for him. He tried to swim the river Göksu, which is deep and wide. In mid-stream he got into difficulties. Perhaps he had a heart-attack. At any rate he was dead or drowned by the time his nobles reached him.

The German crusade, which had done so well, brushing the Byzantines aside with icy efficiency and marching in a disciplined fashion across Turkish Asia Minor, was broken by his death. Some crusaders left at once for home. The rest divided into those who sailed to Antioch and Tripoli and those who marched overland to Syria, losing many of their number in the process. At Antioch the army was further decimated by disease. It began its journey down the coast in late August and early in October arrived before Acre, which had been besieged by the Christians for eighteen months. King Guy of Jerusalem had been released by Saladin in the summer of 1188, but in the following spring Conrad of Montferrat, who denied his right to the kingship, had refused him and Queen Sibylla entry into Tyre. Guy's reaction had been courageous. He had marched south with very few troops to lay siege to Acre. His action had forced his leading vassals, who had remained neutral or had sided with Conrad, to join him and by the following autumn many of them were with him. This so weakened Conrad that in September 1189 he was persuaded to take part in the siege and by the spring of 1190 he had made peace with Guy in return for the promise of a fief in northern Palestine, including Tyre. Guy had been joined over the months by various parties of crusaders, among them a contingent of Germans, Netherlanders and English in September 1189 and a French army under the counts of Champagne, Blois and Sancerre in July 1190. It might be supposed that the arrival of the main German force would have strengthened the besieging host, but the Germans, demoralized and sick, continued to sustain heavy losses, among them the old emperor's son, Duke Frederick of Swabia, who died on 20 January 1191. By the following spring most of them had left for home.

Meanwhile Richard of England and Philip of France, who, like his father forty-three years before, had been presented with the oriflamme in the church of St Denis, had met at Vézelay. On 4 July 1190 they began their march to the Mediterranean coast. Richard was nearly thirty-three years old. His courage, resourcefulness and administrative ability showed up best on the battlefield and on campaign: he was to prove to be the finest crusade commander since Bohemond of Taranto and possibly the best of all. He was vain – he was very good-looking – but he was also efficient and he had a sense of humour. He had inherited a competent and energetic apparatus of government, which had thrown itself into making preparations from the moment his father had agreed to crusade. The archbishop of Canterbury had organized systematic preaching throughout the country and in spite of bitter opposition the Saladin Tithe had been collected. To supplement it Richard had sold everything that could be sold and had ruthlessly exploited every relationship for cash and every opportunity to raise enormous sums of money. He therefore found himself in fairly comfortable circumstances and his superior financial resources were apparent throughout the crusade. Philip was a younger man, still only in his mid-twenties. He was not impressive to look at – he had already lost the sight of one eye – and ten years of government of France had made him cautious and distrustful, cynical and nervous. He was not clever or well educated, but he was sharp, with a practical intelligence, and he had a capacity for hard work and taking pains, combined with self-control, a disposition towards prudence and equity. Ruthless he might be but he was usually ruthlessly fair. He ruled a far less centralized country than Richard did and he could not override the opposition to the Saladin Tithe. He was forced to state publicly that it would never again be levied and outside the royal domain it was collected by his great magnates for their own crusading needs. So he was much less well off than Richard although he led a larger army: about 2,000 mounted men to 800 at the most.

Richard had expected to find an English fleet at Marseille, but it had stopped off in Portugal and had not yet arrived. Hiring other ships, he reached Messina in Sicily on 22 September to find his fleet from England and Philip of France already there. He had business to transact in Sicily which would help him to raise even more cash for his crusade. His sister Joan was the widow of King William II and he wanted her dowry back from Tancred, count of Lecce, who had seized the throne, together with a legacy left by William to his father. He resorted to violence, seizing the Calabrian town of Bagnara, across the straits from Messina, and on 4 October Messina itself, which was sacked by his troops. Tancred was forced to pay 40,000 gold ounces, half for Joan's dowry and half as a marriage portion for his daughter, who was betrothed to Arthur of Brittany, Richard's heir, although Philip managed to get one-third of the gold for himself on the basis of an agreement made by the two kings at Vézelay to share their acquisitions.

Philip sailed for the East on 30 March 1191. Richard, who had stayed to meet his fiancée, Berengaria of Navarre – his betrothal was a delicate issue since he had been engaged to Philip's sister Alice – sailed on 10 April. His fleet cruised by way of Crete and Rhodes to Cyprus, which he reached on 6 May. The Greek ruler of the island, Isaac Comnenus, who had declared his independence of Constantinople in the 1180s, had imprisoned some English crusaders whose vessels, including one of the royal treasure ships, had been wrecked in a storm off the southern coast. The great ship carrying Berengaria and Joan was hove to offshore, fearful of making a landing. Richard at once demanded the return of his men and goods. When Isaac refused, Richard invaded the island and by 5 June, when he left for Acre, it was in his hands. It was to remain under Latin control for nearly four hundred years.

Philip reached Acre on 20 April and Richard on 8 June. They found the city blockaded. Forces had continued to arrive during the autumn, winter and spring of 1190–1, including an English advance party under the archbishop of Canterbury. Like all crusades, the army was a confederation of contingents under different leaders and it was divided over political developments in the kingdom of Jerusalem. Sibylla and the two daughters she had borne Guy had died in the autumn of 1190. This meant, of course, that although Guy was the anointed king, the heiress to Jerusalem was now Isabella, Sibylla's younger half-sister, who was married to Humphrey of Toron. It will be remembered that it had been Humphrey's defection that had destroyed the baronial rebellion in 1186. A group of leading nobles, including Balian of Ibelin, lord of Nablus and the husband of Isabella's mother Maria Comnena, and the lords of Sidon and Haifa, planned to have Isabella's marriage to Humphrey annulled so that she could be wed to Conrad of Montferrat, who was well connected and had proved his ability and the strength of his personality. Isabella was abducted from her tent in the camp before Acre and an ecclesiastical court, dominated by the papal legate, who was a supporter of Conrad, and by Conrad's cousin, the bishop of Beauvais, ruled that her marriage to Humphrey had been invalid, much to the disgust of the archbishop of Canterbury, who represented the sick patriarch of Jerusalem at the hearings. Isabella was hurriedly wed to Conrad. The marriage was later considered to have been bigamous and technically incestuous, since Conrad's brother had been married to Isabella's half-sister. She then formally required the kingdom from the High Court. She was accepted and homage was paid to her. It looked as though Guy of Lusignan was being put aside.

It was certain that the two European kings would be asked to arbitrate in this affair – Richard had been met in Cyprus by Guy, Humphrey of Toron and their supporters – and it was also certain that their responses would be different, because each was entangled in the skeins of western feudal and family relationships. Conrad was Philip of France's cousin. Guy's family, the Lusignans, were feudatories, although extremely difficult ones, of Richard's county of Poitou and they were rival claimants to a prize which had been seized by his father. I have already referred to the fact that the first crusaders Hugh of Lusignan and Raymond of St Gilles had shared the same mother, Almodis of La Marche. Guy and Richard were both descended from her, Richard through his mother Eleanor of Aquitaine. In December 1177 the last count of La Marche of the house of Charroux, whose only son was dead and whose daughter was infertile, had sold his county to King Henry of England for an insignificant sum. There were rumours that Henry had put pressure on him to do so. Geoffrey of Lusignan, Guy's elder brother who headed the family on behalf of his youthful nephew Hugh IX, claimed La Marche for himself and his brothers by virtue of descent from Almodis's eldest son, Hugh VI of Lusignan, whereas Eleanor of Aquitaine could claim descent only through a daughter of Almodis's third son. Geoffrey tried to take La Marche by force. He failed, but the Lusignans did not give up their claims and were denying Richard control of the county, which they eventually got by kidnapping the aged Eleanor of Aquitaine in 1199 and holding her until it was surrendered to them. Given the need to placate an angry family, it is not surprising that during the Third Crusade Richard was to show the Lusignans exceptional marks of favour.

The kings of France and England agreed to adjudicate on the issue of the crown of Jerusalem and the course of events strengthened their hands. Acre capitulated on 12 July, in spite of a last-minute attempt by Saladin to save it, and as conquerors Philip and Richard divided the city between them in accordance with their agreement on the division of spoils. This meant that their decisions on the allocation of what had been royal property could effectively decide the winner in the competition for the throne. On 28 July they announced a compromise. Guy was to have the kingdom for the rest of his life, but after his death Isabella and Conrad would inherit it. All royal rents were to be shared and apanages were to be created in the south – Jaffa and Ascalon – for Guy's brother Geoffrey, and in the north – Tyre, Sidon and Beirut – for Conrad. Philip then gave Conrad his half of Acre, against Richard's wishes, and left for home on 31 July. A large body of French crusaders, under the leadership of the duke of Burgundy, remained in Palestine and was to play an important part in the events that followed.

The terms of the agreement for the surrender of Acre had been that the garrison was to be released on the promise of a ransom of 200,000 dinars; the relic of the True Cross, lost at Hattin, was to be returned; and a large number of Christian prisoners were to be set free. Hostages were to be held by the crusaders pending the fulfilment of these conditions, but negotiations with Saladin broke down when the first instalment of the ransom became due and in a fit of rage Richard ordered the massacre of most of them, some 2,700 men, in the sight of the Muslim army that was still encamped near Acre. He then decided to strike for Jerusalem, which meant first marching to the port of Jaffa, seventy miles down the coast. His army set out on 22 August and was regularly supplied by the Christian fleet. The knights were organized in three divisions, marching in column. Inland from them, on their left flank, there was a protective screen of foot soldiers, who had to ward off most of the attacks. Half of the infantry were periodically rested by allowing them to march with the baggage-train that trundled between the knights and the sea. In what has been described as 'a classic demonstration of Frankish military tactics at their best', the army kept a steady disciplined progress in spite of being continually harassed by Muslim skirmishers and light cavalry. The self-restraint displayed by the infantry was remarkable for the time and in so far as it was a response to Richard's leadership, demonstrated that he was a field commander of the highest calibre. On 7 September Saladin managed to bring him to battle north of Arsuf, where the road passed through a gap between a forest and the sea. He used conventional tactics, seeking to weaken the Christian formation by archery and by attacking its flank and rear. The Hospitallers in the rearguard, maddened by their horses' injuries, launched into a charge too early and Richard had to order a general advance before he was ready, but he was able – and this is further evidence of his quality as a commander – to halt the charge once it had achieved its purpose and to re-form his line to meet a Muslim counter-attack. The Muslims eventually retired, leaving Richard's army, which had sustained comparatively light losses, in possession of the field.

Three days later the crusaders reached Jaffa and began to restore its fortifications. There were three options open to Richard: a treaty with Saladin; an immediate advance on Jerusalem, which was dangerous while there was a large Muslim army in the vicinity; or the occupation and refortification of Ascalon, the walls of which the Muslims were in the process of destroying, since this would limit Saladin's ability to bring up reserves from Egypt. At first Richard did not abandon any of these objectives. He began to concentrate all the troops he could at Jaffa, but he also entered into negotiations with Saladin for the cession of Palestine to the Christians. It was during these that he suggested his sister Joan as a wife for Saladin's brother. Saladin seems to have considered that this offer was not a serious one. By late October Richard had decided to advance on Jerusalem, although he proceeded very cautiously and by 23 December had only reached Latrun, half-way from Jaffa to the holy city. By 3 January he was at Beit Nuba, only twelve miles from Jerusalem, but then, on the advice of the local Christian leaders, he decided to withdraw and refortify Ascalon. On the 20th he reached the place and work on its walls went on until early June; on 23 May the fortress of Deir el Balah further south was taken by storm. Richard then decided to try for Jerusalem once more. His army marched on 7 June and on the 11th again reached Beit Nuba. It halted there until late in the month, but because his line of supplies back to Jaffa was threatened and he realized that his force was not large enough to hold Jerusalem, Richard again withdrew, after considering the option of an invasion of Egypt. On 26 July he returned to Acre.

Richard's withdrawal gave Saladin his chance. On the 27th he launched an attack on Jaffa, which was still weakly fortified. By the 30th the garrison was seeking terms, but Richard was already on his way by sea to relieve it. He arrived the following day to find the Muslims in possession of the town and the garrison in the process of surrendering the citadel. Wading ashore and supported by a sally from the citadel, in which the garrison had rallied, he drove the demoralized Muslims out of the town. An attempt on 5 August by Saladin to surprise Richard's tiny force, including perhaps fifty knights, of whom no more than ten had horses, and a few hundred crossbowmen, faltered as soon as the Muslims saw the Christians drawn up in a solid defensive formation.

Richard was not nearly as successful in local politics as he was on the battlefield. His support of Guy of Lusignan, to whom he was prepared to surrender his conquests, was frustrated by Conrad of Montferrat, the French crusaders and the local lords, who had never really accepted the compromise of 28 July 1191. They set out to undermine his military efforts, since they knew that the territory he gained would be handed over to Guy, and they negotiated behind his back with the Muslims in the hope of getting grants of land directly from Saladin. In February 1192 there was an unsuccessful attempt to seize Acre for Conrad. Richard came to realize that Guy's political situation was hopeless and on c. 13 April he summoned a council of his army and accepted the advice that Conrad should be king. He compensated Guy with the lordship of Cyprus; he had sold the island to the Templars but after a revolt against their rule they were anxious to return it. Within a fortnight, however, Conrad was dead, struck down in Tyre by Assassins. It was never known who had commissioned them, but the seizure of Richard as he returned from the crusade by Leopold V of Austria, who had taken part in the siege of Acre, and his imprisonment by the emperor Henry VI may well demonstrate that they, who were both Conrad's cousins, believed that he had been responsible, although Leopold and Philip of France, who was in touch with the emperor, also considered that they had been humiliated by him during the crusade. At any rate Isabella was now married, with Richard's consent if not on his initiative, to the crusader Count Henry of Champagne, who ruled the kingdom until his death in 1197.

By mid-August 1192 Richard had fallen ill. His crusade had lost impetus and he was worried by news of events in western Europe. On 2 September his representatives signed a truce with Saladin which was to last for three years and eight months. The Christians were to hold the coast from Tyre to Jaffa. Ascalon's fortifications were to be demolished before it was returned to Saladin. Christians and Muslims were to have free passage throughout Palestine. Many of the English crusaders visited the shrines in Jerusalem, although Richard did his best to prevent the French, whom he had not forgiven for frustrating his campaign, from going as well. He sailed from Acre on 9 October.

The crusade of 1197

The Third Crusade had an epilogue. Frederick I of Germany had been succeeded by his eldest son, Henry VI, whose ambitions to turn the western empire into a hereditary monarchy and to pacify Sicily, which he claimed by right of his wife and had to occupy by force, may well have led him to consider the advantages to his international standing of campaigning in the East as soon as Richard's truce with Saladin expired. He must also have shared the enthusiasm for crusading that was almost universal at the time and he may have felt some obligation to fulfil his father's vow, left uncompleted by his death. He took the cross in Holy Week 1195 and on Easter Day summoned his subjects to crusade at a solemn diet at Bari, promising to supplement the crusaders with 3,000 mounted mercenaries. In June he left for Germany to promote the enterprise and on 1 August Pope Celestine III published a new crusade appeal and called on the German clergy to preach the cross. In October and December, at Gelnhausen and Worms, Henry personally witnessed the enrolment of German nobles. At Gelnhausen he also agreed to a proposal from Cyprus that the island should become a vassal-kingdom of the empire and soon afterwards the negotiations began which were to lead to the ruler of Cilician Armenia becoming a vassal-king as well.

At a diet at Würzburg in March 1196 the arrangements for the crusade were completed and a year later an impressive Germany army was assembling in the ports of southern Italy and Sicily. It was led by the archbishop of Mainz, because Henry, who had not been well and had to deal with renewed unrest in southern Italy, had probably given up all hope of commanding it himself. On 22 September 1197 the main German fleet reached Acre. The Germans occupied Sidon and Beirut, which had been abandoned by the Muslims, and laid siege to Toron, but then news from home caused their crusade to disintegrate. Henry VI had died at Messina on 28 September, leaving a baby son. The kingdom of Germany and the empire were bound to be disputed. On 1 July 1198 a truce was made with the Muslims in which the Christian possession of Beirut was recognized and by the end of the summer most of the leading crusaders had left to protect their lands and rights at home.

The Third Crusade and the crusade of 1197 demonstrated what enthusiasm the movement could command in Europe when there was a real crisis and what large forces could be put into the field at such a time. The record of these years, if judged in terms of the men and matériel channelled to the East, is remarkable. And after rather a slow start the crusaders' achievements were outstanding. In 1188 the Christians had been left only with the city of Tyre and one or two isolated fortresses inland; by 1198 they held nearly the whole of the Palestinian coast. This ensured that the kingdom would last for another century, because it removed any threat from a fleet in the Nile Delta to the sea-lanes to Europe at precisely the time when Acre was becoming the chief commercial port in the eastern Mediterranean region. The crusade seems to have been the first to make use of mercenaries on a large scale. In 1191–2 these must have been employed in Palestine, which was always awash with them, but in 1197 Henry VI intended to export an impressive mercenary force from the West. The invasion of Egypt, which had been on the minds of crusaders and settlers in the Levant from the start, moved suddenly to the forefront of thinking. In June 1192, with his sojourn in the East coming to an end, Richard of England had initiated a discussion on the choice of a final goal. A committee, made up of brothers of the military orders, western settlers and crusaders, had decided on Egypt, but this had not been acceptable to the contingent which had been left behind by Philip of France.

The crusaders had showed a new realism in their decision not to risk all in the Judaean hills, but the result was that Jerusalem had eluded them. This helps to explain the obsessive concern with crusading which continued to be displayed at all levels of society.

Pope Innocent III

By the time the Germans were beginning to withdraw from Palestine there was a new pope, for on 8 January 1198 Lothario dei Conti di Segni had been elected and had taken the name of Innocent III. He was then aged 37 or 38 and so was a comparatively young man. Vigorous and quick-witted, his judgements upon others and his decisions, even on points of law, could be hasty. He had an exceptionally high view of his office as a vicariate for Christ, with authority over all aspects of church business and a final say in secular affairs, although it is important to stress that his concerns were primarily pastoral and his decisions were often pragmatic. His ideas and temperament drove him to take far more interest in the management of crusades than had his predecessors, who had been content to leave the planning and conduct to the laity once they had preached them. During the twelfth century leadership of the movement in the field had been assumed by kings: Louis VII of France and Conrad III of Germany; Philip II of France, Richard I of England and Frederick I of Germany. It has often been suggested that Innocent deliberately tried to exclude kings from the conduct of his crusades, but this is misleading. It was rather that he positively set out to manage them himself at a time when Henry of Germany had recently died and Richard of England and Philip of France were not anxious to reassume the cross. Events were to demonstrate, however, that the papacy had not the ability in law nor the organizational powers to direct crusades successfully.

Innocent nevertheless contributed more to the movement than any other individual except Urban II. He could not expect to lead a crusade himself – as early as August 1198 he was admitting that his office was too demanding for him to go to the East in person – but crusading was something that appealed to both the speculative and the political sides of his nature. No other pope seems to have devoted quite so much time to the movement. No other pope preached as many crusades as he did. Perhaps no other pope would have subordinated a fundamental principle of canon law to the needs of crusading as rashly as he did when he decreed that the Holy Land was in such dire straits that a man could take the cross without his wife's consent. He justified this violation of the natural right of married women and the principle of the parity of both partners in a marriage contract in a ruling about which canon lawyers, who never denied its validity, were always uncomfortable, by reference to analogies with the secular world, arguing that since the objections of wives could not overrule the demands of earthly kings for military service they could not be a hindrance to the commands of the heavenly king. In this he developed a theme found in his letters: that, although by its nature voluntary, the vow to crusade was a moral imperative. It was demanded of qualified Christians by God and could not be set aside with impunity:

To those men who refuse to take part, if indeed there be by chance any man so ungrateful to the lord our God, we firmly state on behalf of the apostle Peter that they ... will have to answer to us on this matter in the presence of the Dreadful Judge on the Last Day of Severe Judgement.

On the other hand it would be wrong to suppose that the movement dominated his thinking to the exclusion of everything else. He was one of those enthusiasts with a capacity for concentration on whatever problem he was facing and his pontificate reveals plenty of other examples of major issues in which his guiding hand and individual approach can be discerned. It has been pointed out that he did not come to the papal throne with any preconceived plan for a crusade. It was only in the summer of 1198, six months after his election, that the first signs of one appear, probably in reaction to the collapse of the German crusade.

The Fourth Crusade

In August 1198 he issued *Post miserabile*, his first general crusade letter. He called upon Richard of England and Philip of France to make a truce for five years and he asked Philip to contribute mercenaries, but he made it clear that authority over the crusade in its early stages was to be entirely in his hands. The crusaders were summoned to be ready for two years' service by the following March. Legates were to be sent to Palestine to prepare for their arrival. Prelates of the Church were ordered to send armed men or to contribute their equivalent in cash. There was also a new formulation of the remission of sins. Innocent had opted for the modern theology of penance and for a remission of the type foreshadowed in the writings of Bernard of Clairvaux and Eugenius III. In doing so he definitively established the 'indulgence' as it has been known to Catholics ever since. No longer was the pope simply declaring that a penitential act would be satisfactory. Since he was now promising a sinner the remission on God's behalf, the emphasis was to be no longer on what the sinner did, but on the loving willingness of a merciful God to make good any deficiency by rewarding the devout performance of a meritorious work, following confession and absolution:

We, trusting in the mercy of God and the authority of the blessed apostles Peter and Paul, by that power of binding and loosing that God has conferred on us, although unworthy, grant to all those submitting to the labour of this journey personally and at their expense full forgiveness of their sins, of which they have been moved to penitence in voice and heart, and as the reward of the just we promise them a greater share of eternal salvation.

This formulation made a great impression on contemporaries. Geoffrey of Villehardouin, who played a leading part in the crusade, wrote that 'because the indulgence was so great the hearts of men were much moved; and many took the cross because the indulgence was so great'.

At first Innocent cannot have envisaged a large expedition, because he allowed only six months for the completion of preparations, but later in the autumn he wrote to all archbishops, expanding on the demand he had already made for men and money. He wanted them to summon provincial councils to discuss the issue. At least one of the councils met, in Dijon late in 1198, and many of the bishops present promised to contribute to the crusade as much as a thirtieth – that is over 3 per cent – of the incomes of their dioceses. A year later, on 31 December 1199, Innocent issued another general letter, *Graves orientalis terrae*, which imposed on the whole Church with a few exceptions an income tax of a fortieth – that is 2.5 per cent – 'since the greatest necessity demands it'. The laity were also to be encouraged to give alms and chests were to be placed in churches for this purpose. The proceeds were to be granted to crusaders who could not otherwise afford to go and promised to stay in the Holy Land for at least a year, but allowance was made for those who sent soldiers in their stead.

This was the first step in a process which was to lead to an elaborate system of clerical taxation. It is true that crusading was becoming so expensive that sooner or later a better supplementary resource than the taxes which had been spasmodically levied by twelfth-century monarchs would have to be found, but the transformation within sixteen months of a general demand for cash in support of an *ad hoc* expedition into a tax on the whole Church suggests that the original crusade plan had been abandoned in favour of a much more ambitious one. In fact, within a month or so of the issuing of *Post miserabile* Innocent must have heard of a development which forced him to change his mind. The truce agreed on 1 July 1198 between the kingdom of Jerusalem and al-'Adil, the senior surviving member of Saladin's family, was intended to last for five years and eight months. This made directing a crusade to Palestine inappropriate and when crusaders from the West did arrive they were at first told by the king of Jerusalem in no uncertain terms that military operations were forbidden. News of the truce must have reached Italy in late September or early October 1198. The original project seems to have been revised and expanded; its developed form was revealed in the terms of a treaty made with Venice by representatives of the crusade leaders in the spring of 1201. Venice contracted to transport 4,500 knights, an equivalent number of horses, 9,000 squires and 20,000 'well-armed' foot sergeants to Alexandria in Egypt, which was specified in a secret clause. This was a massive army – thirteen years later at Bouvines, the most important battle of the period in the West, the total of the combatants on both sides was less than 20,000 – and none of the later sea-borne crusading expeditions begins to compare in size with it. The projection of 20,000 foot soldiers is extraordinarily large and is so specific that it is impossible to believe that the emissaries to

Venice, three, perhaps four, of whom had already been crusaders, were thinking only of volunteers. One cannot avoid the conclusion that in hiring berths for so many foot soldiers the negotiators believed that most were going to be paid employees.

It seems that a crusade of the kind foreshadowed in Henry VI's plans of 1195 was being projected, in which a nucleus of crusaders would command a much larger body of mercenaries, engaged in and transported from the West. The decision to use paid soldiers on this scale helps to explain the clerical taxation, which must have been associated with a hunger for cash fuelled by the prospect of their employment. At first sight it must seem odd – and very extravagant, given the costs of transportation – that they were to be hired in Europe. It would have been cheaper to engage them in Palestine, but the reason was that an assault on Alexandria by a force sailing directly from Europe was envisaged. If one was aiming straight for Egypt there would not be the option of engaging men in Palestine.

Egypt had been in Christian sights from the moment the crusaders had entered the Holy Land, as we have seen. The country was to be the target of the Fifth Crusade and of the first crusade of Louis IX of France and it continued to hover like a mirage on the horizon of planners in the early fourteenth century. The interest in it was understandable. It was by far the richest country in the region. It was associated with incidents in both the Old and the New Testaments. It had been part of the Christian Roman empire and still had a large subject Christian population. Its conquest could therefore be justified in terms of the recovery of territory unjustly held by another. Its occupation would be beneficial to western commerce, not only because of its position on the international trade routes, but because of the threat its fleets posed to communications with the West. More important still were the convictions that success in Egypt could lead in the end to the reoccupation of Jerusalem and that as long as westerners held it the Muslims would be on the defensive. It was known that the River Nile had failed to flood and that Egypt was in economic crisis, and it was believed that if Alexandria fell, the rest of the country would be in no condition to withstand an invasion.

Although Alexandria's commercial pre-eminence was now being challenged by Acre, it was the terminus of the most consistently important spice road from the Far East and it was the greatest trading centre known to Mediterranean merchants. One could not imagine a greater prize or at the same time a target which was apparently so soft. Its harbours were not difficult to break into and the ease with which it could be assaulted had been demonstrated on 29 July 1174, when a large Sicilian force had landed before the city, while Christian galleys had roamed one of the harbours at will. The Sicilians had withdrawn abruptly on 1 August, but the city's weakness was to be again apparent when it was temporarily occupied by the crusade of King Peter I of Cyprus in 1365, as we shall see. In 1202 the crusaders were due to muster in Venice in April and the original intention had been for them to sail in late June. This would have meant arrival before Alexandria by late July or early August, at a time when the Nile was normally in flood, making it hard for the Egyptians to relieve the city and allowing for a series of assaults before the receding waters in late October opened the rest of the country to the crusaders.

Much of the planning must have been going on behind the scenes. There was a significant popular response to the sermons of the crusade preacher Fulk of Neuilly, but it has been supposed that enthusiasm was slow to develop among the nobles and knights. This must be an illusion and the sequence of melodramatic cross-takings over the winter of 1199–1200, which appeared to signify the armsbearers' late response, looks like an example of that carefully stage-managed theatre which was a feature of the central middle ages. On 28 November 1199, during a tournament held at Écry (today Asfeld-la-Ville) the young Counts Thibald of Champagne and Louis of Blois took the cross, together with many of their vassals and two important lords of the Île-de-France, Simon of Montfort and Reynald of Montmirail. On the following 23 February, Ash Wednesday, Count Baldwin of Flanders, who was Thibald's brother-in-law, also vowed to crusade, as did his brothers Henry and Eustace and many of his vassals.

The three counts, very closely related and from families with long traditions of crusading, were the natural leaders of the movement and they acted together. A meeting at Soissons decided to delay planning until the number of recruits had grown. Two months later another assembly, held at Compiègne, gave six men, two of whom were chosen by each count, plenary powers to negotiate the best terms they could with one of the maritime cities. The six delegates, two of whom were the famous trouvère Conon of Béthune and the future historian of the crusade, Geoffrey of Villehardouin, decided to approach Venice. Crossing the Alps in mid-winter they put their case in February 1201 to the ducal council and the doge Enrico Dandolo, who was extremely old and partially blind, but experienced, cultured, shrewd and indomitable. They reached the agreement which has already been described and settled on a sum of 85,000 marks of Cologne – not an excessive price – which would have to be paid in instalments by April 1202. The treaty was solemnly ratified at an assembly in the church of St Mark and a copy of it was sent to the pope for his confirmation.

The envoys returned to France to find Thibald of Champagne dying. After the duke of Burgundy and the count of Bar-le-Duc had refused to take his place, an assembly, meeting towards the end of June 1201 at Soissons, decided to offer Marquis Boniface of Montferrat the command of the whole army. Boniface had not crusaded before, but we have already come across one of his brothers, William, marrying Sibylla of Jerusalem and another, Conrad, marrying her half-sister Isabella. A third brother, Renier, had married a Greek princess and had ranked as a Caesar in the Byzantine empire before being murdered in 1183. It has already been pointed out that members of the Montferrat family were very well connected, being cousins of the French and German royal houses; indeed, Philip of France may have suggested Boniface for the leadership of the crusade. Boniface was one of the best-known military commanders of his day and his court was a centre of chivalry. He was also a personal friend and subject of Philip of Swabia, the younger brother of the dead emperor Henry VI. Philip was a contestant for the western empire, to which he had been elected in April 1198, and was therefore in conflict with the pope, who now favoured his rival Otto of Brunswick. He was allied by marriage to the Byzantine imperial house, because his wife was Irene Angelus, whose father, the emperor Isaac, had been deposed, blinded and imprisoned along with her brother Alexius by her uncle, Alexius III. Boniface came to Soissons in the late summer of 1201, accepted the leadership of the army and took the cross. He then went, by way of Cîteaux, where an important cross-taking ceremony coincided with a meeting of the Cistercian general chapter, to Germany to attend Philip of Swabia's Christmas court at Hagenau.

To that court also came the young Alexius Angelus, Philip's brother-in-law, who had escaped his uncle's surveillance and had fled to the West to appeal for help on his father's behalf. It is possible that the expectation of a postponement of the attack on Alexandria and the use of the crusade instead as a means of forcing a change of government in Constantinople was discussed at Hagenau and was raised with the pope by Alexius in the following February and by Boniface in the middle of March. But if so Innocent certainly rejected any such idea and no decision can have been made by the time the crusaders began to reach Venice in the middle of the summer of 1202.

The proposal to attack Alexandria had become such common knowledge that news of it had reached Egypt itself and it was said that the Egyptian government tried to buy the Venetians off. The Egyptians need not have worried. Hiring up to 20,000 foot soldiers was beyond the capabilities and resources of the leaders, particularly as there is no evidence that any proceeds of the clerical fortieth had yet been collected, let alone distributed. Such was the resistance to it that some English assessments were only collected in 1217; by 1208 it had still not been raised in parts of Italy. Even had it been possible to build such an army, the plan to invade Egypt directly from Europe was grossly over-ambitious. It is true that the Sicilians had reached Alexandria in 1174, but their force had probably been much smaller and their assault had been a failure. Lessons were to be learnt after 1204. Neither the Fifth Crusade nor the first crusade of Louis IX were to launch their assaults on Egypt directly from the West. The Fifth Crusade assembled in Palestine before the invasion in 1218 and Louis's crusade wintered in Cyprus in 1248–9.

In April 1202 Innocent was still hopeful, at least on the surface, but a sign of his growing desperation must have been his decretal allowing crusaders to take the cross without their wives' permission, which has been dated to September 1201. It was reported that many crusaders were unhappy with the enterprise. Some did not fulfil their vows; others decided not to travel by way of Venice but to make their own arrangements and go directly to Palestine. Many of those who did not turn up must have supposed that since the leaders had not been able to recruit and pay for the mercenaries required, the plan to invade Egypt directly from Europe would have to be aborted. No one arrived on time and in the early autumn of 1202 it was found that only about one-third of the projected 33,500 men – including perhaps between 1,500 and 1,800 knights – had mustered. The result was that, in spite of every effort and the generosity of the leaders who contributed what they could from their own pockets, the crusaders were left owing the Venetians 34,000 silver marks for shipping which had already been prepared. The Venetians, who had involved themselves in a massive ship-building enterprise to assemble a fleet of about 500 vessels at a cost to their own commercial interests, were determined to get payment and even threatened to cut off supplies to the crusaders, who were encamped on the Lido, the large island closing the lagoon from the Adriatic. Winter was approaching and with it the end of the sailing season. Without even leaving Europe the crusaders had already fallen into the most characteristic trap of crusading, a desperate shortage of cash, in spite of Innocent's revolutionary attempt to tax the Church on their behalf.

It was at this stage that the doge suggested a postponement of the payment of their debt until it could be settled out of plunder, on condition that the crusaders help him recapture the port of Zadar on the Dalmatian coast from the Hungarians. They accepted and found themselves committed to start their crusade by attacking a Christian town which was subject to a fellow-crusader, since King Emeric of Hungary had himself taken the cross. Whatever the rights or wrongs of Emeric's occupation of Zadar the Church was bound to maintain him in his possession of it, just as it was bound to protect the properties of Zadar's assailants while they were away from home. Many crusaders were worried, all the more so since the Venetians refused to accept the credentials of the papal legate, Peter Capuano, and forced him to return to Rome. There were many defections and before he left Venice Peter Capuano, who seems to have been prepared to ignore the plan to attack Zadar, had to insist that some leading churchmen swallow their doubts and remain with the army to assure it of spiritual direction. Even Boniface of Montferrat felt it prudent to leave the crusade and travel to Rome. He did not rejoin the army until after Zadar had fallen.

Once their terms had been accepted Enrico Dandolo and many leading Venetians took the cross. A fleet of over 200 ships, including 60 galleys, left Venice early in October 1202. Many of the ships had been specially designed for a direct attack on Alexandria. An eyewitness remembered that 'in the round ships they carried more than 300 petraries and mangonels and a plentiful supply of all the engines needed to take a city'. The vessels could be arranged side by side to form floating batteries. Besides the artillery for throwing stones and Greek Fire, they were equipped with storming ladders and flying bridges. Some were capable of carrying horses and discharging these, already mounted, down ramps onto a shore. They sailed slowly down the coast in a show of force designed to impress other subject cities before appearing off Zadar on 10 November. The army landed, but it now received a letter from the pope forbidding it to attack any Christian city and referring to Zadar by name. Several leading crusaders, led by the Cistercian abbot Guy of Vaux-de-Cernay and Simon of Montfort, voiced their opposition to the siege in the pope's name and even sent messages to Zadar's defenders encouraging them to resist. They then withdrew some distance and played no further part in the action. On 24 November the city fell and was sacked, the spoil being divided between the crusaders and the Venetians.

The decision had already been taken to winter at Zadar, since it was now too late in the year to continue the voyage, and it was there that Boniface of Montferrat found the army in the middle of December. Close on his heels came envoys from Philip of Swabia proposing, on behalf of Alexius, that if on its way to the East the crusade would restore him and his father to the Byzantine throne the patriarchate of Constantinople would be made to submit to the papacy, 200,000 silver marks would be handed over for division between the crusaders and the Venetians, and the army would be provisioned by the Greeks for an additional year. Alexius would himself join the crusade if his presence was desired and would anyway contribute an army of 10,000 Greeks to it and would maintain a force of 500 knights in Palestine at his expense for the rest of his life.

It is important to bear in mind that the plan to attack Alexandria had not been abandoned. It had merely been postponed. Encamped outside Constantinople eight months later, Count Hugh of St Pol reported that an embassy had been sent to Egypt threatening war. 'You should know', he wrote to Henry of Brabant, 'that we will tourney before Alexandria with the sultan of Egypt'. After the fall of Constantinople Raimbaut of Vaqueiras, a poet in the service of Boniface of Montferrat, was criticizing the new Latin emperor for not launching an invasion of Egypt. At about the same time, on 27 May 1204, twenty ships from the kingdom of

Jerusalem penetrated the Rosetta branch of the Nile and spent two days looting Fuwa. So the king of Jerusalem had been himself involved in the project and his raid must have been planned as a preliminary to the main invasion, which he was still expecting. He cannot have realized that the situation was now so transformed that a full-scale attack on Egypt would have to wait until 1218.

Given the fixation with Alexandria, Alexius's proposal must have seemed a godsend, since it provided the crusaders with a way out of the impasse created by the postponement of the Egyptian venture. The opportunity, for Venice at least, of gaining privileges in Constantinople as a result of setting an ally on the Byzantine throne and then resuming the course for Alexandria with his material support would have seemed to be too good to miss, particularly as its fleet was already equipped to threaten a great fortified port. Alexius's terms were accepted by the Venetians and by most of the greater leaders, but they involved flagrant disobedience to the pope and this weighed heavily with large numbers of their confrères, many of whom appear only to have accepted them because the alternative, the dissolution of the army, was unthinkable. There was general dissatisfaction and anxiety and there were more defections, including that of Simon of Montfort.

The crusaders had incurred automatic excommunication for their insubordination. The bishops in the army were prepared to give them provisional absolution while a delegation visited Rome to explain their action and ask for forgiveness. Innocent found himself caught in a trap. His eyes still seem to have been focused on Egypt. The crusade he had hoped for had at last departed and inflexibility on his part might lead to its dispersal. He was prepared to absolve the crusaders provided they restored what they had taken illegally and did not invade other Christian lands, but he refused to absolve the Venetians and he issued a formal letter of excommunication of them. Now, however, men who were supposed to be directly under his control and had flatly disobeyed him went on to disobey him again in every particular. Zadar was not restored to Hungary. Boniface of Montferrat refused to publish the bull of excommunication of the Venetians on the grounds, he explained, playing on Innocent's fears, that he did not want the crusade to break up; he would only deliver it to the Venetians if the pope insisted. By the time Innocent replied in June 1203, insisting that the bull be published and repeating that the crusaders were not to attack any more Christian territory, referring this time specifically to the Byzantine empire, the fleet was approaching Constantinople.

The crusaders sailed from Zadar late in April 1203 and were joined at Corfu by Alexius. Leaving Corfu on 24 May they passed before the sea-walls of Constantinople before disembarking on 24 June across the Bosporus at Kadiköy. Marching north to Üsküdar (Scutari), they crossed to Galata, on the other side of the Golden Horn, the enormous creek that was Constantinople's chief port, on 5 July. On the 6th they stormed Galata's main defence work and broke the chain that stretched across the entrance to the creek. The crusaders now marched up the shore of the Golden Horn, rounded the end of it and pitched camp outside the city's land-walls, in the angle between them and the water. The Venetian fleet occupied the harbour and prepared to storm the shore defences. On 17 July there was a general assault during which the Venetians occupied about a quarter of the length of these walls, but they abandoned them on hearing of a sortie made by the Greeks against the crusaders which withdrew again without major engagement. Although the attack on the city had failed, the emperor Alexius III fled that night and the blind Isaac Angelus was released from prison. He reluctantly agreed to the terms his son had negotiated and on 1 August the young Alexius was crowned his co-emperor.

By now the number of non-Venetian crusaders had been drastically reduced by defections. In January 1203 only twelve persons had been found to take an oath to sail with the Venetians to Constantinople. In the following May less than twenty, and possibly as few as ten, were reported being in favour of proceeding with the enterprise. It is not surprising that the haemorrhaging of effectives continued and in his letter of c. 1 August 1203 Hugh of St Pol gave the size of the Frankish fighting element before Constantinople as only 500 knights, 500 mounted sergeants and 2,000 foot. Hugh's estimate was confirmed by another eyewitness, Robert of Cléry, who stated, when describing the situation at about the same time, that there were in the Frankish contingent no more than 700 knights, 50 of them fighting on foot. So there remained only 33 per cent of the knights who had left Venice in 1202 and 11 per cent of the number originally envisaged in 1201. On the other hand, the crusaders had every reason to hope that the prologue to their crusade was nearly over, although they agreed to stay on for the winter at the expense of Alexius, who wanted them to prop up his régime in its early months. They wrote to the pope and the western kings explaining what they had done and announcing the postponement of their journey until the following March. At the same time Alexius assured Innocent of his intention of submitting the Orthodox Church to Rome. Innocent hesitated again and did not reply until the following February, when he did no more than reprove the crusaders and the Venetians for their actions and order them to continue with the crusade; he also told the bishops in the army to see that the leaders did penance for their sins.

During the winter, however, the situation at Constantinople had gravely deteriorated. Alexius had paid the first instalments of the money he had promised, but the Greek people and clergy bitterly resented the presence of westerners and rioting and faction-fighting erupted in the city.

Alexius began to cool towards his patrons and the payments dried up. In November, after a delegation of crusaders and Venetians had presented him with an ultimatum, hostilities broke out. Then late in January 1204 a *coup d'état* removed Alexius and his father and a wave of anti-Latin xenophobia elevated to the throne a great-great-grandson of Alexius I, who took the title of Alexius V.

The crusaders could afford neither to proceed nor return to the West. They were in a hostile environment and were short of provisions and forced to forage. In March they decided that there was only one move left for them to make, the capture of Constantinople itself and the subjugation of the Byzantine empire, although this worried and distressed many of them. On the eve of the assault on the city elaborate justifications, based on the Greeks' sin in abetting the murder of their emperor and their schismatic condition, were concocted by the clergy in the army to give some relief to consciences. Enrico Dandolo, representing Venice, and Boniface of Montferrat, Baldwin of Flanders, Louis of Blois and Hugh of St Pol, representing the other crusaders, concluded a treaty to govern the division of spoil once Constantinople was theirs. The Venetians were to have three-quarters of all booty up to the amount still owed them; over and above that there was to be equal division. Venice was assured of all the privileges previously granted her by the Byzantine emperors. Twelve electors, six from either side, were to choose a Latin emperor, who was to have one-quarter of the empire, including the two imperial palaces in Constantinople. The remaining three-quarters were to be equally divided between the parties. The clergy of the party that failed to get the emperorship would have the right to nominate a cathedral chapter for St Sophia in Constantinople, which would choose a Catholic patriarch. Clergy would be appointed by both parties for their own churches, which would be endowed only with enough to enable them to live decently; the residue would be treated as spoil. Both sides agreed to remain in the region for a year to help to establish the new Latin empire and a joint commission was to be set up to distribute titles and fiefs, which would be heritable through the female as well as the male line, and assign services. The doge would not personally owe military service to the emperor, but fief-holders in the Venetian territories would perform it. No citizen of a state at war with Venice would be admitted to the empire. The emperor was to swear to abide by the terms of the treaty and a commission consisting of the doge, Boniface of Montferrat and six councillors from either side would adjust the terms if need be. Both parties agreed to petition the pope to make violations of them punishable by excommunication. It has often been pointed out that this treaty, which established the constitution of the Latin empire, assured it of a weak emperor and an over-powerful Venetian presence.

The number available to take part in the final assault on the city is debatable. To the 3,000 fighting men enumerated by Hugh of St Pol should be added perhaps 1,000 servants and camp followers. Professor Pryor has assumed that the Venetian crews numbered c. 27,000 men, bringing the total surviving the campaign so far to c. 31,000, of whom perhaps 12,000 were combatants. These were to be supplemented by the western residents of Constantinople – perhaps 15,000 of them – who had been expelled from the city by the Greeks in August 1203 and had sought refuge with the crusaders; according to an eyewitness they were of great use to them. As many as 6,000 of these could have been capable of bearing arms. It is not hard, therefore, to imagine a force approaching the 'less than 20,000 armed men *entre uns et altres*' which were described attacking Constantinople.

The action began at daybreak on 9 April against the harbour wall: the land-walls had proved themselves to be very strong in the previous year, while the Venetians had been more successful attacking from the waters of the Golden Horn. The attack failed, but it was resumed on the 12th, with floating freighters grappling the tops of the towers with flying bridges, while troops landed and scaled the walls. By evening the crusaders were in control of a section of the defences and had begun to penetrate the city. Dusk brought the fighting to a close and they slept by their weapons in the flickering light of a fire started by Germans and raging through the wooden buildings in the nearby quarters of the town. They expected renewed resistance in the morning, but there was none, for the emperor had fled. For three days Constantinople was sacked. This was, of course, the usual fate of cities taken by assault, but the Greeks have not forgotten or forgiven it. There may well have been an edge to it. There was in the army an obsession with loot, engendered by the failure of the crusaders to meet their debts to the Venetians, and this, together with the fact that a significant proportion of the assault force was composed of embittered and vengeful ex-residents who were said to have behaved extremely badly, may help to explain some of the excesses that occurred. Constantinople, moreover, was famous for being the greatest storehouse of relics in Christendom. There had grown up among western Christians traditions of *furta sacra*, sacred thefts, in which the stealing of the bones of saints had been justified, if successful, by the proven desire of the saints concerned to have their relics transferred to another place. The sack of Constantinople was a massive *furtum sacrum*, made against the background of the hysteria that had swept western Europe following the loss of the relic of the True Cross at the Battle of Hattin in 1187.

Once the spoil had been divided the crusaders could proceed to the election of a new emperor. Boniface of Montferrat, who had occupied the imperial palace of the Boukoleon and was betrothed to Margaret of Hungary, the widow of the emperor Isaac, must have expected the title, but he found himself baulked in the choice of the six non-Venetian electors, for in the end six churchmen were chosen, only three of whom favoured him. This made it certain that he would not be successful, since the Venetians opposed his candidature. After long debates the electors unanimously announced their choice of Baldwin of Flanders at midnight on 9 May. Baldwin was crowned on the 16th by the assembled Catholic bishops, because there was as yet no Latin patriarch.

The diversion to Constantinople has led to endless and rather pointless historical argument. Was it the result of a conspiracy and, if so, who was involved? Enrico Dandolo, Philip of Swabia, Boniface of Montferrat, even Innocent III, have been named as candidates. And was it the culmination of centuries of growing ill-feeling between Latins and Greeks? In fact, the capture of Constantinople seems to have been the result of a series of accidents, resulting from the postponement of the original plan to attack Alexandria. There can be no doubt that it permanently soured relations between Orthodox and Catholics, but its undoubted ecclesiological importance has led to its place in the history of the crusading movement being ignored. Although in some ways, such as in its internal chains of command, it looked back to the household dominance and committees of the First Crusade, in other ways it broke new ground. The original project was literally breath-taking. A huge army was to be transported across the Mediterranean and was to make a landing before Alexandria. There were plans to employ and transport a large body of mercenaries and the pope tried to tax the Church on its behalf. It attracted a new kind of enthusiast, who was prepared to campaign many times in different theatres of war.

The inclusion of Innocent's name among those responsible for the diversion is particularly unkind, but there is a kind of justice in it. It may well be that the strategy which went awry was his own. He certainly knew and approved of the plan to attack Alexandria and he came to an agreement with the Byzantines over provisions for the fleet on the way. If he was responsible for the idea, it must rank as another of his wildly over-ambitious ones. From the start it proceeded in a way that was galling for him. One act of disobedience led to another. Most of the crusaders, however divided and personally distressed, ignored his advice and prohibitions. While he certainly determined to make the best of things after the event and instructions flowed from Rome with the aim of taking advantage of the fall of the Byzantine empire to bring about, even to enforce, church union, he must have realized that the crusade had ended in a way that was bound to make the unification of the Catholic and Orthodox churches, so dear to his heart, much harder.

> How is the Greek Church [he wrote] so afflicted and persecuted, to return to ecclesiastical union and a devotion for the Apostolic See when she sees in the Latins only an example of perdition and the works of darkness, so that with reason she already detests them more than dogs?

The Baltic crusades

Innocent preached two other crusades while the Fourth Crusade was being prepared. The first was the Livonian Crusade in the Baltic region, which he inherited from his predecessor. It had its origins in a mission to the Livs on the river Dvina patronized by Archbishop Hartwig of Bremen, who saw in the creation of a bishopric at Üxküll the chance of extending his province. The mission made little progress, although it had the personal support of Pope Celestine III. In 1193 and 1197 Celestine was persuaded to grant remissions of sin to those who fought in the service of the new Livonian Church, but in 1198 there was a set-back and the bishop was killed. In his place the archbishop appointed his nephew Albert of Buxtehude. This energetic and rather brutal man, who was to dominate the Baltic crusading movement for thirty years and was to carve a church-state, directly dependent on Rome, out of the pagan communities around Riga, recruited more crusaders and sought authorization from the new pope.

Innocent summoned the Christians of northern Germany to the defence of the Livonian Church on 5 October 1199. He justified the use of force as defence of Christian converts persecuted by their pagan neighbours. The crusaders, however, do not seem to have been granted a full indulgence and only those who planned to make pilgrimages to Rome were allowed to commute their vows to participation in the campaign. In 1204 Innocent issued a more important letter in which he permitted Albert to recruit priests, who had vowed to go to Jerusalem, to work on his mission instead, and authorized laymen who could not go to Jerusalem 'on account of poverty or bodily weakness' to commute their vows to fight the barbarians in Livonia with the full indulgence. He licensed Albert's representatives on recruiting campaigns to open churches once a year throughout the province of Bremen even where there was an interdict. The effect of this letter was to initiate a 'perpetual crusade', which was thenceforward to be a feature of the northern wars, although it was not to be fully developed for another forty years. Albert transferred the capital of his see down river from Üxküll to Riga, which could be reached by cogs (roundships) sailing from Lübeck, and he fostered the cult of Our Lady of Riga and the idea of Livonia as Our Lady's Dowry, which must have been adopted to justify pilgrimages to it. He returned to Germany every year until 1224 to recruit crusaders for summer campaigns. These were supplemented by the members of a small military order, the Sword-Brothers, which he established in 1202. There were probably never more than 120 of these, living in six convents, but they organized the crusaders during the summer and garrisoned strongholds in the winter: the Christians used a strategy that made maximum use of fortified religious communities and small castles. By 1230 Livonia had been conquered in a series of grim annual campaigns against peoples superior in numbers but inferior in the techniques of war.

So had Estonia to the north in campaigns begun by the Danes during Innocent's pontificate. We have already seen that the Danes' eyes were turning to the eastern Baltic in 1184. Although before 1216 they were concentrating on the conquest of the Pomeranian coast from Lübeck to Gdańsk (Danzig), their fleets attacked Finland in 1191 and 1202, Estonia in 1194 and 1197, Saaremaa (Ösel) in 1206 and Prussia in 1210. The attack upon Saaremaa was certainly presented as a crusade and crusading ideas, distorted by the northern concept of missionary war that we have already heard echoed in statements by Bernard of Clairvaux and Eugenius III, are also to be found in a letter from Innocent to King Valdemar II of Denmark in 1209, in which Valdemar was exhorted 'to root out the error of paganism and spread the bounds of the Christian faith. . . . Fight in this battle of the war bravely and strongly like an active knight of Christ'. In letters to Otto of Brunswick and to the Danish Church, written on the same day, Innocent referred to Valdemar's activities as 'so holy a pilgrimage' and mentioned an indulgence. Like Bernard he was sailing close to the wind when he tried to reconcile crusading with the north European missions. It was not until 1219, however, that Valdemar invaded northern Estonia and established a presence at Tallinn (Reval), in response to appeals from Albert of Buxtehude at Riga, who had been alarmed by an incursion from Russian Novgorod, and from Pope Honorius III, who had promised him that he could keep the land he conquered from the heathen. In the following year the Danes, together with the Sword-Brothers, subjugated northern Estonia, but this led to competition with the Germans, who were advancing into Estonia from Livonia to the south, and the Swedes, who were occupying the north-western coast. Valdemar ruthlessly used his naval control of the Baltic and the threat he could pose to shipping out of Lübeck to force his fellow-Christians to agree to his control of northern Estonia, although the settlement there was in fact far more German than Danish.

By the 1220s the idea of a perpetual crusade was taking root. The crusaders were signed with the cross, were referred to as pilgrims and crusaders (*peregrini* and *crucesignati*) and enjoyed the full indulgence. Measures were taken to tax the Church on their behalf. Their crusades were justified as defensive aid to missions and were privileged in much the same ways as crusades to the East.

The crusade against Markward of Anweiler

The other early crusade of Innocent III was preached against Markward of Anweiler, an imperial officer who had tried to maintain a presence in Italy after Henry VI's death. The precedent for such a 'political crusade' had been established by Innocent II at the council of Pisa in 1135, but the step Innocent III took was certainly an extreme one. Determined to recover the papal patrimony in central Italy and acutely sensitive about southern Italy and Sicily, where he was regent for the child Frederick, the pope was galvanized by the activities of Markward and his German followers. On 24 November 1199, having heard that Markward had crossed into Sicily, he wrote to the people there referring to him as 'another Saladin' and 'an infidel worse than the infidels'. He claimed that Markward was allied to the Muslims still living in the centre of the island, who were considered to be quite menacing, and that he was threatening the preparations for the Fourth Crusade. All who resisted him were granted the same indulgence as that enjoyed by crusaders to the East, since the ports of Sicily might be essential to the coming campaign. It is clear from other evidence that for nearly a year the pope had been envisaging a crusade against Markward as a last resort, but in fact the plans came to very little. Only a few men, the most important being Count Walter of Brienne, who was more concerned to assert the rights he claimed to the fief of Taranto, were enlisted – incidentally it was in this crusade that the young St Francis seems briefly to have enrolled – and Markward's death in 1203 ended the reason for the enterprise. But the letter of November 1199 was a straw in the wind, as were Innocent's fulminations at the end of his life against the English barons, 'worse than the Muslims'. By rebelling against King John, who had had the political sense to take the cross, they were believed to be hindering the Fifth Crusade which was in preparation. It has been suggested that the defence of the English kingdom against the rebels, who were in league with Louis of France, had indeed become a kind of crusade and that it was for this that the nine-year-old Henry III took the cross at the time of his coronation on 28 October 1216.

The Albigensian Crusade

Innocent was thinking seriously about another crusade to the East in 1208 and sent appeals to France and northern and central Italy, although the only discernible response came from the passionate crusader Duke Leopold VI of Austria, who was in future to campaign in Spain, Languedoc and Egypt. Innocent responded with one of those deflating letters with which he liked to put high men who were doing their best in their place:

> There is much more merit in the gibbet of Christ's cross than in the little sign of your cross. ... For you accept a soft and gentle cross; he suffered one that was bitter and hard. You bear it superficially on your clothing; he endured his in the reality of his flesh. You sew yours on with linen and silken threads; he was fastened to his with hard, iron nails.

In the meantime events in south-western France were leading to a crisis there. For decades the Church had been worried by the growth of heresy. Since heretics denied the Church's God-given function as the custodian of revelation they were believed to be rebels who had deliberately turned from truth and had chosen to disturb the order established by Christ. Heresy was, therefore, treated as an active, not a passive, force and it came to be associated in many minds with the *routiers*, bands of mercenaries who were already disturbing a region in which it was strong and against whom sanctions, which incorporated crusade ideas, had already been proposed. The Church was particularly worried by the increasing numbers of Cathars, the followers of a type of neo-Manichaeism who believed in two principles, or Gods, of the spiritual and material worlds and saw it as their duty to free their souls from the matter in which they were imprisoned. They renounced as far as was possible everything of this world, including marriage and the eating of meat, milk and eggs, that was considered to be material or procreative in origin. To them the order and life of the Church were vain and belief in the Trinity an error, since Christ had had no material reality. In place of the Church they set up their own hierarchy and liturgy. The demands made by their religion were so severe that only an inner core, the 'perfects', were fully initiated. Most adherents were 'believers', who committed themselves to undergo initiation before death. By the late twelfth century the Cathars, together with the proto-Protestant Waldensians, were the most numerous sectaries the Church had to face and their presence was especially strong in northern Italy and south-western France, both regions where there was no strong central political authority.

That last point is crucial to an understanding of Innocent's thinking. Since the fourth century the Church had normally looked to secular authority to generate the fear which had proved itself to be the most effective remedy to heresy and it is no accident that in the central middle ages nations with strong rulers had very few problems with heretics. The counts of Toulouse, the nominal lords of most of the territory with which we are concerned, had very little control over a region which was one of the most backward in France in terms of political cohesion. Whatever power they did enjoy was further limited by the conflicting allegiances they themselves owed, since they were vassals of the king of France for many of their lands, but also of the king of England in the west, the king of Aragon in the south and the western emperor in the east. The claims and ambitions of these rulers, embroiling themselves in internal conflicts in Languedoc, had led to savage and debilitating wars. The count of Toulouse was in no position to take effective measures. Nor were his overlords. The king of France, in particular, was far too enmeshed in conflict with the English king in the north to cope with heresy in the south, even if he had been capable of tackling it. Innocent was faced by a classic dilemma. Heresy presented a serious challenge. In Languedoc it was permeating all levels of society, including the nobility, and with every year that passed it would be harder to eradicate. Although there were probably fewer than 1,000 perfects in the region between 1200 and 1209 a high proportion of them were from noble families. Of those known by name to us 35 per cent were nobles and it is also significant that a large majority, 69 per cent, were women, preponderantly noblewomen. The sister of the count of Foix was a perfect and another sister, and the count's wife and daughter-in-law were believers. Catholic abbots and bishops had heretical relatives. And the secular powers on which the pope relied could do nothing.

In the course of the twelfth century the Church had resorted to various measures. Preaching missions had been despatched to Languedoc. In 1179 the 27th canon of the Third Lateran Council had called on all Christians to go to the aid of their bishops, if these decided to resort to the use of force. They would enjoy a limited remission of sins for doing this, but were assured of the full remission if they were killed. They would have the same protection of their lands in their absence as had pilgrims to Jerusalem. This was followed in 1181 by a little military campaign in Languedoc under the command of the papal legate Henry of Marcy. In 1184 the bull *Ad abolendam*, issued by Pope Lucius III after a conference at Verona with the emperor Frederick I, set up episcopal inquisitions, abolished all privileges of exemption from episcopal authority in this matter and stressed the need for collaboration between Church and State in the suppression of heretics who, if contumacious, were to be handed over to the secular arm for punishment. It is worth noting that a fierce critic of the Third Crusade, Ralph Niger, argued in the winter of 1187–8 that knights should not be sent overseas because they were needed at home to resist heresy.

Innocent tackled the problem with his accustomed energy. He sent a succession of legates to southern France. He took measures to reform the local church, which was in a bad way – between 1198 and 1209 he deposed seven bishops – and he encouraged the preaching mission of Diego of Osma and Dominic which was to lead to the foundation of the Dominicans; but he gradually came round to the view that the use of force was needed. In May 1204 he called on Philip of France to bring the power of his kingdom to bear in aid of spiritual authority and he went further than any pope had gone before in attaching to this exercise of secular power the full crusade indulgence. This inclusion of the most important crusade privilege in a summons to a king merely to do his duty had no effect. Neither had renewed appeals to Philip in February 1205 and November 1207, the last of which repeated the grant of the indulgence and added the promise to protect the soldiers' properties in their absences. Innocent also sent copies of this letter to the nobles, knights and subjects of France. It was as though he was calling upon the whole French political community to protect the Church, while at the same time making the task more attractive through the granting of crusade privileges. But Philip's reply made much of the difficulties he was experiencing in his conflict with John of England and set conditions for his intervention in the south which the pope was in no position to meet.

On 14 January 1208 Peter of Castelnau, one of the papal legates in Languedoc, was assassinated in circumstances which led the pope to suspect the complicity of Count Raymond VI of Toulouse, already excommunicated for his failure to deal effectively with heresy. As soon as he heard the news Innocent proclaimed a crusade against the heretics and their abettors in powerful letters sent to all parts of France and probably to other regions of western Europe as well. He called for men to take vows, although at this stage he granted them, it is interesting to note, rather an old-fashioned remission, expressed in terms of satisfactory penance for sin; perhaps he was not yet entirely certain of his ground. Three legates were appointed to organize the preaching of the crusade and lead it, and the pope decreed the abolition of usury and a delay in the repayment of debts, the usual way of enabling crusaders to raise money for their campaign. Measures were also taken to tax the churches in the regions from which the crusaders came in order to help finance their expeditions.

The novelty of Innocent's proclamation of the Albigensian Crusade did not lie in his encouragement of the use of force against heretics. That was an issue which had already been comprehensively justified, with reference to historical precedents and authorities stretching back to the fourth century, in Gratian's *Decretum*. It was the use of a crusade in this way that was new, although it was probably inevitable. The category of holy war to which crusading belongs – initially extraliminal, being proclaimed against an external force – seems to have a tendency, as we have seen, to turn inwards sooner or later and to be directed against the members of the very society which has generated it. The belief that any chance of extraliminal victory could be vitiated by corruption or divisions at home, so that only when a society was undefiled and was practising uniformly true religion could a war on its behalf be successful, was being widely expressed following the disasters which overtook the Christian settlements in Palestine in 1187, as we have seen. Everywhere one looks in the West around 1200 one can see evidence of a drive to impose uniformity on a society which was already remarkably monocultural and it is no coincidence that introspective crusades came to the fore, often being preached in the name of the war against Islam.

The Albigensian Crusade came about in 1208, but something similar could have been brought into being at any time, once holy war against external enemies had become the norm and was going badly. The fact that it was an internal war gave it unusual features. Southern France was not Palestine, or even Spain or Livonia, which is why crusaders to Languedoc came to take vows to serve there for only forty days. This short period of service must have diluted the penitential nature of the enterprise. And although the crusaders sometimes called themselves 'pilgrims', the goal of their pilgrimage has never been identified and was perhaps a fiction. The Albigensian Crusade illustrates how crusading was coming to flourish independently of some of the elements that had combined to make it.

The response to Innocent's appeal was enthusiastic, even fervent, and by the spring of 1209 a large force was gathering to attack the south. Raymond of Toulouse hastened to make terms and on 18 June 1209 was reconciled to the Church in a dramatic scene on the steps of the abbey of St Gilles, in front of the great western façade on which the Passion of Christ, in a manifestation of Catholic orthodoxy, is sculpted in stone. He then underwent a penitential whipping inside the abbey church and, because the crowd was so great, had to be led out by way of the crypt, past the new tomb of Peter of Castelnau. The crusade invaded the lands of Raymond Roger of Trencavel, viscount of Béziers and Carcassonne and lord of the Albigeois and of Razès, where the heretics were numerous. Béziers fell on 22 July and large numbers of citizens, both Catholic and Cathar, were massacred in conditions which suggest that the army, which contained many poor people from northern France, had got out of hand – Carcassonne, which held out for two weeks, was treated much more lightly – although the ferocity was exemplary and led to a collapse of resistance.

The time had now come for a secular leader to be appointed to administer the Trencavel lands and set up a permanent base for future operations. The choice fell on Simon of Montfort, who had opposed the attack upon Zadar and the diversion of the Fourth Crusade on principle seven years before. Simon was now in his late forties. Lord of Montfort and Epernon since 1181, he had inherited the earldom of Leicester in 1204 on the death of a maternal uncle. Courageous, tenacious and devout, he was a great military commander and a model husband. He was also ambitious, obstinate and capable of horrifying acts of cruelty. Until his death in the summer of 1218 he had a thankless and lonely task. Every summer parties of crusaders from France and Germany would descend on Languedoc for the campaigning season. Once their forty days' service was completed they would return home, often at most inconvenient times, and during each winter Simon would be left almost entirely alone, trying desperately to hang on to the gains he had made in the previous summer. In a decision, moreover, that must have prolonged the agony by more than a decade, Innocent abolished most of the indulgences for the Albigensian Crusade early in 1213 in favour of his plans for a new crusade to the East. He therefore cut the ground from under Simon's feet and made his position even more precarious.

In 1210 Simon mastered the rest of the Trencavel lands and King Peter II of Aragon, who had earlier refused to acknowledge him, now accepted his offer of homage for them. Raymond of Toulouse had still not fulfilled the promises he had made at the time of his reconciliation with the Church in 1209 and, although he seems to have pursued no consistent policy in the interim, the legates were convinced that he was not to be trusted. Simon, therefore, prepared to attack Toulouse and Raymond's other lands. Throughout 1211 and 1212 he tried to encircle Toulouse itself by taking nearby strongholds, although towns which had adhered to him would defect to Count Raymond when autumn and the end of the campaigning season came. In the winter of 1212–13 Peter of Aragon, his prestige enhanced by the part he had played in the victory of Las Navas de Tolosa, about which more below, approached the pope directly on behalf of his vassals in Languedoc and his brother-in-law the count of Toulouse, and this certainly provided Innocent with the pretext to abolish crusade privileges for outsiders on the grounds that Simon had overreached himself. In the summer of 1213 Peter marched to Raymond of Toulouse's assistance, but on 12 September he was killed and Aragon's expansionist policy north of the Pyrenees was checked, when his army was decisively defeated by Simon's greatly inferior forces at the Battle of Muret. By the end of 1214 Simon was in control of most of Raymond's lands and the expedition to the south of Louis of France, King Philip's heir, in the early summer of 1215 was a triumphal procession. In November the Fourth Lateran Council assigned to Simon those of Raymond's territories which he had taken; the remainder were to be held in trust by the Church for the count's son.

This was the high point of Simon's career, but it was also a turning-point, because the nobles and towns of the region began to rally to the dispossessed count and his son. In September 1217 Raymond entered Toulouse and on 25 June 1218 Simon was killed before the city by a stone thrown by a mangonel. Leadership was assumed by his son Amalric, then twenty-six years old, but he could not reverse the decline, in spite of the fact that in 1218 the crusade in Languedoc was restored by Innocent's successor, Honorius III. Honorius actively encouraged those who had not taken the cross for the crusade to the East to take part and even transferred a substantial proportion of the tax levied in support of the eastern expedition to southern France. But even Raymond's death in August 1222 did not assist Amalric: his son Raymond VII was more popular than he had been. Amalric was at the end of his resources and the situation was saved only by the intervention of the French monarchy. In January 1226 King Louis VIII vowed to crusade in the south. On 9 September the royal army took Avignon after a three-month siege and almost all the region east of Toulouse declared for the king, who left the administration of his conquests to a new lieutenant, Humbert of Beaujeu.

Although Louis died on 8 November in the course of his journey home, Humbert embarked on a policy of ruthless and systematic destruction in response to Raymond VII's attempts to regain his territory, and the end of the crusade came with the Peace of Paris of 12 April 1229. Raymond received the western and northern parts of the domains held by his father at the start of the crusade, with the proviso that Toulouse could be inherited only by his daughter Joan, who was to be married to King Louis IX's brother Alphonse of Poitou, and by their heirs; otherwise it would revert to the king. The Peace also contained clauses dealing with the issue of heresy, of which one of the most interesting was the endowment of a fund to establish the salaries for ten years of four masters of theology, two decretists, six masters of arts and two masters-regent of grammar at Toulouse. This marked the origins of the university there.

The clauses of the Peace of Paris and the decrees of a council held at Toulouse in November 1229 demonstrated that twenty years of violence had not been very effective, since heresy was as much a concern as ever. The fact was that crusading, which was in its nature episodic, could not eradicate deep-rooted heresy. It required the establishment of the inquisition in Toulouse in 1233 and the persistent pressure that such an instrument could bring to bear for headway to be made. From 1250 the Cathar leaders were withdrawing to Lombardy. By 1324 southern French Catharism was dead.

Crusading in Spain

Innocent also proclaimed a new crusade in Spain. In spite of persistent warfare the only crusading activity in the peninsula since the late 1170s had been in 1189, when two fleets of Frisian, Danish, Flemish, German and English crusaders bound for the East had helped Sancho I of Portugal to take Silves and Alvor, and in 1193 and 1197, when Pope Celestine III had issued crusade letters. In the second of these the pope had decreed that residents of Aquitaine might commute to Spain their vows for Jerusalem; presumably these had been made at the time of the Third Crusade and were still unfulfilled. This was in response to the great victory of the Almohad caliph Ya'qub over Alfonso VIII of Castile at Alarcos on 19 July 1195, a defeat which horrified Christian opinion. Ya'qub was seen as a new Saladin. By 1210 Alfonso felt strong enough to renew the offensive and raiding began, fortified by crusade privileges from Innocent and probably based on the Calatravan castle of Salvatierra, well within Muslim territory. The caliph Muhammad an-Nasir resolved to take action and after a siege of ten weeks took Salvatierra in early September, although this success came too late in the year for him to exploit it.

The news of the loss of Salvatierra caused anxiety throughout western Europe and inspired the pope to proclaim a new crusade in the spring of

1212 in letters written to France as well as Spain. In Rome itself fasting and special prayers were ordered for a Christian victory. Although only one northern Frenchman of importance, Bishop Geoffrey of Nantes, seems to have taken the cross, the response was strong in southern France, perhaps as a by-product of the Albigensian Crusade. In June 1212 a large army was mustering around Alfonso of Castile at Toledo: knights from France, León and Portugal; King Peter of Aragon with a strong force; and, of course, the great Castilian nobles, knights and city militias. It set out on the 20th. Alfonso decided to seek engagement and gamble on a decisive battle. Malagón and Calatrava were taken, but on 3 July most of the French deserted, upset by the heat and possibly by the generous terms allowed to the garrison of Calatrava, which had been taken by the Muslims after Alarcos. Only Archbishop Arnold of Narbonne and some 130 French knights stayed to share in the triumph that was to follow. The army went on to capture a string of fortified places and was joined by King Sancho VII of Navarre before hurrying to meet the advancing Muslims at the Despeñaperros Pass. The Almohad army was encamped on the plain of Las Navas de Tolosa, blocking the pass, but the Christians took a secret path through the hills before appearing to face it on the plain. On 17 July battle was joined and the Muslims were routed after an engagement in which the scales were turned by a heroic charge led by the king of Castile himself. After the victory the Christians took the castles of Vilches, Ferral, Baños and Tolosa, opening Andalucia to invasion, and Baeza and Ubeda, which they destroyed.

Like Hattin twenty-five years before, the battle was the result of deliberate risk-taking, but this time the gamble came off. The news of the victory was greeted in Rome with euphoria and inspired one of the finest of Innocent's letters, a paean of triumph and thanks to God:

> God, the protector of those who hope in him, without whom nothing is strong, nothing firm, multiplying his mercy on you and the Christian people and pouring out his anger on races that do not acknowledge the Lord and against kingdoms that do not invoke his most holy name, according to what had been foretold long ago by the Holy Spirit, has made a laughing-stock of the races which rashly murmured against him and a mockery of the peoples thinking empty thoughts by humbling the arrogance of the strong and causing the pride of the infidels to be laid low.

Innocent characteristically refused to congratulate Alfonso of Castile on the success. Victory was to be attributed not to the crusaders but to God, just as defeat was never a failure on God's part but a commentary on the wickedness of crusaders:

It was not your highness's hands but the Lord who has done all these things. . . . For that victory took place without doubt not by human but by divine agency. . . . So do not walk proudly because those who work wickedness have fallen there, but give glory and honour to the Lord, saying humbly with the prophet *the zeal of the Lord of Hosts* has done this. And while others exult in chariots and horses you ought to rejoice and glory in the name of the Lord your God.

Las Navas de Tolosa was a turning-point in the Reconquest, although this would not have been apparent to contemporaries. The Spanish Crusade, like the Albigensian, was set aside, at least as far as outsiders were concerned, by Innocent in 1213 and on several occasions his successor Honorius III expressed the opinion that it should not divert resources from the crusade to the East, although shiploads of Dutch and Rhineland crusaders on their way to Palestine helped the Portuguese take Alcácer do Sal in 1217. Honorius was prepared to grant a partial indulgence to fighters in Spain in 1219, but even then he stressed that this was only to be granted to those who could not travel to Egypt for some good reason. After the capture of Damietta by the Fifth Crusade his attitude changed and he renewed indulgences in 1221 for an enterprise to be led by Alfonso IX of León-Castile and in 1224 for one to be led by Ferdinand III of Castile, although this indulgence, in accord with Innocent's decree of 1213, was confined only to Spaniards. The full renewal of indulgences for the Spanish crusades came in 1229 in a letter from Pope Gregory IX and there were southern Frenchmen on James I of Aragon's expedition of that year to the Balearic islands.

The Children's Crusade and the preaching of the Fifth Crusade

The picture we have of crusading in 1212 is another panoramic one, if not on the scale of 1147–50. War was being waged on three fronts – along the Baltic coast, in Languedoc and in Spain – but there was relative peace in the East where in 1211 the kingdom of Jerusalem had made a six-year truce with the Muslims. During the previous winter northern France and the Rhineland had been in a ferment, as the preaching of men like William of Paris and James of Vitry for the Albigensian Crusade fired popular enthusiasm and gave rise to upheavals of a type to be found occasionally for the next century. The so-called 'popular crusades' were manifestations of the frustration of the poor. Armies for the eastern theatre were increasingly being transported by sea, which meant that the masses could no longer afford to go with them. It was one thing to join a force marching overland – all one needed was health and the use of one's legs – but it was quite another to find the money to pay for a maritime passage. In 1212 a spontaneous movement arose among children, two of whose leaders were said to be Nicholas, a young boy from Cologne, and a French shepherd boy called Stephen, who claimed to have had a vision of Christ and led crowds of children and shepherds to Paris, chanting, 'Lord God, exalt Christianity! Restore the True Cross to us!' They were accompanied by many adults, several of whom were diverted by churchmen into the Albigensian Crusade. The largest band travelled up the Rhine and across the Alps into Lombardy. There many of them dispersed, although a group reached Genoa and some seem to have arrived in Rome, where Innocent dispensed them from their vows, which were not technically valid anyway. Others may have travelled west to Marseille where, the story goes, they were deceived by two merchants into embarking on ships from which many of them were sold into slavery in North Africa.

With the enthusiasm for crusading that seemed to be prevailing at every level of society it is not surprising that Innocent's mind should have been turning again to the idea of a crusade to the East once the truce made there ended in 1217. In the middle of January 1213 he told his legates in Languedoc that he was planning such a crusade and in the following April he proclaimed it, at the same time demoting those in Spain and Languedoc:

> Because ... aid to the Holy Land would be much impeded or delayed ... we revoke the remissions and indulgences formerly granted by us to those setting out for Spain against the Moors or against the heretics in Provence, chiefly because these were conceded to them in circumstances which have already entirely passed and for that particular cause which has already for the most part disappeared, for so far affairs in both places have gone well, by the grace of God, so that the immediate cause for force is not needed. If perchance it were needed, we would take care to give our attention to any serious situation that arises. We concede, however, that remissions and indulgences of this kind should remain available to the people of Provence and to Spaniards.

In the following September he explained to one of his crusade preachers in Germany exactly what this meant:

> Those who have taken the cross and have proposed to set out against the heretics in Provence and have not yet translated their intention into action must be diligently persuaded to take up the labour of the journey to Jerusalem, because this is an action of greater merit. If perhaps they cannot be persuaded, they must be compelled to carry out the vow they have not yet fulfilled.

This delayed the resolution of the Albigensian Crusade for years, as we have seen, and it caused dismay in Spain. At the Fourth Lateran Council in 1215 the Spanish bishops as a body begged the pope to restore full crusade status to the Reconquest. The pope seems to have assured them that according to the terms of his decision indulgences were available, but only to Spaniards. Even the crusade along the Baltic shore, already isolated and self-contained, appears to have come under threat for a time and Albert of Buxtehude was reported making an impassioned, and successful, plea to the pope during the council, using an argument based on his idea of Livonia as Our Lady's Dower:

> Holy Father, just as you take care to concern yourself with the Holy Land of Jerusalem, which is the land of the Son, so you ought not to ignore Livonia, which is the land of the Mother. ... For the Son loves his Mother and just as he would not wish his land to be lost, so he would not wish his Mother's land to be endangered.

Innocent's demotion of the Albigensian and Iberian crusades was the first example of a kind of decision-making that became common in the thirteenth century. The Roman curia was not happy with the dissipation of effort involved in the waging of war on several fronts concurrently and the popes could decide which theatre of war needed their support most at a given moment. The fact that crusaders were increasingly dependent on them for financial subsidies through the taxation of the Church meant that as the century wore on their readiness to intervene grew.

Innocent and his advisers planned the new crusade with great care. *Quia maior*, the new general letter and possibly the greatest of them all, was sent to almost every province of the Church in the second half of April and early May 1213. It opened with an exposition of crusading thought and dwelt on themes that preachers had been putting to their audiences for a long time. Crusading was an act of Christian charity. The summons to crusade was a divine test of an individual's intentions and also a chance to gain salvation; in this respect Innocent went about as far as it was possible to go theologically, referring to the crusade not only as 'an opportunity to win salvation', but also as 'a means of salvation'. The Holy Land was the patrimony of Christ. Innocent had never hesitated to exploit the concept of the crusade as a quasi-feudal service to God, which was recognized by churchmen as being rather a dangerous one, in that a feudal relationship implied mutual obligations between God and man along the lines of those between lord and vassal – God, of course, was not obliged to anyone – and he repeated it here. He included the formulation of the indulgence he had already introduced and also an important new statement on the enforcement of vows. He had already ruled that as pope he could grant deferment, commutation (the performance of another penitential act in place of that vowed) and redemption (dispensation in return for a money payment, theoretically equalling the sum that would have been spent on crusade), but he had formerly allowed these only in the context of a strict enforcement of most of the vows made. *Quia maior* revealed a change of policy, which was partly a measure of the need felt to raise money and partly a means of limiting the role of the unsuitable by indulgencing them without expecting participation, but it was also, it has been pointed out, a means of extending the benefits of the crusade to all Christians. Everyone, whatever his or her condition, was to be encouraged to take the cross, but those who were not suitable could then redeem their vows for money payments:

> Because in fact it would mean that aid to the Holy Land would be much impeded or delayed if before taking the cross each person had to be examined to see whether he was personally fit and able to fulfil a vow of this kind, we concede that anyone who wishes, except persons bound by religious profession, may take the cross in such a way that this vow may be commuted, redeemed or deferred by apostolic mandate when urgent or evident expediency demands it.

A few months later Innocent explained this to a puzzled preacher:

> You can deduce clearly from the letter what you ought to do about women or other persons who have taken the cross and are not suitable or able to fulfil the vow. It states expressly that anyone, except a religious, may take the sign of the cross at will in such a way that when urgent need or evident expediency demands it that vow may be commuted or redeemed or deferred by apostolic mandate.

From this policy originated, of course, the notorious 'sale of indulgences'. Its implementation by the papal legates in France caused a scandal and the abuses to which it was liable led to sporadic criticism throughout the thirteenth century.

Innocent's passion for organization, and perhaps also his experience of the difficulties of recruitment in 1198–9 and 1208, led him to introduce an elaborate system for the preaching of the cross, which resulted in the production in England, France and Germany of handbooks for preachers. He personally oversaw preaching in Italy. In Scandinavia and France papal legates were charged with organizing recruitment. In every other province of Latin Christendom the pope appointed small groups of preachers, many of them bishops, with legatine powers, who were permitted to delegate the task of recruitment to deputies in each diocese. The pope laid down detailed rules for their behaviour and clearly took a great interest in the way they carried out their duties.

Like *Audita tremendi*, *Quia maior* laid great stress on the need for repentance. It decreed monthly penitential processions throughout

Christendom and introduced a new intercessory rite to be inserted into the Mass after the Kiss of Peace and before the reception of Communion. Its penitential sections underlined the conviction that crusading could only be successful if accompanied by a spiritual reawakening of Christendom. Innocent carried the belief of his predecessors in the necessity for general reform to its logical conclusion. *Quia maior* was issued in conjunction with a summons to a general council, the Fourth Lateran Council, the proceedings of which were permeated with crusading themes. The council was opened on 11 November 1215 with a sermon from Innocent in which he stressed the twin aims of crusade and renewal. Among the decrees there was one, *Excommunicamus*, which justified, and laid down rules for, crusades against heretics and led some canonists like Raymond of Peñafort to be concerned lest it would be treated as a standing authorization for crusading of this type.

Even more important was an appendix to the decrees, entitled *Ad liberandam*, which was approved by the council on 14 December and carried the planning of the Fifth Crusade further, giving the date for its departure as 1 June 1217. This, Professor Brundage has pointed out, was 'the most extensive and ambitious catalogue of crusader rights and privileges promulgated by the papacy up to that time and ... its provisions were repeated verbatim in most papal letters throughout the rest of the middle ages'. It legislated for priests in the armies and their enjoyment of their benefices *in absentia*. It included Innocent's classic formulation of the indulgence. It declared the immunity of crusaders from taxes and usury and a moratorium on their debts and it assured them of the Church's protection of their property. It prohibited trade with the Muslims in war-materials and banned tournaments for three years. It decreed peace in Christendom for the duration of the crusade. Most of these provisions had appeared in *Quia maior* and other papal letters, but *Ad liberandam* also instituted another income tax on churchmen. Although in *Quia maior* Innocent had called on them to endow fighting men, he had refrained from reintroducing the tax provisions of 1199, perhaps because they had been so unsuccessful. Now he ordered a three-year tax of a twentieth of all church income, six times more onerous than the earlier one, and he put papal commissioners in charge of raising it: in 1199 he had left the collection of the tax to the bishops, but their lack of cooperation had very soon persuaded him to send officials from Rome to oversee it. Unlike 1199, there was no guarantee in *Ad liberandam* that the tax would not create a precedent. This time, indeed, it was imposed with the approval of a general council and the principle was thereby established that a pope had the right to tax the clergy without any further consent. The ratification of this tax by the general council did not enhance its popularity. It met with fierce opposition in Spain, since it added insult to the injury of the demotion of the Reconquest, and resistance in France, Italy, Germany and Hungary.

Innocent died on 16 July 1216, just after preaching the cross in central Italy and at a time when he was preparing to embark on a tour of northern Italy in the interests of the crusade. With him the various formulae and definitions reached their mature form and his letters became exemplars for future popes. He extended the use of crusading, but within a traditional framework of thought which few expressed as lucidly and beautifully as he, or his draftsmen, did. He was the first pope to tax the Church for crusades, the first to organize a large-scale crusade against heretics, the first to exploit redemptions and the first to build up an elaborate system for preaching the cross. With the Fourth Crusade he probably introduced the idea of a sea-borne invasion of Egypt by a largely mercenary army raised in Europe. With the Fifth, as Professor Powell has written, 'the crusade was being forged into an instrument for the moral transformation of society'. And yet, as with so much else in his pontificate, his ideas were too ambitious and his actual power far too restricted. The Fourth Crusade, in particular, demonstrated the intrinsic weakness of his position. Canon law prohibited priests from military command and the pope was a priest. In spite of his desire to control the greatest instrument at his disposal as 'papal monarch', he had to rely for the implementation of his ideas on secular magnates, who were all too fallible and were often thoroughly incompetent.

The course of the Fifth Crusade

His successor, Honorius III, was an elderly man, who used to be thought to have reigned in his shadow. A new picture of Honorius as an ambitious and independent-minded pope is beginning to emerge. He pressed forward with preparations for the new crusade, trying to cope with the obstacles that so often obstructed the launching of expeditions of this type. Frederick II, the young king of the Romans, had taken the cross at the time of his coronation in Aachen in July 1215, but was unlikely to be able to go while his throne and claim to the western empire was contested by Otto of Brunswick. The papal legates in France, Robert of Courçon and Archbishop Simon of Tyre, had aroused great enthusiasm among the poor, but although the dukes of Burgundy and Brabant, the constable of France, the counts of Bar, La Marche, Nevers and Rodez and the lord of Joinville all took the cross, the French contribution was to be proportionately much less than on the Third and Fourth Crusades. Events in Languedoc, where the Albigensian Crusade was dragging on and would cost the life of King Louis VIII in 1226, the aftermath of the French victory over Otto of Brunswick, John of England and the Flemish in the Battle of Bouvines in 1214 and perhaps knowledge of the planned involvement of Frederick II may have contributed to this. The French lack of commitment worried thoughtful churchmen, but it was more than made up for elsewhere, particularly in Hungary, Germany, Italy and the

Netherlands, where the success of one of the best of the preachers, Oliver of Paderborn, was said to have been literally phenomenal, being accompanied by miracles.

King Andrew of Hungary, who had taken the cross in 1196 but had been granted a series of postponements by the popes, was the first to move. His representatives negotiated with the Venetians for a fleet to meet him at Split, but when his army, containing contingents led by the dukes of Austria and Merano, and the archbishop of Kalocsa and many bishops, abbots and counts from the empire and Hungary, mustered there in late August 1217, it was found that the king's envoys had fallen into exactly the opposite trap to that which had led to the diversion of the Fourth Crusade. Too many soldiers arrived for the ships available and the main body had to wait for several weeks before embarkation. Many knights returned home or made plans for sailing in the following spring.

A large army gathered at Acre in the autumn. It was too large for the food at hand, because a poor harvest had led to famine conditions in Palestine, and crusaders were even being advised to return home. Before they had come the king of Jerusalem, John of Brienne, and the masters of the three military orders of the Temple, the Hospital of St John, and St Mary of the Germans had been considering plans for two separate but simultaneous campaigns: one to Nablus with the intention of recovering the West Bank lands and the other to Damietta in Egypt. Now a council of war met and, putting both of these aside for the time being, decided to promote a series of small-scale expeditions to keep the enemy, and doubtless the troops in Acre, occupied until the rest of the crusade arrived. In early November a reconnaissance-in-force pillaged Bet She'an and crossed the Jordan south of the Sea of Galilee, before marching up the eastern shore of the lake and returning to Acre by way of Jisr Banat Ya'qub. After a brief rest the crusaders marched against Mount Tabor in Galilee, which the Muslims had fortified; the threat from it had been referred to by Innocent III in *Quia maior*. On 3 December they advanced up the mountain in a mist, but their attack failed, as did a second assault two days later. On 7 December they returned to Acre. A third expedition, of not more than 500 men, set out not long before Christmas to attack brigands in the mountainous hinterland of Sidon, but it was ambushed and destroyed.

Meanwhile the king of Hungary, who had played no part in operations after the first reconnaissance-in-force, was making preparations to return home. He left for Syria early in January 1218 and travelled overland to Europe through Asia Minor, taking many of his subjects with him. The crusaders who remained in Acre occupied themselves with the refortification of Caesarea and the building of a great new Templar castle at 'Atlit (Chastel Pèlerin) until fresh reinforcements arrived. These began to sail into Acre on 26 April. With large numbers of Frisians, Germans and

Italians now assembling and, just as importantly, with an impressive fleet at their disposal, the leaders decided that the time had come to invade Egypt. This was in a sense the fulfilment of the Fourth Crusade project. On 27 May the vanguard of the invasion force arrived at Damietta, which as long ago as 1199 had been identified by the patriarch of Jerusalem as the most important target in the Delta. Meeting little resistance, the crusaders chose a site for their encampment, which they fortified with a moat and wall, on an island opposite the city, bordered by the Nile and an abandoned canal.

It was to be eighteen months until Damietta fell. During this period the besiegers were to be reinforced by Italian, French, Cypriot and English crusaders, although there were, of course, also departures: Leopold of Austria in May 1219 for example. King John of Jerusalem was given the overall command, although that seems to have meant little more than the presidency of a steering committee. In September 1218 the papal legate Pelagius of Albano arrived. Pelagius had a strong personality and he was prepared to challenge John's assumption that Egypt would be annexed to his kingdom if it was conquered. His voice became dominant on the committee and John slipped more and more into the background.

In the first stage of the siege the Christians strove to take the Chain Tower, an impressive fortification on an island in the middle of the Nile, from which iron chains could be raised to halt river traffic. Various measures were tried before a floating siege-engine designed by Oliver of Paderborn himself, a miniature castle with a revolving scaling-ladder incorporated into it, was built on two cogs lashed together and was sent against the tower on 24 August 1218. After a fierce fight the crusaders gained a foothold and the surviving defenders surrendered on the following day. The sultan of Egypt was said to have died of shock after hearing the news of this reverse, but the crusaders did not immediately press home their advantage and the Muslims countered the loss of the tower by blocking the Nile with sunken ships. In October the crusaders had to fight off two determined attacks on their camp. They also laboured to dredge the abandoned canal that bounded it so that they could by-pass Damietta and bring their ships up above it. The canal was open by early December, but the winter was exceptionally severe and they suffered intensely from floods which destroyed their provisions and tents and carried over to the Muslim bank of the Nile a new floating fortress, built this time on six cogs, which they had been constructing. In early February 1219, however, the Muslim army facing them abandoned its encampment near the city on hearing of the flight of the new Egyptian sultan, who had uncovered a plot to depose him, and order was restored too late to prevent the Christians crossing the Nile and occupying the same bank as Damietta, together with large stocks of provisions. They now held both sides of the river and built a bridge between them.

At this point the Egyptian government sued for terms, proposing to surrender all the territory of the kingdom of Jerusalem except Transjordan and to adhere to a thirty-year truce in return for the crusaders' evacuation of Egypt. The proposal for a thirty-year truce was an extraordinary concession in the light of the belief in Islamic circles that truces of no more than ten years' duration should be made with infidels. The king of Jerusalem was in favour of acceptance, but Pelagius and the military orders were not, even after the Egyptians added to their offer a rent of 15,000 besants a year for the castles of Karak and Shaubak in Transjordan. The Muslims had, meanwhile, been reinforced by an army from Syria and throughout March, April and May they launched attacks on the new Christian camp. The crusaders built a second pontoon bridge, resting on thirty-eight vessels, below the city and from 8 July made a series of direct assaults on Damietta until a fall in the level of the Nile made it impossible for them to reach the river walls with their scaling-ladders. The Muslims outside the city, who had responded with counter-attacks, penetrated deep into the Christian camp on 31 July before being driven out.

On 29 August the crusaders decided to launch an attack on the Muslim encampment, but, drawn into a trap by a feigned withdrawal, they were badly mauled when their advance faltered. The sultan at once reopened negotiations, adding to his previous proposals the promise to pay for the rebuilding of the walls of Jerusalem and of the castles of Belvoir, Safad and Toron. He also offered the relic of the True Cross which had been lost at Hattin. The king of Jerusalem, the French, the English and the Teutonic Knights were for acceptance, but Pelagius, the Templars and the Hospitallers were adamantly against. In fact the garrison of Damietta was now so weakened by starvation that it could not defend the city properly and on the night of 4 November four Christian sentries noticed that one of the towers appeared to be deserted. Scaling the wall, they found it abandoned and the crusaders quickly occupied the city. The Egyptian army stationed nearby withdrew hastily to El Mansura and by 23 November the Christians had also taken the town of Tinnis along the coast without a fight.

The latent discord between Pelagius of Albano and John of Jerusalem now came to a head. John left, depriving the crusade of its chief military leader, and the tensions at the top manifested themselves lower in the ranks in riots, exacerbated by disputes over the division of the rich spoil found in the city. Rather surprisingly, the Christians made no further move for nearly twenty months, allowing the sultan to turn his camp at El Mansura into a formidable stronghold. Again he renewed, and in fact raised, his offer to them. Again they turned it down. They were now waiting for the arrival of the emperor Frederick II, who at his coronation on 22 November 1220 promised to send part of his army on the next spring passage and to go to Egypt himself in the following August.

The German troops arrived in May 1221 and at last preparations were made for an advance into the interior. On 7 July John of Jerusalem, strictly ordered by the pope to rejoin the crusade, returned and on the 17th the crusaders began to march down the east bank of the Nile. On the 24th, against John's advice, they moved into a narrow angle of land, bounded by two branches of the Nile, opposite El Mansura and then halted. It is possible that they were assuming that the Nile was not going to flood, as it had occasionally failed to do in the past. If so, they were rash, because the river began to rise in August, somewhat later than usual. The Muslims made use of a small canal to bring ships into the main branches, blocking the river route back to Damietta. This unexpected move forced the Christians to withdraw, but the Muslims sent their land forces round behind them, cutting off their retreat, and broke dykes to flood the land. The crusaders were trapped and had to sue for peace. On 30 August they agreed to leave Egypt in return for a truce of eight years and the True Cross, which they were never given, perhaps because the Egyptians did not have it.

The crusade of Frederick II

Reinforcements sent by Frederick had arrived in the middle of this débâcle and their leaders bitterly opposed the terms which had been agreed. When Frederick heard of them he was furious, but he was hardly in the position to criticize. He had not fulfilled his pledge to crusade in the autumn of 1221 and he was being as severely berated as the kings of England and France had been thirty years before. His failure to depart did not mean that he was indifferent. He could certainly be ruthless, but, in spite of the scandalous stories told about him in his lifetime – his was a career that somehow bedazzled contemporaries as well as his biographers – there is no doubt that he was conventionally pious and that he felt deeply committed to the crusading movement. He was still in his twenties and the long civil war in Germany and the anarchy he found on his return to southern Italy explain his delay in fulfilling the vow he had made in 1215. Pope Honorius, however, who had himself been criticized for the crusade's failure, could not refrain from forcefully expressing his feelings. At Ferentino in March 1223 Frederick renewed his vow in the presence of King John, the patriarch of Jerusalem and the masters of the military orders. The date of 24 June 1225 was set for his departure and he was betrothed to the heiress of the kingdom of Jerusalem, for whom her father John was now regent. Frederick offered free transport and provisions to crusaders, but in spite of these generous financial inducements the response was not great and he was forced to suggest a postponement to allow the preaching to have more effect. At San Germano on 25 July 1225 he agreed to leave on 15 August 1227 and he accepted severe conditions imposed on him by the pope. He had to promise to maintain 1,000 knights in the East at his expense for two years and to pay a fine of 50 marks for every man less than that figure, to provide 100 transports and 50 armed galleys and to send 100,000 ounces of gold in advance in five instalments to the leaders of the settlement in Palestine, to meet his war expenses; the money would be returned to him when he reached Acre.

Frederick married Yolande (Isabella) of Jerusalem in Brindisi on 9 November and took the title of king of Jerusalem, having himself crowned in a special ceremony at Foggia. This led to the goal of his crusade being switched from Egypt to Jerusalem. Meanwhile there was quite heavy recruitment in Germany and England and by mid-summer 1227 large numbers of crusaders were assembling in southern Italy. They sailed from Brindisi in August and early September and, although many of them dispersed when the news reached Palestine that the emperor was not joining them after all, the main body marched down the coast to Caesarea and Jaffa to restore the town fortifications, while others occupied and fortified the city of Sidon in its entirety – half of it had been controlled from Damascus – and built the castle of Montfort, north-east of Acre.

Meanwhile Frederick, who had fallen ill, put into the port of Otranto and decided to wait until he was better. Pope Gregory IX responded by excommunicating him. It is hard to decide whether Gregory acted in this way because he was exasperated by yet another delay, which was what he claimed, or whether he was preparing the ground for his invasion of Frederick's south Italian possessions, which would have been impossible had Frederick's crusade been legitimate, since the Church would have been bound to protect his property. At any rate, when Frederick at last sailed for the East on 28 June 1228 he was an excommunicated and unrecognized crusader. On reaching Acre on 7 September, after an interlude in Cyprus which will be described later, he found himself in no position to fight a campaign. His army was small, because so many of the crusaders of the previous year had returned home, and divided, because many elements did not want to be associated with him now that he was excommunicated. Since 1226, however, he had been exchanging embassies with al-Kamil, the sultan of Egypt, who wanted to enter into an alliance with him against his brother, al-Mu'azzam of Damascus. By 1228 al-Mu'azzam was dead, but al-Kamil, who had been given a severe shock by the Fifth Crusade, does not seem to have realized how weak Frederick was and was prepared to use Jerusalem as a bargaining counter to ensure Egypt's security.

Negotiations began at once. In a show of what force he had Frederick marched from Acre to Jaffa in November. On 18 February 1229 a treaty was signed by which al-Kamil surrendered Bethlehem and Nazareth, a strip of land from Jerusalem to the coast, part of the district of Sidon, which had already been occupied by the Christians, the castle of Toron and, above all, Jerusalem itself, although the Temple area was to remain in Muslim hands and the city was not to be fortified. In return Frederick pledged himself to protect the sultan's interests against all enemies, even Christians, for the duration of a truce of ten years; in particular, he would lend no aid to Tripoli or Antioch or to the castles of the military orders of Crac des Chevaliers, Marqab and Safita. It was unlikely, however, that Jerusalem would be defensible and on hearing of the treaty the patriarch of Jerusalem imposed an interdict on the city. Frederick entered it on 17 March and on the following day he went through an imperial crown-wearing ceremony in the Church of the Holy Sepulchre, echoing the ancient prophecy of the last German emperor in occupation of Jerusalem before Anti-Christ, which had been an element in crusading thought from the start and may have motivated his grandfather. Jerusalem was to remain in Christian hands for fifteen years, but it does not seem to have been reincorporated into the kingdom and was treated by Frederick as a personal possession.

On 19 March he returned to Acre, where he faced resistance from the patriarch, the nobles, whose relations with him will be discussed later, and the Templars; the city was in a state of disorder, with armed soldiers roaming the streets. But news of the invasion of Apulia by papal armies forced the emperor to leave hurriedly for home. He tried to go secretly in the early morning of 1 May, but he was pelted with tripe and pieces of meat as he passed the meat markets on his way down to the port.

So the Fifth Crusade had a curious postscript. Jerusalem was recovered in a peace treaty negotiated by an excommunicate, whose crusade was not recognized and whose lands were being invaded by papal forces. The city itself was put under an interdict by its own patriarch. Its liberator left Palestine not in triumph but showered with offal.

CHAPTER 7

Crusading in Maturity, 1229–c. 1291

Crusading thought in the mid-thirteenth century

One hundred and fifty years after its birth crusading thought was given a classic expression in the writings of Pope Innocent IV and his pupil Henry of Segusio (better known as Hostiensis). Both men stressed that the pope was the sole earthly legitimizer. The indulgence, which only he could grant, was an expression of his authority in this matter. The Holy Land, consecrated by the presence and suffering of Christ and once part of the Roman empire, was rightfully Christian and the occupation of it by the Muslims was an offence for which the pope, as vicar of Christ and heir of the Roman emperors, could order retribution. Crusades could also be waged defensively against threats from infidels and by extension against those who menaced Christian souls within Christendom. Hostiensis echoed Peter the Venerable's opinion that crusades against heretics, schismatics and rebels were even more necessary than those to the Holy Land, but he was much more radical than Innocent on relations between Christians and infidels. Innocent was prepared to argue that the pope had a *de jure*, but not *de facto*, authority over infidels, with the power to order them to allow missionaries to preach in their lands and a right in the last resort to punish them for infringements of natural law, but he stressed that Christians could not make war on them for being infidels, nor could they fight wars of conversion. Hostiensis, on the other hand, supposed that the pope could intervene directly in the affairs of infidels and that their refusal to recognize his dominion was in itself justification for a Christian assault upon them. He even suggested that any war fought by Christians against unbelievers was just, by reason of the faith of the Christian side alone. This went too far and Christian opinion since has tended to follow Innocent rather than Hostiensis.

The cerebral and legalistic approaches of Innocent and Hostiensis are rather uninspiring and give no impression of crusading's passionate nature. It is true that its most radical aspect – the fact that it was a personal act of penance – had been gradually diluted by theological developments and by the growth of chivalry and was coming to be seen more in terms of the notion, which stretched back to St Augustine around 400, of service-in-arms for Christ, but one should never exaggerate the extent of the shift away from penance. Crusading remained a penitential activity and this was reflected in the devotional language of thirteenth-century sermons, in which attachment to the cross was central. To the experienced preacher Humbert of Romans it was the cross, the sign of man's redemption, which distinguished Christians from Muslims. It marked the crusader's dedication to the service of Christ and his commitment to some share in the Passion:

> It is just that we wear [Christ's] cross on our shoulders because of him, having it not only in our heart through faith and in our mouth through confession, but also in our body through the endurance of pain.

Of course the cross had always been a major feature of crusading thought, but for the first eighty years of the movement its image appears to have been less significant in the words of preachers and the minds of crusaders (in so far as one can see into them) than the reality of Christ's Tomb in Jerusalem. The triumph of the cross in crusading thought, its transformation from a potent symbol of self-sacrifice to the justification which gave meaning to everything, came about above all because the age was characterized by growing devotion to the Crucifixion and by the appearance of affective imagery relating to it. The stress on the cross reflected a popular religion which was becoming more and more cross-centred.

By the middle of the thirteenth century crusading had become commonplace and many committed families could look back on four or five generations of crusaders. The privileges which regulated crusader status had become formalized. To the greatest of them, the indulgence, were added rights which were elaborations of those traditionally enjoyed by pilgrims: the protection of property and dependants in a crusader's absence; a delay in the performance of feudal service and in judicial proceedings to which he might be a party while he was away, or alternatively a speedy settlement of court cases before his departure; his ability to count the crusade as restitution of theft; a moratorium on the repayment of debts and freedom from interest payments until his return; exemption from tolls and taxes; for a cleric the freedom to enjoy his benefice though not resident and to pledge it to raise cash; and for a layman the freedom to sell or pledge fiefs or other property which was ordinarily inalienable. A further group of rights gave him a privileged legal position in the extraordinary circumstances in which he found himself: release from excommunication by virtue of taking the cross; the ability to count a crusade vow as an adequate substitute for another not yet fulfilled; licence to have dealings with excommunicates and freedom from the consequences of interdict; a guarantee against being cited for legal proceedings outside his native diocese; the privilege of having a personal confessor, who was often permitted to dispense him from irregularities and to grant pardon for sins, like homicide, which were usually reserved to papal jurisdiction.

The machinery for preaching, though never again as systematic as that proposed by Innocent III in 1213, was well established and with the proclamation of indulgences and the appointment of legates it would swing into action, making increasing use of the mendicant friars, who became the normal preachers of the cross. Between 1266 and 1268 Humbert of Romans, who had resigned as master general of the Order of Preachers a few years before and was living in retirement in the Dominican convent in Lyon, wrote *De praedicatione sanctae crucis contra Saracenos*, a portable handbook for them. He wanted them to be well prepared before embarking on their journeys. They should be acquainted with the geography of the world and of the places to which crusades would be directed, particularly those mentioned in the Bible. They should know about Islam – he suggested they should read the Quran – the life of Muhammad and past wars between Christians and Muslims, for which he provided a reading list. They should have the technical knowledge required to give advice and to answer questions on the papal letters which proclaimed crusades and on indulgences, absolutions and dispensations. To help them with their sermons Humbert included 138 scriptural citations as preaching texts, drawn from both the Old and New Testaments to 'provide a panorama of the religious wars of sacred history', as Dr Cole has put it, and anecdotes to arouse an audience's interest extracted from another book list.

He advised his preachers to arrange to meet great lords privately, since these could induce a wide clientage to join them in taking the cross. Private meetings, however, were never more than supplementary to the set-piece public sermon. This should be quite short and should end with an *invitatio*, in which the preacher should implore his listeners to take the cross. Humbert gave twenty-nine examples. Here are the opening sentences of one of them:

> And so it is clear, most beloved, that those who join the army of the Lord will be blessed by the Lord. They will have the angels as companions and they will receive eternal rewards when they die.

Other surviving thirteenth-century sermons contain similar invocations. They are often rather stilted, appearing as they do in carefully written exemplars, but they must usually have been extempore and we can get some idea of how passionate they could become from a report of a sermon preached in Basel by Abbot Martin of Pairis on 3 May 1200. It is punctuated by extraordinarily emotional appeals:

> And so, strong warriors, run to Christ's aid today, enlist in the knighthood of Christ, hasten to band yourselves together in companies sure of success. It is to you today that I commit Christ's cause, it is into your hands that I give over, so to speak, Christ himself, so that you

may strive to restore him to his inheritance, from which he has been cruelly expelled.

Humbert's *invitationes* each end with the word *cantus*. He explained that an *invitatio* should be accompanied by a hymn, referring to the *Veni Creator*, the *Veni Sancte Spiritus*, the *Vexilla regis* and the *Salve crux sancta*, but he added that any other that was suitable could be used. We know that some preachers made use of popular songs. Two of Humbert's hymns were devoted to the cross and two to the Holy Spirit which had always been invoked as the inspirer of crusaders. A choir must have started up as men came forward to commit themselves publicly.

Churchmen were now regularly taxed. Usually apportioned at a tenth, the levies were demanded of the whole Church or of the clergy in particular provinces for periods varying from one to six years. Settlement was usually expected in two equal instalments a year. Grants of subsidies were made to a wide range of individuals from kings to petty lords, often consisting of the cash raised from the churches in their own territories and in those of their relatives. I have already pointed out that this gave the popes a directing power that they could never have hoped for in the twelfth century, because, with crusading so expensive and crusaders patently in need of funds, they could divert their grants and therefore a large part of crusade resources in the direction dictated by their policy at a particular time. In practice, however, their control was never as effective as the theory would suggest. If a grantee failed to fulfil his vow his subsidy, which had been deposited in the meantime in religious houses, was supposed to be sent to Rome, but particularly where kings were concerned the popes seldom got all they should. And the taxation, which tended to become cumulative as new subsidies were demanded while old ones were still in arrears, was extremely unpopular and was strongly criticized on grounds of principle. Papal envoys were greeted with hostility and resistance was such that the returns were often slow in coming and were sometimes not paid at all.

A beneficial result, however, was that the grants of cash enabled crusade leaders not only to employ mercenaries, but also to subsidize subordinate crusaders. From perhaps as early as the Fourth Crusade, and certainly from the later 1230s, kings and greater lords were entering into contracts for service with their followers, granting them money in return for specified service with a known number of men. This system of indentures enabled volunteers to be paid as if they were in the leaders' employment and it made them much more amenable to discipline.

The Barons' Crusade, 1239–41

The truce that Frederick II had made with the sultan of Egypt was due to end in July 1239 and in anticipation Pope Gregory IX issued a new crusade proclamation in 1234. He gave the Dominicans a special commission to preach the cross. In contrast to the Fifth Crusade, the response in France was enthusiastic and in September 1235 Gregory had to order the French bishops to see that crusaders did not leave before the truce in the East expired. He himself had been considering a more ambitious, and far more useful, plan to maintain an army in Palestine for ten years after the ending of the truce, but he had put forward a quite unrealistic proposal, which was to be modified by Gregory X in 1274 and must have been based on the crusade taxes of the twelfth-century kings. Every Christian, male and female, cleric and lay, who did not take the cross was to contribute one penny a week to the cause – a sum that was quite beyond the means of most – and out of this subsidies were to be given to crusaders and to building works in the East. Contributors would be rewarded only with a limited indulgence. It is not surprising that this tax does not ever seem to have been collected.

It had been hoped that the French crusaders would be in the Holy Land before July 1239, but the insistence of Frederick II, on whose ports in southern Italy they might have to rely for shipping and supplies, that no army should set foot in Palestine until after the truce expired, meant that their departure was postponed until August. Much more seriously, the pope changed his mind. The desperate needs of the Latin empire of Constantinople, which will be described in the next chapter, led him in the late summer of 1236 to propose switching the crusade, under the leadership of Peter of Dreux, the count of Brittany, to Constantinople. He asked Count Thibald of Champagne, who had taken the cross for Palestine, to help the Latin empire. He told the archbishop of Reims, who was Peter of Dreux's brother, to finance Count Henry of Bar if he decided to go to Constantinople. He ordered the bishop of Sées to commute his vow to the aid of the Latin empire and authorized the bishop of Mâcon to allow Humbert of Beaujeu, the hammer of Languedoc in 1226, to commute his; the pope is supposed, in fact, to have commuted the vows of 600 northern French knights. He also wrote to Hungary to encourage men there to assist Constantinople. In France there was resistance to this change of goal – in the end even Peter of Dreux and Henry of Bar went to Palestine – and by late May 1237 Gregory seems to have become reconciled to the fact that there were now going to be two crusades. Owing to the efforts of the Latin emperor Baldwin II who led it, the crusade for Constantinople was quite large when it left in the late summer of 1239, although the only great French nobles known to have taken part were Humbert of Beaujeu and Thomas of Marly. It took Çorlu in Thrace in 1240 and its presence bought Constantinople a breathing space.

Meanwhile the French crusaders for the Holy Land, who mustered at Lyon, comprised the most glittering crusading army recruited in France since 1202 and were headed by two peers, Count Thibald of Champagne, who was also king of Navarre and was the son of the early leader of the Fourth Crusade, and Duke Hugh of Burgundy. In their company were the constable Amalric of Montfort, Simon of Montfort's son and inheritor in Languedoc, the butler Robert of Courtenay, and the counts of Brittany, Nevers, Bar, Sancerre, Mâcon, Joigny and Grandpré. Most of them sailed from Marseille in August and reached Acre around 1 September. News soon reached them of a Muslim move against Jerusalem, but their arrival coincided with a debate among the leading settlers over whether to launch an attack on the ruler of Damascus or the sultan in Cairo, who were at odds with one another and could therefore be tackled separately. In the end it was decided to take on both at once. The army would march down the coast to refortify the citadel of Ascalon before campaigning against Damascus. On 12 November a very strong army of c. 4,000 knights reached Jaffa, where they learned that there was a large Egyptian force at Gaza. Ignoring the warnings and even the veto of Thibald of Champagne, Peter of Dreux and the masters of the military orders, a force which included the duke of Burgundy, the counts of Bar, Montfort and Brienne, the last of whom had custody of Jaffa, and the lords of Sidon and Arsuf and Odo of Montbéliard, the constable of Jerusalem, pressed on through the night and camped on the frontier beyond Ascalon. Perhaps its plan was not as rash as it now appears to have been since it had been agreed by leading local nobles, who ought to have known their enemy, but the commanders neglected to post sentries. They consequently found themselves surrounded and, although the duke of Burgundy and lords of the settlement deserted, Henry of Bar and Amalric of Montfort refused to do so. In the engagement that followed they were tricked into leaving their position to charge after a feigned retreat. Henry was killed. Amalric and some eighty knights were captured.

The main body of the Christian army learned of the ambush on reaching Ascalon, but the Egyptians retired without further engagement. The crusaders did not start to rebuild the citadel at Ascalon as they had planned, but withdrew back up the coast to Acre. There they stayed, even after an-Nasir Da'ud, the lord of Transjordan, took Jerusalem and destroyed the Tower of David. In the spring of 1240 Thibald led his forces north to Tripoli, tempted by an offer of conversion to Christianity from the lord of Hama which does not seem to have been serious and stemmed from a desire for aid against his fellow Muslim princes. Nothing of course came of this venture and Thibald was back in Acre in May. He then negotiated an alliance with as-Salih Isma'il of Damascus, who was worried by a turn of political events that had brought his nephew and predecessor as ruler of Damascus the sultanate of Egypt and promised to return Beaufort and the hinterland of Sidon, Tiberias, Safad and all Galilee to the Christians, together with Jerusalem, Bethlehem and most of southern Palestine, once a coalition between Damascus and the Latins had gained victory over Egypt. The treaty was naturally resisted by Muslim religious leaders – as-Salih Isma'il even had to besiege Beaufort before handing it over – and within the Latin kingdom by the party which was still in favour of a treaty with Egypt. But Thibald led his army to a rendezvous with the Damascene forces at Jaffa. As the Egyptians advanced on Palestine large numbers of the troops from Damascus, who were anyway demoralized, deserted, leaving the Christian force isolated. So Thibald was persuaded to enter into negotiations with Egypt. Again there was opposition within the Christian ranks and on the face of it his crusade was becoming somewhat absurd. He had begun by making war on both Egypt and Damascus and was proceeding to negotiate two mutually contradictory peaces. Nevertheless he secured from the Egyptians the promise of the lands in southern Palestine, including Jerusalem, already granted to the Christians by Damascus: that is to say more territory for the settlers than they had held since 1187. After visiting Jerusalem, now back in Christian hands, he departed for the West in September 1240, leaving the duke of Burgundy and the count of Nevers to rebuild the fortress at Ascalon. No sooner had he left than a second wave of crusaders arrived.

There had been a significant response in England to Pope Gregory's appeal. Richard, earl of Cornwall, King Henry III's younger brother, had taken the cross in 1236. He had to resist attempts by his brother and the pope to keep him in England; in 1239 Gregory had even suggested that he send to Constantinople the money he would have spent crusading and had only reluctantly agreed to him making use of the cash which had been collected in England for the Latin empire. He left England on 10 June 1240, accompanied by William, earl of Salisbury, and about a dozen nobles. Simon of Montfort, the earl of Leicester and Amalric's younger brother, who also crusaded at this time, seems to have travelled to the East separately. There were c. 800 English knights in the two parties. Richard reached Acre on 8 October. He found the leadership of the settlement still bitterly divided over relations with Damascus and Egypt, but he decided to follow the advice of the majority, who were for the treaty with Egypt. Marching down to Jaffa, he met the Egyptian envoys and then proceeded to Ascalon to complete the building of the citadel, which he handed over to representatives of the emperor Frederick, the king-regent, ignoring the claims of the baronial opposition which will be described in the next chapter. On 8 February 1241 the truce with Egypt was formally confirmed and on the 13th the prisoners-of-war taken at Gaza were returned. On 3 May Richard sailed for home.

The first crusade of St Louis

Much of the territory gained by Thibald and Richard was lost in 1244 when yet another switch in alliances led to the capture of Jerusalem by the

Khorezmians and the disastrous defeat of the Latin settlers at the Battle of Harbiyah (La Forbie). The news of the fall of Jerusalem probably contributed to King Louis IX of France's decision to take the cross in the following December, but there were also other reasons for his vow. He was seriously ill at the time. It may be that his decision was an act of rebellion against the tutelage of his able and domineering mother, Blanche of Castile, who had held the regency during his minority and had been a great influence upon him even after his coming of age: he was now thirty. She was very upset and with the bishop of Paris's help persuaded him that a vow made during an illness was not binding. His response was to take the vow again once he was well and nothing his mother could say would deter him. It has been pointed out that this defiance of his mother's wishes in a sacred cause echoed the action of his sister Isabella, to whom he was very close, when, eighteen months before, she had rejected the offer of marriage to the emperor's heir – an alliance that had the support of Blanche, Frederick II and the pope – and in the course of a dangerous illness had vowed herself to perpetual virginity. She did not enter a convent but lived at home like a nun, dressing very simply and devoting herself to the care of the poor. The parallels – illness, vow, rejection of their mother's plans for them – may not be coincidental.

Louis's choice of the vehicle for this defiance was a perfectly natural one for a man of his station and inclinations. He was the inheritor of a powerful family tradition. On his father's side almost every generation had produced a crusader since 1095. His great-great-great-grandfather's brother had taken part in the First Crusade. His great-grandfather and grandfather had been leaders of the Second and Third Crusades respectively. His father had died returning from the Albigensian Crusade, which made it natural for Blanche to be so very apprehensive. And through Blanche herself Louis was the heir of another line of dedicated crusaders. The kings of Castile had been leaders of the Spanish Reconquest and Blanche's father had been the victor of Las Navas de Tolosa. By this time the weight of family traditions of crusading was resting heavily on many shoulders and the weight on Louis's was as heavy as any; he was to be accompanied on crusade by three brothers.

At first he does not seem to have been as fervently committed to the needs of the Holy Land as he became. He had backed both sides in the debate over the Barons' Crusade, supporting the pope and his cousin Baldwin II, the young emperor of Constantinople who had been living in the West at his expense, but at the same time providing encouragement, authorization and financial assistance to the crusaders to Palestine. Then an event occurred which seems to have focused his eyes permanently on the Holy Land. In 1238 Baldwin, badly in need of money and military support, raised with Louis the transfer to France from Constantinople of one of the best-known relics of Christ's Passion, the Crown of Thorns. All his life Louis was devoted to relics: he avidly collected them; he built churches to house them and made gifts of them to favoured institutions; his travels were punctuated by visits to shrines. His response to the offer from Baldwin was immediate. He sent a mission to Constantinople, which discovered on its arrival that the Crown of Thorns had been pledged to the Venetians. The mission negotiated the transfer of the pledge to Louis for 135,000 pounds (at a time when the monarchy's annual budget was 250,000). On 11 August 1239 the king and his brothers met the reliquary at Villeneuve-l'Archevêque and carried it barefoot to Sens. Taken by boat to Vincennes, it was again borne by them into Paris where, after being exposed for the veneration of the citizens, it was transferred to the chapel of St Nicolas in the royal palace.

Louis had already learned, probably from Baldwin, of the dispersal of other relics from Constantinople to Palestine, including a fragment of the True Cross which had been pledged to the Templars for a huge sum, and a phial of the Precious Blood. These were redeemed on his behalf and were brought to Paris in 1241. In less than three years the king had acquired a major part of the famous collection from the imperial treasury in Constantinople. It included relics relating to almost every stage of the final hours of Christ's life on earth and many others besides. It rivalled even the ancient treasures in Rome and its provenance was in thirteenth-century terms unassailable. One of several pieces of the True Cross, for example, was probably the famous fragment which had always been stored in the Great Palace of the Byzantine emperors and had helped make Constantinople the chief centre for distribution since the sixth century. Baldwin made the collection over to Louis absolutely in June 1247. To house it Louis had already begun to build the Sainte-Chapelle, which was completed within a decade. His biographers Geoffrey of Beaulieu and William of Saint-Pathus testified to his intense devotion to these relics, but if Baldwin had considered that their transfer would have assisted the cause of his empire by encouraging recruitment to a crusade to save it, his intention spectacularly backfired. Paris became not a reminder of Constantinople, but, in the words of one commentator, 'as if it was another Jerusalem', a phrase which carried enormous weight, given the reoccupation of Jerusalem by the Muslims.

It is probable that Louis had heard of the taking of the city just before he fell into an illness so severe that it was said that at its height Blanche of Castile ordered the relics of the Passion to be brought for him to touch. It is remarkable how often these relics played a part in his crusade preparations thereafter. He timed the solemn *tournée* of his domain before departure on his first crusade so as to be present at the dedication of the Sainte-Chapelle on 25/6 April 1248. As late as June 1270, while at Aigues-Mortes preparing for his last crusade, he was making dispositions relating to the care of the relics in the Sainte-Chapelle. When he was planning that second crusade, John of Joinville, who was going to register a protest against it, found him in the Sainte-Chapelle. 'He had gone up to the platform where the relics were kept and was having the fragment of the True Cross taken down.' The relics answered to the needs of a man with an exaggerated, even histrionic, devotion to the cross which was so well known that Humbert of Romans referred in his advice to preachers to the 'king of France carrying the holy relics of the Crown [of Thorns] and the Cross of the Lord on his shoulders in his chapel'.

Once Louis had made the decision to crusade he threw himself into preparations. Like his great-grandfather he had taken the initiative in advance of a papal proclamation of war. Pope Innocent IV, embroiled in conflict with Frederick II, was in fact to be of very little help to him. Innocent had to flee from Italy and after Louis had refused him asylum at Reims took up residence in Lyon, to which a council was summoned in the summer of 1245. On 17 July Frederick was deposed. This division of Christendom on the eve of the crusade was bad enough – in 1248 it was even rumoured that Frederick was thinking of marching on Lyon – but the situation was made worse by the dispersal of crusading effort, since the pope now authorized the preaching of a crusade against Frederick in Germany and Italy as well as promulgating another in Spain. Louis could expect little help from western Europe beyond the French frontiers; nor could much be hoped for from eastern Europe, which had been shattered by a Mongol invasion in 1241. It says much for his forbearance that he remained on good terms with both the emperor and the pope.

He was going to have to rely on his own resources. He worked hard for order in France – he had suppressed serious baronial uprisings between 1241 and 1243 and seems to have decided to persuade as many of the former rebels as possible to accompany him to the East – and in a way that was typical of any departing crusader and pilgrim anxious not to leave behind ill-feeling or cause for complaints he hit upon a new method of enquiring into the state of the royal administration and its bearing on the ordinary people throughout the royal domain and the apanages held by his brothers. In the early months of 1247 he sent out investigators (*enquêteurs*), mostly Franciscan and Dominican friars, to inquire into grievances against him or his administrators. These men uncovered a great deal that was wrong and their findings shocked the king. The consequences were drastic. There were at least twenty new appointments in the higher ranks of the provincial administration, although the evidence suggests that Louis did not put in new men but made use of experienced and trustworthy officials. A similar attitude was shown by John of Joinville who went with him:

I said [to my men and my vassals], 'Lords, I am going overseas and I do not know whether I will return. Now step forward; if I have wronged you in any way I will make amends to each of you in turn'. ... I made amends to them according to the judgements of all the men of my land and so that I would not influence them in their decisions I rose from the court and accepted whatever they decided without questioning it. Because I did not want to take with me a single penny to which I had no right, I went to Metz in Lorraine to raise a pledge on a large part of my land.

Preaching the crusade had begun in France early in 1245. Odo of Châteauroux, the cardinal-bishop of Tusculum, was given charge of it as legate, while preachers were also sent to England, western Germany and Scandinavia. The army that eventually departed was probably of c. 15,000 men, of whom there were 2,500–2,800 knights. Most of the crusaders were French, although there were also some Norwegians, Germans, Italians, Scots and c. 200 Englishmen. A feature of this crusade was the way Louis underwrote the expenses of the nobles and subsidized a substantial number of knights through contracts of service. He was not the first crusade leader to act in this way, but he was the first to have done so on a large scale. He lent money to leading crusaders, including his brother Alphonse of Poitou, and he continued to lend cash during the crusade. He also arranged for transport and in 1246 he contracted for thirty-six ships from Genoa and Marseille, although his magnates also hired ships on a smaller scale. He concerned himself with port facilities and supplies. Aigues-Mortes, which had already begun to be developed as a royal port, was improved by the construction of an artificial canal and a magnificent tower, to be his residence before departure. Vast stores were sent ahead to Cyprus and it is a measure of the care he took that in spite of the endemic corruption and pilfering of the time his army was nearly always well supplied. When one also considers the cost of his ransom in 1250 and the amount he spent in the Holy Land during his stay there, the expenses borne by him were enormous. It is amazing that he seems to have remained solvent until 1253, when he was forced to borrow from Italian merchants; this was probably due to the effect on the fiscal arrangements in France of the death of his mother and regent in 1252.

It is known that Louis spent over 1,500,000 pounds *tournois* on his crusade at a time when his annual income was c. 250,000 pounds. Steps were taken to reduce royal expenditure, but in fact the money mostly came from sources other than his ordinary revenues, which increased markedly under the new administrators. In 1245 the First Council of Lyon granted him a twentieth of ecclesiastical revenues for three years, which the French clergy voluntarily increased to a tenth; additional tenths for two years were granted in 1251. It is true that for the reasons already given very little reached Louis from outside France, apart from dioceses in Lorraine and Burgundy bordering on his kingdom; but it has been estimated that the French Church itself contributed 950,000 pounds, in other words about two-thirds of his expenses. To church taxation and royal revenues were added cash realized on the properties of heretics – there was a sustained drive to confiscate these – money extorted from Jews, particularly as a result of a campaign against usury, profits accruing from royal licences to certain chapters and monastic communities to elect their bishops and abbots, and the enjoyment of part of the revenues of some vacant benefices. And there were 'voluntary' benevolences which towns in the royal domain were expected to contribute, not once but several times, and which have been estimated to have brought in c. 274,000 pounds.

The king's departure was preceded by a tour of the royal domain early in 1248, the central act of which was the dedication of the Sainte-Chapelle, as we have seen. A solemn exposition of the relics there was followed by the reception by Louis of the pilgrim's scrip and staff in Notre-Dame and a walk barefoot to St Denis, where, like his predecessors, he took possession of the oriflamme. After visiting religious houses around Paris he left for the south, embarked at Aigues-Mortes on 25 August and reached Cyprus on the night of 17 September. He spent eight months on the island while his army, supplemented by troops from Latin Greece and Palestine, gradually mustered. It seems that he was determined not to repeat past mistakes but to invade Egypt with maximum force. His crusade sailed at the end of May 1249, reaching the mouth of the Nile by Damietta on 4 June. The landing began on the 5th – it is a sign of the care he had taken that the crusaders had a large enough number of shallow-draughted vessels to put ashore a strong force at once – and the Muslim opposition was brushed aside. The defenders of Damietta itself, thoroughly demoralized, abandoned the city, which the Christians entered on the following day.

Louis must have been expecting a long siege, since Damietta had held out against the Fifth Crusade for over a year. It is not surprising that his initial success was followed by a long delay, although the possibility of moving in the meantime along the coast to take Alexandria was seriously discussed. The Nile was soon to flood and it was not until 20 November, when the river was subsiding and the weather was cooler, that the march into the interior began, an advance that coincided with the death of the sultan and near panic among the Egyptians. It took the crusaders a month to reach the bank of the Nile opposite the main Egyptian defensive works at El Mansura. On 7 February 1250 the existence of a crossing-place was revealed by a local inhabitant and an advance guard under the king's brother Robert of Artois crossed on the 8th. Without waiting for the rest of the army it charged through the Muslim camp and into El Mansura itself, where it was trapped in the narrow streets and destroyed. Robert was killed. Louis, who had crossed with the main body, fought a dogged battle with the Muslim army all day, before the Egyptians withdrew leaving him in possession of the field. But they had not been broken and were no longer leaderless, for the new sultan reached El Mansura on 28 February. The crusaders, exposed and isolated and now ravaged by disease, were harassed constantly, while the Muslims, transporting ships on camel-back around the Christian position and launching them downstream, cut them off from Damietta and their supplies. At the beginning of April the crusaders recrossed the Nile to their old camp and on the night of the 5th began their retreat to Damietta. They had managed to struggle only half-way when they were forced to surrender. The most carefully prepared and best-organized crusade of all had been destroyed and its leader was a prisoner of the enemy.

On 6 May Louis was released. His ransom had been set at 400,000 pounds, half of which was paid immediately. Damietta, in which his queen had just given birth to a son, was surrendered. Most of the French returned to Europe, but Louis sailed to Acre. He wanted to see that his fellow-crusaders gained their freedom from the Egyptians and he was determined to help defend the Latin settlements against any new Muslim offensives that might result from his failure. He stayed in Palestine for nearly four more years and effectively took over the government of the kingdom of Jerusalem, negotiating a treaty with Egypt in 1252 which included the prospect of an offensive alliance against Damascus – it came to nothing – and in 1254 a two-year truce with Damascus and Aleppo. He refortified Acre, Caesarea, Jaffa and Sidon on an impressive scale. He sailed for home on 24 April 1254, leaving 100 knights to garrison Acre at his expense. This was a very substantial force, comprising more knights than those with which the Hospitallers of St John envisaged garrisoning the fortresses of Crac des Chevaliers (60) and Mount Tabor (40) in 1255 and those in the Templar garrison of Safad (50) in 1260. The knights would have constituted, of course, only a fraction of the personnel involved. There were also crossbowmen and sergeants serving with them. Assuming that each knight would have needed at least three supporters, such as grooms and squires, and that the contingent required some sort of headquarters staff and its own farriers and armourers, perhaps as many as 1,000 persons may have been involved. Louis reached Hyères in Provence early in July, a changed man. The disaster of 1250 was interpreted by him as a personal punishment for his sins. His devotions became more intense and penitential. He dressed and ate simply. He dedicated himself to the poor. He desired death. He sought to make good kingship a kind of expiation for his offences which, he believed, had brought shame and damage on all Christianity.

Crusading in Prussia and Livonia

Competing with the crusades to the East in the thoughts and planning of the popes were those in Europe. Along the shores of the Baltic there had already developed, as we have seen, a kind of perpetual crusade, justified as defensive aid to the little churches growing up in the wake of missionary work among the heathen and, although not entirely confined to Germans and Scandinavians, very much their enterprise. Until 1230 the main thrust had been in Livonia and Estonia, where the foundations of Christian control had now been laid. Although crusading continued in Livonia and in the middle of the century was extended by the Swedes to Finland, it came to be concentrated in Prussia, to the west of those regions. It was again a missionary bishop who got the movement going. Christian, a Cistercian monk of the Polish abbey of Lekno, whose early successes as an evangelist had won the support of the Polish nobles Duke Conrad of Masovia (Mazowsze) and Bishop Goslav of Plock, as well as that of Innocent III, had been consecrated bishop of Prussia in 1215. With his success there came growing hostility from the natives and after several expedients, including the foundation of a new German military order, the Knights of Dobrzyn, had failed, Conrad of Masovia stepped in and in 1225 offered the Teutonic Knights, with whom the subjugation and rule of Prussia was henceforward to be associated, a substantial holding in the region.

Their order, that of the Hospital of St Mary of the Germans of Jerusalem, had its origins in a German field-hospital at the siege of Acre in 1189–90, which was reconstituted in 1198 as a German military order. Like the Hospitallers, the Teutonic Knights had the twin functions of fighting and caring for the sick, but their Rule drew especially on that of the Templars. Until 1291 their headquarters were in Palestine and they were primarily concerned with the defence of the East. They had a large estate near Acre, centred on the castle of Montfort, the building of which has already been mentioned, and important holdings in the lordship of Sidon and in Cilician Armenia. Like the Templars and Hospitallers, however, they were also endowed with properties in Europe and found themselves involved in campaigns there. In 1211 King Andrew of Hungary gave them a stretch of his eastern frontier to defend against the Kipchak Turks, but they made themselves unpopular. They insisted on exemption from the authority of the local bishop and gave the Holy See proprietary rights over their territory. They seem to have increased their holdings by dubious means. They introduced German colonists. The king, who did not want to have an autonomous German religious palatinate on his frontier, abrogated their privileges and when they resisted expelled them by force.

It was at this point that Conrad of Masovia's invitation arrived, and it came to a master, Hermann of Salza, who was exceptionally able and was a close adviser of the emperor Frederick. He wanted a training-ground for his knights before sending them to the East – Dr Christiansen has written that 'the Prussian venture was training for further Jerusalem crusades as cubbing is to foxhunting' – and he was determined to establish the kind of ecclesiastical state which the order had wanted to create in Hungary. The first step was to get authorization from the emperor and in the Golden Bull of Rimini of 1226 Hermann received the status of an imperial prince for the province of Kulmerland (Chelmno) and all future conquests in Prussia. The Teutonic Order, therefore, was the first of the military orders to be given what would later be regarded as semi-sovereign status. The next step was to make the new territory a papal dependence. In 1234 Gregory IX took it into the proprietorship of St Peter and under the special protection of the Holy See, returning it to the knights as a papal fief. Meanwhile Hermann sent his first detachment to the Vistula in 1229 and the conquest began. Potential conflict with the missionary activities of Bishop Christian were resolved in 1233 when Christian was captured by the Prussians. He was held by them for six years, after which, in spite of his protests that the order was more interested in making subjects than converts and was positively hindering conversion, it was too late for him to reverse the subordination of the Church in Prussia to it. He died in 1245, an embittered and disillusioned man.

Under the leadership of the Teutonic Knights the features of the Baltic crusade we have already discerned became more pronounced. Their order was nearly exclusively German and their policies of settlement developed out of those already to be found in the German eastward colonizing drive. Each district was colonized by lay knights and burghers, the latter being generally given customs for settlement based on those of German Magdeburg, which provided a satisfactory means of establishing the order's lordship and a basis for cooperation with the new German towns. And, perhaps because the masters spent so much time in Europe and could liaise directly with the papacy, unlike their opposite numbers in the Temple and the Hospital, the knights were able to formulate more clearly the concept of a perpetual crusade. From the early 1230s a stream of crusaders was flowing into the region. In 1245 Pope Innocent IV granted plenary indulgences to all who went to fight in Prussia, whether it was in response to a specific papal appeal or not:

> We concede the same indulgence and privileges that are granted to those going to Jerusalem to all in Germany who, in response to the appeals of the Teutonic Knights and *without public preaching*, put on the sign of the cross and wish to go to the aid of the faithful against the savagery of the Prussians.

So, unlike those Spanish bishops who had occasionally issued indulgences on their own authority in the twelfth century, the Teutonic Knights were empowered by the very pope who stressed that indulgences could only be granted by him the right to issue them without any reference to papal proclamations of war. Churchmen in northern and central Europe were repeatedly instructed to preach the crusade in the Baltic region.

The strategy employed by the order was based on the building of castles, using forced Prussian labour, alongside which the settlements of German burghers were founded, while Dominican friars under its control Christianized the countryside around. It seems to have planned an advance down the Vistula from Kulmerland to the Zalew Wiślany (Frisches Haff) and then eastwards along the shore in the direction of Livonia, where from 1237 the Sword-Brothers were placed under its rule. After this the conquest of the interior would begin. The Zalew Wiślany was reached in 1236 and by 1239, with most of the shore in its hands, the order began to penetrate the interior. But in the first Prussian revolt of 1242 it lost much of the territory it had gained and had to fight a ten-year war of recovery. A land-bridge linking Livonia to Prussia became a reality with the foundations of Memel (Klaipéda) from Livonia in 1252 and Königsberg (Kaliningrad) by an impressive crusading expedition from Prussia led by King Ottakar II of Bohemia, Rudolf of Habsburg and Otto of Brandenburg in 1254. Then came the second Prussian revolt of 1260, following the defeat of the Livonian Teutonic Knights at Durbe by the Lithuanians. Many of the garrisons and colonies established in Prussia were destroyed and the first group of crusaders marching to their relief was annihilated. Pope Urban IV, who had been planning a crusade against the Mongols, urged all those who had taken the cross to go to the Knights' assistance, offering plenary indulgences for any length of service. A succession of German crusades took place, particularly in 1265, 1266, 1267 and 1272, but the revolt was only crushed in 1283 after warfare of such ruthlessness that it left half of Prussia a wilderness. Civil liberties which had been promised to all converts after the first revolt were now forgotten and most Prussians became serfs on the estates of the Knights and German immigrants and a few collaborators. By the end of the thirteenth century large-scale German colonization of Prussia could begin.

An invasion of Lithuania by the Sword-Brothers from Livonia had been bloodily repulsed in 1236 and the territory south of the Dvina lost at that time was only won back by 1255. The union of the Teutonic Knights and the Sword-Brothers, however, led to proposals for expansion eastwards against nearby Russian principalities, which culminated in the capture of Pskov in 1240. This drive was halted by Alexander Nevski, prince of Novgorod, who retook Pskov and on 5 April 1242 defeated the order in the battle on Lake Peipus. The order's ambitions were already bringing it into conflict with the forces which were to engage much of its attention in the fourteenth century, the Russians, the Poles and the Lithuanians, but at this time more concern was expressed about the Mongols.

The first crusades against the Mongols

The Mongol empire had its origins in an expansionary movement among a group of Turkish and Turco-Mongol tribes north-west of China under a chieftain called Temüjin, who in 1206 took the title of Genghis Khan, or universal emperor, and set out to conquer the world. In 1211–12 northern China fell to his men. The regions east of the Caspian Sea were conquered in 1219–20, after which raids were launched across southern Russia. The death of Genghis Khan in 1227 did not disturb the rhythm of conquest. Between 1231 and 1234 the Kin dynasty of northern China was liquidated, Korea was annexed and Iran was occupied. From 1237 to 1239 central Russia was conquered and in 1240 the Ukraine. In 1241 Poland and Hungary were invaded and a German army was defeated at Legnica (Liegnitz), although the death of Ögödai, Genghis Khan's successor, in 1242 interrupted the invasion of central Europe and may indeed have saved it. Faced with an appalling danger Pope Gregory IX proclaimed a crusade against the Mongols in 1241. This was confirmed in 1243 by Pope Innocent IV and resistance to the Mongols was on the agenda of the First Council of Lyon in 1245. In 1249, when the danger again appeared to be acute, Innocent allowed crusaders to the Holy Land to commute their vows to war against the Mongols. By then he had empowered the Teutonic Knights, to whom he had given the virtual direction of the north-eastern frontier of Christendom, to grant plenary indulgences to all taking the cross against them.

Crusading in Spain

There never was a perpetual crusade in Spain, the second traditional area of crusading activity in Europe, even though there were constant petty wars there against the Muslims. The Almohad empire was now weakening and for over twenty years after 1228 the Iberian Muslims had no help from Africa and had to face the Christians alone. Under two great leaders, James I of Aragon and Ferdinand III of Castile, Christian Spain experienced some of its greatest triumphs, although this extraordinary period has never been studied enough from the point of view of crusading. Crusade privileges were granted to those assisting the Spanish military orders, the activities of which, particularly in the occupation in the 1230s of the region of Badajoz and the Campo de Montiel and Sierra de Segura, are reminiscent of those of the Teutonic Knights. James of Aragon led crusades which took Majorca, 1229–31, and the kingdom of Valencia, 1232–53, reaching a line of demarcation between Aragon and Castile that had been laid down in 1179. The Portuguese reconquest was completed by 1250. In 1230 Badajoz was taken and in 1231 Ferdinand led a crusade which was marked by his brother Alfonso's victory over Ibn Hud, the paramount Muslim king, at Jerez. The way was now open for Ferdinand's conquests of Córdoba, the ancient Muslim capital, on 29 June 1236 and of

Seville, one of the greatest cities in western Europe, on 23 November 1248. Ferdinand was easily the most successful Christian warrior against Muslims of his day. English public opinion maintained that he 'alone has gained more for the profit and honour of Christ's Church than the pope and all his crusaders ... and all the Templars and Hospitallers'. His career demonstrated, moreover, that the Reconquest was now largely a national enterprise. The crusade against Seville was even authorized by the pope in 1246 at the time Louis IX's crusade to the East was being prepared. Few crusaders now came from abroad and the popes recognized Iberian crusading as a royal responsibility, which explains why Ferdinand was able to exploit the Spanish Church for his wars, especially in the form of the so-called _tercias reales_, the third of tithes which should have been spent on the upkeep of church buildings and was increasingly directed his way or seized by him. It has been pointed out that the Reconquest had a cost and that was the impoverishment of the Spanish Church, partly because it had to bear the expenses, partly because the drift of population south into the conquered lands reduced its revenues. This made it very dependent on kings like Ferdinand, who reimbursed himself at its expense, and it also made it insular, reluctant to finance crusades elsewhere.

Then for nearly a century, from 1252 until 1340, the pace of reconquest slowed as new masters of Morocco, the Marinid dynasty, poured troops into what remained of Moorish Andalucia. At first Christian ambitions were high and between 1252 and 1254 a crusade was even being preached to invade Africa. King Alfonso X of Castile tried to recruit King Henry III of England and later King Hakon of Norway for it and in 1260 the city of Salé, which had rebelled against the Marinids, was held for a fortnight. Alfonso had to face a large-scale Muslim revolt in 1264. In response to it he had a crusade preached on the basis of out-of-date papal authorizations and he expelled all Muslims from Murcia, the source of the uprising, when it came into his hands. He was, however, unable to take Granada, partly because Castile was not strong enough to occupy it single-handedly, partly because the Marinid sultan Ya'qub (Abu Yusuf) entered Spain and put the Christians on the defensive.

Crusades against heretics

The Baltic and Iberian crusades deprived the East of recruits and diverted resources, since the local churches contributed to them and the papacy generally allowed them to do so. In Germany the development of a perpetual crusade, something that even the defence of the Holy Land had never been, meant that there was a permanent diversion of effort. In Spain the power of the kings meant that they could, if they so wished, frustrate the transmission of resources to the East. There were other local crusades of less significance. There was a small one authorized by the pope in 1232 against the Stedinger peasants in Germany, whom the archbishop of Bremen had accused of heresy. The bishops of Minden, Lübeck and Ratzeburg were ordered to preach the cross in the dioceses of Paderborn, Hildesheim, Verden, Münster, Osnabrück, Minden and Bremen and the campaign, in which crusaders from the Low Countries as well as Germany took part, was waged early in 1234. In the same category were crusades authorized in 1227 and 1234 by Popes Honorius III and Gregory IX against Bosnian heretics, for which there was also the commutation of crusade vows, and in 1238 against John Asen of Bulgaria's alliance with Byzantine Nicaea, which was ordered to be preached in Hungary. These crusades do not seem to have attracted much criticism or to have created many problems for the papacy, perhaps because they were local.

Political crusades

In quite another class were the crusades in Italy. In a sense the opening campaign had been that conducted by papal armies under John of Brienne in the mainland territories of the kingdom of Sicily from 1228 to 1230. This attack on the emperor's lands while he was in Palestine had been justified by Pope Gregory IX as a war in defence of the Church against a man who had oppressed Sicilian churchmen and had dared to invade the papal states. The soldiers had been promised 'remission of sins' in general terms and had been financed by an income tax levied on the clergy: the churches in Sweden, Denmark, England and northern Italy all paid a tenth in 1229 and French bishops were asked to send to Rome the final payments of a five-year tenth which had been imposed on their dioceses in 1225 in support of the Albigensian Crusade. But full crusade indulgences were not granted and it is noteworthy that the soldiers wore the sign of Peter's keys, not the cross. The campaign looks more like a thirteenth-century version of a war of the Investiture Contest than a crusade.

In 1239–40, however, the crisis was such that a recognizable crusade was preached. Pope and emperor were again in conflict. Frederick had control of southern Italy and he was close to achieving dominance in northern Italy as well. The organization of the crusade began in 1239 and preaching was authorized in northern Italy and Germany. By early 1240 Frederick's army was threatening Rome itself. Gregory preached the cross in Rome and in February 1241 he went so far as to allow his legates in Hungary to commute the vows of crusaders to the East to the war against the emperor. He asked for aid, although not at first linked to crusading, from the universal Church and money was raised, in spite of much reluctance, in England, Scotland, Ireland and France. This crusade achieved little other than checking Frederick's advance on Rome, but it started a train of events that were to dominate Italian politics for almost a century and a half.

The crusade against Frederick was renewed by Innocent IV in 1244 and from 1246, the year after the First Council of Lyon had deposed the emperor, a stream of letters from the pope, addressed particularly to Germany where anti-kings were being set up, urged crusade-preaching. The army which took the old imperial capital of Aachen for the anti-king William of Holland in October 1248 had many crusaders serving in it, but in Germany there were short bursts of enthusiasm rather than sustained commitment. Innocent collected large sums of money from the Church, especially from Italians beneficed in trans-Alpine countries and from dioceses in England, Poland, Hungary and Germany, most of which seem to have gone to finance the German struggle. On the other hand, the papal cause was relatively weak in Italy and a lack of cash seems to have been part of the reason why an invasion of Sicily in 1249 failed.

Frederick died on 13 December 1250. The crusade in Germany was renewed in the following February against his heir Conrad IV and preaching was again ordered there in 1253 and 1254, but with the great emperor dead the eyes of the papacy turned back to the kingdom of Sicily which was, after all, a papal fief. Its invasion would require a large, well-organized and well-financed army, which is one reason why the Italian crusades came to be run on the same lines as those to the East. It would also need a leader of weight and distinction and papal policy in the 1250s was directed towards finding one. Richard of Cornwall was approached; then Charles of Anjou, one of Louis IX's brothers; then King Henry III of England, who had taken the cross in March 1250 on behalf of his younger son, Edmund of Lancaster. When the negotiations with Henry broke down – Henry had agreed to an impossible condition of underwriting all the papacy's war expenses and had had to suffer the imposition of baronial government in England – the pope turned again to Charles of Anjou and between 1262 and 1264 the terms for a transfer of the crown of Sicily to him were hammered out.

The first crusade against Manfred, Frederick's illegitimate son and the upholder of the Staufen cause in southern Italy, was preached early in 1255 in Italy and England. An army under the Florentine cardinal Octavian degli Ubaldini marched to defeat, after which Manfred achieved such dominance that he was crowned king of Sicily in August 1258. Preaching continued while crusading warfare spread into northern Italy – between 1255 and 1260 a crusade in the March of Treviso overthrew the Ghibelline despots Ezzelino and Alberic of Romano – and to Sardinia. Meanwhile Pope Urban IV granted Charles of Anjou's request that a crusade to conquer the kingdom of Sicily be preached in France, the western empire and northern and central Italy. This crusade set out from Lyon in October 1265. On its march it was joined by Italian contingents and it reached Rome in the middle of January 1266, a few days after Charles had been crowned king of Sicily in St Peter's. Being very short of money Charles began his campaign at once and on 26 February defeated and killed Manfred in the Battle of Benevento. The whole kingdom of Sicily was soon under his control, although the crusade had to be revived in April 1268, when Conrad IV's young son Conradin descended on Italy to regain his inheritance. In August he was defeated at the Battle of Tagliacozzo and he was executed in Naples in October. The surrender in August 1269 of the last Staufen garrison at Lucera, a colony of Muslims from the island of Sicily established by Frederick II, ended the first phase of the struggle.

The rise of Charles of Anjou in the Mediterranean political world was meteoric. Already in 1267 William of Villehardouin, the prince of Achaea and Latin ruler of the Peloponnese (the Morea), recognized him as his overlord and the Latin emperor of Constantinople granted him suzerainty over the Greek islands and the Latin holdings in Epirus. In the following year William led 1,100 knights of the Peloponnese to reinforce Charles's army at Tagliacozzo. On William's death in 1278 Charles took over the government of Achaea directly. In 1277, after long negotiations, a claimant to the throne of Jerusalem sold him the crown with the papacy's connivance and support and in September of that year his vicar took up residence in Acre. It is clear that the hopes of the papacy for the survival of the Latin settlement in Palestine rested on the fact that it was now integrated into a huge eastern Mediterranean empire which might, with the active support of Charles's close relative the king of France, provide it with the permanent defensive capability that crusades, of their nature *ad hoc* and temporary, could never give. But on 30 March 1282 the island of Sicily rose against Angevin-French domination in a revolt known as the Sicilian Vespers and the islanders called in King Peter of Aragon, who was married to Manfred's daughter Constance and had the best navy in the western Mediterranean.

Peter's landing at Trapani on 30 August aroused the indignation of Pope Martin IV. The pope was a Frenchman who as legate had concluded the curia's negotiations with Charles in 1264 and had been helped to the pontifical throne by Charles's political intriguing, but any pope, claiming the feudal overlordship of Sicily, would have looked on the Aragonese action as a challenge to his authority. Martin must also have recognized the danger to the papacy's carefully constructed scheme for the preservation of the Christian presence in the Levant. On 13 January 1283 a crusade was declared against the Sicilians, but preaching was at first restricted to the kingdom of Sicily itself and was only extended to northern Italy in April 1284. In November 1282 Peter of Aragon was excommunicated and in March 1283 he was deprived of his kingdom, which was claimed to be another papal fief. A legate was sent to France to organize a crusade against him, while Charles of Valois, the second son of King Philip III, was promised Aragon on terms very similar to those under which his great-uncle Charles of Anjou held Sicily. A four-year tenth was levied on the French clergy and on the dioceses bordering on France to finance the crusade. Preaching in France began in the early months of 1284 and in February King Philip accepted the crown of Aragon for his son.

The crusades in southern Italy and northern Spain were fiascos. In the spring of 1283 the Aragonese themselves carried war onto the Italian mainland and they demonstrated their supremacy at sea, capturing Charles of Salerno, Charles of Anjou's heir, in a naval engagement off Naples in June 1284. Charles of Anjou's death in January 1285, which was followed by that of Martin IV on 28 March, weakened the cause. Charles of Salerno only obtained his liberty and came into his own in October 1288, on terms that involved a commitment from him to work for peace between Aragon, France, Sicily and Naples. Meanwhile Philip of France had invaded Spain with an army of at least 8,000 men in the spring of 1285. The Aragonese in Gerona held up the crusade all summer. In the early autumn their fleet was recalled from Sicilian waters and it destroyed the navy servicing the French and deprived the crusade of its supplies. Philip was forced to retreat and during the withdrawal died at Perpignan on 5 October.

With the Aragonese advance into mainland Italy held at a defensive line south of Salerno everyone seems to have wanted peace, especially after the loss of Palestine and Syria in 1291, which made the diversion of resources look selfish and foolhardy. The papal curia itself was divided, but the election of Pope Boniface VIII in 1294 marked the success of the war-party there. In the summer of 1295 Boniface persuaded King James II of Aragon to withdraw from Sicily, but the king's younger brother Frederick, the governor of the island, rebelled and was crowned king in Palermo in March 1296. So crusading against the Sicilians was renewed in 1296, 1299 and 1302, while it was also proclaimed in 1297–8 against the Colonna cardinals, a faction in Rome composed of personal enemies of Boniface and allies of Frederick. With the help of James II the Angevins cleared Calabria in 1297–8 and won a naval victory at the Battle of Cape Orlando in 1299. But the island was too strong to be reoccupied and the Treaty of Caltabellotta in August 1302 recognized Frederick's rule over Sicily. Although according to the Treaty he was to hold it only for life, the island was destined to remain in Aragonese hands.

These 'political crusades' were justified in traditional ways by the popes, who showed themselves to be acutely aware of the criticism that they were misusing the movement for their own ends at a time when the Christians in the East were in terrible danger. They stressed the need to defend the Church and the faith. They compared their enemies in Italy to the Muslims and they argued that they were hindering effective crusading to the East. They also went to great lengths to build up an efficient machinery for getting their message across. There was, in fact, a fairly large response to their appeals. Preaching in France in the years 1264 to 1268 was particularly successful and the armies of 1265–6 and 1268 contained not only men who had taken the cross for the first time, but also experienced crusaders from the eastern wars like Érard of Valéry, who drew up the battle plan for Tagliacozzo, and Peter Pillart, who wrote to Philip III boasting that 'I have served you and your ancestors in the year they went to Damietta and to Sicily and at the siege ... of Tunis'.

In Italy itself the greatest response came, as might be expected, from Guelf districts that traditionally supported the papacy. Professor Housley is surely right in maintaining that there was enough recruitment to make one doubt the common belief that these crusades had little ideological appeal. The ethos in the armies was typically crusading. The papacy diverted to them a large part of the resources, particularly from clerical taxation, that were available for the eastern theatre of war. Moneys from England, France, the Low Countries, Provence and the imperial dioceses financed Charles of Anjou's campaigns in the 1260s. Between 1283 and 1302 Christendom from the British Isles to Greece was frequently taxed to restore Angevin rule in Sicily. The heavy taxation extended the curia's control over the movement and led to important innovations such as the organization of Christendom into collectorates by Pope Gregory X in 1274, to the increasing reliance of the popes on credit and banking facilities and, in the fourteenth century, to the institution of new taxes to reduce this reliance. But it was understandably unpopular and was resisted, particularly in England in the 1250s and France in the 1260s, and there can be no doubt that it had a bad effect on the relations between the papacy and the Church at large.

The development of the 'political crusades' raises questions that have been hotly debated. Were they perversions of the movement preached simply to further papal policies in Italy? Did they arouse such hostility among the faithful that they damaged the papacy in the eyes of its subjects? The first of these questions has been particularly controversial because of a group of historians who maintain that, whatever the popes and canon lawyers may have said – and they are prepared to admit that the papacy took a broad overall view of crusading – the ordinary faithful did not regard crusades in Europe in the same light as crusades to the East. Their answer to the first question is, therefore, bound up with their answer to the second, since they assume that public opinion was hostile to these diversions.

There can be no doubt that crusades to the East carried the most prestige and were the most appealing. Nor can there be any doubt that expressions of hostility to crusading in Europe can be found. Harsh words were written by Languedociens, not surprisingly, but also by men in northern France and England against the Albigensian Crusade. And in Germany, Italy, France, Spain and the Holy Land there was quite widespread criticism of crusades against Catholic Christians like Frederick II and his descendants. The strongest element in it was that such crusades diverted resources and manpower from the Latin East. Settlers in Palestine, Cyprus and Greece kept up a barrage of complaints, summed up in a rebuke apparently delivered in 1289 by a Templar messenger to Pope Nicholas IV after the fall of Tripoli:

> You could have succoured the Holy Land with the power of kings and the strength of the other faithful of Christ but you have armed kings against a king, intending to attack a Christian king and the Christian Sicilians to recover the island of Sicily which, kicking against the pricks, took up just arms.

When Innocent IV was tactless enough to order the preaching of his crusade against Conrad IV at a time when Louis IX's crusade was in shreds and Louis himself was in Palestine, the French government and people united in fierce opposition to it.

The depth of feeling in France also manifested itself in the Crusade of the Shepherds, an extraordinary reaction to the news of Louis's defeat and imprisonment in Egypt. Its leader was a demagogue called the Master of Hungary, who carried in his hands a letter he claimed to have been given by the Blessed Virgin Mary. His message was that the pride of the French nobles and churchmen had been punished in Egypt and that just as shepherds had been the first to hear the news of Christ's Nativity so it was to them, the simple and the humble, that the Holy Land would be delivered. His army of the poor reached Paris, where it was well received by Queen Blanche. After this it fragmented into different companies and became progressively more violent until, outlawed by Blanche and with the Master killed, it disintegrated. Against this background it was not likely that the French would take kindly to the diversion of resources to Germany or Italy. Blanche took measures to prevent the preaching in France of the crusade against Conrad and threatened to confiscate the lands of any who took the cross for it.

Examples of this sort of reaction have been collected by historians and they were taken seriously by experienced preachers like Humbert of Romans. But they do not in themselves demonstrate that people in general made a distinction in kind between crusading to the East and in Europe; it should not be forgotten that crusading to the East also attracted a measure of criticism. Nor can one create out of them a picture of widespread disillusionment. It has been noted that the critics were on the whole either long-standing opponents of the papacy, who would be expected to be critical anyway, or individuals who had particular reasons for expressing opposition to specific diversions of resources from the East. The French government bitterly opposed the crusade against the Staufen in 1251, but that opposition was not one of principle, since it was brought to support Charles of Anjou's crusade of 1265 into Sicily. Louis was not in favour of the Sicilian venture at first, but his only objections, which were overcome, seem to have concerned the legality of a denial of the Staufen claims to Sicily. A most moral man, he cannot have been opposed to 'political crusades' in principle. There were some signs of disillusionment and there were a few root-and-branch pacifists, horrified by the whole tradition of Christian violence. How numerous they were is open to question, but it is likely that there were very few of them indeed. Dr Siberry has pointed out, moreover, that criticism in the thirteenth century never reached the heights of vituperation that had been scaled in the aftermath of the Second Crusade.

In fact the most striking thing about the movement, wherever it manifested itself, was its continuing popularity. Crusades were waged in all theatres of war and they could not have been fought without crusaders. On the whole the papal arguments for particular ventures, whether in Europe or in the East, were received sympathetically enough for there to be recruits. It is, therefore, impossible to show, and it is hard to believe, that the prestige of the papacy was diminished by the Italian crusades. The popes genuinely perceived the threat to their position in Italy to be so great that they had no option but to preach them. They also believed that the future of the Latin East depended on the integrity of the kingdom of Sicily and therefore on the crusades that followed the Sicilian Vespers. But one cannot deny that the Holy Land suffered from these diversions. It must remain an open question whether the Latin settlements in Palestine and Syria would have survived longer had the popes made more resources available. At the very time when revenue from commerce in the Latin kingdom of Jerusalem was declining because of a change in the Asiatic trade routes, which will be discussed in the next chapter, the settlers were deprived of money and matériel that could have passed to them from Europe.

The second crusade of St Louis

It would be wrong, however, to suppose that the period from 1254 to 1291 was one in which the settlements were starved of European resources. The French crown poured money across the Mediterranean. During Louis's reign resources were focused above all on the standing body of French mercenary troops, to which reference has already been made. This was occasionally supplemented by small bodies of crusaders until it was withdrawn, perhaps early in 1270, to be integrated into the French crusade to Tunis. It is not easy to establish what costs were envisaged by Louis himself at the outset. Very generous sums were entered in a surviving fragment of the king's accounts for the years 1250 to 1253 as subsidies to crusaders and as wages to mercenaries, but it was usual to pay more modest amounts when knights were stationed in a semi-permanent location. Even so, one cannot get away from the fact that Louis was prepared to dip deeply into his pocket. Although according to Professor Strayer the French treasury believed that between 1254 and 1270 the contingent in Acre had cost the king only an average of 4,000 pounds *tournois* a year (or 1.6 per cent of his annual income), Geoffrey of Sergines, who was its captain, estimated in 1267 that he needed the enormous sum of 10,000 pounds a year to retain his knights and c. 1272 Pope Gregory X wrote that some 60,000 pounds sent by Louis to the Holy Land had been lost through the carelessness – doubtless a euphemism for the corruption – of officials. The donation of funds to provide military forces for the defence of the Holy Land was a tradition that stretched back well into the twelfth century, but Louis's provision was unusual in that it was, as far as we know, open-ended.

His commitment was shown at its most intense in his reaction in 1260 to the news of near panic in Palestine. The Mongols, who had already taught everyone in the West a lesson, had broken into the Levant. Appeals were at once despatched to the West. The urgency with which they were sent was exemplified by the case of a Templar messenger, who arrived in London on 16 June bringing letters for King Henry III and the commander of the London Temple. He had broken all records, taking only thirteen weeks to reach London from Acre and only one day to journey from Dover. A letter from the papal legate in Acre was delivered to all European rulers and supplemented by messages from other leading figures in the East, such as the one that survives from the grand master of the Temple. These reported that many Muslims were fleeing for refuge to the Christian territories on the coast. They spelled out the size and potency of the Mongol armies, the reactions of the local Muslim rulers, the speed with which the king of Cilician Armenia and the prince of Antioch-Tripoli had come to terms and the poverty of the Latin settlements.

The reaction of the French government was dramatic. It decreed that the cross was to be solemnly preached throughout France. The king and his nobles agreed to tax themselves at a sixtieth of their income for seven years, while the Church in France was to tax itself at a twentieth. King Louis, assisted by four nobles and four prelates, was going to oversee the collection of the tax personally. All young men aged fifteen and worth 100 pounds per annum in rents and all aged twenty and worth 50 pounds were to be compulsorily knighted. Tournaments were to be banned for two years. To preserve horses, no one, noble or otherwise, would be allowed to buy or own a charger worth more than 100 pounds or a palfrey worth more than 30 pounds; and no ecclesiastic, not even a prelate, was to own a mount worth more than 15 pounds. It was announced that the pope was summoning a meeting in Rome to consider the steps that should be taken.

The crisis passed when the Mongols were halted by the Mamluks in the Battle of 'Ain Jalut on 3 September and it was only a watered down version of these proposals – the banning of tournaments and the imposition of sumptuary laws for two years – which was agreed by an assembly convoked by the king on 10 April 1261. As for the conference at the curia, Pope Alexander IV died before it could be held.

The king of France was not alone in his concern for the settlements, of course. King Edward I of England also gave substantial support. The papacy organized a series of small expeditions, transmitted large sums of cash and through its representative the patriarch of Jerusalem paid for mercenaries to supplement the French regiment. And it continued to plan crusades. In the aftermath of the fall of Constantinople to the Greeks in 1261 Pope Urban IV seems to have been thinking of a crusade to recover it for the Latins, but there was soon a change of plan and in 1263 the pope was again writing of aid to the Holy Land. Until 1266 the crusade of Charles of Anjou into southern Italy had precedence, but in the meantime Mamluk armies from Egypt had begun the systematic reconquest of Palestine. At the news of their advance Louis IX of France took the initiative, as he had done in 1244. Late in 1266 he informed Pope Clement IV of his intention to crusade again and on 24 March 1267 he took the cross at an assembly of his nobles. This time the response in France was apparently not so enthusiastic, although John of Joinville's account of the bitter opposition to it of himself and others may have led to its unpopularity being exaggerated, because the crusade which eventually departed may not have been much smaller than that of 1248. Louis certainly planned it as carefully, if not even more carefully, than he had his first. He was promised a three-year tenth from the French Church and a three-year twentieth from the dioceses bordering on France, to be collected once the Sicilian tax had come to an end. The towns were again asked for aid. His brother Alphonse of Poitou raised well over 100,000 pounds *tournois*, mostly from his own domains. Louis made contracts with Genoa and Marseille for shipping, specifying that the vessels were to be at Aigues-Mortes by the early summer of 1270. It is a tribute to his near-iconic status and organizing ability that some crusading stalwarts, such as Hugh of Burgundy, and some close collaborators in the defence of the Holy Land, such as Érard of Valéry, were engaged. Crusaders were also recruited elsewhere in Europe, particularly in Aragon and England, where the kings wanted to take part, and Charles of Anjou, perhaps somewhat reluctantly, agreed to join his brother.

The Aragonese left first. On 1 September 1269 King James I sailed from Barcelona, but his fleet was so damaged by a storm that he and most of his crusaders returned home. A squadron under two of his bastard sons, the Infants Ferdinand Sanchez and Peter Fernandez, reached Acre at the end of December. Their force, however, was not strong enough to engage the Mamluk sultan Baybars of Egypt when he appeared before the city at the head of a raid and they soon returned to the West with little achieved. In England, in the aftermath of the civil war between Henry III and Simon of Montfort, crusade-preaching had led to the formation of a substantial body of crusaders, among them Henry's eldest son Edward, who took the cross in June 1268 after winning over his father, who had intended to go himself in fulfilment of a vow he had made in 1250, and the pope, who had agreed with Henry that Edward should remain in England. Edward may well have been under Louis's influence; the two men were in touch by late 1267 and in August 1269 Edward went to Paris to attend a council of war. He promised to join Louis's expedition in return for a loan of 70,000 pounds *tournois*. He made widespread use of similar contracts of service to those employed by Louis, binding to himself the crusaders in his following in return for subsidies. It has been suggested by Dr Lloyd that his crusade was 'an extended household operation in all its essentials', but this of course made it expensive and the crown used every measure open to it to raise cash, including a general tax of a twentieth in 1269–70; the Church contributed the grant of a two-year tenth in 1272. Edward left England in August 1270, but by then the crusade was already set for failure.

Louis had sailed from France on 2 July, a month later than he had intended. His original plan had been to sail to Cyprus, but over the previous year a new one had been formulated, involving a preliminary descent upon Tunis in North Africa. It used to be thought that Louis had been persuaded to adopt this course of action by Charles of Anjou, who stood to benefit from a demonstration against the Hafsid ruler of Tunis, but the details of Charles's preparations suggest that he was not *au fait* with the plan to attack Tunis, which must have been decided at the French court. It may be that Louis believed that Tunisia was a major supplier of Egypt, which would be indirectly weakened by such an attack. If so, he was wrong and the Egyptian government was greatly relieved when it heard what he had done. Professor Richard has suggested that we look again at the explanation given by the king's confessor, Geoffrey of Beaulieu. Geoffrey stated that Louis was attracted by the chance of converting the ruler of Tunis, who had let it be known that he would be baptized provided that he had the support of a Christian army. There had, in fact, been a Tunisian embassy in Paris in the autumn of 1269.

The fleet gathered off Cagliari in southern Sardinia and the crusaders landed in Tunisia without serious opposition on 18 July, camping round a fort built on the site of ancient Carthage. They settled down to wait for the arrival of Charles of Anjou, but in the summer heat dysentery or typhus swept through the camp. The king's eldest son Philip was dangerously ill. His youngest, John Tristan, who had been born at Damietta, perished. Louis himself succumbed to sickness and on 25

August he passed away, stretched out penitentially on a bed of ashes. On the night before he died he was heard to sigh, 'Jerusalem! Jerusalem!' Charles of Anjou arrived on that very day and soon decided that the crusade should withdraw. On 1 November he ratified a treaty drawn up with the Tunisian ruler, from which he personally derived most benefit – one-third of a war indemnity the Tunisians were forced to pay, together with a renewal and augmentation of tribute and of Sicilian trading rights and the promise of expulsion from Tunisia of Staufen exiles who were fomenting trouble – and on 11 November the crusaders left for Sicily. They carried with them the remains of the king, whose body had been immediately dismembered. His heart was left in Africa with the remnant of the army. His entrails were deposited in the cathedral of Monreale in Sicily at Charles's request. His bones were brought back to France by his son, Philip III, who led a long cortège, which wound its way through Italy to the Alps and through Savoy, the Dauphiné, the Lyonnais, Burgundy and Champagne, before reaching Paris. After a funeral Mass in Notre-Dame the bones were interred in the abbey of St Denis. Miracles were reported occurring in the course of the journey home: at Palermo, Parma, Reggio Emilia and Bonneuil-sur-Marne, not far from Paris. They multiplied at the tomb, to which the sick pilgrimaged in increasing numbers. These French pilgrims must have been on John of Joinville's mind when he included in his memoirs a story about other pilgrims, Armenians who wanted to see Louis:

> They had asked me if I could show them 'the saintly king'. I went to the king, who was sitting on the sand in a tent, leaning against the tent pole, without a carpet or anything else beneath him. I said, 'Sire, outside there is a crowd of people from Greater Armenia, who are going to Jerusalem and have asked me, Sire, if I can have "the saintly king" shown to them. But I do not want to kiss your bones yet!' The king laughed loudly and told me to send for them.

Edward of England reached North Africa the day before the crusade left and, although he was not happy with what he found, he sailed with Charles of Anjou and Philip of France to Sicily, through a storm off Trapani which did great damage to the fleet. He voyaged on to the Holy Land at the end of April 1271, accompanied by only 200–300 knights and c. 600 infantry, and disembarked at Acre on 9 May. The English remained inactive while the Egyptians took the Teutonic Knights' castle of Montfort, but on 12 July they raided into Galilee and in November, together with local troops and another body of crusaders under Edward's brother Edmund, who had reached Palestine in September, they tried to take the Mamluk castle of Qaqun near Caesarea. They surprised a large Turkoman force nearby, but withdrew at the approach of a Muslim army and any further action was prevented by a ten-year truce, which was agreed between Egypt and the kingdom of Jerusalem in April 1272. There was little Edward could now do. His brother left Acre in May. On 16 June he was severely injured when one of his native servants tried to assassinate him. For a time he was too ill to move, but he eventually left for home and the throne on 22 September.

Pope Gregory X

Louis's second expedition, which accomplished so little, was the last full-scale crusade before the fall of the Latin settlements in 1291, but that was not for want of enthusiasm. Tedaldo Visconti, who had travelled to Acre in the summer of 1270, was elected pope in the following year by cardinals who expressed the hope that he would do all in his power to save the Holy Land. He adopted the name of Gregory X. Before leaving Palestine to take up office he preached a sermon on the text from Psalm 136 (137): 5–6:

> If I forget thee, O Jerusalem, let my right hand forget her cunning. If I do not remember thee, let my tongue cleave to the roof of my mouth; if I prefer not Jerusalem above my chief joy.

In a letter to Edward of England, who was still in Acre, he told how he had hurried directly to the papal curia at Viterbo, not even stopping at Rome, so as to begin work on bringing aid to the Holy Land immediately. Before he had been consecrated he sent a letter to Philip of France with a proposal for fitting out an expedition. He felt, in fact, as obsessively about the movement as Innocent III had done. His first act at Viterbo was to summon a conference of cardinals and of men familiar with conditions in the East and it was at this gathering that he decided to convoke a new general council with the two-fold aim of reforming Christendom and promoting a crusade, which he would lead himself. He tried to prepare carefully for this, the Second Council of Lyon, by calling for written advice from the clergy, and during it, on 18 May 1274, he issued the *Constitutiones pro zelo fidei*, the most imposing crusade document since the *Ad liberandam* constitution of 1215. *Pro zelo fidei* contains many elements found in earlier decrees, especially *Ad liberandam*, but there was also much in it that was new, in particular on the raising of funds. A six-year tenth was to be levied on the whole Church, with exemptions only granted on the strictest conditions. Christendom was to be divided into twenty-six districts staffed by collectors and sub-collectors. Every temporal ruler was to be asked to impose a capitation tax of one silver penny *tournois* a year within his dominions: this was obviously influenced by Gregory IX's attempted levy of 1235. Gregory X's aim was to build up a huge reserve and had he lived a really major enterprise might have been mounted. As it was, his preparations were heroic. Tremendous efforts culminated at the council in the formal reconciliation of the Latin and Greek Churches and the promise from the Byzantine emperor to do all in his power to help the coming crusade. In 1275 the kings of France and Sicily took the cross. So did Rudolf of Habsburg in return for Gregory's agreement to crown him western emperor. The plan was for the pope to crown Rudolf in Rome on 2 February 1277. Then on the following 2 April the pope and the emperor would leave together for the East. There was even discussion with the Greeks about their proposal for the crusade to follow the path of the First in order to reconquer Asia Minor on the way. Gregory was planning an eastern crusade on a more ambitious scale than had ever been dreamed of before, but on 10 January 1276 he died. To a despairing contemporary, 'it does not seem to be the divine will that the Holy Sepulchre should be recovered, since the great number attempting it are seen to have laboured in vain'.

The failure to launch a great crusade after 1276

The huge sums collected for Gregory's crusade were dissipated on the Italian ventures. Although proposals for large-scale expeditions were still put forward – Edward of England bombarded the papacy with them from 1284 to 1293 – it was small parties that sailed to help the kingdom of Jerusalem in its last years. The French regiment had returned to Acre in 1273 and, although it was replaced by one financed by Charles of Anjou in 1277, King Philip IV of France resumed the responsibility for its upkeep on the collapse of Angevin rule in Palestine in 1286. It was to fight heroically in the sieges of Tripoli and Acre which closed the history of the Latin settlements. On 18 June 1287 Countess Alice of Blois landed at Acre with a little crusade which included Count Florent of Holland. It was followed in 1288 by a force under John of Grailly and in 1290 by others of Englishmen under Odo of Grandson and of north Italian crusaders under the bishop of Tripoli.

One reason for the failure to mount a large-scale crusade after 1272 was the increasing complexity, viciousness and cost of inter-state disputes in western Europe. Another was the prevalence of the view that great crusades could be counter-productive. They were difficult to raise, provision and control and could be expected to do little long-term good, since they would conquer but not occupy territory, the defence of which would put additional strains on the already over-stretched resources of the Latin settlement once the crusaders had returned home. What was needed was a strengthening of the permanent garrison and this explains the money sent to Palestine in these years by the papacy, France, and to a lesser extent England. In this respect the popes had pinned their hopes on Charles of Anjou and the integration of the kingdom of Jerusalem into an eastern Mediterranean empire which would be able to defend it, especially since it had the backing of France. The gamble failed. Given the diversion of Charles's interests towards the conquest of Albania and even the Byzantine empire it would probably have failed anyway. But reality dawned in 1286 with the war against the Sicilians and Aragonese going badly, Charles dead and his heir a prisoner of the Aragonese. By then the settlements had only five years of existence left.

CHAPTER 8

The Latin East, 1192–c. 1291

In the third decade of the thirteenth century the settlers in Palestine and Syria were probably more secure than their ancestors had been before 1187. It is true that they controlled much less territory than their great-grandfathers had ruled in the middle of the twelfth century. After Frederick II's treaty with al-Kamil of Egypt in 1229 they held the coast from Jaffa to Beirut, with a tongue of land extending through Ramle to Jerusalem and a somewhat wider salient reaching Nazareth in Galilee. North of Beirut the county of Tripoli remained much as it had been in 1187, but the principality of Antioch was now confined to the neighbourhood of Antioch itself and to a strip of the coast in the south, from Jeble to the Hospitaller castle of Marqab. But Palestine and Syria were no longer lonely outposts in the Levant, since a string of western settlements occupied much of the northern coast of the eastern Mediterranean. The question whether these were or were not expressions of a colonial movement has often been debated. I have already argued against any interpretation of the early crusading conquests in proto-colonial terms and the early Latin states were not classically colonial in that they were politically independent of mother countries. On the other hand, the Holy Sepulchre could never have been held without the occupation and exploitation of the territory around it and up the coast, and the large-scale immigration and the flow of resources to settlements which, if not politically subject to western Europe, were financially dependent make it hard to deny a colonial complexion entirely. However haphazardly they had come into being, moreover, all the settlements to the west of Palestine and Syria were established from 1191 onwards on territory which had been taken not from the Muslims but from fellow-Christians, and certain of them – for example Crete, Euboea and Chios – were politically as well as economically dependent on Venice and Genoa.

Cilician Armenia

North of the principality of Antioch the Cilician Armenian ruler Leo had accepted a crown from the western emperor in 1198, together with a form of submission to Rome which was never very real and has already been described. Cilicia was Latinized in all sorts of ways. Leo took as his second wife Sibylla, the daughter of Aimery of Cyprus and Isabella of Jerusalem, and their daughter and heiress Zabel was therefore the first cousin of the queen of Jerusalem and the king of Cyprus. Leo gave castles and territories to the Hospitallers and Teutonic Knights and privileges to Genoese and Venetian merchants. His court was transformed as offices changed their character at the same time as they adopted western functions and titles. The system of landholding and the relationship between the 'barons' and the crown were modified in imitation of feudalism. Westerners held some of the fiefs and the authority of western law gradually grew until a translation of the *Assises of Antioch* was adopted as their own by the Armenians in the 1260s. In the 1250s King Hetoum entered, as a subject power, into an alliance with the Mongols, but that did not affect Cilicia's relationship with the settlers, which grew even closer. King Toros (1292–4) married Margaret of Cyprus. His sister Isabella married Amalric, the king of Cyprus's younger brother, and in the fourteenth century the Armenian crown passed into the hands of this cadet branch of the royal house of Cyprus, to be held by it until Cilician Armenia was finally destroyed in 1375.

Cyprus

We have already seen how Cyprus, off the Levantine coast, was conquered in 1191 by Richard I of England and was sold to Guy of Lusignan, the rejected king of Jerusalem, in 1192. Guy, who never settled his debt to Richard, died late in 1194 and was succeeded by his brother Aimery of Lusignan, who married Isabella of Jerusalem in October 1197 after the death of Henry of Champagne. At about the same time Aimery paid homage to representatives of the western emperor and received a crown from them, so that from that date he was king of Cyprus in his own right and of Jerusalem by virtue of his marriage. After his death in 1205 the crowns went their separate ways. Cyprus passed to Hugh I, Aimery's son by his first wife Eschiva of Ibelin. Jerusalem was inherited by Maria, Isabella's daughter by Conrad of Montferrat. Hugh of Cyprus married his step-sister, Isabella's third daughter Alice of Champagne, and the crowns were reunited in their grandson, Hugh III of Cyprus and I of Jerusalem, who succeeded to Cyprus in 1267 and to Jerusalem in 1269.

Guy of Lusignan had established a feudal system in Cyprus, peopling it largely with immigrants from Palestine, particularly from those families which had supported him in his struggle to retain the crown of Jerusalem. They were later joined by many of the leading nobles from the mainland – Hugh I's mother, after all, was an Ibelin and therefore a member of the most prominent family in Palestine – and by 1230 many of the great nobles had estates in both kingdoms. The settlers introduced feudal customs from the mainland, and in 1369 a particular interpretation of them, John of Ibelin-Jaffa's great work of jurisprudence, became an official work of reference in the High Court of Nicosia.

There were, however, differences. Cyprus *was* a separate realm, as a representative of its nobility, himself a titular count of Jaffa, stressed in

1271 when he argued that Cypriot knights were not bound by their feudal contracts to serve outside it, in Palestine. It had a different, Byzantine, past. It had a distinct constitutional history, for until 1247 it was a fief of the western empire, whereas Jerusalem was always an independent state. In certain important respects the system of agriculture on which Cypriot feudalism rested was different from that on the mainland. Before the Latin conquest the island had been exposed to the processes of 'manorialization' which had begun to affect Byzantine rural life and many Cypriot villages were markedly more 'manorial' than their Palestinian counterparts, with demesne lands in the possession of landlords and heavy labour services demanded of many of the peasants.

The Latin Church of Cyprus, moreover, adopted a more interventionist attitude towards the indigenous Greek population and clergy. The number of Orthodox dioceses was drastically reduced from fourteen to four and the Orthodox bishops became coadjutors to the four Catholic bishops, with responsibilities for the churches of the Greek rite. There was resistance from the Greeks, occasional brutal countermeasures from the Latins and periods of open hostility, but mostly there was quiet resentment. The *Bulla Cypria*, issued by Pope Alexander IV in 1260, marked the agreement of the higher Greek Cypriot clergy to Uniate status, but, in the words of Dr Coureas, 'with the passage of time it was shown to be increasingly hollow'. The lower clergy and people felt no loyalty towards the westerners, although being poor and deprived of patronage they could not resist Latin cultural influence, manifested most strikingly in the building of a new Orthodox cathedral in Famagusta in the Gothic style in the fourteenth century. On the other hand cultural assimilation was a two-way process. The developing cultural synthesis already in evidence in mainland art gained momentum in Cyprus, while increasing intermarriage meant that from the early fourteenth century there was the real possibility of the Catholics being absorbed into the Orthodox.

Greece

North-west of Cyprus, across the Cretan and Aegean seas, was the Latin empire of Constantinople, bounded by the Greek splinter states of Nicaea and Epirus and the Vlacho-Bulgarian empire. The treaty between the Venetians and the other crusaders drawn up before the capture of Constantinople had been modified by two further treaties, agreed in October 1204 and October 1205, by the way the Greek territories had been conquered and by private arrangements made between individual leaders. The Latin emperor held a triangular block of land in eastern Thrace, together with the north-western edge of Asia Minor and some islands in the Aegean. Venice had part of the European coast of the Sea of Marmara and a corridor of land inland to Edirne, the Ionian islands, where the county of Cephalonia (Kefallinia) was eventually forced to recognize Venetian suzerainty, Methóni and Koróni in the southern Peloponnese, the island of Euboea off the eastern coast of Greece, the island of Crete, and the Cyclades and northern Dodecanese and other islands, assembled by Marco Sanudo into a duchy of the Archipelago centred on Naxos, which was recognized as a fief by the Latin empire. Western Thrace, part of Macedonia and Thessaly made up the kingdom of Thessalonica (Thessaloniki) ruled by Boniface of Montferrat, whose suzerainty extended over Thebes and Athens. South of them lay the Peloponnese, which the Latins began to conquer over the winter of 1204–5 and where William of Champlitte was recognized as prince of Achaea, subject to the Latin empire. William was a grandson of Count Hugh I of Champagne, who, having apparently been told by his doctors that he was incapable of having children, had disowned William's father, his son by his wife Elizabeth of Burgundy.

The settlement of a western super-stratum, drawn not only from Europe but also from Palestine, from whence many sought the relative security of Greece, proceeded along the already well-tried lines of the granting of fiefs. The feudal system that resulted is best illustrated by evidence from the Peloponnese, where the settlement lasted longest and gave rise to a legal collection, the *Assises of Romania*, the final redaction of which was written in French between 1333 and 1346 and was later translated into Venetian Italian, in which language it survives. Below the prince of Achaea were his direct vassals, divided into liege vassals, who were entitled to have vassals of their own, and simple vassals, men not of the knightly class, such as sergeants, who were not. Among the liege vassals were the barons of the principality who enjoyed a special status and were referred to as the 'peers of the prince'. They had the right to judge in their courts according to both high and low justice, whereas the other liege vassals had the right to render only low justice and the simple vassals had jurisdiction only over their peasants. This colonial society was, like that of Latin Jerusalem, highly class-conscious, but the lords in Greece, unlike those in Jerusalem, did not on the whole live down in the cities but above them in the acropolises or in isolated castles and fortified manor-houses: the remains of 150 strongholds have been identified in the Peloponnese alone, mostly thrown up in the early thirteenth century. This, of course, underlined the distinction between them and the Greeks – intermarriage was rare – and it was reinforced by their chivalric culture, the most glittering of the time, expressed in the tournaments they loved and in the histories and French romances they enjoyed. The French spoken at the court of Achaea at Andravidha was reputed to be as pure as that spoken in Paris.

Most of the Greeks sank at first into subservience, being regarded by their western overlords as unfree. The chief exception was a class of *archontes*, great landlords or imperial officials before the conquest, whom the Latins tried to conciliate by promising the maintenance of the Orthodox clergy and the Byzantine legal and fiscal systems, although the use of Byzantine law ceased in the public sphere and the transference of rights of jurisdiction and taxation to private feudal landlords meant the disappearance of the old public system of taxation. The *archontes* ranked as simple vassals, along with the western sergeants, but by the middle of the thirteenth century some of them were receiving fiefs and were beginning to be dubbed knights, thus qualifying for liege vassalage. This paved the way for the occasional Greek who had not been an *archon* to be raised to the highest feudal class. By the fourteenth century Greek liege vassals were to be found and there were Latinized Greeks like the translator of the *Chronicle of Morea* who, writing just before 1388, criticized the Greeks of Constantinople and Epirus and accused the Orthodox of being schismatics.

The conquerors' policy towards the Greeks' Church further humiliated them. In 1204 the Venetians, in accordance with the treaty made between them and the rest of the crusaders, had nominated the cathedral chapter of St Sophia, which then elected Thomas Morosini, of a noble Venetian family and at that time only a sub-deacon, to the patriarchate of Constantinople. Pope Innocent III had to confirm this uncanonical appointment and Thomas's promotion through the clerical orders to priest and bishop, but he also began the long process of wresting the chapter of St Sophia from Venetian control. The Greeks naturally found it hard to recognize the new patriarch, especially after 1208 when the Byzantine emperor in exile in Nicaea assembled a synod to elect a new Orthodox patriarch. Most Greek bishops deserted their sees or refused to recognize Thomas, or, in the few cases in which recognition was given, objected to a reconsecration of themselves according to Catholic rites, which implied that their previous consecration had been uncanonical. The Latins embarked on a policy of substituting Catholic bishops for Orthodox ones, although they could not afford to reproduce the complex Byzantine hierarchy of metropolitan sees with suffragan bishops and autocephalous archbishoprics without suffragans. As in the Levant and in Cyprus, they also introduced western monastic and religious orders. But everywhere Orthodox monasteries and local married clergy survived *in situ*, although the Greeks were forced to pay thirtieths to the Catholic clergy in place of full tithes.

By the treaties of 1204 the Venetians had acquired three-eighths of the empire. They elected their own *podestà*, who was assisted by an administration modelled on that of Venice, although the mother city soon took steps to see that his powers were limited. The treaty of 1205 laid down a procedure for collectively deciding the scale of potential military threats that demanded service from all, whether Venetians or not. A council, made up of that of the *podestà* together with the barons of the empire, would do this and it could require the emperor to follow its advice. It was also to supervise any judges appointed to arbitrate between him and those from whom he desired service. Every time a new Latin emperor was crowned he had to swear to uphold the conditions of the treaties of March and October 1204 and of October 1205, which to the Venetians formed the empire's constitution and which gave them a powerful political position, although they would have had great influence anyway, given the size of their holdings.

The treaties imposed severe limitations on the emperors from which they were never able to escape. This was particularly unfortunate because in the first half of the thirteenth century they were the most insecure and exposed of all the Latin rulers in the East. They had to face threats from the Vlacho-Bulgarians and the Byzantine Greeks, who had established the three *émigré* states of Epirus, Trebizond (Trabzon) and Nicaea, the last under Theodore Lascaris, the son-in-law of the emperor Alexius III. Over and over again the Latins had to fight on at least two fronts. In spite of early successes in Asia Minor, in which Alexius V, the last Byzantine emperor in Constantinople, had been taken – he had already been blinded by his rivals and was now forced to jump to his death from the top of the column in the forum of Theodosius in Constantinople – the ruler of Bulgaria, Ioannitsa, invaded Thrace early in 1205 and ravaged it for nearly a year. He captured the emperor Baldwin, whom he may well have murdered. At any rate Baldwin died in captivity and his brother and regent Henry was crowned emperor on 20 August 1206. A man of remarkable powers of tenacity and leadership, Henry faced an appalling situation, not only in Thrace but also in Asia Minor where by the beginning of 1207 the Latins had only a toe-hold. But Ioannitsa died that summer and on 1 August 1208 Henry defeated the Bulgarians who were anyway divided over who would succeed him. After further victories against the Bulgarians and the Nicaean Greeks in 1211, the Treaty of Nymphaeum gave the Latins the entire Asiatic shore of the Sea of Marmara and a stretch along the Aegean.

Henry died, aged only forty, on 11 June 1216 and his successor Peter of Courtenay, the husband of his sister Yolande, was captured by Theodore Angelus of Epirus, a cousin of the emperor Isaac II, before he ever reached Constantinople. Peter's son, Robert of Courtenay, who came to the throne on 25 March 1221, soon had to face war on two fronts. Theodore Angelus of Epirus was pushing into Thessaly. In 1222 he took Sérrai, in 1224 Thessaloniki and in 1225 Edirne – it is indicative of the situation that he took the last city not from the Latins but from Nicaean Greeks who had crossed the Dardanelles – and he threatened Constantinople itself. In the meantime warfare had again broken out with Nicaea, where John Ducas Vatatzes had succeeded to the throne. By 1226 the Latin settlers had lost all of Asia Minor except Izmit, which they held only until 1235. Probably the only factor that saved Latin Constantinople at this time was the insistence of John Asen of Bulgaria, Ioannitsa's nephew and successor, who wanted the empire for himself, that Theodore of Epirus allow Robert to hold his lands undisturbed.

After a cruel revolt by his own knights at what they regarded as his shameful marriage to a French woman of humble birth – they mutilated her and drowned her mother – Robert fled to Rome. He died in 1228 on his way back to Constantinople. His heir was his brother Baldwin II, who was only eleven years old. Spurning John Asen's attempt to secure Constantinople by a marriage alliance between his daughter and the young emperor, the barons of the empire called in that experienced trouble-shooter, John of Brienne. John had been born c. 1170, the third son of the count of Brienne, and he had spent most of his life in relative obscurity in Champagne before being selected in 1210 to be the husband for Maria, the young heiress of Jerusalem. He had proved himself to be an effective king, although we have already seen him being outmanoeuvred by the papal legate in Egypt during the Fifth Crusade. His wife had died in 1212 and he had ruled as regent for his daughter Yolande until she was married to the emperor Frederick II in 1225. Frederick had refused to allow him to keep the regency and, it was rumoured, had seduced one of his nieces who was in Yolande's entourage. John's fury was such that he had agreed to become commander of the papal forces which invaded Frederick's southern Italian territories while the emperor was in Palestine, but now the barons of the Latin empire offered the hand of their emperor to another of his daughters, by his most recent wife Berengaria of Castile, if he would consent to rule for life as co-emperor. John had arrived in Constantinople by the summer of 1231 with 500 knights and 5,000 men-at-arms, to whom the pope had granted crusade indulgences. The military and political situation, which was already bad, was worsening. In 1230 Theodore of Epirus had been defeated and captured by John Asen, who had swept through Thrace, Thessaly and a large part of Albania. John Asen, who wanted an autonomous Bulgarian patriarchate, opened negotiations with the Nicaeans and in 1235 concluded a pact with John Vatatzes according to which his daughter was betrothed to John Vatatzes's son and Bulgaria gained its own patriarchate. John Vatatzes crossed the Dardanelles, sacked Gallipoli and joined forces with the Bulgarians before being utterly defeated outside the walls of Constantinople by John of Brienne, who had with him only 160 knights.

John of Brienne died on 23 March 1237 and the settlers were saved for a time only by the launching of the crusade from the West in 1239 which has already been described and because the Nicaean Greeks, now established in Europe, were engaged in consolidating their bridgehead in the Balkans and were anxious about the Mongols, who were threatening them from the East. Baldwin II, heavily dependent on French subsidies, made several fund-raising tours of western Europe. The last great relics in Constantinople were disposed of for cash, as we have seen. Baldwin engaged in complex monetary transactions, even resorting to the pledging of the person of his only son, Philip, who spent his childhood and youth in Venice in the custody of his father's creditors. He was redeemed, thanks to King Alfonso X of Castile, in the first half of 1261, but by then Latin Constantinople had only a few months left. On 25 July, while most of the garrison was away on a Venetian expedition to attack the island of Kefken in the Black Sea, a Byzantine force from Nicaea infiltrated the city and occupied it with very little resistance. Baldwin fled and the Venetian fleet was able to save only the wives and children of Venetian residents. On 15 August the Nicaean emperor Michael VIII Palaeologus made his ceremonial entry into the city and was crowned Basileus in St Sophia.

French and Venetian settlers still held southern Greece and the islands in the Aegean. In the middle of the thirteenth century Achaea in the Peloponnese was the most brilliant of all the Latin settlements in the East. The knights gathered round the princes, William of Champlitte, Geoffrey I, Geoffrey II and William of Villehardouin, and the lords of Athens, Othon and Guy of la Roche, engaged in a constant round of chivalric enterprise, including petty war with the Byzantine Greeks to the north. The heyday of Latin rule and prosperity was the early 1250s, but a dispute between William of Villehardouin on one side and Venice and Guy of la Roche on the other gradually engulfed the peninsula and no sooner had that ended when William was defeated by Michael VIII at the Battle of Pelagonia in the summer of 1259. He was imprisoned by the Greeks and in 1261 was forced to surrender to them the strongholds of Monemvasia, Mistra (Mistrás) and Mani in a treaty which was ratified by a parliament composed mainly of the wives of the imprisoned lords. He was dispensed by the pope of the promises he had made under duress, but the two-year war that followed decimated and exhausted the settlers and devastated the principality. Conscious of his insecurity William ceded Achaea to Charles of Anjou, the new king of Sicily, on 24 May 1267, in return for the right to hold it for life. By the terms of the agreement his daughter Isabel was to wed one of Charles's sons, who would succeed him, but if that son died childless Achaea would revert to Charles or his heir. Three days later, as we have seen, the Latin emperor Baldwin confirmed the cession and added to it suzerainty for Charles over the Archipelago, Corfu and the Latin possessions in Epirus, in return for the promise of 2,000 mounted men to help him recover his empire.

So Latin Greece became subject to the kingdom of Sicily. Charles certainly seems to have wanted to go further and to conquer Constantinople, but at first he committed resources to the principality's defence as well as trying to maintain a presence in Albania, where he was recognized as king in 1271. In February 1277 William of Villehardouin's son-in-law and heir presumptive, Philip of Anjou, died and William followed him to the grave on 1 May 1278. The principality now passed directly under Charles's rule, but took second place in his strategic thinking to Albania and especially to his designs on Constantinople. After the Sicilian Vespers in 1282 Latin Greece was left to fend for itself. One of the first acts of Charles II was to restore the government of the principality of Achaea to Isabel of Villehardouin, on the occasion of her marriage to Florent of Hainault, a great-grandson of the emperor Baldwin I, in 1289. Charles later gave his favourite son, Philip of Taranto, immediate overlordship of Florent and Isabel and all Latin Greece. Florent died in January 1297, leaving a three-year-old daughter, Mahaut, and in 1301 Isabel married her third husband, Philip of Savoy, count of Piedmont. He was deposed five years later by Charles for refusing to pay homage to Philip of Taranto and for pursuing policies against Angevin interests. In spite of Isabel's protests, Philip of Taranto took over the direct government of Latin Greece.

I referred in the previous chapter to the Angevins' struggle to recover the island of Sicily from the Aragonese. Now, by an extraordinary turn of events, this conflict was extended into southern Greece. In 1309 Thessaly had been invaded by a band of mercenary adventurers, the Catalan Company, composed of Catalans and other northern Spaniards who were the survivors of various mercenary bands that had been employed in the south Italian wars by the Aragonese princes. The Company had hired itself to the Byzantine emperor Andronicus II to fight the Ottoman Turks, who were making almost their first appearance on the historical scene, but it had quarrelled with him and had pillaged its way through Thrace and Macedonia, for a time serving Charles of Valois, the brother of King Philip IV of France, who was married to a grand-daughter of the Latin emperor Baldwin II and wanted to stake a claim to the empire. Edged by the Greek ruler of Thessaly towards Athens, the Catalans took service with the duke, Walter of Brienne, in 1310, but when he refused them land and would not pay the wages due to them they turned against him. Walter assembled an army from all over Latin Greece and brought them to battle on 15 March 1311 at Halmyros in Thessaly. The result was a sensation. In an engagement typical of a period in which the old chivalry was being overtaken in expertise by new professional soldiers Walter led a charge directly into a swamp which he mistakenly believed was a green meadow. He and almost all his knights were slaughtered. The Catalans themselves took over Thebes and Athens, which were lost to the French and gained by the Aragonese. The knighthood of the Peloponnese was depleted by about a third of its members. An era had ended.

The Italians

Since the Latin East had expanded to comprise several states scattered over a large part of the eastern Mediterranean seaboard it was no longer only a question of safeguarding a lifeline to the West for isolated settlements. Now maritime contacts between many groups of colonists over a large area had to be maintained. The settlers had always been dependent on the sea-power provided by western merchants, particularly those from the Italian ports of Venice, Genoa and Pisa. In the thirteenth century these Italians still provided the sea-power, but with their territorial gains in Greece and the Greek islands they were themselves politically integrated into the framework they helped to bind together. Thenceforward the histories of east Mediterranean trade and east Mediterranean settlement and crusading become virtually indistinguishable.

Italians had been engaged as traders in the region before the crusades. Pisa and Genoa had had few contacts with the great centres of commerce there, for on the whole their activities had been confined to the western Mediterranean, but Amalfi and particularly Venice were already active. The Venetians had gained privileges from the Byzantines, partly because as far as the Byzantine government was concerned they were still subjects of the empire, and a charter issued by Alexius I in 1082, granting them freedom from customs and market taxes in a number of specified ports, was a prototype for the rights later given to Italian merchants by the rulers of the Latin settlements. The Italians had been invited by the pope to take part in the First Crusade and they shared in the conquest of Palestine and Syria. The Genoese arrived in 1098, the Pisans in 1099 and the Venetians in 1100. At a rather later date they were joined by merchants from Languedoc, Provence and Catalonia.

In the twelfth century Venice, Genoa and Pisa had gained rights that may be summarized as follows. First, they were given property, usually quarters in cities, which included administrative buildings, churches, public baths and ovens, although the Genoese family of Embriaco got personal possession of the town and fief of Jubail in the county of Tripoli and in 1124 the Venetians were also given a third of the city-territory of Tyre, in which they settled some of their compatriots as fief-holders. Secondly, they acquired jurisdictional rights, the ability to judge their own nationals and in some cases those living in their own quarters. Thirdly, they were granted commercial privileges: rights to enter, remain in or leave certain ports, the reduction or abolition of entry, exit and sales dues, and sometimes the possession of their own markets. These privileges enabled them to establish their own *comptoirs* or factories (in the old-fashioned sense of this word): quarters in which their merchants could stay when they arrived with the fleets from the West. These were deserted out of season, with only a small resident community – c. 300 persons in the Genoese quarter in thirteenth-century Acre – left to service them.

Although the Italian merchants were highly privileged, this meant less than one might suppose until the 1180s, because the bulk of the spice trade from the Far East, easily the most profitable and attractive commerce, did not pass through the Palestinian and Syrian ports but through Alexandria in Egypt. There was, however, enough of it, together with trade in local products like sugar and cotton and the importation for oriental markets of western manufactures such as cloth, to encourage the trading cities to build up their *comptoirs* and to create administrative structures, establishing in each of them consuls or viscounts or both. These administrators had to cope with the fact that the twelfth-century kings of Jerusalem soon began to adopt a tougher stance towards them with the aim of at the very least keeping them to the letter of the charters of privilege issued to them. The kings insisted that the Italian courts could only deal with their nationals who were visitors; if any Italian settled permanently he was to become answerable to royal justice. They maintained that the Italians only had jurisdiction in low justice: high justice, the justice of blood, was reserved to the crown. They tried to prevent their vassals alienating fiefs to them and sometimes even tried to cut back their privileges. The pressure became at times so intense that Genoa and Venice ceded some of their *comptoirs* and properties to their own vassals, who could fight their battles for them; the Embriaco lordship of Jubail developed in this way.

In the last quarter of the twelfth century, however, the Asiatic trade routes changed course for reasons that are still not clear. After 1180 spices from India and the Far East were increasingly by-passing Egypt and being brought to Syria, where Damascus, Aleppo and Antioch were major centres. Damascus was becoming especially important and its chief ports, Acre and Tyre, were in Christian hands. Acre came to rival and even overtake Alexandria as the chief market on the eastern Mediterranean seaboard and there the western merchants were already ensconced and privileged.

The resulting growth in the volume of trade also benefited the crown. It will be remembered that customs and sales duties were totted up and taken in a single lump sum in the markets, usually expressed as a percentage of the commodity's value. This was, of course, payable by both buyer and seller, so that even if one party to a transaction was exempt from taxation the other, usually a Muslim merchant from the interior, was not. A government, therefore, could never lose more than half the customs and sale tax even if it granted total exemption to one party. The hope was that an increase in traffic, which would never have taken place had not merchants been on hand to carry the goods away, would more than compensate for any losses incurred by granting privileges in the first place. Oriental merchants never seem to have been privileged and they were charged additional exit taxes as they left by the city gates for home, while the rights gained by the Venetians and Pisans in Acre to have their own markets, which could have led to the government losing the ability to levy taxes from those with whom they had dealings, meant in practice that they could sell in them only the goods they had brought from Europe. To fill the holds of their ships for the voyage home they had to buy in the royal markets, where the vendors had to settle their share of the duty. The government, moreover, seems to have strictly enforced the payment of dues by those residents who bought in the Italian markets and it took measures to prevent the Italians circumventing the restraints by themselves travelling to and trading in the Muslim interior. A consequence was that the kingdom of Jerusalem became quite rich. Revenues from trade enabled it to grant additional money fiefs, which made up much of the feudal service lost when the territorial fiefs passed under Muslim control in 1187.

But if the crown was relatively richer, so were the Italians, and their response to increased business and the large number of their merchants now in the East can be seen in the way they centralized the control of eastern *comptoirs*. In the 1190s Venice appointed a *bajulus Venetorum in tota Syria* to be stationed in Acre. At about the same time Genoa and Pisa each appointed two consuls for all Syria, also to be resident in Acre, and in 1248 Pisa put authority into the hands of a single *consul communis Pisanorum Accon et totius Syriae*. Between 1187 and 1192, moreover, Guy of Lusignan and Conrad of Montferrat were prepared to grant more privileges in return for support in their competition for the crown. The Pisans gained rights of jurisdiction, including high justice, over all those living in their quarters and the Genoese were given the privilege that cases involving high justice would be decided by their own and royal judges sitting together. Henry of Champagne tried, not very successfully, to cut back these immunities again and he began to exert a pressure on the Italians that was to be applied sporadically in the thirteenth century, although the long period in which the kings were absent and the fact that in times of financial crisis the Italians had great influence as shippers, money-changers and lenders meant that it was not consistent.

The Ayyubids

If the prosperity of the Latin East in the first half of the thirteenth century and the range and depth of the Latin settlements around the shores of the eastern Mediterranean gave the settlers in Palestine and Syria greater security, they also faced much less aggressive neighbours. Saladin had died on 4 March 1193 and the provinces of his empire – Egypt, Aleppo, Damascus, the Jazira, Transjordan, Hama, Homs and Ba'albek – became independent principalities under his relatives and descendants, one of whom in each generation assumed a precarious paramountcy: al-'Adil (1200–18), al-Kamil (1218–38), as-Salih Ayyub (1240–9). The Ayyubids, of course, had other frontiers to concern them besides that with the settlers. This was also a period of great prosperity for them and for their subjects, partly because of the receptivity of western Europe to Asiatic goods, a receptivity which depended on the transit of those goods through the Christian ports. So, although ideas of *jihad* survived and even flourished, the emphasis was on co-existence and the period was marked by a succession of truces. Jerusalem and Antioch-Tripoli engaged in alliances and counter-alliances like any of the other petty states in the region, but one of these alliances and its consequences provided evidence that appearances were deceptive. In 1244 a party in the kingdom overturned the truce with as-Salih Ayyub of Egypt, which has already been described, and entered into an offensive alliance against him with as-Salih Isma'il of Damascus and an-Nasir Da'ud of Transjordan, which allowed the Christians to extend their control over the Temple area in Jerusalem. Egypt turned to the Khorezmians, the survivors of a state north of Iran which had been broken by the Mongols in 1220. They had been serving as mercenaries in northern Iraq and they now swept down from the north and burst into Jerusalem on 11 July. On 23 August the Tower of David surrendered to them. On 17 October at the Battle of Harbiyah (La Forbie), north-east of Gaza, the Franco-Damascus alliance was shattered by them and the Egyptians. The bulk of the Christian army, possibly comprising 1,200 knights and the largest since Hattin fifty-seven years before, died on the field.

The settlers' knowledge of Muslim politics

It is not surprising that the interest in Muslim politics of the settlers and their correspondents in the West was manifest. Within certain limits their knowledge was accurate and detailed. Between 1196 and 1202, for example, four letters addressed to two correspondents by the Hospitaller master, Geoffrey of Donjon, guided them through a particularly tortuous period in Ayyubid politics. Every now and then, the addressees in Europe were provided with additional titbits of information which might interest them, although how often they were accurate is another matter. Geoffrey had heard that a young Muslim shepherd had adopted Christianity and had engaged in an evangelical preaching campaign among his compatriots, which had led to 2,000 of them being converted. The Templar grand master Armand of Peragors wrote that a grandson of as-Salih Isma'il of Damascus had converted to Christianity and was now called Martin. The Templar grand commander Guy of Basainville had learned in 1256 of an earthquake and volcanic eruption in Arabia which had destroyed Muhammad's tomb at Medina.

The tone adopted by the writers was generally restrained. Many of the letters were, of course, private, but even when they were intended for a wider circulation they were neutrally expressed. It is no exaggeration to say that they contain fewer polemics than one would find in the materials for almost any petty ecclesiastical dispute in Europe. It may be that the relatively neutral language stemmed from the fact that the masters of the military orders and the other managers of crusading violence could not afford to be too emotional. Their responsibility was to defend the frontiers as sensibly as possible, while familiarity with conditions in the East bred a relaxed attitude on their part. But on the other hand they must have believed that the kings, senior churchmen and great nobles with whom they corresponded appreciated their matter-of-fact tone, since if they had been convinced that men from whom they were, after all, soliciting assistance were more likely to be responsive to highly coloured language they would certainly have employed it. The bulk of the correspondence from the West to them has been lost, but circumstantial evidence suggests that it was expressed in the same understated way.

It is natural to wonder which was more typical of western attitudes: the emotionally charged aggression reported of many newcomers to the Levant, or the cooler tone. The answer is probably both. There was not one Christian view of Islam, but several. The calmness of the language which featured in the continuous dialogue kept up between the leaders in the East and the popes and kings in the West made sense in the circumstances in which they found themselves. The hyperbole and exaggeration which was employed by preachers to whip up support and was sometimes expressed by crusaders must have irritated those on whose shoulders the defence of the Holy Land actually rested, because they were faced by unreasonable expectations and were inevitably blamed if the war on God's behalf turned against them.

Antioch-Tripoli

The principality of Antioch and the county of Tripoli came to be united under a single ruler after a war of succession in the early years of the thirteenth century, although each continued to have its own administration and customary law. Raymond III of Tripoli had died in 1187 leaving no direct heirs. Passing over the claims of his relatives in the West, he had designated his godson Raymond, the eldest son of Prince Bohemond III of Antioch, to succeed him, although the prince managed to substitute for him his younger son, the future Bohemond IV. Raymond of Antioch predeceased his father, leaving as his heir to Antioch itself his young half-Armenian son, Raymond Roupen, whose claims had the support of his great-uncle, King Leo of Cilician Armenia. Bohemond III sent Raymond Roupen back to Cilicia with his mother, although Archbishop Conrad of Mainz, who had brought Leo the crown from the western emperor, put pressure on Bohemond to make his vassals swear to uphold Raymond Roupen's succession. This was not popular and the young Bohemond (IV), now count of Tripoli and determined to take over the principality himself, entered Antioch and deposed his father, with the support of a commune, which had already been proclaimed in the city to resist the growing threat of Armenian supremacy, and the Templars, who were in dispute with Leo over his retention of their march around Bağras on the borders of Antioch and Cilicia. The revolt was short-lived, but after Bohemond III's death in 1201 Bohemond IV regained Antioch with the commune's support and held it until 1216 in the face of a series of invasions from Cilicia, a party of opposition within the principality and the peace-making efforts of the leaders of the kingdom of Jerusalem and Pope Innocent III, who excommunicated both him and Leo.

The struggle gave rise to incidents which indicate how integrated Antioch was into the Near Eastern scene. In 1201 Bohemond called in az-Zahir of Aleppo and Sulaiman of Rum to help him against Cilician Armenia and in November 1203 a force, comprising troops from Antioch and Aleppo supplemented by Templars, plundered Armenian villages near Bağras. In 1209 Kai-Khusrau of Rum invaded Cilicia on Bohemond's behalf. Meanwhile Bohemond, who depended on the support of the commune of Antioch, which had a strong Greek element within it, was on bad terms with the Catholic patriarch, Peter of Angoulême. Early in 1207 he connived at the enthronement of the titular Orthodox patriarch and in 1208 entered into an alliance with the Nicaean emperor Theodore Lascaris. When Peter of Angoulême led a revolt in the city, Bohemond threw him into prison and deprived him of food and water. Peter died in agony after drinking oil from the lamp in his cell.

By 1216 Bohemond had become estranged from his Muslim ally in Aleppo and was unpopular in Antioch because of his long absences in Tripoli. A party favouring Raymond Roupen was growing among the nobles, who included Acharie of Sarmin, the commune's mayor. On the night of 14 February Leo of Cilician Armenia entered the city and within a few days was in possession of it. Raymond Roupen was consecrated prince and since at that time he was regarded as Leo's heir there was the prospect of the union of Antioch and Cilicia. But he also proved to be unpopular and in 1219 the city rose against him. Bohemond took it over without resistance and held it thereafter, although he was reconciled with the Church only on his deathbed in 1233. There was an uneasy peace with Cilicia, broken in 1225 when Bohemond invaded it in alliance with Kai-Qobad of Rum after his son Philip, who had married Leo's heiress Zabel, had been murdered in an Armenian revolt.

After 1233 the new prince, Bohemond V, preferred, as his father had done, to live in Tripoli. Antioch was isolated under its commune of Latins and Greeks. Large parts of Christian territory, around Bağras, Marqab, Tartus, Safita and Crac des Chevaliers, were in the hands of the military orders, which pursued their own aggressive policies with regard to the petty Muslim states in their vicinity. The domains of Bohemond V give the impression of being a splintered confederacy, only surviving because of differences between the Ayyubid princelings and their desire for peace.

Constitutional conflict in the kingdom of Jerusalem

There were also serious problems relating to succession to the throne of Jerusalem. I have already described how the competition between Sibylla and Isabella and their husbands had ended in 1192 with Isabella on the throne. She married four times but was survived only by daughters. The eldest of these, Maria, married John of Brienne, but this produced yet another daughter, Yolande, the wife of the emperor Frederick II. Yolande died on 1 May 1228 giving birth to a son, Conrad. Neither he nor his son Conradin ever set foot in Palestine. From 1186 to 1268, therefore, the kingdom was in the hands of heiresses, for whom husbands had to be found, or absentee rulers, for whom regents or lieutenants had to be found. If this was not bad enough, the laws of inheritance and the customs governing the appointment of regents and lieutenants were complicated by the succession of minors and by the way a litigious and clever baronial opposition invented new laws and manipulated existing ones when it suited it to do so. While she lived Yolande, as queen regnant, could legally be represented by lieutenants. After her death her son was a minor and the laws of regency came into operation. A child's father had the first call on the regency, as long as he came to the East to be formally accepted in office, and Frederick II was regent from his arrival in Acre in September 1228, with the right to appoint his own lieutenants on his return to Europe.

Frederick's regency aroused great opposition and in 1241 the approach of Conrad's majority was made an excuse for the invention of the legal fiction that a king who had come of age but did not come to the East to be crowned should be treated as though he was entering a new minority. According to this interpretation Frederick's regency lapsed and was judged to have devolved on Conrad's nearest heir apparent, who was the dowager queen Alice of Cyprus, Isabella of Jerusalem's third daughter. On Alice's death in 1246 the regency passed to her son King Henry I of Cyprus, but he himself died in 1253, leaving a minor heir, Hugh II, who was granted the regency of Jerusalem on behalf of the new minor king, Conradin. Being a minor himself, Hugh needed a regent for his minority-regency and this office was taken by his mother, Plaisance of Antioch, until she died in 1261. The brain-scrambling complications of the regency and succession, with all the opportunities they provided for legal chicanery, were compounded by the fact that the regents were themselves often absentees and so appointed their own lieutenants in Acre, while the interstices between the royal regencies were filled by vassal regents. In the 1260s, moreover, the regency and, after the execution of Conradin, the throne were disputed by various claimants: Hugh of Brienne, the son of

Alice of Cyprus's eldest daughter; Hugh of Antioch-Lusignan, the son of Alice's younger daughter; and Maria of Antioch, Alice's niece through her younger sister Melisende.

The crown of Jerusalem not only carried with it great prestige, but while the trade routes ran favourably it was also quite a rich prize, which explains the interest taken in it by foreigners like Frederick II and even Charles of Anjou. Frederick's policies in Palestine and the residual strength of the crown caused the nobles to fear for what they perceived to be their liberties. The issue was given an additional dimension by the emergence among them of a school of jurists. This had come into existence partly as a result of two features of Jerusalemite and Cypriot law. The first was a usage whereby the king or a lord, as president of a feudal court, could appoint a vassal to help him or another vassal with *conseil* and could demand the acceptance of this duty as a feudal service. A counsellor of this sort, called a pleader, was not an advocate so much as an adviser and so complicated were the procedures in the feudal courts that it was essential for anyone engaged in litigation to make use of an adviser of this sort:

> The master of pleaders ... has very great authority [wrote one of them], for by employing a clever pleader one can sometimes save and preserve in court one's honour and body, or one's inheritance or that of a friend; and through the lack of a clever pleader, when he is needed, one can lose one's honour, body or inheritance.

It followed that those who were skilled in law were greatly in demand, as much by lords as by vassals. It seems to have been common for a man with a reputation of this kind to be granted fiefs in several lordships, which gave him the opportunity of rendering *conseil* in as many feudal courts as were involved. Since the second feature of the law was the *assise sur la ligece* which, it will be remembered, had given the king the right to demand liege-homage from all rear-vassals, a liege vassal could also plead in the king's own court. Although there is evidence that in the thirteenth century many vassals did not make liege-homage to the crown, the openings for a semi-professional class of legal counsellors are obvious. For example, James Vidal, a French knight who was a fief-holder in Palestine by April 1249 and regularly attended the High Court until 1271, also had at one time or another fiefs in the lordships of Caesarea, Arsuf, Iskanderuna and perhaps Nazareth.

The pleaders had prestige before 1187, but the disasters of that year increased it immeasurably. In the thirteenth century it was maintained – whether correctly or not is debatable – that the laws of Jerusalem, or at least some of the more important ones, each written on a separate piece of vellum and sealed by the king, the patriarch and the viscount of

Jerusalem, had been kept in a chest in the Church of the Holy Sepulchre. When Jerusalem had fallen to Saladin the chest and its contents had been lost. At one stroke the character of the law had been changed, since it was no longer based on a corpus of written material – or at least had an important written element – but had become customary. The kingdom's lawyers, therefore, had now to depend for their knowledge on custom and hearsay, as one of the greatest of them pointed out: 'The usages and laws of the kingdom ... are not written down, nor are they made into canons, nor are they authorized by agreement, nor have they been since the land was lost.' So it was to the pleaders, above all to those who moved in circles in which the old laws were remembered and discussed, that vassals sitting in judgment would turn.

The appearance in these exposed frontier marches of pedantic and highly prestigious lawyers, among whom it is probable that knowledge of the law and the ability to plead were more highly regarded, and a more certain way to prominence, than military skill, must seem odd. It should be borne in mind, however, that this was an urban nobility, living off rents and with the leisure to engage in learned debate and, it must be added, factional politics, and that Acre was a much more significant cultural centre than it used to be given credit for. The quality of its buildings are being gradually revealed through archaeology. Art historians have been coming to recognize the importance of its ateliers of manuscript illuminators and icon painters, where work of the highest standard was being produced, not provincial or colonial but with a distinctive style of its own, combining eastern and western elements, although the western, particularly the French, influence was assertive.

The men with legal reputations came from many different groups. Two were rulers, Aimery of Cyprus-Jerusalem and Bohemond IV of Antioch-Tripoli. Others were, at least at times, supporters of Frederick II. Others raised themselves from the burgess class to knighthood through their legal abilities. The most important comprised members of the higher nobility or men closely associated with them and in the early thirteenth century three of them were dominant. They were, according to the jurist Philip of Novara, 'the three wisest men that I have ever seen this side of the sea'. Ralph, lord of Tiberias, was unquestionably the greatest of them, his prestige enhanced by his personal experience of procedures before 1187. John of Ibelin, 'the Old Lord' of Beirut, was the head of the clan that now dominated Palestine and Cyprus and as the son of Balian of Ibelin's marriage to King Amalric's widow Maria Comnena was Queen Isabella's half-brother. Balian, lord of Sidon, was the head of the oldest-established noble family, the Greniers, and was also John of Beirut's nephew through his mother Helvis of Ibelin, although his relations with his uncle do not always seem to have been close. These three magnates, at the centre of a circle of lesser lords, knights and burgesses, gave way to another generation of jurists, most of whom were Ibelins or their relatives: John of Arsuf, John of Beirut's son; John of Jaffa, his nephew and the author of the most famous of the law-books; and Philip of Novara, a vassal of John of Beirut and of his son Balian. In its turn that generation was replaced by another, led by John of Arsuf's son Balian and John of Jaffa's son James.

John of Beirut admitted his debt to Ralph of Tiberias, Philip of Novara his to Ralph of Tiberias, John of Beirut and Balian of Sidon, John of Jaffa his to John of Beirut and Balian of Sidon. So here was a school of law largely, it is true, confined to relatives and dependants. At the centre of the web of relationships were the Ibelins, who by the middle of the century held, or were closely related to the possessors of, the lordships of Beirut, Arsuf, Sidon, Caesarea, Tyre and Jaffa. They and the royal house of Jerusalem were descended from a common ancestress, Maria Comnena, while the royal house of Cyprus was descended from John of Beirut's cousin Eschiva of Ibelin, King Aimery's first wife. The relationship was cemented by the marriages of Kings Hugh II and III to Ibelins and by that of Hugh III's sister Margaret to John of Montfort-Tyre, who had an Ibelin grandmother. It is also noteworthy that the leaders of the first generation of jurists had been associated with the baronial opposition to Guy of Lusignan in the 1180s and 1190s. Ralph of Tiberias was the stepson of Raymond III of Tripoli. John of Beirut was the son of Balian of Nablus. Balian of Sidon was the son of Reynald of Sidon. Since legal ability and political influence went together it is not surprising to find so many members of this school expressing political ideas in opposition to the crown.

Their written output, including several law-books and histories, was unusual for the time. In it were to be found the outlines of a political theory which was closely related to others thrown up elsewhere by baronial movements and, typically, rested on a mythical reading of the past, a legendary golden age, in this case immediately following the First Crusade. The starting-point appears to have been a historical interpretation of the conquest of Palestine in 1099. To the jurists Palestine had been taken by crusaders and was therefore held by the most absolute of rights, that of conquest. But it did not belong to the pope, nor even to the kings: the First Crusade was regarded as a mass migration over which there had been no acknowledged leader. 'When this land was conquered it was by no chief lord, but by a crusade and by the movement of pilgrims and assembled people.' So it belonged by right to God and to the people who had then elected their ruler. 'They made a lord by agreement and by election and they gave him the lordship of the kingdom.'

This did not necessarily mean that the rulers were limited by this contract for government thereafter. The jurists themselves stressed that Godfrey of Bouillon's successors held their kingdom from God and by hereditary right, but they believed that after his election Godfrey had appointed a commission to look into the customs of other lands. On the basis of its reports, together with the results of regular inquiries made later, he had compiled a body of legislation, 'by which he and his vassals and his people ... should be governed, kept, held, maintained, tried and judged'. They stressed that this corpus of law had been established by the decisions of Godfrey's court and in a remarkable passage John of Jaffa suggested a comprehensive body of law drawn up in writing with the agreement of ruler and ruled, in other words a kind of written constitution. The jurists maintained, moreover, that the rulers of Jerusalem had always, or should have always, sworn not only to uphold their ancestors' laws, but also, in accordance with these, only to make judgments through their courts. And it was this last belief that provided them with their point of reference for limitations on the crown.

They were prepared to treat kingship primarily in its feudal and hardly at all in its public aspect. To them the king was, above all, their *chef seigneur*, their feudal overlord, contractually bound to them in the same way as they were bound to him. It followed that disputes between him and them, which would obviously involve their contractual relationship, could only be properly decided in his court, the arena in which such matters should be discussed, and since equity in feudal custom demanded that a party could not be judge in his own suit, judgment in such cases belonged to the court, where the king's vassals, their peers, sat and gave him counsel, rather than to the king himself. This above all applied to the penal element in judgment that might involve bodily punishment or the confiscation of a fief. 'The lord cannot put a hand, or have a hand put, on the body or fief of his vassal unless it is by the judgment [the *esgart* or *conoissance*] of his court'. Such a doctrine was to be found wherever there was feudal resistance to kings, but its strict implementation would have made government impossible. No western king ever kept strictly to the letter of feudal custom and the kings of Jerusalem were no different from others in this respect. Their opponents were cleverer than most, but when it came to putting their ideology into practice they were not very effective, largely because they were blinded by their own ideas.

What they chose to do was to exploit the *assise sur la ligece*, which was originally a law issued by the king for his own benefit. To them the *assise*, which had come into existence because of an act of wrongful dispossession by a lord of Sidon, underlined the condition of the feudal contract that there were no occasions on which any lord, even the king, could take action against a vassal without the formal decision of his court. If a king failed to abide by his contractual obligations the wronged vassal could demand justice according to the law from him; he could withdraw his own service or he could ask his peers to aid him. They would first call upon the king to hear the case properly. If he refused they could use force to release their peer from prison or reoccupy his fief, provided this did not entail raising their hands against the king's person; or they could solemnly 'all together and each individually' withdraw their services from the king. This sounds very impressive and in a frontier state like Jerusalem where there was a heavy reliance on the military services of the vassals it should have been effective. But it had a fatal flaw. It could only be operative in a dreamland in which all the feudatories acted in unison and the ruler was totally dependent on their services. In a perfect feudal world – the world constructed in the law-books – it might have worked. In the reality of the first half of the thirteenth century the feudal class was never really united, while the wealth accruing from commerce enabled the rulers to survive, at least temporarily, without its services.

This was apparent the first time the feudatories resorted to their interpretation of the *assise sur la ligece*. In 1198 King Aimery, convinced that Ralph of Tiberias had had something to do with an attempt on his life, arbitrarily banished him from the country. Ralph responded by asking his peers to demand on his behalf judgment in the High Court. When the king would not be moved they solemnly threatened to withdraw their services to no effect whatever. Ralph remained out of Palestine until Aimery's death.

This fiasco does not seem to have affected the jurists' belief in the efficacy of the *assise*, perhaps because on one later occasion it was successfully used. In July 1228 Frederick II reached Cyprus over which, as the young king's overlord, he had been demanding wardship and its profits during the minority. After what may have been a breach with John of Brienne, the Ibelins had been concentrating their attention on the island and had been possibly misusing their position there. Frederick's determination to enjoy his rights impinged directly on John of Beirut, who had succeeded his brother Philip as guardian of the king on his mother's behalf. Frederick renewed his demands in person in a dramatic scene, in which he surrounded his guests at a banquet with armed men. In the name of the crown of Jerusalem he also ordered John to surrender the fief of Beirut, which he maintained was held illegally. The wrangle was patched up before the emperor sailed on to Palestine, but in the following May he farmed the regency of Cyprus to five leaders of a party of Cypriot nobles who were hostile to the Ibelins and ordered them to disinherit his opponents without reference to the High Court. This was to lead to civil war.

Frederick reached Acre in September 1228 and was recognized as regent. Once he had gained the city of Jerusalem by treaty he returned to Acre, determined to restore to the crown the authority he believed it had lost since the middle of the twelfth century and he took two measures which he could not uphold: he dispossessed the Ibelins and their supporters of their fiefs in the royal domain round Acre; and he tried to enforce the claims of the Teutonic Knights, who were his staunchest backers, to the lordship of Toron, ignoring the rights of the hereditary claimant. In a turbulent few weeks the feudatories adopted the procedures they believed were open to them. They reoccupied the Ibelin fiefs by force and they threatened to withdraw their services, compelling the emperor to back down from his judgment in favour of the Teutonic Knights. In their euphoria at their success they forgot that Frederick, still excommunicated, without troops, worried by the invasion of southern Italy by papal forces and anxious to return home, was in an exceptionally weak position.

After his departure civil war broke out in Cyprus, where the Ibelin partisans refused to recognize the rule of the five imperial 'regents' who had seized their fiefs. John of Beirut fitted out an expedition from Palestine which defeated the imperial forces outside Nicosia on 14 July 1229; the last of the castles in imperial hands surrendered in the following summer. The emperor prepared a strong force under his marshal, Richard Filangieri, whom he had appointed his lieutenant. This sailed for the East in the autumn of 1231. It did not attempt a landing on Cyprus, but occupied John of Ibelin's town of Beirut on the mainland and laid siege to its citadel. Richard demanded the submission of Tyre, which he got, and appeared before an assembly of knights and burgesses of Acre. This probably recognized him as a duly appointed lieutenant of an absent regent, but it was pointed out to him that at Beirut he was trying to dispossess a vassal of his fief by force, which was against the law. Since Richard ignored the request to withdraw, John of Beirut led a force from Cyprus to relieve his fortress early in 1232. By that time a commune, based on a confraternity already in existence, had been established in Acre, the purpose of which seems to have been to act as a focus of resistance to the emperor and to ensure that Acre, the most important part of the royal domain, did not fall into his hands. Although a number of important feudatories, including Balian of Sidon, who had been close to John of Brienne and distant from the Ibelins, now joined John of Beirut's faction, the establishment of the commune and its survival for a decade is a commentary on the failure of the elaborate mechanism provided by the baronial interpretation of the *assise sur la ligece*. John himself did appeal to his peers in accordance with the *assise*, but this time the response was in pathetic contrast to the grandiose pretentions of the theory: only forty-three of his peers rode north to his aid and they did not engage the imperial forces. John had to return to Acre, where he was appointed the commune's mayor and collected a large enough body of men to threaten Tyre. This drew Richard away from Beirut, although a small baronial force left north of Acre was surprised and defeated by him on 3 May. Meanwhile John's absence from Cyprus and his failure to dislodge the imperialists in Palestine encouraged Frederick's supporters on the island to seize control again and they were joined by Richard Filangieri. The Ibelins destroyed them at the Battle of Aghirda on 15 June and with the capture of Kyrenia in April 1233 the civil war on Cyprus was over.

For the next eight years the region settled into an uneasy peace. Cyprus was firmly in the hands of the Ibelins. So was Beirut and many of the fiefs in Palestine. Of the royal domain, Acre was under the control of its commune, but Tyre and Jerusalem were in the hands of the emperor. The years 1232 to 1241 witnessed long and fruitless negotiations between the emperor, the pope and representatives of the nobility. In 1241 support for Frederick, which seems to have been growing and included the Hospitallers, led to a *coup* that very nearly acquired Acre for him, but the fiction was invented by the baronial party that the young King Conrad, who would come of age in the following year, would need a new regent. Alice of Cyprus was appointed and the baronial party at last took Tyre and occupied Jerusalem soon afterwards. The regency of Alice's successor, Henry of Cyprus, was notable for the number of grants made from the royal domain to the greater personalities in the Ibelin faction – Jaffa to John of Ibelin-Jaffa, Achzib to Balian of Ibelin-Beirut, Tyre to Philip of Montfort – and for the way Pope Innocent IV, who deposed Frederick from all government in 1245, supported the regent, confirmed charters, some of them fraudulent, on his own authority and freed Cyprus from imperial suzerainty.

The emergence of the Mamluks

In the 1250s the situation of the settlers in Palestine and Syria changed decisively for the worse because of events beyond their control. The Mongols arrived on the scene. They defeated the Selchükids of Rum at Kös Daği in 1243, after which Anatolia became a Mongol protectorate. In 1256 they destroyed the Assassins' headquarters at Alamut in Iran. In 1258 they took and sacked Baghdad and occupied upper Iraq. In 1260 they invaded Syria, pillaging Aleppo, destroying the petty Ayyubid principalities in the north and terrorizing Damascus into submission.

They were stopped in September of that year in the Battle of 'Ain Jalut in Palestine by the Mamluks of Egypt. Mamluks, specially trained slave-soldiers from the frontiers of Islam, particularly at this time Kipchak Turks from southern Russia, had long been a feature of Islamic armies and they had become powerful in Egypt, where they had formed a picked bodyguard, the *Bahriyah*, of Sultan as-Salih Ayyub. The *Bahriyah* played a distinguished part in the defeat of Louis IX's crusade in spite of as-Salih Ayyub's death on 22 November 1249. But the new sultan, Turan-Shah, distrusted them and wanted to replace them in the offices of state with members of his own military household. They assassinated him on 2 May 1250 and proclaimed as 'queen' as-Salih's concubine, Shajar ad-Durr, who had been a Turkish slave like themselves and had held the reins of power between as-Salih's death and Turan-Shah's arrival. A Turkoman

Mamluk emir, Aybeg, became commander-in-chief and Shajar ad-Durr's husband, while a little Ayyubid prince called al-Ashraf Musa was made sultan and was temporarily associated with their rule for the sake of form. An attempt by the other Ayyubid princes to invade Egypt in the name of legitimism was thrown back. Aybeg's rule, punctuated by violence and revolt, ended on 10 April 1257, when he was murdered in his bath by Shajar ad-Durr, who was herself disposed of soon afterwards. Aybeg was succeeded by his son 'Ali, but this, in a way that was to be typical of the Mamluk sultanate, was a shadow hereditary succession lasting only long enough to allow one of the emirs to emerge as the next ruler, after which the heir by birth was allowed to retire into obscurity. In the face of the threat from the Mongols 'Ali was deposed and the senior of his father's Mamluks, Kutuz, was proclaimed sultan on 12 November 1259. It was Kutuz who defeated the Mongols at 'Ain Jalut, but on his way back in triumph to Egypt he was stabbed to death on 24 October 1260 by a group of emirs under his chief general, Baybars, who had also been a leader of Turan-Shah's assassins. Baybars then usurped the Egyptian throne. Within three months he had secured Damascus and he then extended Mamluk rule over Syria and into northern Iraq. He installed a member of the 'Abbasid family as caliph in Cairo in 1261, making Egypt the seat of the caliphate. And he began to whittle away the Latin settlements.

Changes to the Asiatic trade routes

After 'Ain Jalut the Latins found their hinterland in the possession of two powerful forces, the Mongols and the Mamluks, with the borderlands between them in northern Iraq. Baghdad was in ruins. The trade routes were in chaos. At the same time the unification of central Asia under the Mongols provided the opportunity for the development of new roads to and from the Far East. Two of them were to be important until late in the fourteenth century. One passed from the port of Hormuz (Hormoz) on the Persian Gulf through Iran to Tabriz, after which it divided, with one branch going to Trebizond on the Black Sea, the other bending south to Ayas in Cilicia, which in the late thirteenth century became an important port with direct links with Famagusta in Cyprus. The other passed through central Asia north of the Caspian Sea to a group of ports at the northern end of the Black Sea: Azov (Tana), Feodosiya (Kaffa), Sudak (Soldaia) and Balaklava (Cembalo).

The consequences of this second shift in Asiatic trade routes within a century were even more profound than those of the first had been. The eyes of Italian merchants began to turn from the eastern Mediterranean to the Black Sea and competition bred tension among them. Constantinople, which controlled the narrow channel from the Black Sea into the Mediterranean, took on a new importance and with its loss to the Greeks in July 1261 the Venetians, who had been active in the Black Sea since

1204, suffered a major reverse. Earlier in the year the Byzantine emperor Michael VIII had signed a treaty with the Genoese which gave them much the same privileges as the Venetians had had in the Latin empire. The Genoese never enjoyed the rights they had been promised to the full – in 1264 they were temporarily banished from Constantinople – but they got a quarter at Pera, across the Golden Horn from the city, and they gained access to the Black Sea. The war fleets of the Italian cities were now regularly sent to the Aegean and in the 1260s naval warfare between them spread throughout the eastern Mediterranean. Peace was only made in 1270, mainly because Louis IX insisted on having a fleet for the crusade he was planning; but Genoa was embarking on a period of expansion and this meant further warfare: with Pisa, which spilled into the East in the 1280s, and with Venice, which broke out towards the end of the century.

An early manifestation of this bitter rivalry was urban warfare tearing through the streets of Acre from 1256 to 1258. The conflict, known as the War of St Sabas because it was sparked off by a dispute between the Venetians and Genoese over some property belonging to the monastery of St Sabas, involved so many that it took on some of the features of a civil war. Venice and Genoa, and also Pisa which began by supporting Genoa but went over to Venice in 1257, sent out fleets and soldiers. Siege engines were set up in the streets and the Italian quarters were fortified. The residents of the city found themselves drawn onto one side or the other. The feudatories were divided, reflecting in many cases long histories of differences between individual lords and the Italian communities. Most leading nobles, under John of Arsuf who became regent in 1256, favoured the Genoese, but an important party under John of Jaffa, who had been regent when the war broke out, favoured the Venetians and engineered another change of regencies, bringing in the child Hugh of Cyprus whose mother Plaisance took over the government and swung it onto Venice's side. The war was only settled in June 1258 when a sea-battle between enormous Venetian and Genoese fleets ended with the Genoese losing half their galleys and c. 1,700 men dead or taken prisoner. They decided to abandon Acre and concentrate in Tyre. The Venetians took over part of their quarter, building round their new possession a wall, fragments of which are still *in situ*.

The changes in the pattern of Levantine trade also meant a sharp decline in the volume of goods passing through the Christian ports on the coast. Signs of financial strain were soon evident. In the late 1250s Julian, lord of Sidon, began to give away parts of his lordship to the Teutonic Knights and in 1260 he leased the rest of it to the Templars. He was a heavy gambler, but his territory had suffered greatly from the Muslims and the last straw seems to have been a Mongol raid before 'Ain Jalut. This penetrated Sidon itself and destroyed the town walls which he could not afford to have rebuilt. In 1261 Balian of Arsuf leased his lordship to the Hospitallers. Given the costs of fortification and garrisoning, it is surprising that so many lords held on to their fiefs for so long, although, as Dr Tibble has pointed out, the fact that Sidon and Arsuf were disposed of may simply mean that they were the only lordships with enough assets to be still attractive to potential occupiers.

The Mamluk conquests

Once he had established control over the Muslim regions of Syria Sultan Baybars began systematically to reduce the territory in Christian hands. Like Saladin, he was a foreigner, in his case a Kipchak Turk, but unlike Saladin he did not come from old Islamic territory and he remained very much a Turkish warrior chieftain. He was treacherous and ruthless, but he was a good administrator and a fine general – a much better one than Saladin had been – and his methodical approach to the reconquest of the coast made it possible for his successors to drive the westerners out. He began with a devastating raid into Galilee in 1263, in the course of which he destroyed the cathedral of Nazareth. In 1265 he took Caesarea and Arsuf and temporarily occupied Haifa. In 1266 he seized Templar Safad, in 1268 Jaffa, Templar Beaufort and the city of Antioch, in 1271 Templar Safita, Hospitaller Crac des Chevaliers and Montfort of the Teutonic Knights. By his death on 30 June 1277 the Latin settlers were confined to a strip of coastline from 'Atlit to Marqab, with an enclave further north at Latakia. His campaigns were not indiscriminately destructive. He seems to have been concerned on the one hand to make it hard for Europeans to establish bridgeheads on the parts of the coast he had conquered, but on the other to provide Egyptian shipping with the watering-places of which it had been deprived since 1197. Arsuf, Caesarea, Antioch and Montfort were partially or totally destroyed, but Jaffa survived and estates in the lordships of Arsuf and Caesarea were assigned to his emirs and given a centre at the castle of Qaqun, although the countryside between them and the sea was abandoned to nomadic tribesmen. Crac des Chevaliers, Beaufort and Safad were repaired and garrisoned, as were Hunin and Toron. A ring of fortresses now encircled Acre like a tightened noose, but Baybars never seems to have made a serious attempt to take the city itself. He made several surprise descents on it, but these were really only impromptu raids; a feature of his serious military moves was their careful planning and equipping. He seems to have been conscious of the fact that his empire's prosperity still depended to a large extent on Acre as an outlet for goods and he may have been reluctant to endanger the economic well-being of a large part of his dominions by too hasty an assault on it.

The destruction of the settlements in Palestine and Syria

The settlers were divided over the policy to adopt towards their enemies. Bohemond VI of Antioch-Tripoli, who had succeeded Bohemond V in 1252, joined his father-in-law Hetoum of Cilician Armenia in seeking an alliance with the Mongols and entered Damascus with the Mongol army in March 1260; he was able to increase his holdings in Syria as a result. On the other hand, the government in Acre, considering, probably rightly, that the immediate threat from the Mongols must be countered whatever the cost, allowed the Mamluk sultan Kutuz to camp outside the city for three days before 'Ain Jalut and provisioned his army. Even within the kingdom individual fiefs would go their own way. In the 1250s John of Jaffa appears to have had his county excluded from a truce with Damascus in order to allow him to conduct a series of raids on the Muslims from it. In 1261 and 1263 he, together with John of Beirut and Hospitaller Arsuf, made truces with Baybars and he was even prepared to allow Jaffa to be used as a supply point for the Egyptian field army. In 1269 Isabella of Beirut made an independent treaty with Baybars and this enabled her to defy a demand from the king for *service de mariage* in 1275. Separate truces with Sultan Kalavun, who had usurped the Mamluk throne in 1279, were made by the Templars in 1282 and 1283 and by Margaret of Tyre in 1285. These lords were, of course, exercising their marcher rights, but the large number of independent treaties made with the Muslims shows how weak central government had become.

In fact the settlements were hopelessly split into factions. The county of Tripoli was divided into parties, one of which, made up of Italian immigrants and known as the 'Roman faction', had been introduced by Bohemond V's wife Lucienne of Segni, Pope Innocent III's great-niece, and was headed by her brother, Bishop Paul of Tripoli. It had grown in influence during the rule of her son Bohemond VI. When Bohemond VII came from Cilicia to take over the government in 1277 he found his rule opposed by this party and by the Templars. They were soon joined by Guy Embriaco, the lord of Jubail, who had been estranged by Bohemond's refusal to permit the marriage of his brother to a local heiress. For six years the county suffered a civil war, which ended only when Bohemond immured Guy of Jubail, his brothers John and Baldwin and a relative called William in a pit and left them to starve to death.

The accession to the throne of Jerusalem of Hugh III of Cyprus (Hugh of Antioch-Lusignan) in 1269 – he was the first resident king of the blood-line since Baldwin V in 1186 – did not go unchallenged. His aunt, Maria of Antioch, a granddaughter of Isabella of Jerusalem, claimed the throne as the nearer heiress to Yolande, the last ruler actually present in the East. Maria's case was better in law than Hugh's, but it seems that the High Court, which decided on these conflicting claims by virtue of its corporate decision on the lord to whom homage should be paid, preferred to overlook it in favour of that of a younger man who was already king of Cyprus. Maria appealed to Rome, where her case was being heard in 1272, and on the advice of the Templars, and probably with the pope's support, she offered to sell the kingdom of Jerusalem to Charles of Anjou. The case was withdrawn from the Roman curia in 1276 and in March 1277 the sale of the crown to Charles was completed.

Hugh, meanwhile, had found government of what remained of the kingdom of Jerusalem almost impossible. He tried to act with authority. He may have insisted on the right of his court to deal with cases concerning Italian property outside the communal quarters. He was determined not to sanction automatically those alienations of fiefs or parts of the royal domain made during the years of regency. There are even signs of administrative development: the emergence of an inner council and the use of a privy seal. But at the same time he faced insubordination, such as Isabella of Beirut's refusal to perform *service de mariage*, and hostility from the Templars, whose new grand master, William of Beaujeu, was related to the French royal family and therefore, of course, to Charles of Anjou. Hugh must have known that Charles, whose strength in the eastern Mediterranean region was now formidable, was preparing to enforce his claims and was backed by the papacy, the Templars, the Venetians and, very importantly, by the French soldiers on whom the kingdom had come increasingly to rely since their contingent had first been stationed in Acre in 1254; indeed their captains had been incorporated into the political establishment by being granted the kingdom's seneschalcy *ex officio*. Charles's strength must have seemed to many of the settlers to be providing a lifeline for them, and that was probably how it also seemed to the papacy.

In October 1276 Hugh left Palestine precipitately, stating that the kingdom was ungovernable. Eleven months later, in September 1277, Charles of Anjou's vicar, Roger of San Severino, arrived and claimed the government on behalf of his master. This could have been met with the defiant appeals to law and custom that Frederick II had encountered, particularly as Roger threatened to exile and disinherit those feudatories who stood up to him. In the event there was very little resistance from the vassals of Jerusalem, perhaps because they knew the mind of Rome. The baronial movement, which had given rise to such splendid theories and had put up such dogged opposition in the past, ended with a whimper.

The kingdom of Jerusalem was now part of an eastern Mediterranean empire which could be expected to have the resources to support it, and Charles seems to have taken over the responsibilities for the French regiment in Acre. But Angevin government was not accepted everywhere and in the period from 1277 to 1286 Christian Palestine was more divided than ever. John of Tyre and Isabella of Beirut went their own way. King Hugh, hoping to recover his kingdom, paid visits to Tyre in 1279 and 1284 and to Beirut in 1283. He died in Tyre on 4 May 1284 and was succeeded first by his eldest son John, who lived for only a year, and then by his second son Henry. Meanwhile the Sicilian Vespers were followed by Charles's death and the Angevin empire began to crumble. Opinion in the Holy Land veered back in favour of the Cypriot royal house and it received strong reinforcement from the new king of France, since Philip IV realistically decided to jettison the Angevins in favour of the Cypriot Lusignans and to resume the funding of the French regiment. On 4 June 1286 King Henry landed at Acre and on 15 August he was crowned in the cathedral of Tyre, which had become the traditional place for coronations. The court returned to Acre for a fortnight's feasting, games and pageants, including scenes from the story of the Round Table and the tale of the Queen of Femenie from the Romance of Troy.

This was the last festival in Acre, for the Mamluks had begun to advance again. In 1285 the great Hospitaller castle of Marqab and the town of Maraqiyah (Maraclea) fell. In 1287 Latakia was taken. In 1289 Sultan Kalavun, who had been supporting dissident elements in the county for some years, marched against Tripoli, which was still split by the bitter divisions left by its civil war. Bohemond VII had died on 19 October 1287 and his sister Lucy had only been admitted after long negotiations, since her rights of inheritance had been resisted by a commune with the support of the Genoese. As the siege of Tripoli began the Venetians and Genoese deserted and a general Muslim assault on 26 April met with little organized resistance. The countess escaped with Amalric, the younger brother of King Henry who had come with some Cypriot reinforcements, but most of the defenders were massacred. The Mamluk army moved on to occupy Enfeh and Batroun. All that was left of the county were the important Templar fortress of Tartus in the north and Jubail under John of Antioch, who had married the lord's daughter. He and the Latin residents of Jubail were allowed to remain there under Muslim supervision until perhaps 1302.

The Christians in Acre sent urgently to the West for help. Twenty Venetian and five Aragonese galleys, bringing a force of north Italian crusaders of poor quality, arrived in August 1290. A truce for ten years had been arranged with Kalavun, but the Mamluks were presented with a justification for breaking it when the Italian crusaders rioted and massacred some Muslim peasants who had come into Acre to sell local produce. Kalavun died on 4 November, but his son al-Ashraf Khalil continued with the preparations. In March 1291 his forces left Egypt, to be joined on their march by contingents from all over the Mamluk dominions. On 5 April a huge army with an impressive siege train arrived before Acre. By 8 May the outer fortifications were becoming so damaged that they had to be abandoned and a general assault on the 18th overwhelmed the defenders. King Henry, who had reached the city on the 4th, and his brother Amalric escaped by ship to Cyprus, as did several nobles and their families, but large numbers of Christians perished. By the evening the only part of Acre still in Christian hands was the Templar fortress-convent by the sea. An agreement to surrender it broke down when Muslim soldiers began molesting Christian women and boys who had sought refuge there. The Mamluks mined the building and on the 28th it collapsed, burying defenders and attackers alike in its fall.

Tyre had already been abandoned on 19 May. Sidon was taken at the end of June, although its sea-castle held out until 14 July. Beirut surrendered on 31 July and Tartus and 'Atlit were evacuated by the Templars on 3 and 14 August. Apart from a Templar garrison on the island of Arwad, just off the coast at Tartus, which held out until 1302, and the shadowy rule of the Embriaci in Jubail, the Latin Christian presence in Palestine and Syria had ended, although in the fourteenth century it was rumoured among the Muslims that the kings of Cyprus would secretly cross over to Tyre by night to undergo a silent coronation as kings of Jerusalem in the ruins of the cathedral.

CHAPTER 9

The Variety of Crusading, c. 1291–1523

The range of options

Our understanding of the crusading movement in the later middle ages has been radically altered since the early 1970s. A picture of decline has given way to one of continuing activity. The papal curia was as committed as ever and there was scarcely a year, at least in the fourteenth century, in which there was not crusading somewhere. Many enthusiasts were being presented with the same variety of options as had been available to their ancestors. Humbert of Vienne took part in the Smyrna Crusade in 1345 after showing interest in the proposal for one to the Canary Islands. John Boucicaut, the marshal of France, joined the Prussian *reysen* three times as a young man. He took the cross for King Peter of Cyprus's crusade to Alexandria in 1365 and for Louis II of Clermont's crusade to Mahdia in 1390, although the French king forbade him to go on the second of these; he went to Prussia instead. He was on the crusade of Nicopolis in 1396 and around 1400 he was an active crusader in the eastern Mediterranean region. Henry Grosmont, duke of Lancaster, was reported to have crusaded to Granada, Prussia, Rhodes and Cyprus. Many English noblemen and gentry were, in fact, involved in a range of these enterprises, among them, at the lower end of the scale, Nicholas Sabraham, who had been to Alexandria, Hungary, Constantinople and Nesebŭr. The career of Chaucer's Knight, who had 'reysed' in Prussia, Livonia and Russia and had crusaded in Spain, Egypt and Asia Minor, was, like all good caricatures, close to the truth.

Ful worthy was he in his lordes werre,
And therto hadde he riden, no man ferre,
As wel in cristendom as in hethenesse,
And evere honoured for his worthynesse.
At Alisaundre [Alexandria] he was when it was wonne.
Ful ofte tyme he hadde the bord bigonne
Aboven alle nacions in Pruce [Prussia];
In Lettow [Livonia] hadde he reysed and in Ruce [Russia],
No Cristen man so ofte of his degree.
In Gernade [Granada] at the seege eek hadde he be
Of Algezir [Algeciras], and riden in Belmarye [Morocco].
At Lyeys [Ayas] was he and at Satalye [Antalya],
Whan they were wonne; and in the Grete See
At many a noble armee hadde he be.

It used to be thought that interest was increasingly confined to nobles and the caste of professional soldiers, who were living by a fully developed chivalric code in which crusading ideals played an important part, but the successful recruitment of peasant crusaders in the fifteenth century demonstrated that popular feeling was still finding expression. The more conventional crusading armies seem to have become more 'professional', if one can use that term, because they were more disciplined, through the employment of mercenaries and the use of contracts for service, made possible by the large sums being raised through the taxation of the Church, although it was common for western kings to make false declarations about their intentions in order to get their hands on them.

One can, however, detect signs of decline in the fifteenth century, in spite of the reappearance of the peasant armies. The complexity of European politics, and particularly those of the Italian peninsula, made it almost impossible to present the Turks with a united front. There was weariness, demoralization and a perceptible waning of enthusiasm in those parts of the West which did not directly confront the Muslims.

Crusade theoreticians

Crusading thrived on disasters and it was typical that with the news of the loss of Acre there was a revival of fervour. In 1300 a rumour swept the West that the Mongols had conquered Palestine and had handed it over to the Christians. Pope Boniface VIII sent 'the great and joyful news' to Edward of England and probably to Philip of France as well. He encouraged the faithful to go at once to the Holy Land and he ordered the exiled Catholic bishops to return to their sees. All over Europe men hurriedly took the cross and in Genoa several ladies sold their jewelry to help pay for a crusading fleet, although in the end the project was dropped.

The fall of Acre inspired the writing of a spate of crusade treatises, which continued to appear at intervals throughout the fourteenth century. The authors had to face up to the fact that a major effort would now be required, since it was no longer the case of reinforcing a beach-head but of organizing a full-scale invasion. The ancient Spanish argument that the Reconquest would lead to a liberation of Jerusalem by armies marching overland through North Africa was deployed. Some writers were attracted by the idea of an alliance with one of the powers lurking behind the Levant, particularly the Mongols, and this introduced a train of thought relating to the outflanking of Islam which was to lead to the struggle – as much to do with trade as with Christian strategy – between the Portuguese and Egyptian fleets in the Indian Ocean and to the search for a western route to the Indies.

Four proposals, which were already being bruited on the eve of the fall of Acre, appear over and over again. The first was the suggestion that the military orders should be united and out of them a new super-order created. This was partially achieved when the Templars were suppressed and most of their properties were granted to the Hospitallers. The second, which was related to the first, concerned the government of a future kingdom of Jerusalem. A group of theoreticians put forward the idea of a warrior king, a *Bellator Rex*, the master of a military order that would wage the crusade and then rule Palestine; for one of them, Peter Dubois, this post should always be held by a son of the king of France. The dream climaxed in the vision of the Cypriot chancellor and tutor to Charles VI of France, Philip of Mézières, of a new order, the *Nova Religio Passionis Jhesu Christi*, the members of which would take vows of obedience and poverty, but of conjugal fidelity rather than celibacy, since they would be responsible for colonizing, ruling and defending the Holy Land. Between 1390 and 1395 Philip, who also worked tirelessly for peace between England and France as a prelude to a crusade, recruited the support of over eighty nobles, especially in England and France, but also in Scotland, Germany, Spain and Lombardy. They included Louis II of Clermont and John Boucicaut. The third rested on the conviction that the Muslims' ability to resist invasion could be impaired if their economy was damaged by means of the imposition of an embargo on trade with Egypt, the richest Muslim nation and the reoccupier of Palestine. The fourth distinguished two kinds of crusade, the *passagium generale*, a great international expedition of the traditional kind, and the *passagium particulare*, a preliminary strike on a smaller scale to enforce the embargo, weaken the enemy or gain some specific advantage. It is remarkable how far these ideas were put into practice. In Prussia and on Rhodes order-states came into existence, ruled by the masters of the Teutonic Knights and the Hospitallers of St John. There was an embargo on trade with Egypt. And there were many *passagia particularia*.

The fall of the Templars

The first order-states were established in the wake of one of the most sensational events in late medieval history. Early in the morning of 13 October 1307 nearly every Templar in France was arrested on the charge of heresy and within a matter of days many of them, including the grand master, James of Molay, and his chief representative in north-western Europe, Hugh of Pairaud, had acknowledged their guilt. The vast majority of the brothers interrogated by the inquisitor, by the pope at Poitiers in the summer of 1308, by French bishops in regional inquiries and by a papal commission which sat in Paris also admitted that many of the charges were true. Elsewhere, interrogations of a small number of Templars in various parts of the Italian peninsula produced more evidence. In Britain there were very few confessions, although outside witnesses were more forthcoming. In Castile, Portugal and Cyprus, and in

Aragon and Germany where some of them resisted arrest, the Templars protested their innocence.

Some of the charges laid against the brothers were bizarre in the extreme. They were, it was claimed, actively not Christian. At their reception they were called upon to deny Christ – sometimes being told he was a false prophet who could not redeem mankind – and to spit, stamp or urinate upon a cross or crucifix. They did not believe in the sacraments of the Church and their priests were forbidden to say the words of consecration during the canon of the Mass. Instead they venerated heads or idols of various sorts (or even diabolical cats) and the cords they were accustomed to wear, which seem to have been similar to scapulars, had been laid on a head or idol before being given to them. They hid their infidelity under a cloak of strict secrecy, since they were not allowed to reveal their modes of reception, the debates in their chapters or even their own Rule and were forbidden to confess to any but their own priests. Their deceit was compounded by the fact that their officers, although lay brothers, were in the habit of absolving them from their sins, usurping the sacramental role and canonical prerogative of priests. At reception postulants were forced to kiss their receptors, or to be kissed, not only on the mouth but also on the bare stomach, the base of the spine, the posterior and even the penis. They were told that although their vows of celibacy meant that they could have no sexual relations with women they could, if need be, have them with other brothers; they should suffer the attentions of these brothers if they desired them. They had no novitiate. They were encouraged to augment the order's goods with no thought for justice, while on the other hand they were niggardly in the granting of alms to the poor and did not practise hospitality. The senior brothers had done nothing to reform the order.

For Pope Clement V their arrest was an attack on the Church, an unprecedented denial of the right of professed religious to ecclesiastical justice, particularly since they were members of an order under the protection of the Holy See. But his situation was a delicate one. The pontificate of Boniface VIII had ended only four years previously with the pope dying of shock after being kidnapped by troops led by a minister of the French crown. The curia had been trying to appease France in the intervening years, but Clement, a Gascon and therefore born a French-speaking subject of the king of England, was having to fight off the determined efforts of the French government to have Boniface posthumously condemned. Rome was considered too insecure for residence and after his election in June 1305 Clement lived at Poitiers before moving his court to Avignon in 1309. Meanwhile he tried to seize the initiative in the case of the Templars by establishing an official church inquiry into the allegations. In November 1307 he ordered the arrest of all the brothers outside France. In the following February he suspended the activities of the French inquisition, although this led to conflict with the French crown. The compromise reached was that throughout Christendom there would be episcopal investigations of individuals while concurrently church commissioners would look in to the performance of the order as a whole. The reports of these inquiries and commissions were considered by the council of Vienne in 1311. A majority wanted to give the Templars themselves at least a hearing, but under pressure from France Clement suppressed the order on 3 April 1312. On 18 March 1314 James of Molay and Geoffrey of Charney, the Templar commander of Normandy, having retracted everything they had confessed, were burned at the stake.

The destruction of the Temple has been treated as a good example of what early state machinery could do at a time when a crown, short of cash and with its eyes on rich pickings, controlled the inquisition and when the papacy was on the defensive. Many of the Templars were tortured. All those arrested were put under pressure of various kinds and an attempt at resistance by some of them in 1310 was stifled when under royal influence an episcopal tribunal under the archbishop of Sens and a provincial council under the archbishop of Reims had sixty-seven brothers who were maintaining their innocence burned. Very few historians have believed that the Templars were guilty of the crimes of which they were accused, but although they were certainly innocent of most of the charges laid against them, a close reading of their depositions has led me to the conclusion that in some commanderies new brothers were being forced to deny Christ and spit on a cross or crucifix at the time of, or shortly after, their reception into the order. The practice was probably to be found in a minority of commanderies and among a few receptors in France, but it was not confined to them. It looks as though brothers who believed these demands were customary had carried them to Italy and the Levant; in both regions a large number of French were to be found in Templar houses. On the other hand, Germany appears to have been clear and so were the Iberian peninsula, including Roussillon, and perhaps the British Isles.

It is hard to explain why such odd behaviour had crept into a great and powerful Order of the Church, but it cannot be denied that the inquiries into the Templars demonstrated just how badly in need of reform and reorganization the order had become. In comparison to the Hospitallers, who had a system of smaller provinces and therefore a greater number of senior officials who were in direct and regular communication with the East, representative chapters-general which were also legislatures, a coherent body of law and representation from Europe at magistral elections, the Templars had retained an anachronistic and inefficient system of autocratic management by the grand master and his headquarters. Many brothers had never even heard their Rule read to them and there was no hope whatever of them comprehending the order's supplementary legislation, even had it been available. Incorporated into a collection known as the *retrais*, it was repetitious, muddled, often archaic, and copied with no distinction being made between statute, case law and custom. It is not surprising that it was not always obeyed. The state of the order seems to have been so dire that one wonders how long it could have been allowed to remain in existence, with or without the scandal.

The chaos into which it had descended helps to explain why after the loss of Acre it appeared to be paralysed, particularly once the island of Arwad, which it had fortified and held almost within hailing distance of the Syrian coast, was lost in 1302, in circumstances which were not very creditable; a chapter-general in Paris was marked by a squabble in which Gerald of Villers, the grand commander of France, was blamed for Arwad's fall. There had been a flurry of activity c. 1297, when a chapter-general in Paris ordered 300 brothers to be sent to Cyprus, but the English sergeant Thomas of Thoroldeby, who claimed to have been the order's standard-bearer in the East, was scathing about the failure of his confrères to liaise with other Christian forces in attacks on the Syrian coast. One senses that demoralization was setting in. If so, the order's chains of command would not have been strong enough to pull it together.

The Templars were not alone in being severely criticized at this time. All three major military orders active in the East were blamed for the reverses there. By 1291 the proposals for a union of the Templars and Hospitallers, which had been raised as early as the Second Council of Lyon in 1274, were convincing enough for Pope Nicholas IV to order them to be discussed in all provincial synods. The Teutonic Knights and the Hospitallers must have felt themselves to be very exposed, and rightly so, for serious charges were being brought against them as well. In Livonia the clergy, over whom the Teutonic Knights did not have the control they had in Prussia, were voicing bitter complaints about their behaviour, including their despoliation of the Church, their brutal treatment of the archbishop and citizens of Riga, their failure to defend Livonia properly, their hindering of missionary work – indeed it was claimed, not for the first time, that they alienated the heathen by their cruelty – and their internal corruption. By 1300 the papal curia was concerned about these allegations and in 1310 Clement ordered a full investigation, particularly of the charge that the knights were allying themselves with pagans against their fellow-Christians. The Teutonic Knights did not come at all well out of the Livonian scandal and the final verdict of the Church in 1324 was highly critical of them.

The Hospitallers of St John were also in a bad way, although it is true that at the same time as he was pressing for the dissolution of the Templars Philip of France was backing a crusade to be led by their master. The fourteenth century was punctuated by demands from the popes for their reform – in 1355 Pope Innocent VI even went as far as to threaten to reform them himself if they would not make the necessary changes – and internal inquiries in the 1360s and 1370s revealed a very unsatisfactory state of affairs. Nevertheless both orders survived. There is no immediate evidence even of a decline in their recruitment. An important reason seems to have been that they had a continuing commitment to the poor and to nursing the sick and were, therefore, locked into conventional patterns of religious life and thought in spite of being also 'military'. Through their practical concern for poor pilgrims they could draw on ancient Christian traditions of charity in ways the Temple could not, a point unconsciously underlined by James of Molay himself, when in a memorandum of 1305 he argued against union with the Hospital which, he wrote, 'was founded to care for the sick' – beyond that it engaged in the exercise of arms – whereas the Templars 'were founded solely as a company of knights'. In the short run, moreover, both the Teutonic Knights and the Hospitallers recognized that they must be seen to be doing something positive and it can be no coincidence that in the same year, 1309, the grand master of the Teutonic Knights took up residence at Marienburg (Malbork) in Prussia and the Hospitallers moved their headquarters to Rhodes.

The Teutonic Knights in Prussia and Livonia

To understand the first of these moves something must be said about the continuing crusade in the Baltic region which was, of course, not confined to the Teutonic Knights. In the far north the frontier in Finland between the Catholics and the Russian Orthodox was unstable and in the 1320s, when enthusiasm for crusading was general, a movement got under way in Sweden and Norway to protect the Catholics from the Orthodox schismatics. In 1323 Pope John XXII had a crusade proclaimed in Norway and although war with Novgorod petered out in the mid-1330s crusading was revived in the 1340s by King Magnus of Sweden and Norway, who was under the influence of his cousin St Bridget, an enthusiast. He led a crusade to Finland in 1348 which achieved very little. He campaigned again in 1350 and another crusade was preached on papal authority in the following year. That expedition never materialized and in 1356 there began the internal political convulsions that put paid to Magnus's ambitions. Norway and Sweden passed into the hands of alien rulers for a century and they thwarted at least two papal attempts, in 1378 and 1496, to have new crusades preached against the Russians.

Further south crusading had had to respond to the arrival of the Mongols and the emergence of the powerful state of Lithuania, the creation of a prince called Mindoug who by the time of his death in 1263 had unified his people, a peasantry under the domination of a warrior mounted class, into a strong and comparatively prosperous nation.

Mindoug had accepted baptism and for a short time had professed Christianity, even receiving a crown from Pope Innocent IV, but he had reverted to paganism after the defeat of the Livonian Christians at Durbe. Lithuania was a heathen society and an expansionist and aggressive one at that. Of its neighbours, Poland, which was reunited under a king in 1320 after nearly two centuries without one, was firmly committed to crusading, in spite of almost constant strife with the Teutonic Knights. Its efforts were concentrated in northern Ukraine, where it campaigned against both Lithuanians and Mongols until the latter were decimated by the Black Death. In the fourteenth century it regularly received papal crusade letters, as did the Hungarians, who were also involved in that struggle.

This was the stage on which the Teutonic Knights already stood and where they decided to concentrate their forces. It will be remembered that in 1226 their master had been confirmed in his possession of a march in Prussia and had received from the western emperor the title of imperial prince. After the fall of Acre they had moved their headquarters to Venice, half-way between Palestine and the Baltic, but in September 1309 the grand master Siegfried of Feuchtwangen took up residence at the castle of Marienburg in western Prussia, which henceforth was to be his order's central convent. He came, of course, to the region where the order was most deeply involved, but he also came to a divided and demoralized body of men who were smarting under the Livonian scandal. An attempt by his predecessor Gottfried of Hohenlohe in 1302 to make them live in stricter conformity to the Rule had aroused such opposition that Gottfried had been forced out of office. The response of the Teutonic Knights to their difficulties was to withdraw into their Baltic shell and to extend and reinforce their authority over their semi-sovereign state, while vigorously prosecuting the crusade and attracting to their little wars as many crusaders as they could. The transference of the headquarters was preceded by the acquisition in 1308–9 of eastern Pomerania and Gdańsk by ruthless methods. In Livonia, where authority was shared with three bishops, and in Estonia, where there was a powerful knightly class, the Teutonic Knights established a regime which was semi-independent: after 1438 the Livonian brothers effectively chose their own master. In Prussia, on the other hand, they dominated the secular church and they built up an efficient economy based on the management of their demesne lands and the encouragement of peasant settlement in a region in which there was a vacuum of rural power because of the destruction of so many of the greatest estates. The popes remained suspicious of their motives, but having the right to wage a perpetual crusade, they did not have to seek papal authorization every time they granted indulgences. They could, therefore, recruit lay knights for periods of short service with them.

Throughout the fourteenth century a stream of crusaders from all over

Europe came to fight with them in campaigns, known as *reysen*, which took the form of raids through a frontier wilderness into the areas of Lithuanian settlement: for example, Bohemians in 1323, Alsatians in 1324, Englishmen and Walloons in 1329, Austrians and Frenchmen in 1336. John of Bohemia made three trips, as did John Boucicaut and Count William IV of Holland. Henry of Lancaster went in 1352. Henry of Derby, the future King Henry IV of England, went in 1390 and 1392. In 1377 Duke Albert of Austria came with 2,000 knights for his 'Tanz mit den Heiden (Dance with the Heathen)'. In the following year the duke of Lorraine joined the *winter-reysa* with seventy knights. Shortly after this Albert of Austria turned up again with the count of Cleves and they had a special *reysa* laid on for them so that they could fulfil their vows before Christmas. Count William I of Guelderland went seven times between 1383 and 1400.

The *winter-reysa* was a *chevauchée* of between 200 and 2,000 men with the aim simply of devastating a given area as quickly as possible. There were usually two of these a year, one in December, the other in January or February, with a gap between for the Christmas feast. The *sommer-reysa* was usually organized on a larger scale with the intention of gaining territory by destroying an enemy strongpoint or building a Christian one, although plundering was a feature too. These *reysen* were not unlike sports, subject to the weather conditions in much the same way as horse-racing is today. Those who took part had the right to leave shields painted with their coats-of-arms hanging in Marienburg, Königsberg or other fortresses. Sometimes before, sometimes after, a *reysa* a solemn feast would be held at Marienburg, with a Table of Honour for the ten or twelve most distinguished knights present. In 1375 Grand Master Winrich of Kniprode, under whom this chivalric theatre became most magnificent, presented each of the twelve knights at the Table with a shoulder badge on which was written in gold letters *Honneur vainc tout*. The Order of the Tiercelet, a Poitevin order of knights, had a special augmentation of its insignia, the claws of its emblem of a falcon gilded, for a member who had been on a *reysa*.

Were it not for the brutality and the very real hardships, one is tempted to write of the *reysen* as packaged crusading for the European nobility, and their popularity demonstrated how attractive this package could be when wrapped in the trappings of chivalry. But they depended on the existence of a frontier with paynim and an infidel enemy which could be portrayed as being aggressive. Their *raison d'être* vanished in 1386 when the Lithuanian grand duke Jagiello, who accepted baptism, married the Polish queen Jadwiga in Cracow and took the name of King Vladislav II of Poland. Christianity made slow progress in Lithuania after this dynastic union, but the Lithuanians were now subject to Christian government. A condition of the union, moreover, was that Jagiello would recover for Poland eastern Pomerania and Kulmerland. At Tannenberg (Grunwald) on 15 July 1410 the Teutonic Order's forces were destroyed by a Polish and Lithuanian army which also contained Czech, Moravian, Vlach and Crim Mongol mercenaries. The grand master, the chief officials and c. 400 brother knights lay dead on the field. Marienburg held out and the First Peace of Thorn (Toruń) of 1 February 1411 enabled the order to keep most of its territory, but it was never again to be as great a force, not least because simmering discontent among its subjects, Germans, Prussians and Poles, who were losing their separate identities and evolving into a self-consciously Prussian society, came to the surface. The gentry and townspeople formed themselves into a Union to protect their interests in the face of the order's ruthless attempts to restore control and in the 1450s this Union rejected the order's overlordship and turned to Poland.

Prussia, which had been ravaged by invading armies in 1414, 1422 and 1431–3, was partitioned in the Second Peace of Thorn of 19 October 1466, which ended the Thirteen Years' War with Poland. The order lost Marienburg and was left only with eastern Prussia which it held as a Polish fief. Although it survived until 1525 in Prussia and until 1562 in Livonia, crusading along the Baltic was coming to an end. The 'bulwark of Christendom' was now Poland, which had to confront the Ottoman Turks from the fifteenth century onwards. The last time non-German crusaders came to Prussia seems to have been for the *reysa* of 1413. The order's crusading role was debated, and defended, at the council of Constance in 1415–18, when the Teutonic Knights appealed to the assembled prelates against Poland. In Livonia a certain number of knights still took part in *reysen* against the Russians and Walter of Plettenberg, the Livonian master, organized a heroic defence against a Russian invasion in 1501–2. But it is significant that although his proctor in Rome begged for a crusade letter he never got one: Pope Alexander VI was hoping that the Russians would ally themselves with the Catholics against the Turks.

The Hospitallers of St John on Rhodes

The Teutonic Knights brilliantly exploited their independent situation in the far north to create a type of crusading that was fashionable and gained them public recognition while at the same time exposing themselves to the minimum of interference from the Holy See. The Hospitallers' experience was very different, but their task was much more difficult. On 27 May 1306 their master, Fulk of Villaret, whose headquarters were now at Limassol in Cyprus, came to an agreement with a Genoese admiral called Vignolo de' Vignoli, who claimed rights in the Dodecanese, for the joint conquest of Rhodes and its archipelago. On 23 June a Hospitaller squadron of two galleys and four other vessels, carrying a small force that included thirty-five brothers of the order, left Cyprus and, joined by Genoese galleys, began an invasion of Rhodes which took much longer than anticipated. The city of Rhodes probably did not fall until August 1309 and although the central convent was moved there immediately, the island was not completely subjugated until the following year, its occupation being assisted by a mini-crusade led by Fulk of Villaret which sailed in 1310 from Italy. By the bull *Ad providam* of 2 May 1312 the pope granted the Hospitallers most of the Templars' estates and properties. In the long run this greatly enriched them, although it took them a long time to get control of even a proportion of the lands to which they were entitled. They took over most of those in France on the payment of huge indemnities in 1317. In England they had still not assumed full possession of them by 1338. They failed totally in Portugal and Aragon, where the kings siphoned off the Templar assets to create the new orders of Christ and Montesa. By 1324, however, the Hospitallers' land-holdings had doubled and the Templar properties helped to finance the defence of Rhodes and their active role in military engagements in the eastern Mediterranean region. Even so, the costs of conquering, fortifying and establishing an administration on the island saddled them with crippling debts. The central convent was not solvent until the 1330s and even then its finances were precarious, particularly after huge losses sustained in the 1340s when the leading Florentine banking houses collapsed. Money worries help to explain the comparative efficiency with which the Hospitallers were driven to manage their European estates. Their financial concerns, and the fact that Rhodes was far less secure than Prussia, led the papacy to intervene much more frequently in their affairs than in those of the Teutonic Knights, whom they must sometimes have envied.

Rhodes is a large and fertile island, nearly 50 miles long and 20 miles wide, only 12 miles off the south-western coast of Asia Minor. It dominated one of the most important sea-routes in the eastern Mediterranean and it had a fine harbour. Its population of c. 10,000 Greeks was now joined by western colonists who were offered land on favourable terms. The Hospitallers also held a few neighbouring islands, of which the most important was Cos, and on the mainland after 1408 they built a large castle at Bodrum to replace the one they had lost at Smyrna (Izmir), which will be referred to below. Their relations with the Greek population appear to have been good, but the city of Rhodes, at the centre of which was the enclosure for the conventual brothers (the *collacchio* or rather part of it), also came to have a large West European community. It was strongly fortified by 1356 and the Hospitallers continued to improve its defences and those of other strongpoints throughout the archipelago. By the early fifteenth century Rhodes was one of the most heavily fortified places in the world and the consequent security meant that its commercial importance increased. It had also become a major port of call for pilgrims travelling to the Holy Land. To it, in much the same way as to Prussia although in fewer numbers, came lay knights to campaign with the order and, as they did in Marienburg and Königsberg, they hung their coats-of-arms in a *maison d'honneur* in Rhodes.

After the loss of the Palestinian mainland the order began to build up a navy. In the centuries that followed this was the most distinctive feature of its contribution to crusading, which became as much a naval as a military enterprise since it involved the defence of scattered Christian settlements around the Aegean. The Hospitallers had possessed a number of transports before 1291, but the decision to have war-galleys was made at the bidding of the papacy. In spite of the losses of men and matériel at Acre the brothers had some kind of fleet by 1300, although whether it was built or hired by them is not known. This was a considerable achievement and it demonstrated how the leadership could respond to new demands made of it. On Rhodes the order's battle ground definitely became the sea. It found itself policing the shipping lanes and opposing the Turkish coastal emirates of Asia Minor and later the rapid expansion of the Ottoman state. Its galleys prowled the shipping lanes, protecting European merchantmen and contributing to the naval leagues that struggled for mastery with the Turks. Its fleet was comparatively small, being at the most seven or eight galleys, although three was the more usual number. These were rowed by free Greek islanders, not slaves who were very undependable, and since every brother knight had to serve three *caravans* – naval expeditions of at least six months – to qualify for a commandery in Europe or a captaincy in the navy, every galley carried twenty to thirty ambitious *caravanisti*. The fleet, the maintenance of which was a heavy expense, was supplemented from the late fifteenth century by a carrack, later a galleon.

Rhodes was well situated for offensive operations, particularly against the Turkish emirates of Menteshe (Muğla) and Aydin on the mainland, which in the first half of the fourteenth century threatened Christian shipping, but the Hospitallers were always a significant component in crusade-planning and made an important contribution to the defence of all the Latin settlements in the area. They played a major role in the capture of Smyrna and its defence from 1344 to 1402; indeed from 1374 they were responsible for it. Rhodes was recognized by the Muslims as a threat to their interests and it was attacked by the Egyptians in 1440 and 1444. The most striking demonstration of its reputation throughout Christendom can be seen today on the face of the English Tower at Bodrum, at the south-eastern corner of the *enceinte*: a line of twenty-six English coats-of-arms sculpted in stone, at the centre of which are the royal arms of Henry IV and six other members of his family. No less than seventeen of the individuals represented here were Knights of the Garter and it is likely that the shields record contributions to the building of the tower, probably c. 1414.

It is not surprising that as Turkish power increased the threat to Rhodes grew. By the late 1470s the Hospitallers were expecting to have to meet an invasion sooner or later and were making the best preparations they could for it. From 23 May to late August 1480 the Turks laid siege to the city of Rhodes with a large force before withdrawing exhausted. The successful defence did wonders for the Hospitallers' prestige – in France *Te Deums*, processions and the ringing of church bells were decreed; an account of the siege in English was in print within two years – and the respect with which they were regarded was enhanced when the Turkish prince Jem, Sultan Bayazid's younger brother, fled to Rhodes two years later; he was to be a prisoner first of the order and then of the papacy until his death in 1495. But the Ottoman sultanate under great conquerors like Selim I and Suleiman I was not going to permit this Christian outpost, insignificant in comparison with the territories they had subdued, to exist indefinitely. In July 1522 a large armada under the command of Suleiman himself began to disembark troops on the island. By the 28th Turkish batteries were bombarding the city. The invasion was well planned and was on a very large scale. After months of bombardment, mining and assaults the walls were no longer tenable, the stock of munitions was low and the Greek inhabitants were anxious to give up. On 18 December the grand master Philip of l'Isle Adam surrendered and, permitted to leave with honour, sailed from Rhodes on 1 January 1523.

Features of the order-states

The order-state, developed by the Teutonic Knights in Prussia and the Hospitallers on Rhodes and later on Malta, was a new and distinctive polity. It was a theocracy, governed by an elite class of soldiers, who had taken full religious vows, originated from outside the state's boundaries and isolated themselves from the indigenous population, which was kept at arm's length, although their attitude to those they ruled was generally benevolent. Prussia was divided into commanderies, which were subdivided into *Waldämter* and *Pflegerämter*, all managed by brothers. Supreme authority lay with the grand master and a council of the five great officers (*Gebietigerrat*). Families on Rhodes or Malta who would otherwise be qualified to provide recruits to the Hospital were barred from membership.

An order-state would be established on a Christian frontier and its policy towards its non-Christian neighbours, while theoretically defensive in accordance with Christian war theology, was highly aggressive in practice. This was demonstrated by the raids of the Teutonic Knights into Lithuania, by the caravans of the Hospitallers in the eastern Mediterranean and by their use of the *corso*, a supplement to maritime operations which resembled licensed piracy with the element of holy war added. Regulated by a special tribunal on Rhodes and later on Malta, piratical operations against the Muslims were financed by the Hospitallers and others, with 10 per cent of the spoil going to the master. In 1519 the *corso* was providing the order with 47,000 ducats a year. It also contributed to the Rhodian economy, although the prisoners taken by it and either held on the island or sold on as slaves enraged the Ottoman government and contributed to its decision to invade in 1522.

Cyprus

To the south-east of Rhodes was the kingdom of Cyprus. It was governed by rulers of the Lusignan dynasty – Henry II, Hugh IV, Peter I, Peter II, James I, Janus, John II, Charlotte and James II – until in 1489 it was taken over by Venice in consequence of an extraordinary manoeuvre by which King James II's Venetian queen Catherine Cornaro was adopted by Venice so that in the event of the deaths of both her husband and her heir it would pass to the Republic. In its heyday, in the first half of the fourteenth century, it was very prosperous and the city of Famagusta was a hub of commercial activity, being linked to the Asiatic trade routes through the smaller ports of northern Syria and especially the Cilician port of Ayas, until the latter was occupied by the Mamluks in 1337. The island was now the cultural centre of the Latin East and the royal palace in Nicosia was described by travellers as being the finest in the world. Some of the luxury and splendour is still discernible in surviving churches and other ecclesiastical buildings. The cathedral of Nicosia dates from the thirteenth century, but the cathedral of Famagusta, the churches of St Catherine in Nicosia and St Mary of Carmel in Famagusta, where the great Carmelite Peter Thomas was buried, and the Premonstratensian abbey of Bellapaise are among the most beautiful buildings of the Latin East.

Many of the survivors of the mainland settlements were now in Cyprus. Two of the assassins of Peter I, Philip of Ibelin, titular lord of Arsuf, and Henry of Jubail, had names already familiar to us, and the third, John of Gaurelle, seems to have been a descendant of a Poitevin follower of Guy of Lusignan. Raymond Babin, who was an associate, came from a family settled in Jerusalem in the twelfth century. The feudal system, represented at the apex by the High Court in Nicosia, was, as we have seen, strongly influenced by Latin Jerusalem and it overlay, as on the mainland, a previous administration, in this case Byzantine. The constitutional traditions of the mainland were maintained and at first were strong, manifesting themselves in a typical display of ingenuity, in which the Ibelins played a large part, when in 1306 King Henry II was removed from government and replaced by his brother Amalric, who ruled as governor for four years. But the traditions gradually faded and by the time Venice took over the island the High Court was practically moribund. The Venetian senate imposed its own administrators, who had no legislative powers and from whose courts appeals could be lodged in Venice.

The island was badly hit by the Black Death in 1348 and 1349, and after 1369, the year in which King Peter I, one of the most spectacular figures in the fourteenth-century crusading movement, was assassinated, it suffered a succession of disasters. Since the thirteenth century its economy had been geared to the commodity and commercial needs of the Italians, but this made it peculiarly sensitive to the tensions that existed between Venice and Genoa. It had been turning towards Venice, but in 1372 war broke out with Genoa and a squadron of Genoese galleys burned Limassol, took Paphos and besieged and captured Famagusta, seizing the person of the king. The Genoese later took his uncle James. In October 1374 Cyprus was forced to agree to pay annual tribute and an enormous indemnity against the return of Famagusta. An attempt to take Famagusta by force in 1378 failed and the city, with a zone of two leagues around it, was transferred to Genoa in return for the release of James, who had now inherited the throne. Intermittent hostilities continued on and off for decades, punctuated by Genoese victories after which more indemnities were extracted from the Cypriots. Then in 1425 Mamluk Egypt, responding to Cypriot raids on the Egyptian and Syrian coasts, launched a large-scale attack on the island during which the shoreline between Larnaca and Limassol was pillaged and many Cypriots were enslaved. With the island's weakness revealed, a powerful Egyptian invasion force, probably with the connivance of the Genoese, landed on the southern coast on 1 July 1426. On the 7th, in the Battle of Khirokitia, the Cypriot army was routed and King Janus was taken alive. Nicosia was sacked and Janus was paraded before the crowds in Cairo. He was ransomed for 200,000 ducats, an annual tribute of 5,000 and the acknowledgement of the sultan of Egypt's suzerainty. In 1448 Corycus, the last Cypriot holding on the Cilician mainland, was lost.

Greece

West and north-west of Cyprus was Venetian Crete, the duchy of the Archipelago and the other island-lordships in the Aegean, of which the most important were Venetian Euboea, Lesbos, granted to the Genoese by the Byzantines in 1354 and ruled by the Genoese family of Gattilusio, and Chios, the world centre for the production of mastic, which had been seized by the Genoese in 1346 together with Foça (Phocaea) on the mainland, which was a major source of alum.

In continental Greece the settlements mirrored the political divisions in southern Italy, some recognizing the Angevin kings of Naples, others the

Aragonese kings of Sicily. The overlords of the principality of Achaea in the Peloponnese were, as we have seen, the kings of Naples. In 1315–16 the principality was the scene of armed conflict between two pretenders, Louis of Burgundy, who had married the heiress Mahaut with the support of the French crown and had paid homage to the Angevin Philip of Taranto – himself now married to the Latin empress – and Ferdinand of Majorca, the younger son of King James I of Majorca, who had married a granddaughter of William of Villehardouin. Ferdinand occupied Killini (Glarentsa) in advance of Louis's arrival, but he was killed in the Battle of Manolada on 5 July 1316. The victor was himself dead within a month and Mahaut was forced to surrender the principality in 1322 when it was discovered that she had secretly married a Burgundian knight without her overlord's consent. King Robert of Naples arranged for his youngest brother, John of Gravina, to hold the principality directly from Philip of Taranto. By this time it was a shadow of its former self. In the north the Catalans in Athens posed a constant threat. In the south the Byzantine Greeks at Mistra were expanding the area under their control, so that John of Gravina was recognized only in the western and northern coastal regions where the great lords had nearly independent powers anyway. His suzerainty was also acknowledged by the duchy of the Archipelago, but the islands of Cephalonia and Zante (Zákinthos) remained virtually autonomous under the rule of the Orsini family.

Philip of Taranto died in 1331 and was succeeded as overlord by his son Robert, for whom Philip's widow the empress Catherine acted as regent until her death in 1346. John of Gravina, who did not like the idea of performing homage to his own nephew, surrendered the principality, which therefore passed directly into its overlord's hands. But as the threat to it from the Turks grew the absentee Angevins – Robert, then another Philip of Taranto, then Queen Joanna of Naples herself – could do little to help their subjects, who were increasingly isolated and anarchic. In 1376 the Latin Peloponnese was leased for five years to the Hospitallers, who found its defence a heavy burden, not least because their master, Juan Fernandez of Heredià, was captured and sold to the Turks when he tried to take the Epirote city of Arta in 1378. The rule of Joanna's successors, Charles III and Ladislas of Naples, was shadowy in the extreme, while the claims of a succession of pretenders to the principality were more shadowy still. Effective power came to be exercised by a company of Navarrese and Gascon knights, who had first been employed by the Hospitallers and took control of a large part of the Peloponnese, including the princely domain. In 1396 King Ladislas of Naples recognized the situation by conferring the title of prince on the company's leader, Peter Bordo of St Superan. After Peter's death the head of the oldest and richest of the baronial families, Centurione Zaccaria, persuaded Ladislas to confer the title on him. Centurione, who was able and resourceful, managed to preserve the Latin Peloponnese for a generation, but the *coup de grâce* was delivered by the Byzantine despot of Mistra, Thomas Palaeologus, who forced Centurione to betroth his daughter to him in 1429. Centurione continued to bear the title of prince until 1432, after which Thomas took over the whole principality, except for the Venetian possessions in the south-west and the north-east.

To the north, the Catalan Company which had assumed control of the duchy of Athens in 1311 after the Battle of Halmyros, sought and accepted overlordship from Frederick, the Aragonese king of Sicily, who appointed his younger son Manfred duke. Under a series of able vicar-generals Athens and Thebes were divided among, and run by, members of the Company in spite of the disapproval of much of the West, vigorous string-pulling by the Brienne family they had ousted and even the preaching of crusades against them. Manfred's line held the dukedom until the 1350s, when it passed directly to the throne of Sicily, but internal disputes began to tear the Catalan settlement apart and they were intensified after 1377 by a dispute within the Aragonese royal family for the Sicilian throne. From 1379 Athens was annexed to the crown of Aragon itself, but in that year the Navarrese Company, with the connivance of the Hospitallers, took Thebes. Then in 1385 Nerio Acciaiuoli, the lord of Corinth and a member of a Florentine banking family which had risen to prominence in Angevin service in the Peloponnese, entered the duchy and in 1388 occupied the acropolis of Athens, thus ending Catalan rule. When Nerio died in 1394 he left no legitimate male heirs. His son-in-law, the Byzantine despot, Theodore of Mistra, seized Corinth. Venice held Athens for a time until forced out by Nerio's bastard son, Antonio Acciaiuoli, who ruled the duchy from 1403 to 1435, a period that was comparatively peaceful and prosperous. The government of Antonio's successors was ended when the Turks occupied Athens on 4 June 1456.

The history of the Latins in the eastern Mediterranean region in the fourteenth and fifteenth centuries is one of squabbling petty states, some under absentee dynasties, bound together by religion and by little else and faced with a growing threat from the Ottoman Turks. A feature of their history is the decline of the old feudal, chivalric culture in the face of independent mercenary companies and Italian money. Active at every stage one finds Italians, whose commercial concerns gave them an interest in the maintenance and even the government of the settlements and whose shipping provided the means of communication, and Hospitallers of St John, who were the region's trouble-shooters.

Crusading in Spain, 1302–54

Although in 1309–10 the kings of Castile and Aragon waged an unprofitable crusade against the Moors, which certainly impeded, as was intended, the *passagium particulare* of the Hospitallers to the East, and there was some activity in 1318–19, there was a stalemate in Spain in the early fourteenth century, in spite of regular grants of money and authorizations of crusade-preaching. The popes were highly suspicious of the Iberian kings, who seemed to be cynically manipulating crusade appeals for their own purposes. But in 1312 Alfonso XI, who was to prove himself to be the best military leader in the peninsula since Ferdinand III, inherited the throne of Castile. From 1328 a series of papal grants concerning crusade-preaching and the collection of tenths and *tercias* evidenced a revival of activity on the frontier with Granada. This attracted interest from across the Pyrenees and in 1326–7 and 1331 King Philip VI of France (in 1326 still count of Valois), in 1328–9 King John of Bohemia and King Philip of Navarre and in 1330 Count William of Jülich were enthusiastic enough to plan to bring parties of crusaders. The period was one in which crusading fervour was at a high level in western Europe and outsiders had not shown so much interest in the Reconquest for a century, although it subsided on the news of a short-lived truce made with Granada in 1331.

In 1340 the Marinid sultan 'Ali began to move troops across the straits from Africa and a Marinid army of c. 67,000 men besieged Tarifa. Alfonso, leading about 21,000 men, mostly Castilians and Portuguese, took the same sort of gamble by seeking engagement that his ancestor had taken at Las Navas de Tolosa. On 30 October he won a major victory on the banks of the little river Salado, returning to Seville with so much booty that in Paris the price of gold and silver fell. In August 1342 he laid siege to Algeciras with soldiers from all over Europe, including Genoese and nobles from France, Germany and England, King Philip of Navarre, Gaston of Béarn, Roger Bernal of Castielbon and the earls of Derby and Salisbury among them. The city fell in March 1344, the Straits of Gibraltar were won and the flow of African invaders into Spain was dammed. In 1350, however, Alfonso died of the Black Death while besieging Gibraltar and thereafter the Reconquest flagged for a century. Christian Spain, riven by internal disputes, was not strong enough to take Granada. Realism gave way to dreams, like Peter I of Castile's proposal to crusade in Africa in 1354, which had been foreshadowed by the planning of a crusade to the Canary Islands ten years earlier.

Crusading in Italy, 1302–78

From the point of view of the papacy the same conflicts of crusading interest prevailed as in the thirteenth century and threats from political opponents in Europe were at times believed to pose a greater danger to Christendom than the lengthening shadow in the East. The Italian crusades in support of the Angevin rulers of Naples had ended in 1302. After that date others were directed against the Ghibelline supporters of imperial claims, which had been revived in northern and central Italy, although the first significant crusade of the new period was preached in 1309 against Venice, not a Ghibelline city at all, after a dispute over the succession to Ferrara, a place of strategic importance to both sides. Venice submitted in 1310, but Ferrara, which from 1317 was under a regime hostile to the papacy, was also involved in the next crusade, which was proclaimed in December 1321 against its Estensi rulers, together with Matthew Visconti of Milan and Frederick of Montefeltro, and Frederick's brothers and supporters in the march of Ancona and the duchy of Spoleto. Frederick of Montefeltro was defeated and the Visconti regime in Milan went under, but the continuing resistance of the Ghibellines meant that papal authority was not restored in the region. In 1324 the crusade was extended to cover Mantua as well, but the resulting campaigns, although enormously costly, only achieved a precarious balance of forces, which was broken in 1327 by King Louis IV of Germany's descent on Italy. Louis's initial success, his deposition of the pope and appointment of an anti-pope and his occupation of Rome, led to a crusade being declared against him in 1328, but lack of money and supplies forced him to leave Italy, the Ghibelline coalition collapsed and many of its leaders, including Azzo Visconti and the Estensi, changed sides.

Pope John XXII now lent his support to a plan to establish a kingdom in Lombardy for John of Bohemia, the son of the former emperor Henry VII and a committed crusader, to hold as a papal fief. In September 1332 the League of Ferrara was formed to oppose this and the pope's desire to dominate northern and central Italy was thwarted. The papacy tried again in 1353, when Pope Innocent VI sent Cardinal Gil Albornoz, who as archbishop of Toledo had celebrated Mass before the Battle of Salado, to Italy to regain control of the Papal State. Gil Albornoz was successful in the western provinces, but he could not overcome the Romagna. In October 1354 Francesco Ordelaffi of Cesena and the Manfredi of Faenza were declared to be heretics and in the winter of 1355–6 a crusade was proclaimed against them. Gil Albornoz completed the reconquest of the Romagna in 1357 at a huge cost.

In 1360, however, the Church went to war with the Visconti of Milan and in 1363 declared Bernabò Visconti to be a heretic. The crusade was renewed and although peace was concluded in 1364 it was again revived in 1368 when preaching was organized in Italy, Germany and Bohemia. A feature of these wars of the 1350s and 1360s was the use by both sides of mercenary companies. Crusades, which provided models for further crusading activity against *routier* bands in France in the 1360s, were in turn preached against the companies when they got out of hand. For almost the whole of the pontificate of Gregory XI (1371–8) the Church was at war in Lombardy and Tuscany, although Gregory, who commuted vows, resorted to crusade terminology and transferred certain crusade taxes, does not seem to have launched fully privileged crusades there, preferring to grant limited indulgences which were applicable only in the case of death.

This endemic crusading was given impetus by the exile of the popes in Avignon from 1309 to 1378. Under strong pressure to return to Rome, yet reluctant to do so until order had been restored to the Papal State, fearful of the emperors, particularly in the light of Louis IV's invasion, they pressed on when they could. They could not avoid criticism for this, particularly in France, which was swept by crusading fever in the 1320s and could not accept that a crusade to recover the Holy Land should be postponed in Italy's favour. In 1319 Pope John XXII even diverted to his Italian wars a Franco-papal fleet of ten ships intended for the eastern crusade, and in response Philip V of France went so far as to take the Visconti and the Ghibelline league under his protection. Nor could the popes avoid having to pay for these enormously expensive wars: nearly two-thirds of John's revenue was spent on them. It is remarkable how they managed to meet the bills and remain solvent; to do so they drew on their experiences in the thirteenth century and elaborated a system of extraordinary taxes, especially caritative subsidies ('voluntary' donations), annates (taxes on the first year's income of the new holder of a benefice) and intercalary fruits (income from benefices during vacancies), to supplement the income taxes they were levying on the clergy. This led to the system of clerical taxation that prevailed to the end of the middle ages.

The fourteenth-century popes tended to associate Ghibellinism with heresy, or at least with schism, and this featured alongside traditional references to the defence of the rights of Christendom's mother church in their justification of the Italian crusades. The popes were genuinely worried about heresy and schism at that time and by the 1320s charges of heresy were being levelled forcefully and elaborately, backed by references to the Ghibellines' denial of papal authority and their association with known heretics like the Franciscan Spirituals. In this respect these crusades were large-scale versions of a type of crusading which included a savage little war against the followers of Fra Dolcino in Piedmont in 1306–7, the proclamation of a crusade against Cathars in Hungary in 1327 – cancelled when it was realized that it encroached on the authority of the inquisition – and a minor campaign against heretics in Bohemia in 1340.

Crusading to the East in the aftermath of the fall of Acre

A threat to Europe itself was now growing, more serious than any faced since the eighth century. The West became really worried about the Ottoman Turks in 1369, when the Byzantine emperor John V journeyed to Rome to appeal for help against them. So the history of crusading in the East between 1291 and 1523 falls into two periods. The first was one in which the aims were the reconquest of Palestine, but also the crushing of Mamluk Egypt, which was a necessary prerequisite, and the defence of the remaining Latin settlements, particularly against the piratical activities of the Turkish emirates of Menteshe and Aydin. This meant that crusading moved to the sea and became very largely naval. In the second period the defence of Christian Europe against the Ottomans became the priority.

After 1291 the policies of the papal curia involved providing aid to Cilician Armenia, which was still holding out against the Mamluks, enforcing an economic blockade of Egypt, which most men agreed was a necessary prelude to a crusade, and organizing support for Latin Greece. From Boniface VIII's pontificate onwards the popes promulgated decrees of increasing severity on the blockade. Clement V authorized the Hospitallers on Rhodes to capture the vessels of Christian merchants trading with the Mamluks and sequester their cargoes. Strict embargoes were imposed from the early 1320s, when it was laid down that merchants who infringed them were to be excommunicated. These measures were accompanied by direct approaches to western trading communities which were often persuaded to legislate for their merchants in the way the popes wanted. The effectiveness of the blockade has been debated. Ports like Ayas which could act as intermediaries between Christians and Muslims grew in importance, but direct trading with Islamic centres continued, if on a reduced scale, and when the Mongol routes across Asia came to be temporarily disrupted in the 1340s with effects on the Black Sea traffic the Italians insisted that trade relations with the Mamluks be reopened. From 1344 the Holy See, which was beginning to abandon hope for the recovery of the Holy Land, granted licences for such commerce.

After the death of Boniface VIII the growing French influence on the curia manifested itself in support for Charles of Valois, the king of France's brother, who in 1301 had married Catherine of Courtenay, the heiress to the Latin empire, and wanted to recover it. In 1306 the collection of crusade tenths in France, Sicily and Naples was authorized in favour of Charles and in 1307 crusade-preaching was ordered in Italy. Charles delayed so long that the coalition of powers against the Byzantine emperor on which he was relying collapsed, but meanwhile Clement V had been considering the preaching of a general passage with the purpose of recovering Palestine. The attitude of the French and the Templar scandal made this impossible, except as a long-term goal, so he turned to the organization of a *passagium particulare*, which was to consist of 5,000 troops, was to remain in the East for five years under the command of the Hospitaller master, was to defend Cyprus and Cilicia and prevent Christian merchants engaging in illicit trading. The pope had to face the fact that King James of Aragon's crusade against Granada, planned at the same time, was siphoning off potential recruits, although it is indicative of the general enthusiasm for ventures in the East that in the spring and summer of 1309 large numbers of rural and urban poor in England, Flanders, northern France and Germany were taking the cross and gathering in disorderly groups. It was said that 30–40,000 of them arrived at Avignon demanding a general passage. In fact the expedition which sailed from Brindisi early in 1310 did little more than help consolidate the Hospitaller occupation of Rhodes, as we have seen.

In the years after 1310 the papacy was still concerned about the future of Latin Greece, granting Philip of Taranto crusade tenths and indulgences and authorizing crusades in favour of the Brienne pretenders to the dukedom of Athens against the Catalan Company: one was approved as late as 1330. But with the accession of Pope John XXII in 1316 crusading further to the east again came to the forefront of curial planning, in response to the enthusiasm that was showing itself in France, where in 1320 there was another outbreak at a popular level in a movement of shepherd crusaders. At the council of Vienne in 1312 Philip IV had agreed to prepare a crusade and a six-year tenth had been levied on the whole Church, of which the French contribution, increased for a seventh year, had been conceded directly to the king. At Whitsun 1313, at a great assembly held in Paris to witness the knighting of his sons, Philip himself, his sons and his son-in-law Edward II of England had all taken the cross. Philip had since died, but his son Philip V, one of those who had taken the cross in 1313, was committed to the project and to assist him Pope John not only confirmed a new four-year tenth to be levied on the French Church, but also made a four-year grant of annates; this was followed in 1318 by another two-year tenth. The French crown had been given eleven years of tenths and four years of annates since 1312 and the tenths alone would have raised 2,750,000 pounds *tournois*. But rebellion in Flanders held the king back and, with Cilicia again under threat, the various parties began to think of another *passagium particulare*, to be led by Louis I of Clermont. It was the naval vanguard of this which John directed in 1319 to the Italian wars, where it was lost. The French reaction was strong and King Philip, who was a committed crusader, took a very hard line, as we have seen. He left 100,000 pounds in his will to a future *passagium* and might well have gone on crusade if he had not fallen mortally sick in 1321. Over the winter of 1319–20 he held a number of assemblies, to some of which he summoned many old war-horses from the provinces – among them probably Odo of Grandson – to advise him.

Crusading to the East, 1323–60, and the emergence of leagues

In January 1323 the new king of France, Charles IV, formulated another detailed proposal, this time for a three-part crusade: a *primum passagium*, to sail in the same year to the aid of Cilicia; a *passagium particulare* in the following year or soon afterwards; and, in the very long term, a *passagium generale* to reconquer the Holy Land. The planning ground to a halt over finance, since it was certain that the bulk of the costs would have to be borne by the French Church, which was in no state to take on such a commitment, and it was not until 1328 that King Philip VI, who was another enthusiast, revived the project. In 1331 the pope gave his consent to the preaching of an expedition to leave before March 1334. Philip's plan, which at first took the pope by surprise, was a very ambitious one, involving, again, a three-stage crusade, for which the main French contribution would be to a general passage proposed for August 1336 under the command of the king himself as captain-general of the Church. On 1 October 1333, in another great Parisian ceremony held in the meadows near St-Germain-des-Près, Philip and many of his nobles took the cross.

The first of the two preliminary *passagia* was launched in 1334 and constituted a significant development in crusading, because the result was a naval league designed to deal with the pirate emirates of Menteshe and Aydin. This was the first example of a mutation of crusading which was to become increasingly important. A defining feature of crusades had always been that they were supranational, representing in theory, if not always in practice, the 'Christian Republic'. The leagues, on the other hand, never claimed to be representing the whole of Christendom. Called by one historian 'frontier crusades', they were alliances of those front-line powers which felt themselves to be most threatened or whose rulers were most enthusiastic, but their campaigns were authorized by the popes and their forces were granted crusade privileges.

The first of these leagues was built on an agreement drawn up on Rhodes in September 1332 between Venice, the Hospitallers and the Byzantine emperor Andronicus III to maintain a force of twenty galleys in the area for five years. In the autumn and winter of 1333–4 Philip VI of France, Hugh IV of Cyprus and Pope John agreed to supply more galleys, bringing the total, at least on paper, to forty. This fleet inflicted a heavy defeat on the Turks in the Gulf of Edremit.

The league was also going to be involved in a second *passagium*, a force of 800 men-at-arms under Louis of Clermont, which was to invade Asia Minor in 1335: 400 men were to be sent by France and the papacy, 200 by the Hospitallers and 100 each by Cyprus and the Byzantine empire, while Venice and Naples would contribute additional shipping. But Pope John died at the end of 1334 and the alliance came to nothing as relations between France and England degenerated. Under John's successor, Benedict XII, the plans for the second *passagium* were shelved, but an attempt was made to revive the naval league, it seems unsuccessfully, although at one point the papacy, the Byzantine empire and France were preparing ships. In 1336 Benedict recognized that political conditions in western Europe were so unfavourable that the general passage would have to be cancelled as well, although he sent some limited aid to Cilicia. This led to bitter reproaches and disillusionment.

In May 1342 Benedict was succeeded by Clement VI, who had been a leader of the French delegation which had negotiated on behalf of Philip VI in the early 1330s. Clement made no plans for a general passage, the organizing of which would now have been quite impossible, given that France and England were at war and western Europe was suffering from a general economic depression, but in its place a new strategy, based on the successes of 1334, was hammered out. Responding to appeals from Venice, Cyprus and Rhodes, Clement sent a legate to Venice to reconstruct a new naval league against the Turkish emirates, now at their most aggressive: the papacy and Cyprus would each provide four galleys, the Hospitallers and Venetians six each. The pope paid for his galleys by levying a three-year tenth, later supplemented by another two-year one, on certain provinces of the Church and by crusade-preaching to raise money through the sale of indulgences. In the spring of 1344 twenty-four galleys assembled off Euboea. They defeated the Turks at sea and on 28 October took the port of Smyrna, the emirate of Aydin's principal harbour.

Smyrna was to be held until it fell to the Mongol Timur in 1402. Its capture led to yet another outburst of crusading fever in the West and in response to a set-back early in 1345, when the leaders of the crusade were killed in an engagement with the Turks, the dauphin of Viennois, Humbert II, volunteered to defend the new beach-head and led an expedition which sailed from Venice in the middle of November. Humbert returned to the West in 1347 and the league broke up in 1351, by which time Venice was at war with Genoa, which had been granted indulgences to defend its Black Sea station of Feodosiya against the Mongols in 1345. In a Europe coping with the Black Death and against the background of the Hundred Years' War Pope Innocent VI spent most of his ten-year pontificate trying to revive the league, since it was still officially in being and was still jointly responsible for the defence of Smyrna; but it was not until 1359 that it was put on a more active footing. Crusade-preaching was authorized and a tenth was levied. Peter Thomas, the great Carmelite preacher and diplomatist, was appointed legate and with Venetian and Hospitaller ships he won a victory that autumn at Lâpseki in the Dardanelles.

Peter I of Cyprus

During the next decade, however, the old idea of a general passage to Jerusalem was revived through the efforts of King Peter I of Cyprus. In 1359, the year he succeeded to the throne, he used Cypriot ships abstracted from the league to occupy Corycus in Cilicia and in 1361 he captured Antalya. On 15 June 1362 he addressed a circular letter to the

West announcing his intention of leading a crusade to liberate Jerusalem. In October he set off to raise money in Europe and he met the new pope, Urban V, at the end of March 1363. A general passage was planned for March 1365. King John II of France was a fervent supporter and took the cross, together with several of his nobles. He was granted a six-year tenth and other revenues and was appointed captain-general, but he died on 8 April 1364 a prisoner of the English, to whom he had surrendered himself when one of the hostages for his ransom after his capture in the Battle of Poitiers had broken his parole.

The dream of a general passage was unrealistic, given the economic conditions in France. Peter, leading what was originally envisaged as a *passagium particulare* in advance of it, left Venice on 27 June 1365 with the crusaders he had recruited. With an army estimated as consisting of c. 10,000 men and 1,400 horses he adopted the old expedient of attacking Alexandria, perhaps, it has been suggested, with the aim of at least strengthening the standing of the Cypriot ports by destroying a major rival. He launched his attack to take advantage of the Nile floods, which would have hindered the Egyptians bringing up reinforcements. Sailing into the Old Harbour on 9 October, he landed on a strip of beach near the city wall on the following morning. At the same time a Hospitaller contingent of 100 brothers in four galleys under the order's admiral landed on the shore of the New Harbour so as to be able to attack the Muslim defenders from the rear. What then happened is rather confused, but finding a gate which was not well defended the crusaders set fire to it and broke into the city. Peter could not hold his prize and his expedition, laden with plunder, withdrew to Cyprus six days later. In the following year Count Amadeus of Savoy left Venice with another fragment of the crusade, an army of 3–4,000 men. After retaking Gallipoli from the Turks in August he campaigned on the Black Sea coast against the Bulgarians, who had been holding up the return overland of the Byzantine emperor John V from Buda (Budapest): the towns of Nesebŭr and Sozopol were restored to the empire. Peter of Cyprus went on to lead a raid on Cilicia and Syria in 1367, but after his assassination in 1369 the liberation of Jerusalem became a secondary goal, as Christian Europe began to worry about its future.

Concern about the Turks

In the following year there was a new pope, Gregory XI, under whom the power of the Ottoman Turks became for the first time a dominant factor in curial thinking. The Ottomans had emerged from the confusion in Asia Minor that had followed the collapse of Selchük rule. After their defeat at the hands of the Mongols in 1243 the authority of the Selchüks had declined and there had been a fragmentation of the Turkish polity into principalities, of which the emirates of Menteshe and Aydin, although not the most powerful, were for a time the ones that concerned westerners the most. Among the frontier princes was a man called Ertugrul who by the time of his death in 1280 seems to have founded a little state of his own. His son Osman came to prominence early in the fourteenth century; it was against him that the Catalan Company was employed by the Byzantines. Before he died, shortly after taking Bursa in 1326, Osman had extended his authority over a significant part of north-western Asia Minor, as far as the Aegean, the Sea of Marmara and the Black Sea. Under his son Orkhan the Ottoman state, well governed and with a disciplined army, began to expand rapidly. In 1331 Nicaea was taken, in 1337 Izmit and in 1338 Üsküdar, just across the Bosporus from Constantinople. Invited into Thrace as mercenaries, the Turks had established a beach-head in Europe by 1348 and they occupied Gallipoli, at the mouth of the Dardanelles, in 1354. By Orkhan's death in 1360 his rule stretched from western Thrace to Eskişehir and Ankara. Hordes of Turks were now pouring into Europe. Edirne was taken in 1361, Plovdiv in 1363 and in 1371 victory at Maritsa gave Sultan Murad I most of Bulgaria and Serbian Macedonia. The Turks achieved dominance of the Balkans after the Battle of Kosovo in 1389, on the morning of which Murad was assassinated. His elder son and successor, Bayazid I, took what was left of Bulgaria in 1393, invaded the Peloponnese in 1394, reducing the Christian lords to vassaldom, and defeated the crusade of 1396 at Nicopolis (Nikopol).

Turkish expansion was halted for a time by the Mongol Timur's victory at Ankara in 1402 and by succession disputes in the Ottoman family which lasted until 1413. But then, and particularly under Murad II (1421–51), the Turks resumed their advance, laying siege to Constantinople in 1422 and taking Thessaloniki in 1430. Eastern Anatolia was absorbed or cowed and in 1444 a crusade was routed at Varna. The Peloponnese was ravaged in 1446. Hungarian military power was decimated in a second battle at Kosovo in 1448. Under Mehmed II (1451–81) the Turks then prepared to turn on Constantinople itself. In spite of the efforts of the papacy and last-ditch attempts to unite the Catholic and Orthodox Churches, which split the Greeks themselves, the western response was inadequate. Constantinople fell on 29 May 1453, after a siege of nearly two months, and the last Byzantine emperor, named, extraordinarily enough, Constantine, died in the fighting. In 1456 Athens was annexed and although Belgrade was held by the Hungarians until 1521, Serbia succumbed in 1459 as did most of the Peloponnese in 1459–60. Trebizond fell in 1461 and Lesbos in 1462. Euboea was taken in 1470 and under Bayazid II (1481–1512) Lepanto (Návpaktos), Koróni and Methóni in 1499–1500. Under Selim I (1512–20) it was the Muslim Near and Middle East that felt the weight of Turkish assault, but with the accession of Suleiman I (1520–66) the Ottomans turned again on the West and, as has already been described, Rhodes was taken in 1522.

This inexorable advance provides the background to the efforts of the papacy from 1370 onwards. Pope Gregory XI, who came from a family with crusading traditions, had in mind the preaching of a general passage to the Balkans to defeat the Turks; here for the first time the defence of Europe against them came to the fore. The Anglo-French war made this impossible and the pope therefore tried to unite those powers which were directly threatened and to encourage them to help themselves. This meant leagues. Plans for a new one had been hatched in 1369. They were revived in 1373 and 1374, but the proposals foundered on the refusal of the powers involved – Venice, Genoa, Naples, Hungary and Cyprus – to unite. Gregory's attempt to organize a Genoese expedition in 1376 came to nothing and another one forced on him by the Hospitallers in 1378 ended disastrously in Epirus as we have seen.

Crusades engendered by the Great Schism

Then came the Great Schism and from 1378 to 1417 there were two (later three) lines of popes, in Rome and Avignon. Europe was split between those adhering to one line or the other – even the Hospitallers on Rhodes were divided among themselves – and there came to be internal crusades generated by the Schism itself. Attempted crusades against Naples in 1382 and 1411–12 and France in 1388, and in Italy in 1397 and Aragon in 1413, came to nothing, but in the early 1380s England, which backed Urban VI in Rome, was swept by crusading fervour and two expeditions were planned, one under Henry Despenser, the bishop of Norwich, against the 'Clementists', the supporters of Clement VII in Avignon, wherever they might be found, and the other under John of Gaunt, duke of Lancaster, against Castile. The crusade of the bishop of Norwich was a lost cause. It left for Flanders, which was subject to the Clementist French, on 16 May 1383 with massive demonstrations of popular support and, after taking several seaside channel towns, laid siege to Ypres. In early August the approach of a French army caused the siege to be abandoned and the English crusade withdrew. John of Gaunt's campaign, heralded by a ceremony in which his nephew King Richard II recognized him as king of Castile, began on 9 July 1386, when he sailed from England. A year later he had withdrawn to Gascony, having received a rich indemnity in return for his renunciation of the crown.

The crusades of Mahdia and Nicopolis

A united response to any threat should have been an impossibility, but two major ventures in this period demonstrated that the crusading movement was strong enough to rise even above the Schism. In 1390 continuing interest manifested itself in a scheme, proposed by the Genoese, who supported Pope Boniface IX, to King Charles VI of France, who supported Pope Clement VII, for a crusade against the town of Mahdia in the Hafsid kingdom of Tunisia, which was a centre for what would later be called Barbary corsairs. These pirates had been raiding Genoese shipping. The Genoese, Sicilians and Pisans had already been involved in a major engagement and had occupied the island of Jerba in 1388. Pope Clement VII authorized the crusade, for which there was great enthusiasm in France, even though the king stipulated that knights must equip themselves at their own expense and that the number of *gentilshommes* in the army must not exceed 1,500. Genoa contributed 1,000 crossbowmen and 2,000 men-at-arms in addition to 4,000 sailors. Crusaders also came from England, Spain and the Low Countries. The fact that this venture was seen to transcend the Schism was demonstrated by an order from the high command that no one should refer to it, but that in a spirit of fraternity all should unite to defend the Catholic faith. Louis II of Clermont, an experienced soldier, was appointed leader. In July 1390 the French and Genoese fleets made for the island of 'Consigliera', possibly Kuriate, where they halted for nine days. Late in the month they landed on the mainland, but the North Africans had had time to organize resistance and after nine or ten weeks besieging Mahdia both sides were exhausted. The Genoese secretly negotiated a renewal of an earlier treaty they had had with the Tunisians and Louis of Clermont returned to Europe in October with nothing achieved.

Perhaps because it had been a demonstration of Christian unity, perhaps because France and England were once again caught up in a bout of crusading zeal, this curious side-show actually fired more interest and Gregory XI's project for a general passage against the Turks in the Balkans, which had been held up since 1370, was revived. The governments of France and England were actively discussing plans for a crusade either to the East or to Prussia from 1392 onwards and early in 1393 a small Anglo-French force was sent to Hungary, to be followed in 1394 by ambassadors from England, Burgundy and France. It was in response to them that King Sigismund of Hungary sent embassies to western Europe to appeal for help. The reaction in France, particularly in Burgundy, was strong and many leading nobles were recruited, including the counts of Nevers, La Marche and Eu, and Henry and Philip of Bar, all cousins of the king. Large numbers of men also took the cross in Germany. Charles of France himself wrote to Richard of England, suggesting that they both enrol, and it seems that the crusade which came into being was envisaged as a preliminary passage, in advance of a *passagium generale* which was to be led in person by the kings of France and England. The pope in Rome, Boniface IX, proclaimed the crusade in 1394 and he was joined by the pope in Avignon, Benedict XIII, who granted indulgences to the French crusaders.

An army of c. 10,000 men mustered around Sigismund at Buda in the late summer of 1396, before advancing to Orşova and crossing the Danube at the Iron Gate (Portile de Fier). In the second week of

September they came before the city of Nicopolis (Nikopol), where they were joined by Venetian and Genoese ships and by a Hospitaller squadron under the master, Philibert of Naillac, which had sailed up the Danube. The Turkish sultan Bayazid was besieging Constantinople when the news of the crusaders' advance reached him. He at once marched to relieve Nicopolis, which he approached on 24 September. On the following day, in one of those futile acts of stupid bravery typical of feudal chivalry in the period of its decline, the French knights, in spite of their inexperience of the enemy or the conditions, insisted on being placed in the front line. They then charged up a hill straight for the Turkish position which was fortified by stakes and, slowed down by these obstacles, they were exhausted by the time they came face to face with the main body of Muslims. In the confusion the crusaders began to recoil and their withdrawal degenerated into a rout during which John of Nevers and many of the leaders were taken prisoner.

Crusading against the Turks, 1397–1413

The downfall of western chivalry at Nicopolis opened the rest of the Balkans to the Turks. In this moment of crisis the Hospitallers accepted the custody of Corinth from the Byzantine despot, Theodore of Mistra, who was even prepared to consider the sale of his entire despotate to them; he bought Corinth back from them in 1404 when the immediate danger had passed. Boniface IX issued general crusade letters in favour of Byzantine Constantinople in 1398, 1399 and 1400, although the last of these was suddenly withdrawn, perhaps because the Roman curia had heard that the Byzantine emperor was appealing to his rival in Avignon. King Charles of France turned to John Boucicaut, who had been captured at Nicopolis but had been ransomed. John Boucicaut set sail in late June 1399 with c. 1,200 men. Joined by ships from Genoa, Venice, Rhodes and Lesbos he broke the Turkish blockade of Constantinople and with his substantial fleet of twenty-one galleys, three large transports and six other vessels pillaged the coasts in Turkish hands. After relieving Constantinople he brought the Byzantine emperor back to the West with him to appeal for help.

Eastern Europe was, however, only saved by the Mongol Timur's invasion of Anatolia. In its wake and with the temporary eclipse of Turkish power there was a revival of Christian activity. John Boucicaut, who had been appointed governor of Genoa, arrived at Rhodes with a Genoese fleet of ten galleys and six large transports in June 1403, with the intention of enforcing Genoese claims in Cyprus but also raiding the Muslim coastline. He ravaged the port area of Alanya and then, unable to reach Alexandria because of contrary winds, he and the Hospitallers attacked Tripoli, pillaged Batroun and sacked Beirut; most of the loot appears to have been Venetian merchandise. After an unsuccessful descent on Sidon he returned to Genoa, fighting a sea-battle with the Venetians on the way. In 1407 he may have been planning a new attack on Egypt.

The Hussite crusades

The restoration of Turkish power after 1413 and the ending of the Great Schism in the West meant a revival of crusading plans. In 1420 Pope Martin V tried without much success to organize a crusade in aid of the Latins in the Peloponnese and in 1422, when Constantinople was being besieged by the Turks, he tried to arrange a league of Hospitallers, Venetians, Genoese and Milanese to go to its assistance. The problem at this time was that the western empire was caught up in the Hussite crusades, the last great series of crusades against heretics. Although John Hus, who had criticized the granting of crusade indulgences by Pope John XXIII to those who waged war on King Ladislas of Naples, had been burned for heresy in 1415 on the judgment of the council of Constance, Hussite strength in Bohemia was growing and the Hussite demands – communion in both kinds; the public suppression of sin, particularly among the clergy, with the threat of non-clerical jurisdiction in the field of morals; freedom to preach; and a review of the Church's temporal possessions – were sharpened by their association with Czech nationalism at a time when the emperor-elect, Sigismund, was laying claim to the throne of Bohemia. In 1418 Martin V, who seems to have been particularly determined throughout, charged one of his cardinals with the preparation of a crusade. In March 1420 Sigismund held an imperial diet at Breslau (Wrocław) during which the papal legate publicly read the pope's proclamation of a crusade against Wyclifites, Hussites and their supporters. Early in May Sigismund led an army of c. 20,000 men into Bohemia, but many of them deserted and he suffered a series of defeats at the hands of the Hussites under their able leader Jan Žižka.

A feature of these crusades, however, was the energy with which they were organized. By the time Sigismund was pulling out in March 1421 another crusade was being prepared. Two armies entered Bohemia, although they had withdrawn before Sigismund re-entered Hussite territory in the following October, only to be comprehensively defeated and forced out in January 1422. In the next autumn two more armies marched; they had withdrawn within months. A fourth crusade invaded Bohemia in July 1427, but it dissolved in panic after an engagement near Tachov and suffered huge losses, after which the Hussites themselves advanced into German territory. A plan to raise an English crusade in 1428–9 under Cardinal Henry Beaufort, who had been legate on the crusade of 1427, ended with Henry's army, financed with crusade taxes, being put at the disposal of the duke of Bedford in France and being swallowed up by the French war. Against this background of failure a great imperial diet took place at Nuremberg in February and March 1431 and planned yet another crusade. In the summer three armies mobilized. One concentrated on retaking those German territories which had been lost, the second, under Albert of Austria, raided Moravia, but the third, under Frederick of Brandenburg, was annihilated by the Hussites on 14 August.

The five Hussite crusades, which included in their ranks participants from many parts of Europe, were almost the most futile of the whole movement. Crusading, of its nature spasmodic, was, we have already seen, an uncertain instrument with which to confront heresy, but it has been pointed out that the fact that the armies were so often routed, rather than merely defeated, suggests a major collapse in morale. The crusades simply reinforced the links between heresy and Czech nationalism and in the end the Hussites were only brought under some measure of control by the Bohemian nobles themselves, although they were still worrying the papacy in the 1460s. On the other hand the crusades demonstrate how completely everything could be subordinated to a drive for uniformity within Christendom. Sigismund had been the king of Hungary who had been the instigator of the crusade of Nicopolis. If anyone had first-hand knowledge of the Turkish threat it was him, and yet he was prepared to divert energy and resources into an internal struggle. This helps to explain why a century later, in spite of the Turkish menace, crusading would falter when the Latin Christian world was to be much more seriously divided by the Reformation and the ensuing wars of religion.

The crusade of Varna

By 1440 Turkish power was even more threatening, but the union of the Catholic and Orthodox Churches, for which the papacy had been working hard, looked promising. On 1 January 1443 Pope Eugenius IV issued a new letter, calling on all the faithful to defend the Christian East against the Turks. The response came from Poland, Wallachia, Burgundy and Hungary, where John Hunyadi, the ruler of Transylvania, had been engaged in heroic resistance. He and King Ladislas of Hungary planned a great expedition for the summer of 1443. They were joined by crusaders, routed the Turks at Niš and entered Sofia, after which they withdrew. The Balkans were now up in arms and although the king of Hungary may have been induced to pledge himself to a ten-year truce with the Turks in June 1444, he had already sworn to renew the war against them. A Christian army of c. 20,000 men advanced through Bulgaria and besieged the coastal town of Varna. At the same time a new naval league – twenty-four galleys provided by the pope, Duke Philip of Burgundy, Venice, Dubrovnik (Ragusa) and the Byzantine empire – sailed for the Dardanelles. Sultan Murad hurried to Varna's relief with a much larger army, some of it transported, it was rumoured, in Genoese ships, and on

10 November destroyed the Christians in a battle in which Ladislas of Hungary and the papal legate were killed.

Reactions to the loss of Constantinople and the reappearance of peasant armies

Varna paved the way for the final onslaught on the Byzantine empire. The news of the fall of Constantinople on 29 May 1453 was a sensation and the remaining Christian settlements in the Aegean were thrown into a state of terror: in November 1455 the pope was persuaded to grant plenary indulgences to the defenders of Genoese Chios. There followed seventy years of intense activity and propaganda on the part of the papal curia, in which the recovery of Constantinople became an ideal similar to the liberation of Jerusalem in earlier periods. The news had reached Rome in early July 1453 and on 30 September Pope Nicholas V issued a new general crusade letter and sent appeals to the courts of western Europe. For the first time printing-presses in Germany were used to advertise the crusade and print indulgences and propaganda. On 17 February 1454 Duke Philip the Good of Burgundy and his Knights of the Golden Fleece swore to take the cross at a magnificent feast in Lille during which a live pheasant, decked with jewelry, was brought to the table; among the side-shows an elephant was depicted carrying the Holy Church appealing for aid. A few weeks later there opened the first of a series of crusade assemblies in Germany, marked by intrigue and divisions of opinion, which in 1455 concluded by postponing the crusade for a year after the news of the pope's death had reached the participants.

The new pope, Calixtus III, was even more committed than his predecessor had been and was reported to be 'always talking, always thinking about the expedition'. On 15 May 1455 he confirmed Nicholas's general letter and he set 1 March 1456 as the date for the crusade's departure. Legates and preachers, especially recruited from among the Franciscans, were sent throughout Europe and a commission of cardinals under the Greek Bessarion oversaw planning. On 14 February 1456 the great preacher St John of Capistrano took the cross at Buda and was empowered to preach the crusade: he was said to have recruited 27,000 men in Hungary alone. A major Turkish threat was developing against Belgrade. John himself led a force of 2,500 men to the town where he was joined by other Hungarian crusaders under John Hunyadi, who broke the Muslim blockade. In an engagement reminiscent of those on the First Crusade a huge Turkish army was repulsed by inferior Christian forces on 22 July. The Turks left their equipment in their disorderly flight and John of Capistrano went so far as to claim that the time had now come to recover Jerusalem and the Holy Land. In the following summer a papal fleet of sixteen galleys captured more than twenty-five Turkish ships at Mitilíni and occupied Samothráki, Thásos and Limnos (Lemnos), for the defence of which Pope Pius II was later to found a new military order, of Our Lady of Bethlehem.

John of Capistrano had recruited and led to Belgrade an army of the poor. Unlike the rabbles of the past here was a popular crusade which was successful and was characterized by piety, discipline and good internal organization. Hungarian peasants had been accustomed to bear arms in popular levies, but the Belgrade Crusade was not the only example in the fifteenth and early sixteenth centuries of the recruitment of the poor. A sequence of occurrences culminated in a 'crusade revolt', the Dósza uprising in Hungary in 1514, in which a huge peasant crusade totalling c. 50,000 men recruited by Franciscan Observants turned on the nobles, who were condemned as *infideles*. The reappearance of the poor in the movement was a remarkable development and came about presumably because crusades were no longer being transported by sea, but were fighting on European ground. The common people, called to combat on their own soil, were coming back into the picture, but really too late to make much of a contribution, since crusading was now in obvious decline.

Pius II

The stand at Belgrade was not enough to stop the Turks, of course. The European powers were not prepared to sink their differences and give full-hearted backing to a crusade, as the experiences of Calixtus's successor Pius II show. Pius had been a fervent supporter of the movement from the start. Almost his first act as pope was to summon a crusade congress to Mantua. This dragged on for eight months, largely because the envoys of Germany and France, who were anyway inadequately empowered, arrived so late, but by Christmas 1459 a total of 80,000 men had been promised. On 14 January 1460 a three-year crusade against the Turks was proclaimed, but by March 1462 Pius was very nearly in despair:

> If we think of convening a council, Mantua teaches us that the idea is vain. If we send envoys to ask aid of sovereigns, they are laughed at. If we impose tithes on the clergy, they appeal to a future council. If we issue indulgences and encourage the contribution of money by spiritual gifts, we are accused of avarice. People think our sole object is to amass gold. No one believes what we say. Like insolvent tradesmen we are without credit.

In fact, apart from a declaration of war on the Turks by Venice, the results of all the papal diplomatic activity were nugatory.

Pius, however, was determined that there should be a crusade and, like Gregory X two centuries before, he wanted to lead it himself, doing battle as a priest 'with the power of speech, not the sword'. He took the cross on 18 June 1464 in St Peter's and left Rome on the same day for Ancona, where he expected to be joined by a Venetian fleet. Companies of Spanish, German and French crusaders arrived – more men than is usually supposed – and so did the fleet, but plague broke out and Pius died on 15 August.

With the fall of the island of Euboea, Venice's chief naval station after Crete, the newly elected Pope Sixtus IV published a general letter on 31 December 1471 and hurriedly went into league with Venice and Naples, spending more than 144,000 florins on a papal squadron under Cardinal Oliviero Carafa. The league's fleet, a really large one which comprised some eighty-seven galleys and fifteen transports, assembled off Rhodes in the late summer of 1472 and attacked Antalya and Smyrna, burning the latter town to the ground. Pieces of the chain from the entrance to Antalya's harbour were brought back in triumph and until recently could be seen hanging over a door in St Peter's.

When it came, the response of the Turks was startling and a display of the power now at their disposal. In 1480 they besieged Rhodes and at the same time their forces landed in Italy itself, near Otranto, which fell to them on 11 August. They had established a beach-head in western Europe and Sixtus, who even contemplated flight to Avignon, at once appealed for aid. He followed this by issuing another general letter on 8 April 1481, but on 3 May the great sultan Mehmed II died and on 10 September Otranto surrendered to Christian forces.

The conquest of Granada and the invasion of North Africa

In the midst of all the activity and propaganda the Reconquest in Spain, which had been dormant for over a century, was renewed. Since 1344 it had had a low priority in the minds of kings and frontier-fighting had been left to local nobles. In 1475 Pope Sixtus had gone as far as appropriating for the wars against the Turks half of the *tercias reales*, which had long since ceased to be used for conquest. But with the union of Aragon and Castile in the persons of Ferdinand and Isabella in 1479 and the resurgence of crusading ideas that had followed the loss of Constantinople the Spanish court, with Isabella taking the lead, began to seethe with fervour, nationalistic as well as religious. The paraphernalia of crusading – papal letters and crusade privileges – were in evidence. Huge sums of money were spent and large armies raised and the war was pursued with a remarkable single-mindedness at the expense of almost all the country's other interests. The Christians were helped by the fact that Granada, which by seizing Zahara provided a *casus belli*, was torn by dissension set off by the rebellion of the king's son in 1482. Alhama fell to the Christians in that year and the western half of the kingdom, comprising Zahara, Alora, Setenil, Benameji and Ronda, was occupied between 1483 and 1486. Malaga was taken in 1487 and Baza, Almería and Guadix in 1488–9. Ferdinand and Isabella laid siege to Granada itself in

April 1490 and when their camp was destroyed they replaced it with a town, Santa Fe, the building of which demoralized the Muslim defenders.

Granada surrendered on 2 January 1492 and the Spanish king and queen entered it on the 6th. On 4 February the Vatican and Castel St Angelo in Rome were illuminated with torches and bonfires and on the next day a solemn procession of thanksgiving was held and the first bullfights in Rome were organized by Cardinal Rodrigo Borgia. It was said somewhat grandiloquently that the taking of Granada offset the loss of Constantinople and it was assumed that this would be a prelude to the liberation of North Africa. The invasion of Africa began in 1497 with the occupation of Melilla and this was followed by a notable series of conquests, authorized by the popes and justified by the ancient idea of reaching the Holy Land by way of the African coast: Mers el-Kebir in 1505, Gomera (the Canary Islands) in 1508, Oran in 1509 and the Rock of Algiers, Bejaïa (Bougie) and Tripoli in 1510.

Crusade plans, 1484–1522

The Spanish advance in the far west was the only concrete result of all the papal efforts, in spite of the curia's continuing commitment. Capitulations agreed by the cardinals before proceeding to the election of Pope Innocent VIII on 29 August 1484 included the pledge to summon a general council to reform the Church and initiate a new crusade, an old programme that was to be revived in the sixteenth century. As soon as Innocent had been elected the curia began to make plans, but it was not until 1490 that the political situation in western Europe began to look favourable; and that was deceptive. A congress to discuss a crusade was opened in Rome in March and was attended by representatives of all the major powers except Venice. It put forward very detailed proposals for two land armies, one comprising German, Hungarian, Bohemian and Polish crusaders, the other French, Spanish, Portuguese, Navarrese, Scottish and English, together with a fleet which was to be provided by the Holy See and the Italian states. The whole campaign was to be under the general command of the emperor Frederick III or his son Maximilian, the king of the Romans. One army was to attack the Turks on the Hungarian frontier while the other would land in Albania. The fleet would operate in the Aegean. The Turkish prince Jem, who was now being held by the papacy, was to accompany the crusade: everyone seems to have been convinced that his presence would be a major political bonus. No crusade resulted from these ambitious proposals – although plenary indulgences were given to those who went to the defence of Hungary in 1493 – and they were overtaken by the French invasion of Italy in 1494. But crusading was so much in the air that King Charles VIII of France, who was asserting his claims to the throne of Naples, seems to have been genuinely absorbed in the dream that his conquest of southern Italy would be a prelude to an invasion of Greece in the company of Jem, whom he collected in Rome. Jem soon died, the crusade plans faded away and although Charles entered Naples in triumph on 22 February 1495 and was crowned king on 12 May the hostility of Venice and Milan made it impossible for him to stay. He withdrew to France in November.

In 1499 news of extensive Turkish preparations reached Italy. It was feared that an attack on Rhodes was imminent, but in fact the assault was targeted at the Venetian possessions in Greece. Lepanto fell in August and Methóni, Pilos (Navarino) and Koróni a year later. Pope Alexander VI commissioned preparatory studies for a crusade and Europe seemed to be again aroused, with Henry VII of England expressing real concern. The pope tried to assemble another congress and on 1 June 1500 he issued a new general letter. Substantial sums were raised from a three-year crusade tenth and in the spring of 1502 a papal squadron of thirteen galleys sailed to supplement the Venetian fleet. But France and Spain were at each other's throats over the kingdom of Naples and the next few years were taken up with much talk and little action. Popes Julius II and Leo X were indefatigable planners and propagandists, but the constant warring in Italy, the French invasions and the League of Cambrai against Venice nullified their efforts. Henry VII of England, Manuel of Portugal and James of Scotland pressed for a new crusade, while at one time or another Ferdinand of Spain and Louis XII of France were prepared to commit themselves to the enterprise. Crusading was discussed at the first, sixth, eighth, tenth and twelfth sessions of the Fifth Lateran Council between 1512 and 1517, with the stress on the old association of reform and crusade. Leo X issued another letter for eastern Europeans in 1513 and a crusade army was certainly being raised in the following year. Leo pressed the political powers on the need to resolve their differences and in 1516 he even summoned the French to a crusade under their king, Francis I, whom he had persuaded to take personal leadership.

Then in 1516 and 1517 came the Ottoman conquests of Syria and Egypt. Public opinion was aroused and people were terrified. The papal curia responded with a further burst of activity. On 11 November 1517 a special crusade indulgence was issued and the pope established a commission of eight cardinals which, after stressing the need for a general armistice in Europe, to be guaranteed by solemn oaths taken by all the princes in a sworn alliance entitled the *Fraternitas Sanctae Cruciatae*, proposed the raising of an army of 60,000 infantry, 4,000 knights and 12,000 light cavalry, together with a fleet. One force should land at Durazzo while the other advanced on Thrace from the north. The pope himself would accompany the crusade. Copies of this memorandum were sent to the western kings. The responses of King Francis and the emperor Maximilian underlined their conviction that peace in the West was a prerequisite and on 6 March 1518 the pope declared a five-year truce in

Europe and sent prominent cardinals as legates to secure the adherence of all the powers. So concerned were people at this time that it really looked as though the pope's appeal would be heeded. France, the western empire and Venice agreed to the five-year truce and in October France and England made the Treaty of London, establishing a defensive union which other powers could join. The pope ratified it on 31 December and King Charles of Spain a fortnight later. The Field of the Cloth of Gold in June 1520 was a demonstration of this new alliance. Plans for raising money and military forces went ahead, but with the news of Sultan Selim's death in 1520 the preparations faltered and the crusade passed out of the limelight. The Christian princes were not to know that Selim's successor Suleiman was to be just as formidable a conqueror and they turned their minds to their political interests nearer home, the rival claims for the empire and Naples of Charles of Spain and Francis of France, and the Lutheran revolt in Germany.

The inability of the popes and the Roman curia, in spite of continuing enthusiasm and tremendous efforts over seventy years, to unite the West behind a crusade reminds one of the periods 1150–87 and 1272–91. The nature of inter-state politics and the chaos into which Italy fell from 1494 onwards made it impossible to persuade the princes to sink their differences for long enough. They could always be convinced that a dispute with a neighbour or a justifiable claim was more important than the Turkish threat to Europe. The crusading movement was now in serious decline. In so far as it was associated with the papacy and the papacy was no longer respected or really trusted it seems that in Germany and perhaps also in France papal appeals no longer met with a ready response. It was also obvious that sections of intellectual opinion were turning quite radically against the movement. One can exaggerate the decay – at times real enthusiasm could still be aroused not only among the nobles but also at a popular level – but one can also discern an ebbing of the ideal in those regions distant from the Mediterranean and eastern Europe, where the powers which had to face the Turks were still quite highly committed.

CHAPTER 10

The Old Age and Death of the Crusading Movement, 1523–1798

The Reformation

After the seventy years of intense effort, pressure for crusading relaxed in the third decade of the sixteenth century. The curia was distracted by the French and imperial invasions of Italy and by anxiety about the activities of the reformers as the Lutheran revolt in Germany began to gain momentum. Pope Adrian VI's reaction to the news of the fall of Belgrade in 1521 and of Rhodes in 1522 had been to declare a three-year truce in Europe to allow the mustering of forces to fight the Ottomans. Francis of France was reminded by the Sacred College that the glory of his house rested not on wars with its neighbours but on the part it had played in crusades against the infidel, but the project collapsed in the face of yet another French assault on Italy. Adrian's successor, Clement VII, set out to organize a pan-European league against the Turks and it was no doubt with reference to this that Francis I and Charles V expressed their desire for a 'general crusade' to be summoned by the pope in their Treaty of Madrid in 1526. On 26 August of that year a Hungarian army under King Louis II was destroyed by the Ottomans in the Battle of Mohács and Louis was killed. It is not surprising that the pope was still discussing the formation of a crusade league in spite of the growing imperialist threat to Italy which was to lead to the German occupation of Rome in 1527. The emperor Charles V's agents demanded of Clement the summoning of a general council to reform the Church and extirpate Lutheranism, and linked this with the preparation of 'the most desired expedition against the infidels'. This very conventional programme was proposed again in the abortive plans for a council at Mantua in 1537 and yet again in the summons to the council of Trent (Trento) in 1544, which was convoked to resolve those matters 'which relate to the removal of religious discord, the reform of Christian behaviour and the launching of an expedition under the most sacred sign of the cross against the infidel', an agenda which differed from those of the councils of the thirteenth century only in its reference to Protestantism.

Catholics tended to believe that the Protestants were at least as dangerous as the Turks, if not more so. In February 1524 Clement VII was expressing anxiety about both the Turkish threat to Hungary and the activities of Martin Luther, and the proposal for a general crusade incorporated in the Treaty of Madrid between Charles V and Francis I two years later expressed the twin aims of 'the repelling and ruin ... of the infidels and the extirpation of the errors of the Lutheran sect'. Although for political reasons the Catholics avoided introducing crusade ideas into the Schmalkaldic War (1546), the English rebels against King Henry VIII in the Pilgrimage of Grace (1536–7) adopted badges depicting Christ's Five Wounds which had been worn on crusade in North Africa. The exiled Cardinal Reginald Pole called for a crusade against England and this was eventually realized in the Spanish Armada of 1588, which was indulgenced and was partly financed by crusade taxation. In 1551 Pope Julius III threatened King Henry II of France with a crusade for aiding the Protestants as well as the Turks. Crusade confraternities were much in evidence in the first three outbreaks of civil war in France in the 1560s. In 1566 King Philip II of Spain's spokesman had stated that the Turks were less of a menace than the 'internal evil' of heretics and rebels. This was typical. We have seen over and over again that internal threats were almost invariably treated more seriously by the popes, and indeed by most Catholics, than external ones. Crusading elements were to surface as late as the Thirty Years' War (1638–48).

Protestant doctrines spread rapidly and by the end of the century a significant minority of western Christians were lost to Catholicism and therefore to the crusading movement. Many of the reformers were quite happy with the idea of righteous wars. While Martin Luther rejected expressions of the papal *magisterium* and examples of salvation through works – and indeed, in a sort of negative echo, portrayed the bishop of Rome as worse than the Turks – in preaching the right of Christians to take up arms in defence of their lands and families against the Muslims his approach, Professor Housley has pointed out, 'resembled the Catholic crusade in a number of key respects, notably its emphasis on repentance and prayer', and this 'enabled Lutheran communities to work alongside their confessional foes in times of crisis'. The Lutheran princes and estates voted the emperor grants of supplies to fight the Turks and in Protestant England a Form of Thanksgiving was said thrice weekly in the churches for six weeks after the successful defence of Malta in 1565. The Huguenot captain, Francis of La Noue, spent his time in prison in the early 1580s writing his *Discours politiques et militaires* which contained a project for a modified *passagium generale*, without an indulgence, to recover Constantinople. He hoped this would unite Christendom and end the religious wars. But the Protestants naturally rejected the notion of a holy war under the aegis of the pope and the appeal of crusading must have faded rapidly among them, although in the following centuries they were still occasionally to be found serving with the Hospitallers on Malta.

Although the Reformation obviously weakened Christian resistance to the Turks, the advance of the Ottomans, however potent and terrifying they appeared to be, was becoming spasmodic, at least on the eastern land frontier, where rapid moves were followed by intervals of relative peace. By 1541 the Turkish frontier had been established in central Europe with its capital at Buda. Vienna was besieged in 1529 and again in 1683. A grim battle raged in North Africa where the local Muslims recognized Ottoman overlordship and gained Turkish support in their struggle with the Spaniards. In the Mediterranean itself the Turks were mopping up the islands and the remaining mainland holdings of the Latin Christians. Návplion and Monemvasia were surrendered in 1540, Chios fell in 1566 and Cyprus in 1570–1. Although Malta, an important link in the Christian defensive line from central Europe to North Africa, fought them off in 1565, Crete was to fall in 1669.

It was understandable for the Christian powers to try to limit the damage through diplomacy as well as meeting the Turks head on. Venice and the empire, which were bearing the heaviest losses, had to be prepared to make truces with Constantinople and the Venetians went as far as to congratulate Suleiman on his capture of Rhodes and his victory at Mohács. France actually allied herself to the Turks as part of a strategy to protect herself against the power of Charles V, although it is fair to say that the entente of 1536, reinforced by Selim II's capitulations of 1569, put her in the position to act as protector of Catholic merchants and pilgrims travelling in the Ottoman empire and her role in this respect was to prove beneficial. More surprising was the attitude of Pope Paul IV (1555–9), whose obsession with heresy left him with little time for crusades, although he threatened Charles V and Philip II, whom he feared and hated, with one. He even considered an alliance with the Turks against the Habsburgs and this was among the charges for which his nephew Cardinal Carlo Carafa, who, incidentally, had been a Hospitaller, was later sentenced to death.

The military orders

The military orders were, in fact, seriously weakened, and not just by the Reformation. Although in 1562 a new military order, that of Santo Stefano, was founded by the duke of Tuscany, with knights who could be married and a well-organized fleet based at Livorno, the nationalization of the Castilian orders was well underway before 1500. Between 1489 and 1494 King Ferdinand received their administration, with a royal council set up to control them. In 1523 Pope Adrian VI incorporated them into the crown in perpetuity, granting the king their masterships and incomes. Montesa was later incorporated into the crown of Aragon and the Portuguese orders, including that of Christ, also passed under the control of the kings. Other papal letters freed the brothers from restrictions relating to almost every aspect of the religious life. The orders became Orders of Chivalry, with their knights permitted to marry – those of Santiago had always been allowed to wed – their habits sold and their titles conferring honour and prestige. Their role, it has been written, was now 'one of social orientation and definition', although a few knights still performed service in war against the infidel. Pope Pius V (1566–72) ordered the Portuguese military orders to take up position on the North African frontier and even decreed that no brother could be professed until he had served for three years there; he wanted to establish a seminary in Africa for the training of young brother knights. From 1552 Santiago maintained three or four galleys, which were incorporated into the Spanish Mediterranean fleet. After the failure of an attempt in 1489 to incorporate it in the Hospital of St John, what was left of St Lazarus was progessively secularized.

The surviving military orders were hit hard by the Reformation. In 1525 the grand master of the Teutonic Order, Albert of Brandenburg, adopted Lutheranism and was enfeoffed by the king of Poland as hereditary duke of Prussia. In 1562 the last master of Livonia, Gotthard Kettler, also became a Lutheran duke. The commandery of Utrecht adopted Calvinism and still exists as a prestigious charitable body in the Netherlands. The rest of the order survived as a Catholic institution only in southern Germany, where from its headquarters at Mergentheim its grand master ruled over a little court. It continued to play a part in the Habsburg wars against the Turks and Protestants, maintaining from 1696 a regiment in the Habsburg army. It was now relatively small – in 1699 it comprised only 94 knights and 58 priests – but it remained a functioning military order, moving its headquarters to Vienna after 1809. It is still in existence, although now its membership consists only of priests.

Although the Hospital of St John survived, and even flourished, as we shall see, it lost its northern provinces. The North German brothers, who had already carved out for themselves a separate province in 1382, adopted Lutheranism and formed a Protestant bailiwick which eventually bought itself freedom from the grand magistry on Malta and survives today as a Protestant institution. In Denmark the order also lived on for a time as a Lutheran establishment, but then gradually ceased to function. In England, Norway and Sweden it was dissolved and its property was confiscated, although it was briefly revived in England under Queen Mary. In Scotland the last Hospitaller commander, James Sandilands, converted to Calvinism and was granted the order's lands as a secular barony in 1564.

North Africa

Crusading was now confined to three zones. One of these was North Africa, where Spanish beach-heads had been established along the northern coast as centres of conversion and as bases for the mastering of the shoreline. The vast conquests in the Americas absorbed much of the energy of Castilian society – there is, in fact, evidence that crusading ideas were transferred across the Atlantic – but the efforts and resources put into the struggle for North Africa were striking. The Spanish crusading movement was a national enterprise under royal control and it was self-reliant enough to be less affected by events elsewhere in Europe than was crusading to the East, but sooner or later it was bound to come up against the Turks, who had been casting their eyes westwards since their occupation of Egypt.

An early leader of resistance to the Spaniards was a man called Aruj Barbarossa, a native of Lesbos and possibly originally a Greek, who took control of Miliana, Médéa, Ténès and Tlemcen. He was killed in 1518, but his younger brother Khair ad-Din Barbarossa took over, subjected the territories he ruled to the Turks and with their help took Collo, 'Annaba (Bône), Constantine, Cherchell and in 1529 the Rock of Algiers, which became his base. He soon built a reputation for himself as one of the most feared pirate captains in the western Mediterranean, leading large fleets of freebooters on raids as far as Italy. He was such a menace that in 1533 the imperial envoys treating with the Ottoman government on the exchange for Hungary of Koróni, which had been retaken by the Christians in 1532, wanted the Turks to include in the bargain the surrender of the Rock of Algiers to the Spaniards.

In August 1534 Khair ad-Din occupied Tunis, providing himself with a base of operations uncomfortably close to southern Italy. The emperor Charles V's response was to organize an expedition to take it. A crusade was preached and indulgences were offered. The emperor himself took command under 'the Crucified Saviour' and like many crusaders before him made a preliminary pilgrimage, in his case to Montserrat to invoke the aid of the Blessed Virgin Mary. Pope Paul III sent money and six galleys; the Hospitallers sent four; and the Portuguese provided galleons and caravels. On 16 June 1535 a fleet of 74 galleys and 330 other ships disembarked an army under the emperor's command not far from the spot where Louis IX of France had landed in 1270. In a great crusading victory, which Charles claimed liberated 20,000 Christian captives, the fortress of La Goulette was taken on 14 July, most of the Barbary fleet was captured, Khair ad-Din's troops were defeated and on the 21st Tunis was sacked. The lock and bolts of its gate were sent to St Peter's in Rome where Charles enjoyed an imperial triumph. Khair ad-Din withdrew, by way of Mahón on Minorca which he ravaged, to Algiers. He went on to become a Turkish admiral and the scourge of Christians throughout the Mediterranean region until his death in 1546.

In October 1541 Charles led the forces of his empire on an assault on Algiers, which was unsuccessful because a gale scattered his fleet and convinced him that he could not properly supply the army he had landed. Among those with him who tried to persuade him to persist with the enterprise was Hernando Cortes, the conqueror of Mexico. Then in June

1550 Charles sent a fleet to besiege Mahdia which had been the goal of Louis of Clermont's crusade in 1390. It had recently become the base of Khair ad-Din's successor as the leading Barbary corsair, a native of Asia Minor called Turghud Ali (Dragut). The Christians took the town on 8 September, although Turghud Ali slipped away. The sultan appointed him governor of Tripoli, which had been given to the Hospitallers in 1530 but was surrendered by them to the Turks on 14 August 1551.

The Hospitallers, whose reputation had not been enhanced by their lacklustre defence of the place – 200 of them had surrendered – pressed King Philip II of Spain to reoccupy it. Pope Paul IV granted crusade indulgences which were renewed by Pope Pius IV and in February 1560 a fleet of at least forty-seven galleys, provided by Spain, Genoa, Florence, Naples, Sicily, the papacy and the Hospitallers, together with forty-three other ships, carried an army of 11–12,000 men – Italians, Spaniards, Germans, Frenchmen, Hospitallers and Maltese – to the island of Jerba at the southern entrance of the Gulf of Gabès and took possession of its fortress on 13 March as a first step towards the recapture of Tripoli. The Christians knew that there would be a Turkish counter-stroke and they worked hard to improve the fortifications, although many of them were being struck down with typhus. In May the bulk of the army began to re-embark, planning to leave behind a garrison of 2,200 Spaniards, Italians and Germans, but there was no time to complete an orderly embarkation before a Turkish armada was upon it. On the 11th the Christian fleet was destroyed with the loss of twenty-seven galleys. The garrison of Jerba had very little water because the two cisterns in the castle were almost dry, but it managed to produce about thirty barrels a day through distillation. By 27 July it had run out of the wood needed to heat the stills and many men were dying of thirst and scurvy. The siege was over by the 31st. Many of the defenders, including the wounded, were massacred; 7,000 prisoners, of whom 5,000 had been captured in the destruction of the fleet, were taken to Constantinople.

Spain and Portugal were more concerned about North Africa than the eastern Mediterranean and the papacy understood this. In the period leading up to the Battle of Lepanto in 1571 Spain was persuaded to subordinate its interests in favour of naval campaigns in the East, but this did not alter the fact that Tunis, which Charles V had restored to a dependent Muslim ruler in 1535, posed a constant threat to the Christian outpost at La Goulette. In 1569 Tunis was occupied by Uluj-Ali, another Algerian corsair and Ottoman admiral who, incidentally, was to be the loser at Lepanto, and this convinced the Spaniards that something must be done. With the collapse of the Holy League, which will be described below, Don John of Austria took Tunis with hardly a fight on 11 October 1573 and went on to capture Bizerte. The Turkish response was immediate. On 13 May 1574 an enormous fleet of 240 galleys left

Constantinople for the Barbary coast. After a month's siege La Goulette was taken on 25 August and Tunis was recaptured on 13 September.

The Christians had now been pushed into the far west. The Turks strengthened their grip on the North African coast and began to press on the Christian holdings in Morocco, assisting their own candidate for the sharifate to take Fez in 1576. The Spanish government began to look secretly for peace with them, but King Sebastian of Portugal, a romantic figure who was obsessed with the idea of crusading, launched himself into what may have been the last old-fashioned crusade – as opposed to a league – against Muslims, fortified with indulgences and accompanied by papal legates. He landed at Asilah, in command of an army of 15,000 foot and 1,500 horse – Portuguese, Spaniards, Germans, Netherlanders and a papal force originally destined for Ireland under the command of the Englishman Sir Thomas Stukeley – together with several thousand non-combatants. By 3 August 1578 he had reached Ksar el-Kebir (Alcácer-Quivir), but he was now out of touch with his fleet and out of provisions. On the 4th he was faced by a greatly superior Moroccan army and in the ensuing battle 'of the Three Kings', Sebastian, the Ottoman puppet sharif and his predecessor, to whom Sebastian was allied, all succumbed. Stukeley and some 8,000 Christians were also killed; nearly 15,000 were taken prisoner.

The eastern theatre

The two other theatres of war, Hungary and the eastern Mediterranean, were linked strategically and so can be treated together. It is surprising how much activity there was in the Mediterranean in spite of the fact that the papacy and the western European powers were becoming increasingly hamstrung by the growth of Protestantism. In the autumn of 1529 Sultan Suleiman laid siege to Vienna for three weeks and anxiety about his advance impelled Pope Clement and the emperor Charles into an alliance. Francis of France, who had been at war with Charles, was forced to make peace with him. As far as the pope was concerned, therefore, a threat to the heart of Europe had brought into existence the general peace for which he had been striving and now at last Christian arms could be turned against the Turks. On 2 February 1530, three weeks before the emperor was to be crowned by Clement in Bologna, the representatives of a dozen states, mostly Italian but also including the empire and Hungary, were asked by the pope to secure the necessary authority to commit their masters to a 'general expedition against the infidels'. Clement authorized crusade-preaching in the empire and for the next two years worked hard to get an expedition going, but his efforts were nullified by hostility between France and the empire and by the Lutheran problem.

Charles's triumph at Tunis revived the hopes for a crusade to the East. In January 1536 Pope Paul III assured King Sigismund I of Poland that he was working for the recovery of Constantinople and in the middle of September 1537 a Veneto-papal league was formed and a commission of cardinals was appointed to plan a campaign, although this coincided with an extraordinary alliance between France and the Turks to attack Italy, which in the event was a failure because their moves were not synchronized. In February 1538 Charles joined the league. If it was successful he was to become emperor in Constantinople and the Hospitallers were to get back Rhodes. He was to pay half the expenses, the Venetians a third and the papacy one-sixth. The pope managed to persuade France and the empire to sign a ten-year truce, but in September the league's fleet was defeated by a Turkish navy under Khair ad-Din's command off Préveza at the entrance to the Gulf of Arta. The pope, who intended, he said, to go on crusade himself, encouraged Charles to take up arms again in the following spring, but the league faded away and in 1540 the Venetians made peace with the Turks, paying an indemnity of 300,000 ducats and ceding to them Návplion and Monemvasia, their last fortresses in the Peloponnese. They were not to recover any important holdings in continental Greece until 1685.

The disaster at Préveza put paid to crusading in the eastern Mediterranean for some time. In the late 1550s Paul IV was not interested and although Pius IV was more conventional – he said he would like to accompany the expedition of another league, for there was no more glorious way to die than on a crusade – the imperial government was anxious for peace on its eastern frontier. Truces, interspersed, it is true, with outbreaks of war, were arranged with the Ottomans in 1545, 1547, 1554, 1562, 1565 and 1568. By the late 1560s, however, it was clear that the Turks were preparing to seize Venetian Cyprus. On 25 March 1570 their demands for its surrender reached Venice. The Republic, which had sought to avoid committing itself to an alliance with Spain since that would involve it in the defence of the Spanish possessions in North Africa, now turned in desperation to King Philip II. A large fleet of papal, Genoese, Venetian, Sicilian and Neapolitan ships was hurriedly assembled, but after reaching Rhodes it withdrew to Crete on hearing of the fall of Nicosia. The Turks had landed on Cyprus on 1 July. Nicosia had fallen on 9 September. Famagusta surrendered after a heroic defence on 5 August 1571.

On the previous 25 May a Holy League of the papacy, Spain and Venice had been formed after intense diplomatic efforts. As in 1538 Spain would pay half the costs, Venice a third and Pius V one-sixth. The Venetians would assist in the defence of Spanish North Africa. This was to be a perpetual alliance, committed to annual campaigns in the eastern Mediterranean, and Don John of Austria, Charles V's bastard son and so Philip of Spain's half-brother, was to be its first commander-in-chief. John reached Naples on 9 August 1571 and was ceremonially presented with the standard which was to fly over his ship: an enormous embroidery of the Crucifixion, embellished with the arms of the three allies. His command, the largest fleet assembled by the Christians in the sixteenth century, supplemented by vessels provided by Savoy, Genoa and the Hospitallers, consisted of 209 galleys, 6 galleasses, 27 large ships and many smaller ones, carrying 30,000 men, 28,000 of whom were professional infantry. It set sail on 16 September from Messina with the aim of engaging a Turkish armada of 275 vessels which had been cruising destructively in the southern Aegean and the Adriatic. Battle was joined on 7 October at the point near Lepanto where the Gulfs of Corinth and Patras (Pátrai) meet. John had more heavy cannon and his gunners were better trained. The Turks were overwhelmed by the Christian gun-fire. Their losses were immense and were said to include 30,000 men killed or captured, 117 galleys taken and 80 vessels destroyed. Lepanto is not regarded nowadays as the watershed it once was, but the effect on Christian morale can scarcely be exaggerated and in a sermon that was printed and widely circulated the French humanist Mark-Anthony Muret declared that the Christians must now push on to Judaea and liberate the Holy Sepulchre. In the Catholic Church the anniversary is still celebrated as the Feast of Our Lady of the Rosary.

The Holy League was reaffirmed on 10 February 1572. Pope Pius made great efforts to extend its membership and on 12 March he issued a long brief addressed to all the faithful, in which he renewed the crusade in terms that would have been familiar to Innocent III nearly four centuries before:

> We admonish, require and exhort every individual to decide to aid this most holy war either in person or with material support. ... To those who do not go personally but send suitable men at their expense according to their means and station in life ... and to those similarly who go personally but at another's expense and put up with the labours and peril of war ... we grant most full and complete pardon, remission and absolution of all their sins, of which they have made oral confession with contrite hearts, the same indulgence which the Roman pontiffs, our predecessors, were accustomed to concede to crusaders going to the aid of the Holy Land. We receive the goods of those going to war ... under the protection of St Peter and ourselves.

A large advance fleet engaged the Turks in early August. The encounters were inconclusive, although they again demonstrated the superiority of Christian gunnery. Joined by John of Austria and with the number of vessels swelled to 195 galleys, 8 galleasses, 25 galleots and 25 other ships, the Christians then tried to take Methóni and Pilos in the Peloponnese. But they failed and in spite of the efforts of the papacy the Holy League dissolved in 1573 with the Venetians making peace with the Ottomans and the Spaniards turning their attention back to North Africa. Pope Gregory XIII spent the rest of his pontificate trying to form another league, but he was not successful.

The general acceptance that crusade ideas were still alive, if decaying, in the sixteenth century is due to the work of Professor Setton, who uncovered enormous quantities of material to support the case. Examples of the traditional language of holy war and grants of indulgences and crusade tenths which, for instance, were being regularly given to Venice, are now known to be abundant, although some elements were now solidifying into forms in which their original functions were obscured. Parts of the Spanish *cruzada*, a tax which originated in the sale of crusade indulgences in return for privileges, were diverted in the sixteenth century to defray the costs of the rebuilding of St Peter's in Rome; indeed the *cruzada* became so divorced from its original purpose that its privileges were issued regularly until the twentieth century and were only abrogated in the diocese of Pueblo, Colorado, in 1945. Since the indulgence was being granted to all who fought the Turks, whether they had taken the cross or not, and the vast majority of the men employed by the leagues were professional soldiers and sailors, it is not entirely clear how many crusaders, that is to say volunteers who had taken the vow, were to be found by the 1570s. Nevertheless, crusading was still too living a force to be ignored by any Catholic ruler. Given the general fear of the Turks, it was anyway in everybody's interest. It is no longer possible for any historian to echo Karl Brandi's view that in the Treaty of Madrid the agreement of Charles V and Francis I to crusade was a 'strange reversion to the outworn beliefs of medieval France and Burgundy!'

On the other hand, no one could deny the fact that the movement was now decaying fast. The treaties and peaces made with the Muslims by those states like Venice and the empire which were in direct contact with the Ottomans are not evidence of this – in the course of this book there have been many references to truces made with the Muslims from the earliest times by rulers whose commitment was incontrovertible – but the Franco-Turkish entente belongs in a different category. The fact that a nation which had been the chief upholder of crusading for so long was now indulging in this kind of *Realpolitik* is evidence that change was in the air. Although Muslim power had been directed by Christian rulers against their co-religionists as early as the twelfth century, the scale of its use in the sixteenth century is a signal that the commitment to an ideal was no longer as strong as it had been.

The movement was decadent but it was not yet dead, although once we pass 1578 we move into evidential twilight. A few examples suggest that crusading was still a force, even if it is impossible to make much of them in the present state of our knowledge.

In 1645 the Turks invaded Venetian Crete. In nearly twenty-four years of war, until Iráklion (Candia) surrendered on 26 September 1669, the Venetian fleet, supplemented by galleys and other ships provided by the popes and the Hospitallers, undertook a series of aggressive operations in the Aegean, with the aim of blocking the Dardanelles. In 1656 the islands of Bozcaada (Tenedos) and Limnos near the mouth of the Dardanelles were taken and were held for a year.

In March 1684, following the second unsuccessful Turkish siege of Vienna, a new Holy League with Poland, the empire and Venice was formed by Pope Innocent XI. It was supported by preaching, crusade tenths, enthusiastic recruitment and prayers of intercession at home, reminiscent of earlier centuries. The League embarked on a war which lasted until 1699 and impoverished the papal curia. Buda was taken in 1686, Belgrade was held from 1688 to 1690 and there was a consolidation of Christian gains in Hungary and Transylvania. Between 1685 and 1687 the Venetians occupied almost the whole of the Peloponnese and they held Athens from October 1687 to April 1688, blowing up the Parthenon in the process of taking it. They seized the island of Levkás in 1684 and they held Chios for five months in 1694–5.

The Turks went to war again in 1715, reoccupying the Peloponnese and taking the island of Tínos, which the Venetians had ruled for over five hundred years. In 1716 the emperor Charles VI made an alliance with Venice. A Christian army under Prince Eugene of Savoy inflicted severe defeats on the Turks in the Balkans, taking Petrovaradin, Timişoara (Temesvár), the last Muslim fortress in what was then Hungary, and Belgrade in 1716–17.

Indulgences were issued for the defence of Crete and Vienna. Thousands of 'volunteers' fought in Crete and in the armies of the Holy League of 1684, which was a good deal more successful than the leagues of the sixteenth century. Were these volunteers crusaders? No researcher has yet examined these seventeenth-century conflicts in terms of crusading, but it seems that we are justified at least in supposing that the movement was still being expressed in them.

The Hospitallers of St John and Malta

It certainly survived in the last order-state. Within a year of their evacuation of Rhodes the Hospitallers of St John were negotiating for a new base. On 23 March 1530 the emperor Charles V granted them the islands of Malta and Gozo and the North African city of Tripoli, putting them in the front line of the defence of the Spanish African holdings in just the way his predecessors the kings of Castile had used the Spanish military orders. Eighteen months later the Hospitallers tried to demonstrate their worth to the general Christian cause by sacking Methóni in the Peloponnese. The pope was not particularly impressed and said that it would have been better for them to have occupied the place instead of looting it, but this raid probably led to the suggestion in 1533 that they be given charge of Koróni, which had recently been recaptured. Their surrender of Tripoli to the Turks in 1551 has already been mentioned, but any loss of prestige was more than compensated for by their heroic defence of Malta in 1565 against an enormous and well-equipped Turkish army, sent to clear Constantinople's line of communication with North Africa. On 19 May the invasion force of 25,000 men began to land. To resist them the grand master, John of la Valette, had 8–9,000, including c. 500 brother knights and some brother sergeants-at-arms, 4,000 arquebusiers and 3–4,000 Maltese irregulars. The assault lasted until 8 September when, having sustained very heavy losses, the Turks withdrew in the face of a relief force of c. 12,000 Spaniards and Italians. They left a scene of ruin and desolation on the shore of the Grand Harbour, in the midst of which stood only 600 of the original defenders still capable of bearing arms. Of the 500 brother knights at the start of the siege, 300 were dead and most of the rest were wounded.

The Hospitallers had not been enthusiastic about Malta, a small and infertile island of ninety-five square miles with its fortifications in poor repair. Memories of the past were kept alive by the way the churches built by them – of St John, St Catherine, Our Lady of Victory – were given the same patrons as churches on Rhodes. Nor were they prepared to embark on an ambitious building programme at first: they satisfied themselves with a few simple conventual buildings and the construction of two forts. After 1565, with their reputation enhanced and so much energy expended and blood spilt, their attitude changed. A new city, designed by Francesco Laparelli, decorated by Girolamo Cassar and named after John of la Valette, was built on the peninsula overlooking the Grand Harbour which had been the scene of some of the fiercest fighting. A feature of it was the incorporation of the conventual buildings into the town rather than in a separate compound, so that the whole city became as it were a monastic enclosure. It was massively fortified and the Hospitallers continued to improve the fortifications around the Grand Harbour in the seventeenth and eighteenth centuries; in fact, although there was a large Turkish raid in 1614, no serious invasion came before 1798.

Since the early 1990s the internal history of the order in the early modern period has been revised and a far more positive picture is being drawn of it. It is true that the brothers' vows were being fulfilled in a more flexible manner, that many commanders were absentee, that others lived alone on the orders' estates the lives of affluent country gentlemen and that the order's government was increasingly autocratic and geronto-cratic, since seniority was everything. Although between 1526 and 1612 chapters-general met on average every six years, none was summoned between 1631 and 1776, when financial concerns forced one on the grand master. For most of the seventeenth and eighteenth centuries, therefore, the order's management depended solely on the master, whose title had been elaborated into grand master during the Rhodian period. But it was far from being decadent. In 1700 it still had 560 commanderies throughout Catholic Europe. Its devotional life benefited from Counter-Reformation ideas. There was the serious pursuit of pious, charitable and missionary goals, often in collaboration with the Jesuits, alongside the traditional concerns for the care of the sick poor and the defence of Christendom. The order still attracted recruits and between 1635 and 1740 the number of brothers, predominantly knights, rose from 1,715 to 2,240. Dr Anthony Luttrell has pointed out that although it was a noble corporation the Hospital attracted 'entrants with a remarkable and vigorous range of thoroughly up-to-date military, diplomatic, scientific and artistic interests and talents'. The order's magnificent library in Valletta still testifies to the cultured interests of many brothers, who included men like Louis de Boisgelin and Déodat de Dolomieu. A corollary, of course, was the arrival of Enlightenment ideas, and even freemasonry, among them.

The Hospitallers remained a foreign elite, a closed oligarchic caste which refused to admit into its higher ranks even the Maltese nobles, whose sons could only enter as chaplains, although families did sometimes arrange for children to be born in Sicily in the hope of qualifying them for admission. The grand masters ruled their order-state as benevolent, if rather unimaginative, despots. They built hospitals, encouraged works of art, founded a famous school of anatomy in 1676, to supplement their hospital, and a university in 1768. They ran a health service for the population, which rose from c. 20,000 in 1530 to over 90,000 in 1788, mainly in response to the employment provided by the dockyards and arsenals. After 1566, when the decision to found Valletta was taken, the building campaign attracted labourers from the countryside and about 8,000 workers from Sicily, and the urban complex around the Grand Harbour grew rapidly. By 1590 there were 7,750 residents in Valletta and 'The Three Cities', by 1614 c. 11,200 and by 1632 c. 18,600. Like Rhodes, Malta became an important commercial centre, handling a growing volume of shipping and acting as the entrepôt for eastern goods on their way even to the Americas; the United States established a consulate there as early as 1783. The quarantine service was internationally regarded as the most efficient in the Mediterranean. Commercial relations with France were particularly close and half the shipping which called at Malta in the eighteenth century was French. It was from this that Napoleon's ambitions partly sprang.

Malta was not legally autonomous. It was a fief of the kingdom of Sicily and there was a political crisis as late as 1753 when King Charles VII of Naples claimed his rights as sovereign. Stage by stage, however, the grand masters had been assuming the attributes of sovereignty. They had begun to mint their own coinage as soon as they had conquered Rhodes and from that island they had sent ambassadors to the courts of Europe, whose function was often to defend their estates and privileges from predators. Their ambassadors from Malta were officially received in Rome, France, Spain and Austria. From perhaps as early as the fifteenth century they were creating honorary knighthoods for laymen closely associated with their work. Their claims to sovereignty were to some extent recognized in 1607 when, nearly four hundred years after the grand master of the Teutonic Knights, the grand master of the Hospitallers was made a prince of the empire, but it was Grand Master Manoel Pinto (1741–73) who completed the process by adopting the closed crown, the signifier of full sovereignty.

The Hospitallers continued to fulfil their military role effectively. They played a part in nearly all the leagues and major campaigns against the Turks. To this day the keys of the fortresses of Passava, Lepanto and Patras in Greece and Hammamet in Tunisia, which were stormed between 1601 and 1603, hang in the chapel of Our Lady of Philermos in their conventual church in Valletta. In 1664 they attacked Algiers and in 1707 they helped the Spaniards hold Oran. Their ships were regularly at sea, cruising along the North African coast and throughout an area bordered by Sicily and Sardinia in the west and Crete and the Peloponnese in the east, with the aim of clearing the Mediterranean of Muslim pirates. As we have seen, they had a fleet of seven or eight war-galleys; after 1705 they gradually replaced these with a squadron of four or five ships of the line, mounting fifty or sixty guns each. Although the maintenance of this force was a very great expense – in the seventeenth century an average of 45 per cent of the headquarters' revenues was spent on it – the Hospitallers kept up an aggressive and quite damaging onslaught on Muslim shipping. The Turkish attack on Tripoli in 1551 was partly in retaliation for a series of assaults by them on neighbouring Muslim ports. In the years from 1722 to 1741 their line ships accounted for one Turkish and fifteen Barbary vessels and their galleys for a further five ships from Tripoli. Their fleet was still actively engaged in 1798, the year Malta fell. The naval training they gave their knights was much admired. When the empress Catherine the Great of Russia wanted a galley fleet in the Baltic she asked for the assistance of a knight of St John. Famous French sailors who were brother knights included the Chevaliers Tourville and d'Hocquincourt and the marquis of Valbette in the seventeenth century and the great Bailiff de Suffren in the eighteenth. Their formal naval actions were supplemented by the *corso*, 38 per cent of the operations of which were under Hospitaller command in the earlier eighteenth century, although the indigenous Maltese also played a full part. As late as 1675 there were between twenty and thirty active corsairs operating out of Malta, although the numbers later declined. By 1740 there were only between ten and twenty; thereafter they dwindled almost to nothing.

By the middle of the eighteenth century, in fact, the war with the Ottomans was dying away and the Hospitallers' role was rapidly becoming out-of-date. Their order was devastated by the French Revolution and the revolutionary wars; it was, after all, one of the classic expressions of the *ancien régime*. In 1792 all its property in France was seized and by 1797 it had lost all its estates west of the Rhine, in Switzerland and in northern Italy. Its revenues fell by two-thirds. A new grand master, Ferdinand of Hompesch, made approaches to Austria and Russia which alarmed the French and in June 1798 Napoleon, who had his eye on Malta for commercial and strategic reasons, brought his fleet into Maltese waters on his way to Egypt and demanded admission to the Grand Harbour. When the knights tried to stand on their rights as neutrals he attacked and it is evidence of the extent to which the order had decayed that it was in no state to resist him. Of the 332 knights on the island 50 were too old or ill to fight and the rest were divided as to what to do. Command was in the hands of brothers chosen for seniority and not merit. The guns were ancient and had not been fired in anger for a century; the powder was found to be rotten and the shot defective. The urban militia was inexperienced and undisciplined. It is hard to say who were the more frightened: the militia of the French, or the order, which had recently faced a popular uprising, of the militia. Obsolete defensive plans were put into operation. In two days and with hardly any bloodshed the garrison, which was scattered throughout the island rather than concentrated in Valletta, had been overcome. Hompesch and his brother knights were ignominiously expelled.

The crusading movement ended with the fall of Malta on 13 June 1798, although the Order of the Hospital of St John survives today, still recognized as sovereign by many states, still an Order of the Church but, although technically still a military order, now devoting itself entirely to the care of the poor and the sick. Like the Teutonic Order, it is associated with non-Catholic chivalric Orders of St John which share its history. There is real irony in the last act on Malta. Just over 700 years after Pope Urban II had called for the service of Christian knights, here these knights still were, still predominantly French and obsessive about their status, as the armigerous mosaic memorials carpeting the floor of their conventual church in Valletta, the cenotaph of chivalry, testify. The order-state of these brothers, heirs of the men extolled by St Bernard, many of them descendants of twelfth-century crusaders, was a survival of the type of crusading polity proposed by the theoreticians of the fourteenth century. It collapsed before the fleet of a French general bound for Egypt of all places. Napoleon, of course, was not a crusader, but he was more successful in Egypt than Louis IX had been. And the story has a final twist to it. Napoleon confiscated the precious stones and metals that adorned the Hospitallers' relics, many of which they had carried with them all the way from Palestine to Malta, by way of Cyprus and Rhodes. A lot of this treasure still lies at the bottom of Aboukir Bay, to which it was sent when Nelson attacked the French fleet, but Napoleon disposed of some of it in the markets of Alexandria and Cairo to pay for his troops. So precious metal acquired in the East by representatives of the crusading movement returned six centuries later.

The death of crusading

The crusading movement died a lingering death. By the fifteenth century growing disinterest in Germany and perhaps in France witnessed to disillusionment with the papacy. In the sixteenth century the Reformation reduced the Catholic population of Europe and involved everyone in introspective and bitter conflict. By the seventeenth century adherence to crusading was confined to the popes, those nations directly confronting the Turks and those families from which the Order of the Hospital of St John and the Teutonic Order recruited their members. The last crusades were that of Sebastian of Portugal in 1578 and the Spanish Armada ten years later. The last crusading league was the Holy League from 1684 to 1699. The last crusade vows may well have been made in the late seventeenth or early eighteenth century. The last functioning order-state was Hospitaller Malta until 1798.

In the light of the evidence presented in the last two chapters the old explanations of decline are no longer convincing. Failure in the East cannot have bred too much disillusionment and the rise of nation-states in the West cannot have created too alien a climate for survival if the movement kept going for another five hundred years. Even the Reformation and Counter-Reformation did not kill it off. It had, of course, changed by the sixteenth century, but that only demonstrates its adaptability. It is surely the case that its demise was the result of something more fundamental than sentiment or political environment. The moral theology on which it rested passed out of currency in two stages. In the sixteenth century Christ's authority for the use of force came to be challenged. A catalyst for this was the critical reaction of the Dominican Francisco de Vitoria to atrocities committed by his compatriots against the New-World Indians. For Vitoria and his followers, particularly Francisco Suarez and Felipe Ayala, the chief justification of violence could not be divine plan, but had to be 'the common good', an Aristotelian concept expressed in an embryonic form in the work of Thomas Aquinas. To Vitoria, Suarez and Ayala it was the defence of the common good, which was the prerogative of every community, that provided authority and some of the justification. Just-war arguments moved quickly from the field of moral theology to that of international law, a step developed within decades by Alberico Gentili and Hugo Grotius. God was removed from the equation and just war lost the lustre of divine approval. The next stage in the evolution of modern justifications of violence was reached in the nineteenth century and was probably an achievement of the peace movement which swept Europe and America after the Napoleonic Wars and split in the 1830s into two wings, pacifist and moderate. The conviction that violence was intrinsically evil, unrecognized by earlier war theorists, was borrowed from pacifism and the argument was developed that force could nevertheless be condoned as the lesser of evils.

At any rate, holy war was becoming unfashionable by the eighteenth century and was being regarded as the product of a fanatical and quaintly superstitious age. Intellectuals looked on crusades with a mixture of sorrow and contempt. For Denis Diderot, the *encyclopédiste*, the consequences for Europe of 'these horrible wars' were 'the depopulation of its nations, the enrichment of monasteries, the impoverishment of the nobility, the ruin of ecclesiastical discipline, contempt for agriculture, scarcity of cash and an infinity of vexations'. To David Hume they 'have ever since engaged the curiosity of mankind, as the most signal and most durable monument of human folly that has yet appeared in any age or nation'. Edward Gibbon's judgement was that they

> have checked rather than forwarded the maturity of Europe. The lives and labours of millions which were buried in the East would have been more profitably employed in the improvement of their native country: the accumulated stock of industry and wealth would have overflowed in navigation and trade; and the Latins would have been enriched and enlightened by a pure and friendly correspondence with the climates of the East.

Despised by fashionable opinion the last vestiges of crusading were too demoralized to survive. 'Malta [wrote Napoleon] ... certainly possessed immense physical means of resistance, but no moral strength whatever.'

Afterword

Although trenchant views of the kind expressed by the Enlightenment thinkers were occasionally voiced in the early nineteenth century, a romantic penumbra began to envelope Europe's crusading past now that Christian holy war had been extinguished as a living force. Romance was fanned by the prevailing obsession for genealogy, by freemasonry and its supposed roots among the Templars and by the continuing existence of the Teutonic Order and the Hospital of St John of Jerusalem (now known as the Order of Malta). The crusades soon began to attract the interest of writers and historians. Friedrich Wilken, who knew Arabic and Persian and whose *Geschichte der Kreuzzüge* appeared in seven volumes between 1807 and 1832, was the first scholar to combine western and eastern materials in a critical source-based account up to the early fourteenth century. Sober and careful blow-by-blow narrative was already becoming a feature of German history. It is still to be found today, in a form called micro-history by Wilken's heirs in America, where his scholarship has been very influential. One cannot get away from the fact, however, that micro-history can be very dull, an adjective which would never be used of two other works written at about the same time as Wilken's: Sir Walter Scott's novel *The Talisman*, which was published in 1825, and Joseph François Michaud's six-volume *Histoire des croisades*, which appeared between 1812 and 1822.

The critical romantics

At the heart of Scott's *The Talisman* is the story of a friendship between an apparently poor Scottish knight serving on the Third Crusade, who turns out to be a prince and wins the love of the lady he admires, and Saladin, who appears in a bewildering array of disguises, including that of a skilled physician who cures King Richard I of England. It is striking that throughout the novel the Muslims are portrayed in a far better light than the crusaders, whose personalities range from the brash, intemperate and childish to the proud and deceitful. In his introduction Scott wrote that

the warlike character of Richard I, wild and generous, a pattern of chivalry, with all its extravagant virtues and its no less absurd errors, was opposed to that of Saladin, in which the Christian and English monarch showed all the cruelty and violence of an Eastern Sultan; and

Saladin, on the other hand displayed the deep policy and prudence of a European sovereign.

Scott may have been a romantic, but he was also an heir of eighteenth-century intellectual opinion and he represented a school of thought which treated the subject at the same time both romantically and critically. Its disapproval was reinforced by a Protestant conviction that crusading was yet another expression of Catholic bigotry and cruelty. It was not hard for Scott and others to portray crusaders as brave and glamorous but backward and unenlightened, crudely assailing more sophisticated and civilized Muslims. Leaving aside the actual state of cultural development in western Europe and the Near East respectively in the twelfth century – and they were not nearly as far apart as the romantics supposed – any reading of history which placed the crusaders in one context – the central middle ages – and their opponents in another – the nineteenth century – was anachronistic. Under his faux-oriental clothing Scott's Saladin was not so much an eastern figure as a liberal European gentleman, beside whom medieval westerners would always have made a poor showing.

Nevertheless, *The Talisman* was Scott's most popular crusade novel after *Ivanhoe*, in which crusaders were also harshly portrayed. It was dramatized on many occasions and was translated into many European languages. It inspired painters in Britain, France and Italy and its picture of Saladin influenced generations of writers and politicians. Saladin's ruinous tomb in Damascus began to feature on European sight-seeing tours, but it took an overblown act of homage by Kaiser Wilhelm II of Germany, on a visit in 1898 which will be described later, to bring him fully to the attention of the Muslim public, which had almost completely forgotten him.

The potency of the critically romantic approach was demonstrated by the way that it continues to suffuse writing on the crusades, scholarly as well as popular. Indeed the most widely read and prestigious history in English, that published in the early 1950s by Sir Steven Runciman, another Lowland Calvinist, was almost what Walter Scott would have written had he been more knowledgeable. In it the crusaders were characterized as courageous and colourful, but at the same time boorish and not very bright, and Scott could himself have written the peroration with which it famously ended.

There was so much courage and so little honour, so much devotion and so little understanding. High ideals were besmirched by cruelty and greed, enterprise and endurance by a blind and narrow self-righteousness; and the Holy War itself was nothing more than a long act of intolerance in the name of God, which is a sin against the Holy Ghost.

The romantic imperialists

On the other hand, the epic *Histoire* of Joseph François Michaud, which went through four editions under the Restoration and a further five under the July Monarchy, was imbued with a passionate nationalism. A fervent royalist who began his researches under a Napoleonic régime he despised, Michaud believed that crusading had enriched all the European nations engaged in it:

> Names made famous by this war are still today objects of pride to families and country. The most positive of the results of the First Crusade is the glory of our fathers, this glory which is also a real benefit for a nation.

He went further and maintained that of all European countries France had benefited the most:

> France would one day become the model and centre of European civilization. The holy wars contributed much to this happy development and one can perceive this from the First Crusade onwards.

His *Histoire* made much more of a splash than did Wilken's with the European public and the nationalist euphoria it generated in France found expression in the Salles des Croisades in the Château of Versailles. These formed part of King Louis Philippe's scheme of decoration for the palace, which was to become a museum dedicated to the glories of France. The five rooms contained over 120 paintings illustrating scenes from crusading history, of which the most famous is Eugène Delacroix's *Entry of the Crusaders into Constantinople on the Fourth Crusade* (now in the Louvre), and the coats-of-arms of families whose ancestors had been crusaders. There was fierce competition among French nobles to be included. When the galleries opened in 1840 a total of 316 families were represented, but a storm of protest was whipped up by others who demanded inclusion and produced documents, many of them forged, attesting to crusading ancestry. The rooms had to be closed and were only reopened in 1843 after further coats-of-arms had been added.

The French were the first to describe their contemporary imperialist ventures in crusading terms. Their occupation of Algeria in 1830 was compared to Louis IX's descent on Tunis in 1270 and in an abridged edition of Michaud's *Histoire* published in 1838 his collaborator Jean-Joseph Poujoulat averred that 'the conquest of Algiers in 1830 and our recent expeditions in Africa are nothing other than crusades'. Two rooms at Versailles were dedicated to critical moments in the Algerian campaign and on seeing Horace Vernet's painting of the French assault on Constantine in 1837 a contemporary exclaimed that:

We find there again, after an interval of five hundred years, the French nation fertilizing with its blood the burning plains studded with the tents of Islam. These men are the heirs of Charles Martel, Godfrey of Bouillon, Robert Guiscard and Philip Augustus, resuming the unfinished labours of their ancestors. Missionaries and warriors, they every day extend the boundaries of Christendom.

French knights of Malta, whose minds had been awash with a half-baked scheme to assist Greek rebels against the Turks and recover the island of Rhodes for their order, proposed that they be given Algeria to manage as an order-state. In the 1850s French military campaigns in south-east Asia were bathed in crusading rhetoric and when the government of Napoleon III decided to intervene in Lebanon on behalf of the Maronites there was talk of actually proclaiming one. In 1860 Napoleon addressed the French troops leaving for the Levant in Michaud-like language:

> You are leaving for Syria. ... On that distant soil, rich in great memories ... you will show yourselves to be the worthy descendants of those heroes who carried the banner of Christ gloriously in that land.

Charles-Martial Allemand-Lavigerie, archbishop of Algiers from 1867 and cardinal from 1882 until his death ten years later, whose brain was saturated with crusading imagery, drew up a Rule for a new military order which was to operate in North Africa and he proposed sending members of the surviving military orders – elderly gentlemen who now hardly qualified as warriors – to protect Catholic missionaries in East Africa.

France was by no means the only country to develop a myth of national crusading history and to associate it with the imperialist present. Belgium adopted Godfrey of Bouillon. Norwegian nationalists looked to King Sigurd. Germany had eight crusading rulers, above all Frederick Barbarossa. Spain had the glories of the Reconquest, a national war of liberation fought against the Moors, with heroes like Ferdinand III of Castile; its invasion of Morocco in the 1850s was also described as a crusade. England had Richard I, Coeur-de-Lion. Feelings were running so high over atrocities reputedly committed by the Ottomans in Bulgaria in 1876 that the author of a pamphlet written for English Catholics had to explain why a crusade could not be launched against the Turks. Thirty-six years earlier Sir Richard Hillary, an enthusiastic member of the body which was to become the Most Venerable Order of St John, one of the non-Catholic Orders of Chivalry upholding the traditions of the Hospitallers, publicized an impractical project for the liberation of the Holy Land and its government by the Order of Malta.

The idea of the crusade as an instrument of nationalism and imperialism was reinforced by the First World War and its aftermath.

A British army invaded Palestine and in the dismemberment of the Ottoman empire which followed Britain and France occupied Palestine and Syria and Lebanon under mandate from the League of Nations. Although the British commander, General Allenby, never made the remark 'today the wars of the crusaders are ended' attributed to him – indeed steps were taken to avoid giving offence, particularly as Muslims were serving with the British forces – the magazine *Punch* published a cartoon entitled 'The Last Crusade', which had Richard I gazing at Jerusalem from a distance with the caption: 'At last my dream come true.' On arriving in Damascus in 1920 the first French military governor of Syria, General Henri Gouraud, was heard to say, 'Behold, Saladin, we have returned.'

The establishment of the French Mandate generated a wave of historical literature, one theme of which was that the achievements of the crusaders provided the first chapter in a history which had culminated in modern imperialism. Jean Longnon wrote that: 'The name of Frank has remained [in the Levant] a symbol of nobility, courage and generosity ... and if our country has been called on to receive the protectorate of Syria, this is a result of that influence.' Referring to the end of the Latin settlements in Palestine and Syria, René Grousset concluded his three-volume *Histoire des croisades* (1934–6) with the words: 'The Templars only held until 1303 the islet of Ruad, south of Tortosa, from where one day – in 1914 – the "Franks" would again set foot in Syria.' The American heirs of Wilken disapproved strongly of Grousset's tone and planned to counter it with an American general history, which took so many decades to complete that many of the original contributors had died before their chapters were written and several Europeans, including pupils of Grousset, had to be enlisted.

The romantic imperialists believed that the crusaders' achievements were now being replicated and that backward Muslim societies were going to benefit from Christian rule. François René de Chateaubriand, Michaud's friend and another Frenchman for whom the history of the crusades recalled national glory, was of the opinion that their true purpose had been the destruction of an Islam which was an enemy of civilization, since it knew nothing of liberty. This idea, Edward Said has written (in *Orientalism*), acquired 'an almost unbearable, next to mindless, authority in European writing'. The flavour of positive imperialism was particularly apparent in Sir Claude Conder's *The Latin Kingdom of Jerusalem* (1897):

The Crusades were no wild raids on Palestine resulting only in misery and destruction. The kingdom of Jerusalem was the model of just and moderate rule, such as we boast to have given to India, under somewhat similar conditions.

Conder's publisher, the Palestine Exploration Fund, advertised his book by recalling that 'The condition of the Orientals [is] almost the same as that when Europe intervened in the Eastern question in the days of Godfrey of Bouillon and of King Richard Lionheart'.

Neo-imperialists: Liberal, Marxist, Zionist, Muslim

Romantic imperialism was clothing European colonial expansion inappropriately in crusading armour at a time when the crusading movement was extinct. It was bound to suffer as imperialism itself came to be reviled, opening the way for searing critics like Norman Daniel, for whom western assumptions of Islamic inferiority were based on perverse ideas generated in the period of the crusades. French imperialistic history, which was associated with conservative Catholicism, had stressed the ideological forces motivating crusaders, but by the 1920s and 1930s the crusades, stripped of their ethic, were being interpreted in social and economic terms by Liberal as well as Marxist economic historians, all of whom had inherited from the imperialists the belief that crusading was an early example of colonialism.

This neo-imperialistic and materialistic interpretation became popular orthodoxy, although specialists on the crusades had played no part in its development and no one has even half-proved it by research. It seems to have gained currency among crusade historians only in the 1950s, when in the vanguard were the Israelis, particularly the best known of them, Joshua Prawer, for whom the portrayal of the crusaders as proto-colonialists was in accord with Zionism's interpretation of the history of the Promised Land since the diaspora. Prawer's powerful adoption of neo-imperialism helped to impress it on the mind of the general public.

Among the most enthusiastic proponents of the neo-imperialistic interpretation have also been Muslim historians. Their writing of crusade history originated in the 1890s, when the Ottoman empire was in crisis. Faced by revolt and disintegration in the Balkans and under pressure from Britain, France and Russia, the empire had been forced to recognize the independence of Romania, Serbia and Montenegro, and the autonomy of Bulgaria, and to surrender territories to the Russians, Greeks, French and British. The response of Sultan Abdulhamid II to this chain of disasters had been to turn to pan-Islamism, an ideology enshrining the unity of all Muslims under one world authority. He was a pious man who took his role as caliph very seriously, particularly as his right to hold the caliphate was being challenged. But he went further. He publicized his conviction that the Europeans had embarked on a new 'crusade'. In using this term he was only echoing the rhetoric that had washed round western Europe for more than half a century, but his language was taken up by the pan-Islamic press and in his introduction to the first Muslim history of the crusading movement, published in 1899, the author, Sayyid 'Ali al-Hariri, wrote that 'Our most glorious sultan, Abdulhamid II, has rightly remarked that Europe is now carrying out a crusade against us in the form of a political campaign'.

This was an entirely new development. One often reads that Muslims have inherited from their medieval ancestors bitter memories of the violence of the crusaders. Nothing could be further from the truth. Muslims had not hitherto shown much interest in the crusades, on which they looked back with indifference and complacency. They believed, after all, that they had beaten the crusaders comprehensively. They had driven them from the lands they had settled in the Levant and had been triumphant in the Balkans, where they had occupied far more territory than the western settlers had ever ruled in the East.

The sudden awakening of interest among them was reinforced by the behaviour on a visit to Damascus in November 1898 of Kaiser Wilhelm II of Germany, who laid a satin flag and a wreath, with an inscription dedicated to 'the Hero Sultan Saladin', on Saladin's delapidated tomb. He was to pay for the restoration of the mausoleum and the construction of a very un-Islamic marble tomb-chest, on which rested another wreath, this time bronze gilt and inscribed 'From one great emperor to another'. At a banquet afterwards the kaiser expressed his delight at treading the same soil as Saladin, 'one of the most chivalrous rulers in history', who, he added, had been 'a knight without fear or blame, who often had to teach his adversaries the true nature of chivalry'. In this bombastic echo of *The Talisman* Saladin was reintroduced to the Muslims in the Levant. A year later the Egyptian poet Ahmad Shawqi asked how it could be that Saladin's greatness had been ignored by Muslim writers until they had been reminded of it by Kaiser Wilhelm.

At any rate, the Islamic world was aroused by an authoritative statement by the caliph that crusades were still in train at a time when two popular but contradictory western constructs were being widely disseminated. In the critically romantic version established by Walter Scott, barbarous and destructive crusaders, morally and culturally inferior, had faced civilized and modern-thinking Muslims. In the romantic imperialistic one, originating in the writings of Joseph François Michaud, these same crusaders had brought enlightenment to a heathen world and their heirs were now returning to complete the work they had begun. It was easy to gloss this with the view that Europe, having lost the first round in the crusades, had embarked on another, a conspiracy theory which struck a chord in Arab Nationalism, beginning to emerge in response to the British and French occupation of much of North Africa and the Levant and the settlement of Jews in Palestine.

From the first approach the Muslims took the idea of a destructive and savage West, which had benefited by absorbing their civilized values while at the same time leaving a trail of wreckage in its wake.

Is it possible to imagine [asked one North African historian] any substantial advantage that the Islamic world has drawn from the crusades? Indeed, how could Islam benefit from contacts established with an inferior, backward civilization?

Within fifteen years of the kaiser's visit an Arab author, warning against the threat posed by Zionist settlement in Palestine, had adopted Saladin's name as a *nom de plume* and a university named after him was opened in Jerusalem in 1915. In the account by the Lebanese novelist Mahmoud Darwish of the invasion of Lebanon by the Israelis in 1982 their actions, described in much the same terms as Scott's crusaders, are compared unfavourably to the courtesy of Saladin: 'Our water has been cut off by those acting on behalf of leftover crusaders, yet Saladin used to send ice and fruits to the enemy.'

From romantic imperialism Muslim writers took the idea of a continuing western assault on them. Already in 1920 one author praised Saladin for thwarting the *first* European attempt to subdue the East. Under the influence of the economic historians to whom I have already referred, Arab Nationalists saw the crusades as manifestations of western colonialist avarice conducted under the guise of religion and constituting the first chapter in European colonial expansion. In 1934 it was being suggested that 'the West is still waging crusading wars against Islam under the guise of political and economic imperialism'. Others developed the theme that after losing the first round the West was consumed with a spirit of vengeance; indeed, the creation of the state of Israel on the very ground occupied by the kingdom of Jerusalem had been an act of vengeful malice. Mahmoud Darwish wrote of the Israeli siege of Beirut in 1982 as 'revenge for all medieval history'.

The Islamization of neo-imperialistic history

To the Nationalists, their struggle for independence was a predominantly Arab riposte to a crusade which was still being waged against them. From the 1970s onwards, however, they were being challenged by a renewed and militant pan-Islamism, the adherents of which, believing Islam to be an indivisible entity, a brotherhood dedicated to the worship of the one God embracing all races, anathematized Nationalism because it was often secular and was, of its nature, divisive. This did not prevent them from adopting the Nationalist interpretation of crusade history. They then globalized it. Whereas the Nationalists' vision of a crusading past and present underwrote an Arab struggle for freedom from colonial oppression, to the Islamists western agression and, above all, infidel penetration into any part of the *dar al-Islam* justified the waging of *jihad* on a world scale. Inspired by the arguments of their leading ideologue, Sayyid Qutb, they maintained that 'crusading' was a term that could be applied to any offensive, including a drive for economic or political hegemony, against Islam anywhere by those who called themselves Christian or were in the Christian tradition and to any aggressive action by their surrogates, like Zionists or Marxists. Indeed 'international Zionism' and 'international Communism' were ideologies employed by the imperialism of the outside world to mask its 'Crusaderism': the ambition of the old Christian enemy to subvert Islam and destroy believers.

The militant wing of Islamism, composed of the so-called jihadist-salafists, was also inspired by the writings of a figure from the middle ages, the charismatic Ibn Taymiyya. For him the priority of the *jihad* in his day was not to wage war beyond the frontiers but to purge Sunni Islam of alien elements, such as heretics and infidels. So the *jihad* was to turn inwards and create by force a united and purified society dedicated to God, which could then focus its attention on the world beyond. Jihadist-salafists were, therefore, particularly emotional about infidel penetration, which they believe defiled Islam.

> The Arabian Peninsula has never – since Allah made it flat, created its desert, and encircled it with seas – been stormed by any forces like the crusader armies, spreading in it like locusts, eating its riches and wiping out its plantations.

Crusading was expressed no less in the Soviet invasion of Afghanistan than in American activities in the Near and Middle East.

> This is a battle of Muslims against the global crusaders. . . . God, who provided us with his support and kept us steadfast until the Soviet Union was defeated, is able to provide us once more with his support to defeat America on the same land and with the same people.

In a war of civilizations,

> our goal is for our nation to unite in the face of the Christian crusade. . . . This is a recurring war. The original crusade brought Richard from Britain, Louis from France and Barbarossa from Germany. Today the crusading countries rushed as soon as Bush raised the cross. They accepted the rule of the cross.

It was this radical Islamist version of neo-imperialist crusade history which suddenly and spectacularly forced itself on the world outside, since it provided the historical and moral justification for acts of extreme violence.

The challenge to historiographical tradition

So far I have traced the critically romantic, romantic imperialistic and neo-imperialistic lines of crusade historiography since 1800, the last being shared by Marxists, Liberals, Zionists and Arab Nationalists, who interpreted crusading in materialistic terms, and Islamists, who did not, since they tended to recognize that crusaders were motivated by ideology. In western academic circles, however, or at least in those in which historians of the crusades are to be found, the various mutations in the line of descent from Michaud are now facing a serious challenge.

This originated in intellectual developments after the Second World War, which generated a re-examination of the history of Christian violence. A renewed interest in the theory of just force, fuelled by controversy over the Nuremberg Trials and by debates about nuclear deterrence and proportionality, coincided with the re-emergence in the militant wing of the movement for Christian Liberation of violence as an attractive and theologically viable option. The use of force on behalf of the poor was justified by some Christians, particularly in Latin America, as an act of charity in accordance with Christ's intentions for mankind and as a moral imperative. But as academic interest grew it did not take long for a major question to be asked: What was a crusade anyway?

Finding an acceptable general definition of crusading has always been so difficult that it has often been considered best to leave it well alone. The writers of the multi-volume histories of the twentieth century – René Grousset in the 1930s, Steven Runciman in the 1950s and the team led by Kenneth Setton in the 1960s – never explicitly stated what they stood for and there was anyway a school of thought, represented by a party now known as the generalists, which believed that any attempt at definition was more limiting than helpful and held that any Christian religious war fought for God, or in the belief that its prosecution was furthering his intentions for mankind, could be described as a crusade. Its most influential representative was Carl Erdmann, a German nationalist who at the same time hated Naziism and wrote, possibly deliberately, an extraordinarily unideological study of the development of crusade ideas. Another group of scholars, mostly French and known today as the popularists, proposed that the essence of crusading lay not with the popes or the knights, but in a prophetic, eschatological, collective exaltation arising in the peasantry and the urban proletariat.

Although there have been recent attempts to revive them, generalism and popularism were always advocated by a minority. Most scholars are nowadays classed rather crudely as either traditionalists or pluralists. Traditionalists treat as authentic only the campaigns fought for the recovery of Jerusalem, or in its defence. For them, therefore, crusading is essentially to be seen in the context of the warfare between Christianity and Islam which has been endemic since the seventh century. Pluralists, on the other hand, follow the medieval popes in maintaining that an array of campaigns, preached as crusades and fought by men and women who had taken crusade vows and enjoyed crusade privileges, were as authentic as those to or in aid of Jerusalem, although many of them took place in other theatres of war and many were preached long after Jerusalem had faded from the scene.

Pluralism is potent enough to have upset many of those who hold to traditional views. Jean Richard, the last surviving representative of the old French imperialist line, reluctantly accepted it, but went on to argue that crusades to the East were characterized by 'a visceral attachment to the Holy Land', which gave them their particular features. This of course put them back into a special category of their own. Hans Mayer rejected pluralism utterly in favour of the conviction that only expeditions with a Levantine goal were authentic. Otto (R. C.) Smail was fiercely opposed to it towards the end of his life. So was Joshua Prawer. The intensity of the feelings of these well-known scholars was an indication of the seriousness of a challenge which is based on the fact that pluralists do not share their conviction that crusading is defined by its hostility towards Islam and by its theatres of operation in the Levant. The Muslims become less significant. Although they remain the most important of the counter-forces, consideration has also to be given to other theatres of war and other enemies: Pagan Wends, Balts and Lithuanians, Shamanist Mongols, Orthodox Russians and Greeks, Cathar and Hussite heretics and even Catholic political opponents of the papacy.

There are signs that younger historians, whose priorities are diferent, are turning away from what is in danger of becoming a sterile debate, but it is heartening to find the 200-year-old historiographical tradition, which originated in Scott, Wilken and Michaud, being questioned.

Bibliography

A select bibliography of secondary works

BIBLIOGRAPHIES

The best bibliography is H. E. Mayer, *Bibliographie zur Geschichte der Kreuzzüge* (1960), supplemented, for works published 1958–67, by Professor Mayer's 'Literaturbericht über die Geschichte der Kreuzzüge', *Historische Zeitschrift* Sonderheft 3 (1969) and for the years 1967–82 by a 'Select Bibliography of the Crusades', in collaboration with J. McLellan, in K. M. Setton (editor-in-chief), *A History of the Crusades* 6 (1989). Mayer's regular short reviews for *Deutsches Archiv für Erforschung des Mittelalters* are worth consulting. The lists of recent publications and the accounts of work in progress in the *Bulletin of the Society for the Study of the Crusades and the Latin East* are a good guide to what is being brought out year by year. The *Bulletin* has now been incorporated in a journal, entitled *Crusades*, which has been appearing since 2002 and also includes reviews.

For Islamic history J. Sauvaget, *Introduction to the History of the Muslim East*, recast by C. Cahen (1965) is still useful and there are good modern bibliographies in the *New Cambridge Medieval History*.

HISTORIOGRAPHY

The best treatment of historiography has been written by G. Constable, 'The Historiography of the Crusades', *The Crusades from the Perspective of Byzantium and the Muslim World*, ed. A. E. Laiou and R. P. Mottahedeh (2001). A more limited approach is that in J. S. C. Riley-Smith, 'Islam and the Crusades in History and Imagination, 8 November 1898 – 11 September 2001', *Crusades* 2 (2003).

Ideas about, and images of, crusading in the last two centuries are described by E. Siberry, *The New Crusaders: Images of the Crusades in the 19th and early 20th centuries* (2000).

C. J. Tyerman (*The Invention of the Crusades* (1998)) suggests that 'crusade history' is a modern construct.

GENERAL HISTORIES

Two large-scale histories in English are

S. Runciman, *A History of the Crusades*, 3 vols (1951–4), which is now fifty years old, favours the Byzantine Greeks and concentrates on crusading to the East;

K. M. Setton (editor-in-chief), *A History of the Crusades*, 2nd edn, 6 vols

(1969–89), is also rather dated and variable in quality, although it gives some space to crusades in Europe.

Of the single-volume studies, H. E. Mayer, *The Crusades*, tr. J. B. Gillingham, 2nd edn (1988) and J. Richard, *The Crusades, c. 1071 – c. 1091*, tr. J. Birrell (1999) contain first-class treatment of the Latin East from the traditionalist perspective, whereas J. S. C. Riley-Smith (ed.), *The Atlas of the Crusades* (1991) and (ed.), *The Oxford Illustrated History of the Crusades* (1995) are pluralist.

A mass of new material on the later crusades was presented in

K. M. Setton, *The Papacy and the Levant (1204–1571)*, 4 vols (1976–84), a work that is impossible to read and is quite without analysis.

Sense of the subject is made by

N. J. Housley, *The Later Crusades, 1274–1580: From Lyons to Alcazar* (1992).

A feature of the last few years has been many good collections of articles covering the whole subject, among which are

A. Sapir Abulafia (ed.), *Religious Violence between Christians and Jews* (2002)

M. Balard (ed.), *Autour de la Première Croisade* (1996)

M. Balard, B. Z. Kedar and J. S. C. Riley-Smith (eds), *Dei gesta per Francos* (2001)

M. Bull, N. Housley, P. W. Edbury and J. Phillips (eds), *The Experience of Crusading*, 2 vols (2003)

Ecole Française de Rome (ed.), *Le concile de Clermont de 1095 et l'appel à la croisade* (1997)

P. W. Edbury (ed.), *Crusade and Settlement* (1985)

J. France and W. G. Zajac (eds), *The Crusades and their Sources* (1998)

L. García-Guijarro Ramos (ed.), *La Primera Cruzada novecientos años después* (1997)

B. Z. Kedar, H. E. Mayer and R. C. Smail (eds), *Outremer* (1982)

B. Z. Kedar (ed), *The Horns of Hattin* (1992)

B. Z. Kedar, J. S. C. Riley-Smith and R. Hiestand (eds), *Montjoie* (1997)

H. E. Mayer (ed.), *Die Kreuzfahrerstaaten als multikulturelle Gesellschaft* (1997).

CRUSADING IDEAS

Crusade ideology has been approached in two ways. One of these is through canon law. For this, see

J. A. Brundage, *Medieval Canon Law and the Crusader* (1969)

J. Muldoon, *Popes, Lawyers and Infidels* (1979)

M. Purcell, *Papal Crusading Policy 1244–1291* (1975)

J. S. C. Riley-Smith, *What Were the Crusades?*, 3rd edn (2002)

F. H. Russell, *The Just War in the Middle Ages* (1975)

R. H. Schmandt, 'The Fourth Crusade and the Just-War Theory', *Catholic Historical Review* 61 (1975)

M. Villey, *La croisade: essai sur la formation d'une théorie juridique* (1942).

A second way is to look at crusading against a wider theological background:

H. E. J. Cowdrey, 'Christianity and the morality of warfare during the first century of crusading', *The Experience of Crusading. 1: Western Approaches*, ed. M. Bull and N. Housley (2003)

E. Delaruelle, *L'idée de croisade au moyen âge* (1980)

C. Erdmann, *The Origin of the Idea of the Crusade*, tr. W. Goffart and M. W. Baldwin (1977), which was a work of seminal importance, first published in 1935.

J. Flori, *Le guerre sainte: La formation de l'idée de croisade dans l'Occident chrétien* (2001)

E. D. Hehl, *Kirche und Krieg im 12. Jahrhundert* (1980)

N. J. Housley, *Religious Warfare in Europe 1400–1536* (2002)

B. Z. Kedar, *Crusade and Mission* (1984)

J. S. C. Riley-Smith, 'Crusading as an act of love', *History* 65 (1980).

For the critics of crusading in the twelfth and thirteenth centuries, see
E. Siberry, *Criticism of Crusading 1095–1274* (1985).

New fields of study are now opening up. One of these is preaching:
P. J. Cole, *The Preaching of the Crusades to the Holy Land, 1095–1270* (1991)

G. Dickson, 'Revivalism as a Medieval Religious Genre', *Journal of Ecclesiastical History* 51 (2000)

C. T. Maier, *Preaching the Crusades: Mendicant Friars and the Cross in the Thirteenth Century* (1994)

——, *Crusade Propaganda and Ideology: Model Sermons for the Preaching of the Cross* (2000).

The other is liturgy for which see
C. Dondi, *The Liturgy of the Canons Regular of the Holy Sepulchre of Jerusalem* (2004)

A. Linder, *Raising Arms: Liturgy in the Struggle to Liberate Jerusalem in the Late Middle Ages* (2003).

For the theoreticians of the late thirteenth and fourteenth centuries, see
S. Schein, *Fideles Crucis: The Papacy, the West, and the Recovery of the Holy Land 1274–1314* (1991)

J. N. Hillgarth, *Ramon Lull and Lullism in Fourteenth-century France* (1971)

N. Iorga, *Philippe de Méziéres (1327–1405) et la croisade au XIVe siècle* (1896)

A. Leopold, *How to Recover the Holy Land: The Crusade Proposals of the Late Thirteenth and Early Fourteenth Centuries* (2000).

THE POPES AND THE CRUSADES

For Gregory VII:
H. E. J. Cowdrey, 'Pope Gregory VII's "Crusading" Plans of 1074', *Outremer*, ed. B. Z. Kedar, H. E. Mayer and R. C. Smail (1982) and *Pope Gregory VII, 1073–1085* (1998).

For Urban II:
A. Becker, *Papst Urban II (1088–1099)*, 2 vols (1964–88)
H. E. J. Cowdrey, 'Pope Urban II's Preaching of the First Crusade', *History* 55 (1970).

For Innocent III:
C. R. Cheney, *Pope Innocent III and England* (1976)
M. Maccarone, 'Studi su Innocenzo III: Orvieto e la predicazione della crociata', *Italia sacra* 17 (1972)
H. Roscher, *Papst Innocenz III und die Kreuzzüge* (1969).

For Honorius III:
R. Rist, 'Papal Policy and the Albigensian Crusades: Continuity or Change?', *Crusades* 2 (2003).

For Gregory X:
P. A. Throop, *Criticism of the Crusade* (1940), which is no longer acceptable for its conclusions on the critics, but it still contains the best treatment of Gregory's policies.

For Clement V:
S. Menache, *Clement V* (1998)
L. Thier, *Kreuzzugsbemühungen unter Papst Clemens V, 1305–1314* (1973).

The best study of the fourteenth-century popes is in
N. J. Housley, *The Avignon Papacy and the Crusades, 1305–1378* (1986).

For the taxation of the Church, see
P. Guidi (ed.), 'Rationes decimarum Italiae nei secoli XIII e XIV. Tuscia. I: La Decima degli anni 1274–80', *Studi e Testi* 58 (1932)
W. E. Lunt, *Papal Revenues in the Middle Ages*, 2 vols (1934)
——, *Financial Relations of the Papacy with England*, 2 vols (1939–62).

For the most detailed treatment of the papal embargoes of the early fourteenth century, see
E. Ashtor, *Levant Trade in the Later Middle Ages* (1983).

CRUSADE LITERATURE

A starting-point is M. Routledge, 'Songs', *The Oxford Illustrated History of the Crusades*, ed. J. S. C. Riley-Smith (1995). See also
M. Böhmer, *Untersuchungen zur Mittelhochdeutschen Kreuzzugslyrik* (1968)
C. T. J. Dijkstra, *La chanson de croisade* (1995)
P. Hölzle, *Die Kreuzzüge in der okzitanischen und deutschen Lyrik des 12. Jahrhunderts: das Gattungsproblem 'Kreuzlied' im historischen Kontext*, 2 vols (1980)
M. de Riquer, *Los Trovadores: Historia literaria y Textos*, 3 vols (1983)
S. N. Rosenberg and H. Tischler, *Chanter m'estuet: Songs of the Trouvères* (1981)

D. A. Trotter, *Medieval French Literature and the Crusades (1100–1300)* (1988)

F.-W. Wentzlaff-Eggebert, *Kreuzzugsdichtung des Mittelalters: Studien zu ihrer geschichtlichen und dichterischen Wirklichkeit* (1960).

RECRUITMENT IN THE WEST

Interesting work on the response in the West is to be found in

M. Bull, *Knightly Piety and Lay Response to the First Crusade: The Limousin and Gascony, c. 970–c. 1130* (1993)

G. Constable, 'The Financing of the Crusades in the Twelfth Century', *Outremer*, ed. B. Z. Kedar, H. E. Mayer and R. C. Smail (1982)

——, 'Medieval Charters as a Source for the History of the Crusades', *Crusade and Settlement*, ed. P. W. Edbury (1985)

A. J. Forey, 'The Crusading Vows of the English King Henry III', *Durham University Journal* NS. 34 (1973)

M. Keen, 'Chaucer's Knight, the English Aristocracy and the Crusade', *English Court Culture in the Middle Ages*, ed. V. J. Scattergood and J. W. Sherborne (1983)

S. Lloyd, 'The Lord Edward's Crusade, 1270–2: its setting and significance', *War and Government in the Middle Ages*, ed. J. B. Gillingham and J. C. Holt (1984)

——, *English Society and the Crusade* (1988)

C. J. Tyerman, *England and the Crusades* (1988).

For women and crusading, see

S. B. Edgington and S. Lambert (eds), *Gendering the Crusades* (2001)

S. Geldsetzer, *Frauen auf Kreuzzügen 1096–1291* (2003).

CRUSADES TO THE EAST BEFORE 1274

Contributions to the study of crusading in the period 1095–1274 include the following:

For the First Crusade:

R. Chazan, *European Jewry and the First Crusade* (1987)

——, *God, Humanity and History: The Hebrew First Crusade Narratives* (2000)

J. Flori, *Pierre l'Ermite et la Première Croisade* (1999)

J. H. and L. L. Hill, *Raymond IV de Saint-Gilles* (1959)

H. E. Mayer, 'Mélanges sur l'histoire du royaume de Jérusalem', *Mémoires de l'Académie des Inscriptions et Belles-Lettres* NS 5 (1984), which contains interesting studies of Godfrey and Baldwin of Boulogne.

A. V. Murray, *The Crusader Kingdom of Jerusalem: A dynastic history 1099–1125* (2000), which is also relevant to the early years of the settlement.

J. Phillips (ed.), *The First Crusade: Origins and Impact* (1997)

J. Prawer, 'The Jerusalem the Crusaders Captured: A Contribution to the Medieval Topography of the City', *Crusade and Settlement*, ed. P. W. Edbury (1985)

J. S. C. Riley-Smith, *The First Crusade and the Idea of Crusading* (1986)

——, *The First Crusaders* (1997)

R. Somerville, *The Councils of Urban II. 1: Decreta Claromontensia* (1972)

——, 'The Council of Clermont (1095) and Latin Christian Society', *Archivum historiae pontificiae* 12 (1974)

——, 'The Council of Clermont and the First Crusade', *Studia gratiana* 20 (1976).

For the attempt to reinstate Peter the Hermit as originator of the First Crusade, see
E. O. Blake and C. Morris, 'A Hermit Goes to War: Peter and the Origins of the First Crusade', *Studies in Church History* 22 (1984)
J. Flori, *Pierre l'Ermite* (1999).

For the Second Crusade:
G. Constable, 'The Second Crusade as seen by Contemporaries', *Traditio* 9 (1953)
M. Gervers (ed.), *The Second Crusade and the Cistercians* (1992)
J. Phillips and M. Hoch (eds), *The Second Crusade: Scope and Consequences* (2001).

For the Third Crusade:
J. B. Gillingham, *Richard I* (1999)
P. Munz, *Frederick Barbarossa* (1969)
J. Richard, '1187: Point de départ pour une nouvelle forme de la croisade', *The Horns of Hattin*, ed. B. Z. Kedar (1992).

For the Fourth Crusade:
M. Angold, *The Fourth Crusade* (2003)
J. Longnon, *Les compagnons de Villehardouin* (1978)
D. E. Queller and T. F. Madden, *The Fourth Crusade: The Conquest of Constantinople*, 2nd edn (1997).

The views in this book are justified in an article which will appear in a collection of papers edited by Professor A. Laiou.

For the Children's Crusade:
G. Dickson, 'The Genesis of the Children's Crusade (1212)' and 'Stephen of Cloyes, Philip Augustus and the Children's Crusade of 1212', both in G. Dickson, *Religious Enthusiasm in the Medieval West* (2000)
——, 'Pope Innocent III and the Children's Crusade', *Innocenzo III: Urbs et Orbis* 1, ed. A. Sommerlechner (2003).

For the Fifth Crusade:
J. M. Powell, *Anatomy of a Crusade, 1213–1221* (1986).

For the Barons' Crusade:
M. Lower, 'The burning at Mont-Aimé: Thibaut of Champagne's preparations for the Barons' Crusade of 1239', *Journal of Medieval History* 29 (2003).

For the crusades of Louis IX:
W. C. Jordan, *Louis IX and the Challenge of the Crusade* (1979)
J. Richard, *Saint Louis*, tr. S. Lloyd (1992)
D. Weiss, *Art and Crusade in the Age of Saint Louis* (1998)
D. Weiss and L. Mahoney (eds), *France and the Holy Land* (2004).

THE LATER CRUSADES, 1274 ONWARDS

In addition to Setton, *The Papacy and the Levant* and Housley, *The Avignon Papacy and the Crusades*, *The Later Crusades* and *Religious Warfare in Europe*, see

M. Barber, 'The pastoureaux of 1320', *Journal of Ecclesiastical History* 32 (1981)

A. C. Hess, 'The Battle of Lepanto and its place in Mediterranean History', *Past and Present* 57 (1972)

J. J. N. Palmer, *England, France and Christendom, 1377–99* (1972)

P. Rousset, 'Sainte Catherine de Sienne et le problème de la croisade', *Revue Suisse d'histoire* 25 (1975)

——, 'Un Huguenot propose une croisade: le projet de François de la Noue (1580–1585)', *Revue d'histoire écclesiastique suisse* 72 (1978)

S. Schein, 'Gesta Dei per Mongolos 1300', *English Historical Review* 94 (1979)

K. M. Setton, *Venice, Austria and the Turks in the Seventeenth Century* (1991).

THE MILITARY HISTORY OF THE CRUSADES AND THE LATIN EAST

R. C. Smail's magisterial study of warfare in the twelfth-century Latin East, *Crusading Warfare (1097–1193)* (1956) has a sequel in C. Marshall, *Warfare in the Latin East, 1192–1291* (1992).

J. France, *Victory in the East* (1994) is dedicated to the military history of the First Crusade. See also

J. France, *Western Warfare in the Age of the Crusades, 1000–1300* (1999)

Y. Friedman, *Encounter between Enemies: Captivity and Ransom in the Latin Kingdom of Jerusalem* (2002)

P. Herde, 'Die Kämpfe bei den Hörnern von Hittin und die Untergang des Kreuzritterheeres (3. und 4. Juli 1187)', *Römische Quartalschrift für christliche Altertumskunde und Kirchengeschichte* 61 (1966), which is the best analysis of the Battle of Hattin

D. C. Nicolle, *Arms and Armour of the Crusading Era 1050–1350*, 2nd edn, 2 vols (1999)

J. Pryor, *Geography, Technology and War* (1988)

J. S. C. Riley-Smith, 'Casualties and the Number of Knights on the First Crusade', *Crusades* 1 (2002) and 'The Crown of France and Acre, 1254–1291', *France and the Holy Land*, ed. D. Weiss and L. Mahoney (2004)

R. Rogers, *Latin Siege Warfare in the Twelfth Century* (1992)

R. C. Smail, 'The Predicaments of Guy of Lusignan, 1183–1187', *Outremer*, ed. B. Z. Kedar, H. E. Mayer and R. C. Smail (1982).

For the service of *milites ad terminum* in the East, see

G. Ligato, 'Fra Ordine Cavallereschi e crociata: "milites ad terminum" e "confraternitates" armate', *Militia Christi e Crociata nei secoli XI–XIII* (1992). For confraternities, see also

J. S. C. Riley-Smith, 'A Note on Confraternities in the Latin Kingdom of Jerusalem', *Bulletin of the Institute of Historical Research* 44 (1971).

THE BYZANTINE GREEKS AND THE CRUSADERS

A far more realistic attitude is now being taken towards their relationship. See

M. Angold, *The Byzantine Empire, 1025–1204*, 2nd edn (1997)

C. M. Brand, *Byzantium Confronts the West, 1180–1204* (1968)

J. Harris, *Byzantium and the Crusades* (2003)

R.-J. Lille, *Byzantium and the Crusader States, 1096–1204*, tr. J. C. Morris and J. E. Ridings (1993)

J. Shepard, 'When Greek meets Greek: Alexius Comnenus and Bohemond in 1097–8', *Byzantine and Modern Greek Studies* 12 (1988) and 'Cross-purposes: Alexius Comnenus and the First Crusade', *The First Crusade*, ed. J. Phillips (1997).

For the centuries after 1204, see

K. M. Setton, *The Papacy and the Levant*

M. Angold, *A Byzantine Government in Exile* (1975)

J. W. Barker, *Manuel II Palaeologus (1391–1425)* (1969)

D. J. Geanakoplos, *Emperor Michael Palaeologus and the West* (1959)

A. E. Laiou, *Constantinople and the Latins: The Foreign Policy of Andronicus II, 1282–1328* (1972).

THE MUSLIMS

The starting-point must now be C. Hillenbrand, *The Crusades: Islamic Perspectives* (1999), in which there is the first scholarly attempt to provide a general treatment of the crusades to the East through the Arabic sources. See also

M. Brett, 'The Near East on the Eve of the Crusades', *La Primera Cruzada Novecientos años Después*, ed. L. Garcia-Guijarro Ramos (1997)

——, 'Abbasids, Fatimids and Seljuqs', *New Cambridge Medieval History*, ed. D. Luscombe and J. S. C. Riley-Smith, 2 (2004)

C. Cahen, *Pre-Ottoman Turkey* (1968)

N. Daniel, *Islam and the West: The Making of an Image* (1960; revised edn, 1993)

N. Elisséeff, *Nur ad-Din*, 3 vols (1967)

S. D. Goitein, *A Mediterranean Society*, 6 vols (1967–93)

H. L. Gottschalk, *Al-Malik al-Kamil von Egypten und seine Zeit* (1958)

M. G. S. Hodgson, *The Order of Assassins* (1955)

P. M. Holt, *The Age of the Crusades: The Near East from the Eleventh Century to 1517* (1986)

——, *Early Mamluk Diplomacy (1260–1290)* (1995)

R. S. Humphreys, *From Saladin to the Mongols: The Ayyubids of Damascus 1193–1260* (1977)

H. Inalcik, *The Ottoman Empire* (1973)

R. Irwin, *The Middle East in the Middle Ages: The Early Mamluk Sultanate 1250–1382* (1986)

M. A. Köhler, *Allianzen und Verträge zwischen fränkischen und islamischen Herrschern im Vorderen Orient* (1991)

M. C. Lyons and D. E. P. Jackson, *Saladin* (1982), which is much the best biography of him.

S. J. Shaw, *History of the Ottoman Empire and Modern Turkey* 1 (1976)

E. Sivan, *L'Islam et la croisade* (1968)
P. Thorau, *The Lion of Egypt: Sultan Baybars I and the Near East in the Thirteenth Century*, tr. P. M. Holt (1987).

THE MONGOLS

P. Jackson, 'The Crisis in the Holy Land in 1260', *English Historical Review* 95 (1980)
D. O. Morgan, *The Mongols* (1986).
For the first crusade against them, see
P. Jackson, 'The Crusade Against the Mongols', *Journal of Ecclesiastical History* 43 (1991).

CRUSADING IN SPAIN

E. Bernardet, 'Croisade (Bulle de la)', *Dictionnaire de droit canonique 4*, ed. R. Naz (1949), pp. 773–99
R. I. Burns, *The Crusader Kingdom of Valencia*, 2 vols (1967)
——, *Islam under the Crusaders* (1973)
——, *Medieval Colonialism* (1975)
——, *Muslims, Christians and Jews in the Crusader Kingdom of Valencia* (1984)
R. A. Fletcher, *Saint James's Catapult: The Life and Times of Diego Gelmírez of Santiago de Compostela* (1984)
——, 'Reconquest and Crusade in Spain c. 1050–1150', *Transactions of the Royal Historical Society*, 5th ser., 37 (1987)
J. Goñi Gaztambide, *Historia de la Bula de la Cruzada en España* (1958)
P. Linehan, 'The Synod of Segovia (1166)', *Bulletin of Medieval Canon Law* NS 10 (1980)
——, *The Spanish Church and the Papacy in the Thirteenth Century* (1971).

The Reconquest from 1274 onwards is treated by Professor Housley in *The Avignon Papacy* and *The Later Crusades*. Its extension into North Africa in the sixteenth century is described by Professor Setton in *The Papacy and the Levant* and Professor Hess in 'The Battle of Lepanto', *Past and Present* 57 (1972). Works on the Spanish military orders are included in the section on the military orders.

THE BALTIC AND THE NORTH-EASTERN CRUSADES

Central to this topic is the history of the Teutonic Knights. Works on them are included in the section on the military orders. Professor Housley has interesting things to say in *The Avignon Papacy* and *The Later Crusades*, as has M. Keen, *Chivalry* (1984). See also
H. Beumann, *Heidenmission und Kreuzzugsgedanke in der deutschen Ostpolitik des Mittelalters*, 2nd edn (1973)
E. Christiansen, *The Northern Crusades* (1980)
F. Lotter, *Die Konzeption des Wendenkreuzzugs* (1977), although some of his conclusions have been challenged.

CRUSADES AGAINST HERETICS AND OPPONENTS
OF THE CHURCH

The best study to date of the Albigensian Crusade is M. Roquebert, *L'Épopée Cathare*, 3 vols (1970–86), though H. Roscher, *Papst Innocenz III* (1969) is also useful. A brief introduction can be found in M. Barber, *Cathars* (2000). See also

R. Rist, 'Papal Policy and the Albigensian Crusades: Continuity or Change?', *Crusades* 2 (2003).

A good short treatment of the crusades against the Hussites is to be found in
F. G. Heyman, 'The Crusades against the Hussites', *A History of the Crusades* 3, ed. K. M. Setton (1975).
See also Professor Housley in *The Later Crusades* and *Religious Warfare*; also
G. A. Holmes, 'Cardinal Beaufort and the crusade against the Hussites', *English Historical Review* 88 (1973).

The standard work on the political crusades in Italy is N. J. Housley, *The Italian Crusades* (1982). Professor Housley continues the story in *The Avignon Papacy*. See also
N. J. Housley, 'Crusades against Christians: their origins and early development, c. 1000–1216', *Crusade and Settlement*, ed. P. W. Edbury (1985)
——, 'The Mercenary Companies, the Papacy and the Crusades, 1356–1378', *Traditio* 38 (1982)
S. Lloyd, '"Political Crusades" in England, c. 1215–17 and c. 1263–5', *Crusade and Settlement*, ed. P. W. Edbury (1985).

THE LATIN SETTLEMENTS ON THE LEVANTINE MAINLAND

There are no good studies of the county of Edessa and outside the general works there is little to recommend on Cilician Armenia, except
T. S. R. Boase (ed.), *The Cilician Kingdom of Armenia* (1978).

The groundwork on Antioch-Tripoli was laid in
C. Cahen, *La Syrie du Nord à l'époque des croisades et la principauté franque d'Antioche* (1940), the study that began the revolution in the history of the Latin East.
J. Richard, *Le comté de Tripoli sous la dynastie toulousaine (1102–1187)* (1945).
The history of Antioch has been carried further in
T. S. Asbridge, *The Creation of the Principality of Antioch* (2000)
H. E. Mayer, *Varia Antiochena* (1993).

The best introduction to the constitutional history of the kingdom of Jerusalem is still in many ways
J. Richard, *The Latin Kingdom of Jerusalem*, tr. J. Shirley, 2 vols (1979), although it was first published in 1953.
See also
J. Prawer, *Histoire du royaume latin de Jérusalem*, 2 vols (1969–70)
——, *The Latin Kingdom of Jerusalem* (1972)

——, *Crusader Institutions* (1980), a most important collection of articles, of the writing of which Prawer was a master.
J. S. C. Riley-Smith, *The Feudal Nobility and the Kingdom of Jerusalem, 1174–1277* (1973).

Recently Professor Mayer has been leading studies away from political and constitutional history and back to the detailed examination of individual lordships. His articles have been collected in a series of volumes:
H. E. Mayer, *Kreuzzüge und lateinischer Osten* (1983)
——, *Probleme des lateinischen Königreichs Jerusalem* (1983)
——, *Kings and Lords in the Latin Kingdom of Jerusalem* (1993)
S. Tibble, *Monarchy and Lordships in the Latin Kingdom of Jerusalem, 1099–1291* (1989) reaches much the same conclusions.

For the kingdom's political, legal and administrative history, see
P. W. Edbury, 'Feudal Obligations in the Latin East', *Byzantion* 47 (1977)
——, *John of Ibelin and the Kingdom of Jerusalem* (1997), which is a preliminary study to Professor Edbury's edition of the great lawbook of John of Jaffa: *John of Ibelin, Le Livre des Assises* (2003).
B. Hamilton, 'The elephant of Christ: Reynald of Châtillon', *Studies in Church History* 15 (1978)
——, *The Leper King and his Heirs. Baldwin IV and the Crusader Kingdom of Jerusalem* (2000)
P. Jackson, 'The End of Hohenstaufen Rule in Syria', *Bulletin of the Institute of Historical Research* 59 (1986)
B. Z. Kedar, 'On the Origins of the Earliest Laws of Frankish Jerusalem: The Canons of the Council of Nablus, 1120', *Speculum* 74 (1999)
H. E. Mayer, 'Jérusalem et Antioche au temps de Baudouin II', *Comptes rendus de l'Académie des Inscriptions et Belles-Lettres* (1980)
——, 'The Succession to Baldwin II of Jerusalem: English impact on the East', *Dumbarton Oaks Papers* 39 (1985)
——, 'Studies in the History of Queen Melisende of Jerusalem', *Dumbarton Oaks Papers* 26 (1972)
——, 'Kaiserrecht und Heiliges Land', *Aus Reichsgeschichte und Nordischer Geschichte*, ed. H. Fuhrmann, H. E. Mayer and K. Wriedt (1972)
——, 'Ibelin versus Ibelin: the struggle for the Regency of Jerusalem, 1253–1258', *Proceedings of the American Philosophical Society* 122 (1978)
——, 'The Concordat of Nablus', *Journal of Ecclesiastical History* 33 (1982)
——, *Die Kanzlei der lateinischen Könige von Jerusalem*, 2 vols (1996), which is one of the most important works to appear since the early 1980s.
J. Phillips, *Defenders of the Holy Land: Relations between the Latin East and the West, 1119–1187* (1996)
S. Reynolds, 'Fiefs and Vassals in Twelfth-Century Jerusalem: a View from the West', *Crusades* 1 (2002), which in my opinion does not take into account the experimental nature of Frankish government in Palestine and the self-conscious approach of the settlers to their institutions.
J. S. C. Riley-Smith, 'The motives of the earliest crusaders and the settlement of Latin Palestine, 1095–1100', *English Historical Review* 98 (1983)

——, 'The survival in Latin Palestine of Muslim administration', *The Eastern Mediterranean Lands in the Period of the Crusades*, ed. P. M. Holt (1977)

——, 'Further Thoughts on Baldwin II's *établissement* on the Confiscation of Fiefs', *Crusade and Settlement*, ed. P. W. Edbury (1985).

For the Church in the Latin patriarchates of Jerusalem and Antioch, see
P. W. Edbury and J. G. Rowe, *William of Tyre* (1988)
B. Hamilton, *The Latin Church in the Crusader States: The Secular Church* (1980)
K. Elm, *Umbilicus Mundi* (1998)
A. Jotischky, *The Perfection of Solitude: Hermits and Monks in the Crusader States* (1995)
B. Z. Kedar, 'The Subjected Muslims of the Frankish Levant', *Muslims under Latin Rule, 1100–1300*, ed. J. M. Powell (1990)
H. E. Mayer, *Bistümer, Klöster und Stifte im Königreich Jerusalem* (1977)
——, Das Pontifikale von Tyrus und die Krönung der lateinischen Könige von Jerusalem', *Dumbarton Oaks Papers* 21 (1967)
J. Richard, *La papauté et les missions d'Orient au moyen âge (XIIIe–XVe siècles)* (1977)
J. S. C. Riley-Smith, 'Latin Titular Bishops in Palestine and Syria, 1137–1291', *Catholic Historical Review* 64 (1978)
——, 'Government and the indigenous in the Latin kingdom of Jerusalem', *Medieval Frontiers: Concepts and Practices*, ed. D. Abulafia and N. Berend (2002)
J. G. Rowe, 'The Papacy and the Ecclesiastical Province of Tyre (1100–1187)', *Bulletin of the John Rylands Library* 43 (1960–1).

On schools and learning, see, besides A. Jotischky, *The Perfection of Solitude*,
P. C. Boeren, *Rorgo Fretellus de Nazareth et sa description de la Terre Sainte* (1980)
R. B. C. Huygens, 'Guillaume de Tyr étudiant', *Latomus* 21 (1962)
B. Z. Kedar, 'Gerard of Nazareth: A neglected twelfth-century writer in the Latin East', *Dumbarton Oaks Papers* 37 (1983)
R. C. Schwinges, *Kreuzzugsidee und Toleranz: Studien zu Wilhelm von Tyrus* (1977).

For the culture of the nobility, see
D. Jacoby, 'La littérature française dans les états latins de la Méditerranée orientale à l'époque des croisades: diffusion et création', *Actes du IXe Congrès International de la Société Rencesvals pour l'Étude des Épopées Romanes* (1982).

On art and architecture, see
K. M. Setton, *A History of the Crusades* 4 (1977), which is devoted to the subject.

On art, the most important work is
J. Folda, *The Art of the Crusaders in the Holy Land*, 1 vol. so far; another to come (1995–).
See also
H. Buchthal, *Miniature Painting in the Latin Kingdom of Jerusalem* (1957)

J. Folda, *Crusader Manuscript Illumination at Saint-Jean d'Acre,* 1275–1291 (1976).

For coins and seals, see
H. E. Mayer, *Das Siegelwesen in den Kreuzfahrerstaaten* (1978)
D. M. Metcalf, *Coinage of the Crusades and the Latin East,* 2nd edn (1995)
G. Schlumberger, F. Chalandon and A. Blanchet, *Sigillographie de l'Orient latin* (1943).

For religious architecture, see, besides J. Folda, *The Art of the Crusaders,*
M. Biddle, *The Tomb of Christ* (1999)
R. W. Edwards, 'Ecclesiastical Architecture in the Fortifications of Armenian Cilicia', *Dumbarton Oaks Papers* 36 (1982), 37 (1983)
R. Ellenblum, 'Frontier Activities: the Transformation of a Muslim Sacred Site into the Frankish Castle of Vadum Jacob', *Crusades* 2 (2003)
C. Enlart, *Les monuments des croisés dans le royaume de Jérusalem: Architecture religieuse et civile,* 2 vols (1925–8)
D. Pringle, *The Churches of the Crusader Kingdom of Jerusalem: A Corpus,* 2 vols so far; 2 more to come (1993–), which is the definitive survey of all the church buildings in the kingdom.

For castles, see
M. Benvenisti, *The Crusaders in the Holy Land* (1970)
P. Deschamps, *Les châteaux des croisés en Terre Sainte,* 3 vols (1934–77)
R. W. Edwards, *The Fortifications of Armenian Cilicia* (1987)
R. P. Harper and D. Pringle, *Belmont Castle* (2000)
H. Hellenkemper, *Burgen der Kreuzritterzeit in der Grafschaft Edessa und im Königreich Kleinarmenien* (1976)
H. Kennedy, *Crusader Castles* (1994)
W. Müller-Wiener, *Castles of the Crusaders* (1976)
D. Pringle, *The Red Tower* (1986)
——, *Secular Buildings in the Crusader Kingdom of Jerusalem: An Archaeological Gazetteer* (1997).

Recent works on social and economic history, including trade, are
C. Aslanov, 'Languages in Contact in the Latin East: Acre and Cyprus', *Crusades* 1 (2002)
R. Ellenblum, *Frankish Rural Settlement in the Latin Kingdom of Jerusalem* (1998), which is seminal.
M.-L. Favreau, *Die Italiener im Heiligen Land vom der ersten Kreuzzug bis zum Tode Heinrichs von Champagne (1098–1197)* (1989)
D. Jacoby, 'L'expansion occidentale dans le Levant: les Vénitiens à Acre dans la seconde moitié du treizième siècle', *Journal of Medieval History* 3 (1977)
——, 'Crusader Acre in the Thirteenth Century: Urban Layout and Topography', *Studi Medievali,* Ser. 3, 20 (1979)
J. H. Pryor, *Geography, technology and war: Studies in the Maritime History of the Mediterranean 649–1571* (1988)
J. S. C. Riley-Smith, 'Government in Latin Syria and the Commercial Privileges of

Foreign Merchants', *Relations between East and West in the Middle Ages*, ed. D. Baker (1973)

I. Shagrir, *Naming Patterns in the Latin Kingdom of Jerusalem* (2003).

LATIN CYPRUS

The best introduction is

P. W. Edbury, *The Kingdom of Cyprus and the Crusades, 1191–1374* (1991). It can be supplemented by

G. F. Hill, *A History of Cyprus* 2–3 (1948). See also

D. and I. Hunt (eds), *Caterino Cornaro* (1989)

D. Jacoby, 'The Rise of a new Emporium in the eastern Mediterranean: Famagusta in the late thirteenth century', *Meletai kai Upomnemata* 1 (1984)

J. Richard, *Chypre sous les Lusignans: Documents chypriotes des archives du Vatican (XIVe et XVe siècles)* (1962).

For the Latin Church, see

N. Coureas, *The Latin Church in Cyprus, 1195–1312* (1997).

For art and architecture, see

C. Enlart, *Gothic Art and the Renaissance in Cyprus*, tr. D. Hunt (1987).

LATIN GREECE

The history of Latin Greece has had detailed, if rather unanalytical treatment, in various chapters in Professor Setton's *A History of the Crusades* 2–3 and *The Papacy and the Levant*. See also

P. Argenti, *The Occupation of Chios by the Genoese and their Administration of the Island, 1346–1566*, 3 vols (1958)

M. Balard, *La Romanie génoise (XIIe–début du XVe siècle)* (1978)

A. Bon, *La Morée Franque: Recherches historiques, topographiques et archéologiques sur la principauté d'Achaïe (1205–1430)* (1969)

N. Cheetham, *Mediaeval Greece* (1981)

G. Fedalto, *La chiesa latina in Oriente*, 3 vols (1973–8)

D. Jacoby, *La féodalité en Grèce Médiévale: Les 'Assises de Romanie': sources, application et diffusion* (1971)

——, 'The Encounter of Two Societies: Western Conquerors and Byzantines in the Peloponnesus after the Fourth Crusade', *American Historical Review* 78 (1973)

——, 'Catalans, Turcs et Vénitiens en Romanie (1305–1332): un nouveau témoignage de Marino Sanudo Torsello', *Studi Medievali*, Ser. 3, 15 (1974)

P. Lock, *The Franks in the Aegean, 1204–1500* (1995)

J. Longnon, *L'empire latin de Constantinople et la principauté de Morée* (1949)

F. Thiriet, *La Romanie vénitienne au moyen âge* (1959).

THE MILITARY ORDERS

A good introduction to the military orders in general is to be found in the chapters by A. J. Forey and A. T Luttrell in *The Oxford Illustrated History of the Crusades*, ed. J. S. C. Riley-Smith (1995). See also

A. Demurger, *Chevaliers du Christ: Les ordres religieux-militaires au Moyen Âge* (2002)

J. Forey, *The Military Orders* (1992)

——, 'Recruitment to the Military Orders', *Viator* 17 (1986)

——, 'Novitiate and Instruction in the Military Orders during the Twelfth and Thirteenth Centuries', *Speculum* 61 (1986)

L. García-Guijarro Ramos, *Papado, cruzadas y órdenes militares, siglos XI–XIII* (1995).

Conferences on the military orders are becoming increasingly common and are generating collections of papers. Examples are

M. Barber (ed.), *The Military Orders: Fighting for the Faith and Caring for the Sick* (1994)

H. Nicholson (ed.), *The Military Orders. Volume 2: Welfare and Warfare* (1998)

A. T. Luttrell and L. Pressouyre, *La Commanderie, institution des ordres militaires dans l'Occident médiéval* (2002).

A reliable general history of the Templars is

M. Barber, *The New Knighthood: A History of the Order of the Temple* (1994). See also

M. Barber, *The Trial of the Templars* (1978)

M. L. Bulst-Thiele, *Sacrae Domus Militiae Templi Hierosolymitani Magistri* (1974)

S. Cerrini (ed.), *I Templari, la guerra et la santità* (2000)

A. Demurger, *Vie et mort de l'ordre du Temple* (1985)

A. J. Forey, *The Templars in the Corona de Aragon* (1973), which is the best book on their provincial structure.

A. T. Luttrell, 'The Earliest Templars', *Autour de la Première Croisade*, ed. M. Balard (1996)

H. Nicholson, *The Knights Templar: A New History* (2001)

J. S. C. Riley-Smith, 'The Templars and the Teutonic Knights in Cilician Armenia', *The Cilician Kingdom of Armenia*, ed. T. S. R. Boase (1978)

——, 'Were the Templars Guilty', *Medieval Crusade*, ed. S. Ridyard (2004)

——, 'The Structures of the Orders of the Temple and the Hospital in c. 1291', *Medieval Crusade*, ed. S. Ridyard (2004).

The best general history of the Hospitallers of St John is

H. Sire, *The Knights of Malta* (1994). See also

H. Nicholson, *The Knights Hospitaller* (2001)

J. S. C. Riley-Smith, *Hospitallers* (1999).

For the Hospitallers of St John before the fourteenth century, see

S. Edgington, 'Medical Care in the Hospital of St John in Jerusalem', *The Military Orders. Volume 2*, ed. H. Nicholson (1998)

A. J. Forey, 'Constitutional Conflict and Change in the Hospital of St John during the Twelfth and Thirteenth Centuries', *Journal of Ecclesiastical History* 33 (1982)

B. Z. Kedar, 'A Twelfth-Century description of the Jerusalem Hospital', *The Military Orders. Volume 2*, ed. H. Nicholson (1998)

A. T. Luttrell, 'The Earliest Hospitallers', *Montjoie*, ed. B. Z. Kedar, J. S. C. Riley-Smith and R. Hiestand (1997)

——, 'The Hospitallers' Early Written Records', *The Crusades and their Sources*, ed. J. France and W. G. Zajac (1998)

J. S. C. Riley-Smith, *The Knights of St John in Jerusalem and Cyprus, c. 1050–1310* (1967).

Good work is being done on the management of the Hospitallers' European estates. See especially:

P. Bonneaud, *Le prieuré de Catalogne, le couvent de Rhodes et la couronne d'Aragon 1415–1447* (2004)

M. Gervers (who has edited *The Cartulary of the Knights of St John of Jerusalem in England: Secunda Camera Essex* (1982)), *The Hospitaller Cartulary in the British Library (Cotton MS Nero E VI)* (1981)

——, '*Pro defensione Terre Sancte*: the Development and Exploitation of the Hospitallers' Landed Estate in Essex', *The Military Orders*, ed. M. Barber (1994)

A.-M. Legras, *Les Commanderies des Templiers et des Hospitaliers de Saint Jean de Jérusalem en Saintonge et en Aunis* (1983).

For the history of the order's occupation of Rhodes one should first read the many articles written by Dr A. T. Luttrell, the world's leading authority on the subject. Some of these have been collected in four volumes:

A. T. Luttrell, *The Hospitallers in Cyprus, Rhodes, Greece and the West (1291–1440)* (1978)

——, *Latin Greece, the Hospitallers and the Crusades, 1291–1400* (1982)

——, *The Hospitallers of Rhodes and their Mediterranean World* (1992)

——, *The Hospitaller State on Rhodes and its Western Provinces, 1306–1462* (1999).

Also consult

A. T. Luttrell, 'The later History of the Maussolleion and its utilization in the Hospitaller castle at Bodrum', *The Maussolleion at Halikarnassos* (1986)

——, 'English Contributions to the Hospitaller Castle at Bodrum in Turkey: 1407–1437', *The Military Orders. Volume 2*, ed. H. Nicholson (1998)

——, *The Town of Rhodes, 1306–1356* (2003).

See also the comments in Professor Housley's, *The Avignon Papacy* and *The Later Crusades*, and

A. Gabriel, *La cité de Rhodes (1310–1522)*, 2 vols (1921–3)

J. Sarnowsky, *Macht und Herrschaft im Johanniterorden des 15. Jahrhunderts* (2001)

N. Vatin, *L'Ordre de Saint-Jean-de-Jérusalem, l'Empire Ottoman et la Méditerranée orientale entre le deux sièges de Rhodes (1480–1522)* (1994).

For the order's occupation of Malta, see

D. Allen, 'The Social and Religious World of a Knight of Malta in the Caribbean, c. 1632–1660', *Malta: A Case Study in International Cross-Currents*, ed. S. Fiorini and V. Mallia-Milanes (1991)

——, '"A Parish at Sea": Spiritual Concerns aboard the Order of St John's Galleys in the Seventeenth and Eighteenth Centuries', *The Military Orders*, ed. M. Barber (1994)

——, 'The Order of St John as a "School for Ambassadors" in Counter-Reformation Europe', *The Military Orders. Volume 2*, ed. H. Nicholson (1998)

R. Cavaliero, *The Last of the Crusaders* (1960)

J. O. Hughes, *The Building of Malta during the Period of the Knights of St John of Jerusalem, 1530–1795* (1956)

A. Hoppen, *The Fortification of Malta by the Order of St John, 1530–1798* (1979)

A. T. Luttrell, 'Eighteenth-Century Malta: Prosperity and Problems', *Hyphen* 3 (1982)

V. Mallia-Milanes, *Venice and Hospitaller Malta 1530–1798: Aspects of a Relationship* (1992)

——, (ed.), *Hospitaller Malta 1530–1798* (1993).

For the Teutonic Order and the other German orders, one should consult, besides Christiansen, *The Northern Crusades* and Housley, *The Avignon Papacy* and *The Later Crusades*,

U. Arnold (ed.), *800 Jahre Deutscher Orden* (1990)

F. Benninghoven, *Der Orden der Schwertbrüder* (1965)

M. Burleigh, *Prussian Society and the German Order* (1984)

M.-L. Favreau, *Studien zur Frühgeschichte des Deutschen Ordens* (1974)

K. Forstreuter, *Der Deutsche Orden am Mittelmeer* (1967)

P. Hilsch, 'Der Deutsche Ritterorden im südlichen Libanon', *Zeitschrift des Deutschen Palästina-Vereins* 96 (1980)

W. Paravicini, *Die Preussenreise des Europäischen Adels*, 2 vols (1989–95)

M. Tumler, *Der Deutsche Orden im Werden, Wachsen und Wirken bis 1400* (1955)

M. Tumler and U. Arnold, *Der Deutsche Orden vom seinem Ursprung bis zur Gegenwart*, 5th edn (1992).

For the Order of St Lazarus, see now

D. Marcombe, *Leper Knights* (2003).

For the Spanish Military Orders, see

A. J. Forey, 'The Military Orders and the Spanish Reconquest in the Twelfth and Thirteenth Centuries', *Traditio* 40 (1984)

D. W. Lomax, *La Orden de Santiago, 1170–1275* (1965)

J. F. O'Callaghan, *The Spanish Military Order of Calatrava and its Affiliates* (1975)

L. P. Wright, 'The Military Orders in Sixteenth- and Seventeenth-century Spanish Society', *Past and Present* 43 (1969).

For the English Order of St Thomas of Acre, see

A. J. Forey, 'The military order of St Thomas of Acre', *English Historical Review* 92 (1977).

Some sources in translation

Many medieval texts have now been translated, although it is still rare to find collections of documents, as opposed to narrative sources. Two such collections are

N. J. Housley, *Documents on the Later Crusades, 1274–1580* (1996)
L. and J. Riley-Smith, *The Crusades, Idea and Reality, 1095–1274* (1981).

Eyewitness accounts of the First Crusade are
Gesta Francorum et aliorum Hierosolimitanorum, ed. and tr. R. Hill (1962)
Raymond of Aguilers, *Historia*, tr. J. H. and L. L. Hill (1968)
Fulcher of Chartres, *A History of the Expedition to Jerusalem 1095–1127*, tr. F. R. Ryan, ed. H. S. Fink (1969)
Anna Comnena, *The Alexiad*, tr. E. A. S. Dawes (1928).
See also
E. Peters, *First Crusade* (1998).
And for the Hebrew sources on the pogroms that marred the First and Second Crusades, see
S. Eidelberg, *The Jews and the Crusaders* (1977).

Two of the main sources for the Second Crusade, one covering the fighting in Asia Minor, the other the engagements in Portugal, are
Odo of Deuil, *De profectione Ludovici VII in orientem*, ed. and tr. V. G. Berry (1948)
De expugnatione Lyxbonensi, ed. and tr. C. W. David (1936).

For the Third Crusade, see
Ambroise, *The Crusade of Richard Lion-Heart*, tr. M. J. Hubert and J. L. La Monte (1941)
Chronicle of the Third Crusade, tr. H. J. Nicholson (1997)
The Conquest of Jerusalem and the Third Crusade, tr. P. W. Edbury (1996)
Baha' ad-Din, *The Rare and Excellent History of Saladin*, tr. D. S. Richards (1997).

For the Fourth Crusade, see
A. J. Andrea, *Capture of Constantinople: the Hystoria Constantinopolitana of Gunther of Pairis* (1997)
——, *Contemporary Sources for the Fourth Crusade* (2000)
Geoffrey of Villehardouin, *The Conquest of Constantinople*, tr. M. R. B. Shaw (1963)
Robert of Cléry (Clari), *The Conquest of Constantinople*, tr. E. H. McNeal (1936).

For eyewitness accounts of the Fifth Crusade, see
Oliver of Paderborn, *The Capture of Damietta*, tr. J. J. Gavigan (1948)
E. Peters, *Christian Society and the Crusades, 1198–1229* (1971).

A marvellous eyewitness account of St Louis's first crusade is
John of Joinville, *The Life of Saint Louis*, tr. M. R. B. Shaw (1963).

For the Albigensian Crusade, see
Peter of Les Vaux-de-Cernay, *The History of the Albigensian Crusade*, tr. W. A. and M. D. Sibly (1998)
The Song of the Cathar Wars, tr. J. Shirley (1996).

For the Hussite Crusades, see
The Crusade against the Heretics in Bohemia, 1418–1437, tr. T. A. Fudge (2002).

For the German crusades of the thirteenth century, see
Henry of Livonia, *The Chronicle*, tr. J. A. Brundage (1961).

For the Latin East, see
The Assizes of the Lusignan Kingdom of Cyprus, tr. N. Coureas (2002)
Crusaders as Conquerors: The Chronicle of Morea, tr. H. E. Lurier (1964)
Fulcher of Chartres, *History*, tr. F. R. Ryan (see above)
Leontios Machairas, *Recital Concerning the Sweet Land of Cyprus*, ed. and tr. R. M. Dawkins, 2 vols (1932)
Philip of Novara, *The Wars of Frederick II against the Ibelins in Syria and Cyprus*, tr. J. L. La Monte and M. J. Hubert (1936)
The 'Templar of Tyre', tr. P. Crawford (2003)
Walter the Chancellor, *The Antiochene Wars*, tr. T. S. Asbridge and S. B. Edgington (1999)
William of Tyre, *A History of Deeds Done Beyond the Sea*, tr. E. A. Babcock and A. C. Krey, 2 vols (1943).

For Muslim accounts of relations with the settlers, see
Abu'l-Fida', *The Memoirs of a Syrian Prince*, tr. P. M. Holt (1983)
Baha' ad-Din, *The Rare and Excellent History of Saladin*, tr. D. S. Richards (1997)
F. Gabrieli, *Arab Historians of the Crusades* (1969)
P. M. Holt, *Early Mamluk Diplomacy (1260–1290): Treaties of Baybars and Qalawun with Christian Rulers* (1995)
Ibn 'Abd al-Zahir, *Sirat al-Malik al-Zahir*, part ed. and tr. S. F. Sadeque (1956)
Ibn al-Furat, *Ayyubids, Mamlukes and Crusaders*, part ed. and tr. U. and M. C. Lyons, 2 vols (1971)
Ibn Jubayr, *Travels*, tr. R. J. C. Broadhurst (1952)
Ibn al-Qalanisi, *Chronicle of Damascus*, tr. H. A. R. Gibb (1932)
Usamah ibn Munqidh, *An Arab-Syrian Gentleman and Warrior in the Period of the Crusades*, tr. P. K. Hitti (1929).

Itineraries and pilgrimage descriptions of the Holy Land were translated by the *Palestine Pilgrims Text Society*, 14 vols (1896–1907), but many have been superseded by the descriptions in *Jerusalem Pilgrimage 1099–1185*, tr. J. Wilkinson, J. Hill and W. F. Ryan (1988).

For the internal legislation of the Templars and Hospitallers of St. John while their headquarters were in Palestine and Cyprus, see
The Rule of the Templars, tr. J. M. Upton-Ward (1992)

The Rule, Statutes and Customs of the Hospitallers, 1099–1310, tr. E. J. King (1934).
See also
The Templars, tr. M. Barber and K. Bate (2002)
The Fall of the Templars in the Crown of Aragon, tr. A. Forey (2001).

An account of the siege of Rhodes in 1480 was translated within two years:
William Caoursin, *The dylectable newesse and tythinges of the glorious victorye of the Rhodyans agaynst the Turks*, tr. J. Kaye (1482).
There is an edition by H. W. Fincham (Order of St John of Jerusalem, Historical Pamphlets no. 2, 1926).

For the siege of Malta, see
Francisco Balbi de Corregio, *The Siege of Malta, 1565*, tr. E. Bradford (1965).

Index